World Tourism Cities

World Tourism Cities: A Systematic Approach to Urban Tourism is a unique and contemporary textbook that addresses the particular situation of urban tourism destinations in the 2020s by reviewing key issues, trends, challenges and future opportunities for urban tourism destinations worldwide, as well as city destination management.

The book is divided into four parts, with Part I providing background chapters on world tourism cities. It begins by clearly defining world tourism cities and explaining the impacts of globalisation and urbanisation on these cities. The subsequent chapter explains the urban tourism phenomenon and traces its growth. Part II presents city destination management, planning and development and the marketing and branding of cities, offering practical solutions and approaches. Part III discusses major issues and trends in world tourism cities including resident well-being and quality of life, sustainability, smart tourism, crises and the rise of tourism in Asian cities, and the final part identifies the future opportunities for city tourism.

Written in a student-friendly tone, the book is richly illustrated and contains several engaging features, including Sweet tweets (snippets of information on cities) and Short breaks (detailed case studies on cities). This will be essential reading for all tourism students.

Alastair M. Morrison, PhD, is Research Professor in Marketing, Events and Tourism at the Greenwich Business School, University of Greenwich. Formerly, he was Distinguished Professor at Purdue University, USA, specialising in the area of tourism and hospitality marketing. He has published approximately 300 academic articles and conference proceedings and is the author of six books on tourism marketing and development. Prof. Morrison is the co-editor-in-chief of the *International Journal of Tourism Cities* and co-editor of the *Routledge Handbook of Tourism Cities*.

Cristina Maxim, PhD, is Senior Lecturer in Tourism at the University of West London. Her research interests are focused on destination management, cities, sustainability, tourism planning and management, regional development and local government. She has published a number of academic papers on urban tourism, including a recent article in *Current Issues in Tourism* on the challenges faced by world tourism cities, and has contributed a chapter to the *Routledge Handbook of Tourism Cities* titled "Challenges of world tourism cities: London, Singapore and Dubai".

"This is a timely book set to become a seminal contribution to urban tourism. The authors, who are prolific researchers and consultants in this field, build on scholarly work published in the *International Journal of Tourism Cities* over the last six years, whilst adding to the latest research on urban tourism and tourism cities with valuable insights from practice around the world. *World Tourism Cities* will be of interest not only to students and academics alike, but also to practitioners and policy makers eager to capitalise on the latest knowledge related to the management of urban tourism destinations in all their different dimensions – from capacity management and innovative destination marketing practices to smart tourism".

Dr J. Andres Coca-Stefaniak, *Professor in Tourism, Events and Sustainability, University of Greenwich (London, UK); and co-editor of the* Routledge Handbook of Tourism Cities

"This is a timely book that provides an extensive overview of tourism in world cities. By taking a systemic approach, the authors provide much needed new insights and perspectives on urban tourism. The book is written in an accessible way with plenty of real-life examples that help clarify the comprehensive insights and ideas put forward in the book. As such, the book acts as an important source of reference for researchers, students as well as engaged practitioners".

Dr Ko Koens, *Professor of New Urban Tourism, Inholland University of Applied Sciences, the Netherlands*

World Tourism Cities

A Systematic Approach to Urban Tourism

Alastair M. Morrison and
Cristina Maxim

Routledge
Taylor & Francis Group

LONDON AND NEW YORK

First published 2022
by Routledge
2 Park Square, Milton Park, Abingdon, Oxon OX14 4RN

and by Routledge
605 Third Avenue, New York, NY 10158

Routledge is an imprint of the Taylor & Francis Group, an informa business

British Library Cataloguing-in-Publication Data
A catalogue record for this book is available from the British Library

Library of Congress Cataloging-in-Publication Data
A catalog record has been requested for this book

ISBN: 9780367629137 (hbk)
ISBN: 9780367629120 (pbk)
ISBN: 9781003111412 (ebk)

DOI: 10.4324/9781003111412

Typeset in Frutiger
by Deanta Global Publishing Services, Chennai, India

Access the Support Material: www.routledge.com/9780367629120

Sheng Hua, Alick and Andy
Ovidiu and Philip

Contents

Figures

Figures

Tables

Preface

World Tourism Cities: A Systematic Approach to Urban Tourism is a unique and contemporary textbook that addresses the particular situation of urban and metropolitan tourism destinations in the 2020s. Much of the world's leisure and business tourism is focused on cities, and this book defines the features of tourism cities and is built around a structured approach to urban tourism planning, management and marketing. Major trends, issues, challenges and opportunities are discussed with many interesting supporting international city examples in each chapter. Written in a student-friendly tone, the book is richly illustrated and contains several engaging features.

Maxim (2020) describes the world tourism cities concept as follows:

> The concept of world tourism cities can be understood to refer either to those cities that depend on tourism for their global profile such as Venice (Ashworth 2010), or to world cities as environments were tourism occurs (Maitland and Newman 2009).

Rationale for the book

There is a gap in the textbook market for a work dealing with tourism cities on a global scale. In fact, most of the leading books on tourism tend to focus on countries, states and provinces and resorts rather than on urban areas. This is rather curious since there are many more urban settlements.

The most quoted figures on urban areas are from the United Nations (UN), which generally uses populations of 150,000 and 300,000 and over for its urban statistics. For example, in its 2019 reports, the UN quoted a figure of 4,220 urban settlements in the world, of which 529 were megacities of 10 million or more, 325 were large cities of 5 to 10 million, 926 were medium-sized cities of 1 to 5 million, 415 were cities with 500,000 to 1 million, 275 were cities with 300,000 to 500,000 and 1,750 were urban settlements with fewer than 300,000 inhabitants.

What then is a world tourism city? Maxim's (2020) definition is above cited. Public recognition of the term tourism city came in 2012. Then, tourism cities had their own representational body through the World Tourism Cities Federation (WTCF) headquartered in Beijing. Tourism cities are places where tourism is important and in which city governments put a high priority on this economic sector. Additionally, these urban areas are the ones that get the most tourists. Using these parameters, it is easy to say that London, New York and Paris are tourism cities; however, what about less famous "provincial" cities like Anqing in China, Portland in the USA and Dundee in the UK?

There are quantitative and qualitative criteria that determine tourism cities. Considering the volumes of tourists and expenditures is an example of one of the potential quantitative metrics. As an example of this, a ranking of the world's top tourism cities is produced each year in Mastercard's *Global Destination Cities Index* (GDCI). Some 167 cities were in the results for 2019, and Bangkok, London and Paris were the top three. The GDCI ranks the cities by their total volumes of international overnight visitors. GDCI also reports on the spending of international visitors in cities. Bangkok in 2019 welcomed 22.78 million international visitors. Euromonitor International publishes an annual ranking of the *Top 100 City Destinations*, which also uses the total number of international tourist arrivals. The company's 2019 rankings had a top ten that included five cities in Asia (Hong Kong as #1 in the world; Bangkok, #2; Macau, #4; Singapore, #5; Kuala Lumpur, #9). The other top-ranking cities were London (#3), Paris (#6), Dubai (#7), New York City (#8) and Istanbul (#10) (Euromonitor International, 2020).

On the business tourism side, GainingEdge, a consulting company based in Melbourne, Australia, has developed a city-based *Competitive Index* with respect to international conventions. For 2019, the index ranked 103 cities worldwide, with Paris, Barcelona, Singapore, Tokyo, New York and Beijing receiving the highest scores (GainingEdge, 2019). Additionally, the International Congress and Convention Association (ICCA), based in Amsterdam, and the Union of International Associations (UIA) (Brussels) produce annual statistics on international conference and conventions by city.

Another potential measurement, and one that is more subjective, is to examine the polls of popular and "bucket list" city destinations prepared by travel magazines and guidebooks, and other sources. Entities that prepare these include *Travel + Leisure*, *Condé Nast*, *National Geographic Traveler*, *Frommer's*, *Tripadvisor* and *Lonely Planet*. Getting on these lists is surely an indicator that the cities are popular and desirable for visitors and that these authoritative sources are recommending them as destinations. However, as with most of the aforementioned city ranking systems, some of the results are quite predictable as the most famous and highly visited cities are usually listed, such as London, Paris, Rome, Tokyo and Venice. Less well-known cities seldom feature in these rankings.

Another group that definitely has tourism city members is the BestCities Global Alliance. Eleven cities around the world are cooperating in this initiative through their destination management organisations (DMOs), and they are Berlin, Bogotá, Cape Town, Copenhagen, Dubai, Houston, Madrid, Melbourne, Singapore, Tokyo and Vancouver (BestCities Alliance, 2020). This alliance focuses on serving international business events.

Surely, tourism cities must have many hotels and rooms, convention facilities, attractions for tourists and significant transport access and capacity. Nowadays, cities like Las Vegas, Orlando, Beijing and Shanghai are thought to have the largest hotel capacities.

The academic literature is not particularly helpful in answering the question although many articles can be found when searching by "tourism city" in the Web of Science, Scopus and Google Scholar. For example, there are now a significant number of research articles on "smart tourism cities" as well as many case examples about individual places identified as "tourism cities".

So, after all of this has been said, what is a tourism city? Once more, let's be honest and say that all urban areas are potentially tourism cities. However, some cities demonstrate qualities and characteristics that make them stronger tourism cities, and the authors consider these to be:

- Have a formal or official priority on tourism (such as a tourism policy statement or tourism plan/strategy).
- Have a dedicated and official organisation with responsibility for city destination and management, such as a DMO.
- Have significant numbers of visitors (business, holiday/vacation, visiting friends and relatives (VFR) and others).
- There are significant levels of tourist expenditures.
- Tourism supports significant levels of employment.
- Have significant levels of tourism capacity in respect to, for example, hotel rooms, convention/conference facilities, attractions and transport.
- Have a concerted effort in marketing, branding and promotion to attract visitors.
- Have developed a professional city or destination brand.
- Possess "bucketability" or the popularity of cities as expressed by the media, influencers and others.

Abbreviations

10 AS	Awareness, accessibility, availability, attractiveness, activities, appearance, assurance, appreciation, accountability, action
ADVICE	Authority, destination, visitor, industry, community, environment
ASEAN	Association of Southeast Asian Nations
CAV	Connected and autonomous vehicle
CDME	Certified Destination Management Executive (Destinations International)
CDMO	City destination management organisation
CLIA	Cruise Lines International Association
DMO	Destination management organisation
ECM	European Cities Marketing
EWOM	Electronic word of mouth
GDCI	Global Destination Cities Index
GDP	Gross domestic product
HDI	Human Development Index
ICCA	International Congress and Convention Association
IMC	Integrated marketing communication
KPI	Key performance indicator
LCC	Low-cost (airline) carrier
MICE	Meetings, incentives, conventions, exhibitions
NIMBY	Not in my backyard
OECD	Organisation for Economic Co-operation and Development
PATA	Pacific Asia Travel Association
PESTEL	Political, economic, social, technological, environmental, legal
PESTEL-RV	Political, economic, social, technological, environmental, legal, resident, visitor
PESTEL-RVS	Political, economic, social, technological, environmental, legal, resident, visitor, stakeholder
PIB	Positioning, image and branding
PPP	Public-private partnership
QOL	Quality of life
SAARC	South Asian Association for Regional Cooperation
SDGS	Sustainable Development Goals (UN)
SMART	Specific, measurable, attainable, relevant, timely

Abbreviations

SWOT	Strengths, weaknesses, opportunities, threats
TBL	Triple bottom line
UCCN	UNESCO Creative Cities Network
UNCTAD	United Nations Conference on Trade and Development
UNDP	United Nations Development Programme
UNESCAP	United Nations Economic and Social Commission for Asia and the Pacific
UNESCO	United Nations Educational, Scientific and Cultural Organization
UNWTO	United Nations World Tourism Organization
USP	Unique selling proposition
VOA	Visa on arrival
WEF	World Economic Forum
WHL	World Heritage List (UNESCO)
WTCF	World Tourism Cities Federation
WTTC	World Travel & Tourism Council
WOM	Word of mouth

Part I

Background

Part I begins by defining tourism cities and world tourism cities. Fourteen criteria and features of such cities are identified. The term world tourism city is treated as being aspirational rather than as fixed forever. They act as transport gateways and are influential, impactful, cosmopolitan and recognised. They must also be practitioners of sustainable tourism, launching efforts to enhance economic, socio-cultural and environmental sustainability.

Part I provides a rationale for considering world tourism cities and shows how globalisation and urbanisation are accelerating the rate of change in urban areas. It highlights that urban tourism has been somewhat neglected in the recent past; however, now it is a topic receiving much greater attention from city leaders, industry practitioners and academic scholars. Others are engaging in a broader debate about the merits of developing tourism within cities and the commentators include proponents of tourism as an economic sector and an anti-tourism lobby. These conversations have been lively and have spawned new expressions such as overtourism, touristification and gentrification. The COVID-19 pandemic and its drastic consequences have only heated up this discussion, with many asking for a "new normal" and more sustainable future for city tourism. Rather than deepening the debate, the authors choose to segue into how city tourism can become more professional in the future in Part II.

Chapter 1 identifies the characteristics of tourism cities and world tourism cities and provides clear definitions of the two terms. There is no universal consensus on which urban areas are world tourism cities. So, the relevance and roles of various city rating schemes are considered. Several organisations representing tourism cities are profiled.

Chapter 2 highlights how the process of globalisation affects cities, tourism in general and world tourism cities in particular. The glocalisation concept is also discussed as how cities and tourism companies have adapted global concepts and ideas to better fit local circumstances. The connection of globalisation and world tourism cities is reviewed, and a summary is provided of the advantages and disadvantages of globalisation for tourism and world tourism cities across eight dimensions and perspectives.

Chapter 3 has a focus on urbanisation and how it contributed to the development of towns and cities around the world. It discusses urban tourism, which has been neglected by researchers and academics until only a few decades ago. It also reviews the complex nature of urban tourism and the evolution of this field of study.

DOI: 10.4324/9781003111412-1   1

Unique concepts in Part I:

Definition of world tourism cities – 8 + 5 + 1 (Chapter 1)
PESTEL-RV dimensions of globalisation (Chapter 2)
Evolution of urban tourism studies (Chapter 3)

Short breaks: Part I

1. Orlando
2. Cape Town
3. Dubai

Sweet tweets: Part I

1. WTTC reports on the economic impact of tourism on cities
2. Gothenburg, Sweden, tops the Global Destination Sustainability Index
3. More megacities on the horizon
4. Newly emerging first-tier cities in China
5. The Historic Urban Landscape approach
6. The GDS-Index (GDSI)
7. UNWTO-World Tourism Cities Federation (WTCF) city tourism performance research
8. Preserving culture in a major world tourism city (Shanghai)
9. Jollibee rules fast food in the Philippines
10. Migrant workers in the hotel industry
11. The man who drove McDonald's out of Iceland
12. Exporting Las Vegas
13. Transnational urbanism and tourism in New Delhi
14. What is economic globalisation?
15. The World Trade Organization
16. The C40 network
17. The Nature Conservancy and Hong Kong – building healthy cities
18. Cruise Lines International Association (CLIA) policies
19. Capital cities significantly contribute to the country's GDP
20. The transformation of the city of Pittsburgh
21. New technologies and tourism in cities
22. Tourism as an inextricable part of the life of the city
23. Urban tourism – an under-researched area

Chapter 1

What is a world tourism city?

Abstract

This introductory chapter identifies the characteristics of tourism cities and world tourism cities and provides clear definitions of the two terms. Eight criteria that underpin tourism cities are identified. World tourism cities are described as transport gateways and as influential, impactful, cosmopolitan and recognised. They are also places that have great concern for the sustainable development of tourism. Examples are provided so that readers have a clear understanding of world tourism cities.

Recognition is one of the factors that defines a world tourism city. As such, the concept of a World Heritage (List) city via UNESCO designation is also reviewed, as is UNESCO's Creative Cities Network (UCCN). Cities also receive recognition from the media and other sources including travel magazines. Social media customer engagement is specified as a further indicator of recognition.

There is no universal consensus on which urban areas are world tourism cities (or even tourism cities). So, the relevance and roles of various city rating schemes are considered. These systems produce results that often do not match as the criteria applied are dissimilar.

Several organisations representing tourism cities are profiled. One of these is the World Tourism Cities Federation (WTCF) based in Beijing and another is European Cities Marketing with its offices in Dijon, France.

Keywords: Global Cities Index (GCI); Global Destination City Index (GDCI); Global Destination Sustainability Index (GDSI); tourism city; UNESCO Creative Cities Network (UCCN); urban tourism; World Heritage (List) city; world tourism city.

DOI: 10.4324/9781003111412-2

Learning objectives

Having read this chapter, you should be able to:

- Explain the concept of urban tourism.
- Define a tourism city and world tourism city.
- Explain the concept of a World Heritage city.
- Identify and profile various city rating schemes.
- Describe organisations representing tourism cities and their activities.

The authors decided to write this book based on one assumption – in the future, cities will become the most significant and influential destinations for tourism in the world! A bold statement indeed and especially since many scholars have neglected urban tourism in favour of rural areas and natural landscapes. There are possibly many reasons for overlooking urban tourism research; however, having a greater focus on city tourism in the decades ahead is firmly justified as the world continues on the path to greater urbanisation. Also, it needs to be realised that urban areas are crucibles of leisure, recreation and tourism, and are not for tourism alone. City-dwellers use leisure time and participate in recreational activities in locales frequented by out-of-town visitors. These crucibles are containers of pleasure and enjoyment, but they are also carriers of discontent. The paradoxes of urban tourism justify a much deeper treatment and investigation of tourism cities.

The authors' concept for a world tourism city is an aspirational one and not a fixed notion embedded in the present day. Many different (and sometimes contradictory) criteria can and are applied to identify and rank cities, and these criteria reflect the perspectives taken by the parties involved. Some rank cities by numbers of tourist arrivals and spending; others by sustainable initiatives including efforts on climate change. So, this chapter reviews city ranking systems and the results are quite revealing, as is what you will read later in Chapter 7 about the quality of life and well-being of urban residents.

The first chapter draws from previously published works by the two authors (Maxim, 2015, 2019, 2021; Morrison, 2019, 2021; Morrison and Coca-Stefaniak, 2021). Cristina Maxim has researched and written extensively on world tourism cities; Alastair M. Morrison has focused on destination management and marketing in urban tourism. The chapter begins by describing urban tourism, tourism cities and world tourism cities, and then reviews cities on the World Heritage List and the UNESCO Creative Cities Network. Thereafter, various city ranking systems are profiled. Organisations representing tourism cities are discussed.

Urban tourism, tourism cities and world tourism cities

What is urban tourism? Chapter 3 explores this topic in detail. However, the straightforward answer for now is that it is tourism that happens in a city or within an urban area. Morrison et al. (2018) suggest that it is more than just activities and that there are tourism systems in cities consisting of four interconnecting parts (destination, marketing, demand and travel). These three authors emphasise that tourism systems are open and are affected by external environmental factors. The devastating impacts on cities of the COVID-19 pandemic are witness to the influence of factors beyond the control of those in tourism. Chapter 2 explores the effects of globalisation on tourism cities, and Chapter 3 looks into urbanisation.

The destination system part means that cities have tourism products that include attractions and events, built facilities, transportation, infrastructure and service quality and friendliness. Morrison (2021) highlights eight specific types of city tourism products: (1) history, heritage, culture and creativity; (2) events and festivals; (3) business tourism and events; (4) sport; (5) shopping, entertainment and dining; (6) built contemporary leisure attractions; (7) architecture; and (8) ethnicity, diasporas and visiting friends and relatives (VFR). Apart from these products, cities often have tourism policies and plans, purpose-specific tourism organisations (destination management organisations, DMOs), legislation and regulations and sustainable tourism guidelines. So, in essence, cities have tourism "hardware" and "software" which, in many instances, are shared by visitors and city residents.

Marketing involves communicating with target markets to convince people to visit the city, and this effort is often coordinated by city DMOs. Positioning, image and branding (PIB) are critical to successful marketing (Morrison, 2019). City and place branding are well-researched and discussed concepts, as is destination branding. Chapter 6 is devoted to the marketing and branding of world tourism cities.

Demand includes the visitors to cities as well as factors that influence people in making travel decisions, how they make bookings, travel and recall their memories of trips. Cities draw visitors with dissimilar purposes that include business and meetings, incentives, conventions and exhibitions (MICE) travel, pleasure, VFR and personal. Some cities have a focus on leisure travel and attract people on holidays or vacations. These include Las Vegas, Macao and Orlando that specialise in entertainment. Other cities have diversified markets, and some, for example, are recognised for their attractiveness for international meetings such as Paris, Vienna, Madrid, Barcelona and Berlin (ICCA, 2019).

The fourth system part, travel, encompasses online and offline travel distribution channels and modes of transportation. Transportation and mobility are particularly critical aspects of cities. For example, the World Travel & Tourism Council (WTTC) identified 33 major port cities with significant levels of tourism (WTTC, 2019). Included among these were Barcelona, Cancún, Hong Kong, Miami and Singapore. Leading world tourism cities often have busy airports that may serve as international or regional airline hubs. Some of these are Dubai International Airport, London Heathrow Airport and Paris Charles de Gaulle Airport.

Thus, city tourism is a system that involves a great deal more than just what visitors do in urban areas. The system needs careful planning and management as there are multiple stakeholders to be considered, including visitors, residents and tourism sector owners and staff. Also, making tourism sustainable for the longer term needs to be prioritised.

Is tourism important to cities? From all the information available, tourism is of great significance to many cities around the world. This point is confirmed by statements made by the World Conference of Mayors, which includes tourism in its "7 T" goals – "to stimulate increased tourist travel between cities of the world". The other six Ts are trust, trade, technology transfer, twin cities, treasury and training (World Conference of Mayors, 2021).

Sweet tweet 1

WTTC reports on the economic impact of tourism on cities

The WTTC analysed the economic impact of travel and tourism on 73 cities around the world. The results underlined the great importance to major urban centres. A selection of the key findings included:

- Almost half of global international travel occurs in cities.
- Cities rely more on international travel demand than broader economies, with international visitor spending accounting for 45% of tourism spending across the 73 cities, compared to 29% globally.
- Seven of the 15 fastest-growing cities in terms of travel and tourism GDP were in the Asia-Pacific region.
- Some cities have very high proportions (more than 95%) of total tourism spending from international visitors and these include Macao, Dublin (Ireland) and Dubrovnik.

Source: WTTC (2019). Figures are based on 2018.

Now, what is a tourism city? This is a tough question to answer as all cities welcome some level of visitors. It could be argued that tourism cities are places where tourism is important and in which city governments put a high priority on this economic sector. Additionally, it could be said that these urban areas are the ones that get the most tourists. Using these parameters, it is easy to say that London, New York and Paris are tourism cities; however, what about less famous "provincial" cities like Anqing in China, Portland in the USA and Dundee in the UK?

There are undoubtedly both quantitative and qualitative criteria that determine tourism cities. Considering the volumes of tourists and expenditures is an example of one of the potential quantitative metrics. As an example of this, a ranking of the world's top tourism cities is produced in Mastercard's *Global Destination Cities Index* (GDCI) (Mastercard, 2019). Some 167 cities were in the results for 2019 and Bangkok, London and Paris were the top three. The GDCI ranks the cities by their total volumes of international overnight visitors. GDCI also reports on the spending of international visitors in cities. Bangkok in 2019 welcomed 22.78 million international visitors.

Euromonitor International publishes an annual ranking of the *Top 100 City Destinations*, which also uses the total number of international tourist arrivals. The company's 2019 rankings had a top ten that included five cities in Asia (Hong Kong as #1 in the world; Bangkok, #2; Macao, #4; Singapore, #5; Kuala Lumpur, #9). The other top-ranking cities were London (#3), Paris (#6), Dubai (#7), New York City (#8) and Istanbul (#10) (Euromonitor International, 2020).

On the business tourism side, GainingEdge, a consulting company based in Melbourne, Australia, has developed a city-based *Competitive Index* with respect to international conventions (GainingEdge, 2020a). For 2020, the Index ranked 101 cities worldwide, with Paris, Singapore, New York, Barcelona and Tokyo receiving the highest scores (GainingEdge, 2020b). Additionally, the International Congress and Convention Association (ICCA), based in Amsterdam, and the Union of International Associations (UIA) (Brussels) produce annual statistics on international conferences and conventions by city.

Another potential measurement, and one that is more subjective, is to examine the polls of popular and "bucket list" city destinations prepared by travel magazines and guidebooks, and other sources. Entities that prepare these include *Travel + Leisure*, *Condé Nast*, *National Geographic Traveler*, *Frommer's*, *TripAdvisor* and *Lonely Planet*. Getting on these lists is surely an indicator that the cities are popular and desirable for visitors and that these authoritative sources are recommending them as destinations. However, as with most of the aforementioned city ranking systems, some of the results are quite predictable as the most famous and highly visited cities are usually listed such as London, Paris, Rome, Tokyo and Venice. Less well-known cities seldom feature in these rankings.

Greater legitimacy to the term tourism city arrived in 2012. Since then, tourism cities have had their own representational body through the WTCF headquartered in Beijing. Through self-selection, the cities that belong to WTCF consider themselves to be tourism cities.

Surely, it might also be said that tourism cities must have many hotels and rooms, convention facilities, attractions for tourists and significant transport access and capacity. Later in this chapter, it will be seen that the *Global Power City Index* (GPCI) uses some of these metrics in its ranking systems. Nowadays, cities like Las Vegas, Orlando, Beijing and Shanghai are thought to have the largest hotel capacities.

The academic literature is not helpful in answering the question although many articles can be found when searching by "tourism city" in the Web of Science, Scopus and Google Scholar. For example, there are now a significant number of research articles on "smart tourism cities" as well as many case examples about individual places identified as "tourism cities". While authors often use these as keywords to give the context for their research, they do not clearly define the term "tourism city".

So then, what is a tourism city? It is correct to argue that all urban areas are potentially tourism cities. However, some cities demonstrate qualities and characteristics that make them stronger tourism cities, and these are illustrated in Figure 1.1.

An explanation of the eight qualities, characteristics or criteria depicted in Figure 1.1 follows:

- *Support and involvement of city residents* (unnumbered): Not every city can claim to have this; however, it is a baseline requirement for a successful tourism city. The

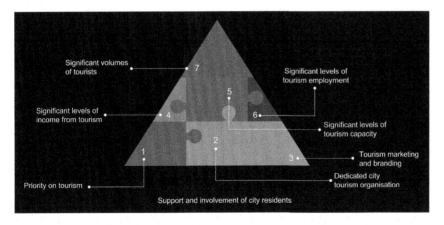

Figure 1.1 Tourism city criteria.

lessons learned from the overtourism issue are that tourism cities must give a higher priority to residents and their quality of life.

- *Priority on tourism* (1): The city has a formal or official priority on tourism such as a tourism policy statement or tourism plan. The planning and development of city tourism destinations are covered in Chapter 5.
- *Dedicated city tourism organisation* (2): The city has a dedicated and official organisation with responsibility for city destination management. The concept of city destination management is the topic of Chapter 4.
- *Tourism marketing and branding* (3): The city has implemented a concerted effort in marketing, branding and promotion to attract visitors. City destination marketing and branding are described in detail in Chapter 6.
- *Significant levels of income from tourism* (4): The city receives significant tourism expenditures.
- *Significant levels of tourism capacity* (5): The city has a significant supply of hotel rooms, convention/conference facilities, attractions, dining and entertainment facilities and transport.
- *Significant levels of tourism employment* (6): The city has significant numbers of jobs that are directly and indirectly supported by tourism.
- *Significant volumes of tourists* (7): The city has significant numbers of visitors (business, holiday/vacation, VFR and personal).

Another criterion that might be added is the attractiveness or "bucketability" of cities as expressed by the media, influencers and others. This point is discussed later in the chapter as some of the city rating systems attempt to select cities with the greatest tourist appeal.

As a footnote to the tourism city criteria, the authors are not advocating that cities should attract significant volumes of visitors, nor that they solely should be concerned with creating significant income and employment from tourism. Rather, the intention here is to indicate that these tend to be characteristics of tourism cities.

What now is a world tourism city? Maxim (2019, p. 1006) described these cities as follows:

> World tourism cities perform multiple functions and exhibit various characteristics that influence tourism development within their boundaries. They are the main gateway for tourists visiting a country and their success has a direct impact on the visitor economy of that destination.

Maxim specifically identifies Dubai, Hong Kong, Las Vegas, London, Paris and Singapore in her *Current Issues in Tourism* (2019) article as examples of world tourism cities. Barcelona, Berlin and New York were also referenced in the article. Later, she used Dubai, Hong Kong, London, New York and Paris as examples of world tourism cities (Maxim, 2021) in the *Routledge Handbook of Tourism Cities*.

It could be said that world tourism cities are tourism cities plus, but what does the "plus" represent in terms of additional features or criteria? Maxim's definition has certain key messages that are expressed in the phrases of "perform multiple functions", "influence tourism development", "gateway for tourists" and "impact on visitor economy". Figure 1.2 provides five essential descriptors of a world tourism city and adds "cosmopolitan" and "recognised" to Maxim's three features (Figure 1.2).

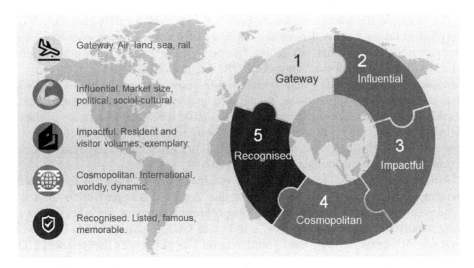

Figure 1.2 Features of world tourism cities.

- *Gateway*: Highly convenient transportation accessibility is a significant feature of world tourism cities. Many of these cities are hubs for airlines, railways or ships, or are strategic points in national highway systems. Orlando, Florida, is a good example of the latter. Dubai is a case where the city has developed into a major airline hub. Shanghai with its Hongqiao transportation hub is now a major airline and rail gateway. Singapore has become a major Asian port for cruise ships.
- *Influential*: World tourism cities are multi-functional and influence other places within their countries. Of course, this is partly due to their population densities and market size. They are significant generators of domestic tourists as well as being sources of international visitors. They may be centres of industry, services, finance and banking, government or hubs for the MICE markets. London is a wonderful case here based on its influence on the rest of the UK.
- *Impactful*: These cities economically impact other areas within nations. They may also be capital cities that have political power. World tourism cities are key centres of culture and heritage that are shared by all citizens of particular countries. Sustainable and smart tourism policies and initiatives can provide exemplars for others to try to emulate. These cities can be particularly innovative and creative. Gothenburg and Copenhagen, two major Scandinavian cities, are highly influential in terms of their sustainability initiatives. Edinburgh, the capital of Scotland, has become the "festival city" with a worldwide impact due to its success.
- *Cosmopolitan*: The Cambridge Dictionary defines this as "containing or having experience of people and things from many parts of the world". Worldly is thus a good synonym for cosmopolitan. World tourism cities attract visitors from abroad in addition to domestic travellers. There may also be significant immigrant populations within the cities. They tend to be lively and dynamic places because of the mixtures of peoples and cultures. According to WorldAtlas (2021), the most cosmopolitan cities in the world are Dubai, Brussels, Toronto, Auckland, Sydney and Los Angeles.

An example for measuring cosmopolitism is provided in Resonance's *World's Best Cities* rating system. Under the category of people, there is a criterion of the percentage of foreign-born residents. The presence of people from other countries tends to make a city more cosmopolitan (Resonance, 2021).

- *Recognised*: It is easy to say that world tourism cities are famous, but that falls short of a comprehensive definition of recognised in the context of tourism. Later, the World Heritage List recognitions are discussed, and it is noted that many of the cities included are not famous household names. Recognition can be received in a variety of ways such as through government or official organisations, accreditations, media companies and various polls and ranking systems.

    Another indicator of recognition is the volume of people liking, sharing and commenting on the social media profiles of cities. Again, this is part of the Resonance city rating system and included within the promotion category. Specifically, the company measures Facebook check-ins, number of Google search results, Tripadvisor reviews, Instagram hashtags and popularity on Google Trends (Resonance, 2021).

Before leaving this discussion of features of world tourism cities, it needs to be said that they must be concerned about *sustainability* and have implemented initiatives to support sustainable development. Taken together with the 8 criteria for tourism cities, there is a set of 14 indicators for world tourism cities (including sustainability and resident support) (Figure 1.3). The chapters which follow elaborate on these indicators and present a systematic approach to urban tourism management.

Sweet tweet 2

Gothenburg, Sweden, tops the Global Destination Sustainability Index

The *Global Destination Sustainability Index* (GDS-Index) is a destination-level programme that "measures, benchmarks and improves the sustainability strategy and performance of meetings, events and business tourism destinations". It assesses four areas that are vital to the sustainability performance of a destination: Environmental strategy and infrastructure, social sustainability performance, industry supplier support and the DMO's strategy and initiatives. For 2019, Gothenburg was the highest ranked for the fourth year in a row, scoring 89.64 out of a total possible of 100 points.

Source: Global Destination Sustainability Movement (2021).

It also must be realised that not all tourism cities and world tourism cities are the same and they can be classified in various ways. For example, WTTC (2019) formed five categories – capital cities, largest cities, port cities, secondary cities and leisure cities. There were 11 leisure cities including Antalya, Cancún, Dubrovnik, Fort Lauderdale, Honolulu, Las Vegas, Macao, Marrakech, Miami, Orlando and Venice. These cities were defined as places "where leisure travel is the dominant segment … and include cities where over 80% of travel spending is from leisure visitors while they must also be

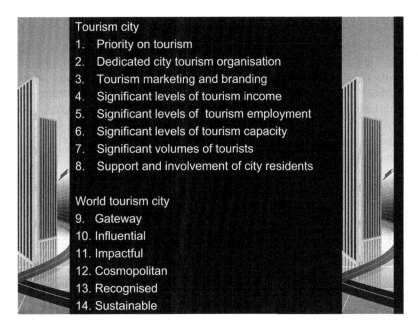

Figure 1.3 Combined tourism city and world tourism city criteria.

an important leisure destination within the country". The WTTC findings for these and 62 other cities underlined the significance of world tourism cities being cosmopolitan and impactful.

SHORT BREAK 1

Orlando: From swampland to a world entertainment capital

It was said earlier that the term world tourism city was aspirational; in other words, some cities can have a vision to become important global tourism hubs. One shining example of this notion is Orlando in the central part of Florida. The opening of Walt Disney World in 1971 was the beginning of an era in which Orlando would become the "theme park capital of the world". The affordability of land, location at the intersection of two major highways, the availability of an airport and good access to markets in the Southeast USA were reasons for Walt Disney selecting Orlando to build Walt Disney World.

Since 1971, Orlando has become one of the world's most vibrant leisure cities. The attendance figures for Orlando's theme parks in 2019 were Magic Kingdom – Walt Disney World (20.96 million), Disney's Animal Kingdom – WDW (13.89

million), EPCOT – WDW (12.44 million), Disney's Hollywood Studios (11.48 million), Universal Studios Florida (10.92 million), and Universal's Islands of Adventure (10.38 million). According to Visit Orlando, it received approximately 75.8 million visitors in 2019. In 2018, around 6.5 million were international visitors with over 1 million coming from the UK. STR (2020) found that the greater Orlando region had 486 hotels with 127,809 rooms at the end of 2019. CBRE estimated that 53 new hotels with 10,863 rooms would open in 2021.

Orlando may now be the leading leisure world tourism city drawing visitors from around the globe. However, it must also be acknowledged as a major centre for conventions, exhibitions and other types of meetings. The Orange County Convention Center (OCCC) hosted 172 events in 2018–2019 and had a total attendance figure of 1.235 million people (Orange County Convention Center, 2019). OCCC has a total square footage of seven million.

Discussion points:

1. What are the key factors leading to Orlando becoming a world tourism city?
2. Why do leisure cities also tend to be successful MICE destinations?
3. Orlando has been able to sustain and grow its tourism for 30 years. Given its reliance on entertainment, what strategies must the city take to make tourism sustainable in the future?

Sources: CBRE (2021); CultureTrip.com (2021); HVS (2020); Orange County Convention Center (2019, 2021); TEA/AECOM (2019); Visit Orlando (2021).

Three associated terms that need to be mentioned here for further clarification are "world cities", "global cities" and "national capital cities". While the latter is self-explanatory, the other two terms are not and there are differing and contesting definitions for them. For global cities, however, the Global Cities Index (GCI) by Kearney is the most cited source, and this city rating scheme is discussed in more detail later. The sociologist Sassen (2002, 2005) is often quoted in connection with the concept of global cities, and she uses the backdrop of globalisation to hone her definition of these cities. In her 2001 book, London, New York and Tokyo are the examples chosen to represent global cities (Renn, 2013). Global cities are population centres that are highly competitive and significant to the worldwide networks of industry, finance, technology and services.

Yuen and Ooi (2009, p. 1) say that "World cities compete in the global arena on the basis of connectivity and their contributions to the international networks and flows of goods, services and finance which constitute the world economy". Hall (2009) argued that the most successful cities in the future were likely to be "world cities that are already integrated in different ways with the world economy". So, world cities are highly networked and connected with the global economy (Beaverstock, Taylor & Smith, 1999) .

A megacity according to the United Nations is a city with a population of ten million or more. Table 1.1 shows 30 of the world's megacities ranked by population. It is noteworthy that four countries (Bangladesh, China, India and Pakistan) account for 14 of these 30 megacities.

Table 1.1 World's largest urban agglomerations in 2020

Rank	City	Country	Millions
1	Tokyo	Japan	37
2	Delhi	India	30
3	Shanghai	China	27
4	São Paulo	Brazil	22
5	Ciudad de México (Mexico City)	Mexico	22
6	Dhaka	Bangladesh	21
7	Al-Qahirah (Cairo)	Egypt	21
8	Beijing	China	20
9	Mumbai (Bombay)	India	20
10	Kinki M.M.A. (Osaka)	Japan	19
11	New York-Newark	USA	19
12	Karachi	Pakistan	16
13	Chongqing	China	16
14	Istanbul	Turkey	15
15	Buenos Aires	Argentina	15
16	Kolkata (Calcutta)	India	15
17	Lagos	Nigeria	14
18	Kinshasa	Congo	14
19	Manila	Philippines	14
20	Tianjin	China	14
21	Rio de Janeiro	Brazil	13
22	Guangzhou, Guangdong	China	13
23	Lahore	Pakistan	13
24	Moskva (Moscow)	Russia	13
25	Los Angeles-Long Beach-Santa Ana	USA	12
26	Shenzhen	China	12
27	Bangalore	India	12
28	Paris	France	11
29	Bogotá	Colombia	11
30	Chennai (Madras)	India	11

Source: United Nations (2021).

Sweet tweet 3

More megacities on the horizon

There were 34 megacities in the world in 2020 with populations above ten million. The United Nations expects this to grow saying that

> By 2030, the world is projected to have 43 megacities with more than 10 million inhabitants, most of them in developing regions. However, some of the fastest-growing urban agglomerations are cities with fewer than 1 million inhabitants, many of them located in Asia and Africa. While one in eight people live in 34 megacities worldwide, close to half of the world's urban dwellers reside in much smaller settlements with fewer than 500,000 inhabitants.

Source: United Nations (2021).

The United Nations classifies cities into six groups based on population: (1) 10 million or more (megacities); (2) 5 to 10 million; (3) 1 to 5 million; (4) 500,000 to 1 million; (5) 300,000 to 500,000; and (6) fewer than 300,000. The UN's figures for 2020 indicated that there were 51 cities (agglomerations) in the second group; 494 in the third; 626 in the fourth; and 729 in the fifth. The number of cities with fewer than 300,000 was not specified.

Tiering is another classification concept used with the cities in certain countries. China is one of the nations that puts its cities into tiers, although these are not officially sanctioned by the Central Government. Also, there are differing approaches to the tiering of China's cities, some using population and GDP, others using more complex algorithms (*South China Morning Post*, 2016; TheBiggestCitiesinChina.com, 2020). Generally, Beijing, Guangzhou, Shanghai and Shenzhen are considered to be China's first-tier cities. The USA is another country where cities are placed into tiers, and this is applied in the real estate market and for conventions and meetings. Shimasaki (2015) defined first-, second- and third-tier cities in the USA based upon their capacities to accommodate conventions and meetings. Citing Chicago, Las Vegas and Orlando as examples of Tier 1 convention cities, she indicated that they must have at least 10,000 rooms and a convention centre with a minimum of 500,000 gross square feet of exhibit space. Chen (2020) suggested that Tier 1 cities have developed and established real estate markets and tend to be highly developed, with desirable schools, facilities and businesses. These cities have the most expensive real estate properties.

Sweet tweet 4

Newly emerging first-tier cities in China

The argument is made in this chapter that cities are rapidly changing and so it is advisable to have a flexible definition of a tourism city. The Yicai Media Group ranks China's cities into tier levels, and 337 cities in total are analysed.

There is little argument about Beijing, Guangzhou, Shanghai and Shenzhen being China's four first-tier cities; however, 15 other cities are hot on their heels. These are (in order) Chengdu, Chongqing, Hangzhou, Wuhan, Xi'an, Tianjin, Suzhou, Nanjing, Zhengzhou, Changsha, Dongguan, Qingdao, Hefei and Foshan. Yicai calls these the "new first-tier cities". Some of these are hardly "household names" in Western countries and the same is true of many large cities in India as discussed later in Chapter 11. As these cities grow in size and power, they are also becoming increasingly viable and competitive tourism destinations.

Source: Yicai Media Group (2020).

This book is about tourism cities and the emphasis is on tourism as the qualifier. It is not a text on global cities, world cities or megacities as described earlier. The criteria for inclusion are not the same. However, this does not mean that global cities, world cities and megacities are not also world tourism cities. For example, Nara in southern Honshu, Japan, is a world tourism city, but it is not a critical centre for globalisation. Tokyo, however, is both a global city and a world tourism city. The population of Nara is under 400,000; for the Tokyo agglomeration it is almost 40 million. Here, it must be emphasised that world tourism cities are not necessarily the largest cities on the globe.

Having discussed urban tourism, tourism cities and world tourism cities, the next topic is city recognition through UNESCO's World Heritage List and the UNESCO Creative Cities Network.

UNESCO World Heritage List and UNESCO Creative Cities Network

Recognition is one of the features of world tourism cities. Official recognition is a most powerful way for a city to be recognised, and UNESCO is one of the official agencies that grants such designations. There is substantial evidence that the UNESCO recognitions attract visitors to the cities that have earned them (Pulido-Fernández et al., 2019; Ramires et al., 2018). Three of UNESCO's programmes are now discussed.

UNESCO World Heritage List

UNESCO says that "What makes the concept of World Heritage exceptional is its universal application. World Heritage sites belong to all the peoples of the world, irrespective of the territory on which they are located". The World Heritage List (WHL) was initiated in 1972. At the time of writing, there were 1,121 WHL properties, of which 869 were cultural and 213 were natural (UNESCO, 2021c).

There are many urban areas around the globe that are designated as World Heritage cities by UNESCO. Some of these are famous places such as Budapest, Macao, México City, Prague, Rome, Vatican City and Venice, while many others are not as widely known. Two examples of the latter are Augsburg, Germany, and Dujiangyan in Sichuan Province, China. These two cities were placed on the WHL due to their exemplary water management (Augsburg, Figure 1.4) and irrigation (Dujiangyan) systems.

Figure 1.4 Augsburg, Germany, is on the World Heritage List due to its water management system. (Author: Ruth Plössel; copyright: Stade Augsburg; source: UNESCO, https://whc.unesco.org/en/documents/166554.)

World Heritage Cities Programme

The UNESCO World Heritage Cities Programme was established to assist with the challenges of protecting and managing urban heritage (UNESCO, 2021b). This initiative has several thematic programmes which include Urban Notebooks, World Heritage City Webinar, World Heritage City Lab, International Experts Meeting and World Cities Day. A Historic Urban Landscape approach also has been developed.

Sweet tweet 5

The Historic Urban Landscape approach

In 2011, the UNESCO World Heritage Cities Programme released the Historic Urban Landscape approach which "moves beyond the preservation of the physical environment and focuses on the entire human environment with all of its tangible and intangible qualities". Among the approach's key recommendations for cities are:

- To undertake comprehensive surveys and mapping of the city's natural, cultural and human resources.
- To reach consensus using participatory planning and stakeholder consultations on what values to protect for transmission to future generations and to determine the attributes that carry these values.

- To assess the vulnerability of these attributes to socio-economic stresses and impacts of climate change.
- To integrate urban heritage values and their vulnerability status into a wider framework of city development, which shall provide indications of areas of heritage sensitivity that require careful attention to the planning, design and implementation of development projects.
- To prioritise actions for conservation and development.
- To establish the appropriate partnerships and local management frameworks for each of the identified projects for conservation and development, as well as to develop mechanisms for the coordination of the various activities between different actors, both public and private.

Source: UNESCO (2021b).

The World Heritage Cities Programme in conjunction with its partners produces other reports and recommendations for urban areas. One of these is the report, *Community-centred urban development: A paradigm of inclusive growth* (UNESCO Cities Platform, 2020). Essentially, this document is part of the dialogue led by UNESCO to create greater community involvement in urban development and also to enhance resident quality of life.

UNESCO Creative Cities Network

UCCN was started in 2004, and there were 246 city members in 2021 (UNESCO, 2021a). Seven creative fields are included (crafts and folk arts; design; film; gastronomy; literature; media arts; and music). All of these fields have an appeal to tourists and city residents. For gastronomy, there are 37 cities recognised in UCCN, and some are well known including Macao, San Antonio and Tucson (Figure 1.5). Other cities are not as famous, such as Alba (Italy), Bendigo (Australia) and Cochabamba (Bolivia). Whether famed or not, the inclusion in UCCN potentially puts all these cities on the world stage.

City rating systems

Not all cities and urban areas are alike. However, they all attract residents, visitors, investors, companies, students and other groups and individuals. Due to the magnetism of cities, several ranking schemes have developed to rate them on various criteria. Most of these include some measures of tourism and the cultural offers within specific cities, as will now be highlighted.

Non-tourism rating systems

The *A.T. Kearney 2020 Global Cities* report uses several metrics to rank many of the world's most recognised urban areas. In the following quote from the firm's 2019 report, use of the words "vibrancy" and "competitive" is noticeable, as is the bottom-line statement that global cities attract people and businesses:

Figure 1.5 An example of the food in Tucson, Arizona.
(Photo: unsplash.com; courtesy: Travis Yewell.)

> The vibrancy of the world's most competitive cities – places such as London, New York, Singapore, and San Francisco – is no happy coincidence. With a focus on human capital, thoughtful municipal policies, smart corporate investment, and a commitment to building a technology pathway into the future, these cities have become bustling, global hubs that attract people and businesses alike.
>
> *(Kearney, 2020)*

The top ten ranked cities for 2020 were New York, London, Paris, Tokyo, Beijing, Hong Kong, Los Angeles, Chicago, Singapore and Washington, DC.

The 2020 report ranked 151 cities with 29 metrics divided into five categories – business activity (30%), human capital (30%), information exchange (15%), cultural experience (15%) and political engagement (10%). In the 2019 report, London ranked first for cultural experience which had the six metrics of museums, visual and performing arts, sporting events, international travellers, culinary offerings and sister cities. London received the highest scores for four of these six criteria (museums, sporting events, international travellers and culinary offerings).

The GPCI is operated by the Institute for Urban Strategies of the Mori Memorial Foundation in Japan (Institute for Urban Strategies, 2021). It measures city magnetism defined as their "power to attract people, capital, and enterprises from around the world". The six criteria that GPCI covers are the economy, research and development, cultural interaction, liveability, environment and accessibility. Within cultural interaction, the measurements include several tourism-related items including tourism resources (tourist attractions, proximity to World Heritage sites, nightlife options), visitor amenities (number of hotel rooms, number of luxury hotel rooms, attractiveness of shopping options, attractiveness of dining options), cultural facilities (number of museums, number of theatres, number of stadiums), international interaction (number of foreign visitors, number of foreign residents) and trendsetting potential (number of international conferences, number of cultural events, cultural content export value, art market environment). These are great indicators for assessing tourism in cities; however, the GPCI only reports on 48 cities worldwide. The GPCI had London, New York, Tokyo, Paris and Singapore in the top five slots for 2019.

Liveability (or livability) is a quality often ascribed to cities, and there are also several polls that measure this construct. The *Global Liveability Index* is published annually by the Economist Intelligence Unit (EIU) (Economist Intelligence Unit, 2019) . Thirty criteria (quantitative and qualitative) are used in five categories (stability, healthcare, culture and environment, education and infrastructure) to rank 140 cities around the world. Within the culture and entertainment category, there are nine indicators, three of which are cultural availability, food and drink and sporting availability. There are transportation-related indicators within the infrastructure category. Ranked highest in 2018 and in order were Vienna (Austria), Melbourne (Australia), Osaka (Japan), Calgary (Canada), Sydney (Australia), Vancouver (Canada), Toronto (Canada), Tokyo (Japan), Copenhagen (Denmark) and Adelaide (Australia).

The *Mercer's Quality of Living Ranking* was produced in its 21st annual edition for the year 2018 (Mercer LLC, 2020). Some 231 cities were ranked and once again Vienna came out on top and Baghdad was 231st. The other top-ranked cities, in order, were Zurich (Switzerland), Vancouver, Munich (Germany), Auckland (New Zealand), Düsseldorf (Germany), Frankfurt (Germany), Copenhagen, Geneva (Switzerland) and Basel (Switzerland). The ranking criteria used by Mercer are not easily determined; however, in their rankings for 2018, the company measured personal safety and provided separate statistics for it. Helsinki (Finland), Luxembourg, Bern, Basel and Zurich were ranked as the best for personal safety (Mercer LLC, 2020).

There are other city rating systems that adopt different measurement criteria. For example, there is the *Global Happiness Report* (Sustainable Development Solutions Network, 2020) and the *City Wealth Index* (Harley, 2021). De Neve and Krekel have a section in the *World Happiness Report* on *Cities and happiness: A global ranking and analysis*. Rather than using factors and scales developed by the researchers, De Neve and Krekel used city resident self-reported measures. Mentioned again in Chapter 7, Helsinki, Aarhus, Wellington, Zurich, Copenhagen, Bergen, Oslo, Tel Aviv, Stockholm and Brisbane obtained the highest scores for subjective well-being. London, New York, Paris, Tokyo and Hong Kong ranked at the top in the *City Wealth Index*. The Brookings Institute (2018) produces the *Global Metro Monitor* that ranks 300 metropolitan areas in the world by rate of GDP growth.

Resonance, a planning and consulting company based in Vancouver, British Columbia, prepares the *World's Best Cities* which it says is "a global ranking of place equity" (Resonance, 2021). The six core categories used in this ranking system are place, people, programming, product, prosperity and promotion. Although the Resonance system covers more than just tourism, there are many individual criteria that fit within tourism. For example, programming includes culture, nightlife, dining and shopping. Within the place category, there are sights and landmarks, weather, safety and parks and outdoors. Products include airport connectivity, attractions and museums. The results for 2020 had the top ten cities as London, New York, Paris, Moscow, Tokyo, Dubai, Singapore, Barcelona, Los Angeles and Madrid. The Resonance ranking system is a "hybrid" assessment of liveability, leisure, recreation and tourism, and is very robust.

Tourism rating systems

There are several systems that rank cities based on their attractiveness in tourism. These are another form of recognition for world tourism cities. The GDCI by Mastercard, Euromonitor International and GainingEdge systems are previously mentioned.

One of these is the *Best 150 Cities to Visit in the World* (World Cities Ranking, 2021). Using 13 criteria (sights, location, pedestrian zones, affordability (value for money), safety, cleanliness, shopping, climate, people, nightlife, transport, size and ease of travel) the top 10 cities in 2020 were Venice, Paris, Barcelona, Rome, London, Florence, Istanbul, St. Petersburg, Madrid and New York.

The *Global Destination Sustainability Index* (GDSI) is operated by the Global Destination Sustainability Movement and it was launched in 2015. The focus of GDSI is on meeting destinations and business travel. The top-rated cities in 2019 were Gothenburg, Copenhagen, Zurich, Glasgow, Aalborg, Reykjavik, Malmö, Sydney (Australia), Upsala and Melbourne (Australia).

Sweet tweet 6

The GDS-Index (GDSI)

The Global Destination Sustainability Movement states that the "GDS-Index is the world's leading benchmarking and performance improvement program for business tourism and events destinations. Its purpose is to engage, inspire and enable destinations to become more regenerative, flourishing and resilient places to visit, meet and thrive in".

Source: Global Destination Sustainability Movement (2021).

Some travel magazines conduct polls with experts or readers as their respondents. For example, *Condé Nast Traveler* magazine published the *2020 Readers' Choice Awards* for the *Best Cities in the World* (Marino, 2020). The winners were divided into small and big cities. For the larger urban areas, those ranking highest for 2020 were Kyoto, Lyon, Singapore, Sydney (Australia), Vienna, Tokyo, Porto, Helsinki, Copenhagen and Lisbon. San Miguel de Allende in Mexico was the top-ranked small city destination followed by Chiang Mai, Mérida, Monte Carlo, Valetta, Salzburg, Siena, Victoria (British Columbia), Florence and Edinburgh. *Travel + Leisure* is another magazine that produces an annual ranking of best cities to visit. For 2020, these were Oaxaca, San Miguel de Allende, Hoi An, Chiang Mai, Florence, Kyoto, Udaipur, Luang Prabang, Ubud and Istanbul (*Travel + Leisure*, 2020).

These ranking systems, most if not all owned by commercial interests, demonstrate a high level of interest in cities as well as the desire for city governments to have competitive benchmarks. Their limitation is that they only cover a small portion of the world's urban areas and do not offer much guidance on how to manage and improve tourism in cities. Also, they do not classify urban areas by their economic emphasis on tourism and their related policy-making and planning. In addition, it is noteworthy that the results are very varied, and this reflects the differing methods and criteria applied to do the ranking.

While there is no agreement on the number of cities in the world, the figure is certainly in the thousands. Recent estimates indicate that there are as many as 10,000 cities globally (OECD, 2020; Scruggs, 2020; United Nations Human Settlement Programme, 2021). This means that many of these cities are not included in the city rating systems just reviewed. However, for those that are, these ratings represent a form of recognition that can be significant to their roles as world tourism cities.

Self-recognition as tourism cities is another way of identifying urban areas that have accepted their significance as destinations. Next, there is a discussion of the organisations that represent such cities.

Organisations representing city tourism

Global and regional organisations such as United Nations World Tourism Organization (UNWTO), UNESCO, WTTC, Pacific Asia Travel Association (PATA) and Association of Southeast Asian Nations (ASEAN) have profound impacts on tourism cities; however, their mandates include more than just urban areas. This chapter began by asserting that cities as destinations had for many years been a neglected topic in research and practice. The recent emergence of organisations serving city destinations is evidence of this argument.

A brief discussion of seven organisations with stronger mandates vis-à-vis cities now is provided, beginning with the World Tourism Cities Federation.

> [The] World Tourism Cities Federation (WTCF), voluntarily formed by famous tourism cities and tourism-related institutions in the world under the initiative of Beijing, is the world's first international tourism organization focusing on cities. Established on 15 September 2012 in Beijing, the headquarters and Secretariat of WTCF are based in Beijing, and Chinese and English are its official languages.

Information on WTCF's website at the time of writing indicated that it had around 150 member cities. While this number is growing as is WTCF itself, it still represents only a minor proportion of the world's urban areas. WTCF has produced several expert and research reports including the *Report on Recovery and Development of World Tourism amid COVID-19* and the *Action Guide on Recovery and Revitalization of City Tourism amid COVID-19*, both published in 2020.

Sweet tweet 7

UNWTO-WTCF city tourism performance research

In 2019, UNWTO and WTCF released a joint report consisting of a compilation of 15 city case studies. The case studies were based on an assessment of the performance of tourism in the cities in five aspects: Destination management, economic impact, social and cultural impact, environmental impact, and technology and new business models.

This report is mentioned again in Chapter 6, citing the 10 success factors that were extracted from the analysis of the 15 case studies. At least 3 of the 14 requirements for tourism cities outlined in this chapter were among these success factors, including a city priority on tourism (long-term vision and strategic planning), community engagement and a policy for sustainable development and management. The 292-page report is an excellent reference tool for world tourism cities.

Source: UNWTO/WTCF (2019); UNWTO (2020a, 2020b).

The World Cities Culture Forum (WCCF) "provides a way for policy makers in 38 key cities to share research and intelligence and explore the vital role of culture in their future prosperity" (BOP Consulting, 2021). The members include major cities such as London, New York and Paris, as well as less well-known urban centres including Abu Dhabi, Lagos and Oslo. WCCF has produced a number of useful reports related to culture and cities, including *Culture and Climate Change* and the *Transformational Cultural Projects Report* (World Cities Culture Forum, 2021).

Sweet tweet 8

Preserving culture in a major world tourism city

Tianzifang is an area within Shanghai's French Concession (Figure 1.6). A report by the World Cities Cultural Forum says, "Tianzifang is special in a city whose physical form has changed in almost direct correlation with its rapid economic growth, deindustrialisation and the voracious development of its land assets".

With cities becoming increasingly concerned with maintaining their authenticity, it is extremely challenging to preserve traditional districts with their unique architecture and ways of living. Tianzifang is a great case where local residents and business owners banded together to conserve what they had.

Source: BOP Consulting (2014).

The World Conference of Mayors was created in 1984 and is a non-profit, non-political conference of current and former mayors. Its objective is to "stimulate positive and constructive relations between mayors internationally, based on interlocking interests and concerns" (World Conference of Mayors, 2021). As previously mentioned, its 7 T goals include tourism.

The Urban Land Institute (ULI) is a membership organisation of cross-disciplinary real estate and land use experts, established in 1936 (ULI, 2021). Located in Washington, DC, it has more than 4,500 members worldwide. ULI has several publications and has arranged events related to tourism in cities. For example, it currently has an online course called *Tourism and the City* that is part of its *RE:SHAPING CITIES – Post-Pandemic Perspectives* series.

Destinations International is a major association of DMOs that includes many city organisations. Its four cornerstones are community, advocacy, research and education

Figure 1.6 Shanghai's characteristic *Shikumen* architecture can be found in Tianzifang and other historic districts such as *Xintiandi*. (Photo: unsplash.com; Courtesy: Mathew Waring.)

(Destinations International, 2021). It has around 600 member organisations. The *Certified Destination Management Executive* (CDME) programme is one of its major educational offerings, and Destinations International also operates the *Destination Marketing Accreditation Program* (DMAP). Destinations International has developed highly useful criteria for measuring the performance of city DMOs. Also, like European Cities Marketing, it produces estimates of DMO budgets and funding sources. For 2021, it provided a figure of $3.28 million as the median destination organisation budget.

European Cities Marketing is an association of European city DMOs with its office in Dijon, France. ECM states that it "is a non-profit organisation improving the competitiveness and performance of the leading cities of Europe. ECM provides a platform for convention, leisure and city marketing professionals to exchange knowledge, best practice and widen their network to build new business" (European Cities Marketing, 2021). ECM has approximately 120 members, most of whom are city DMOs. The organisation produces expert reports and statistics and in 2020 produced *A new tomorrow* which included the thoughts of six experts on tourism after the COVID-19 pandemic. ECM publishes a regular *DMO Funding Survey* and for 2020 found the average DMO budget to be 5.9 million euros with 46 staff members.

BestCities Global Alliance is another group that definitely has tourism city members. Eleven cities around the world are cooperating in this initiative through their DMOs, and they include Berlin, Bogotá, Cape Town, Copenhagen, Dubai, Houston, Madrid, Melbourne, Singapore, Tokyo and Vancouver (BestCities Alliance, 2021). This alliance focuses on serving international business events. The Alliance has been active recently in promoting work to measure the legacies of meetings within communities. It defines meeting legacies as "the long-term impacts which a meeting has on wider society". Meeting legacy goals can be defined for both the destination in which the meeting is held as well as for the association holding the meeting (BestCities Alliance, 2020). There are five categories of legacies – environmental, political, economic, sectoral and social. Another group that advocates for the measurement of legacies is ICCA (Fred Production Company, Ltd., 2021).

These seven non-profit organisations are all making significant contributions to the development of world tourism cities and are growing in stature. They provide research and expert opinions that increase the knowledge of tourism cities and help them to become more professional. Several of them have an emphasis on sustainability, and most have education, training and professional development as prominent activities. The community building and networking that they foster are a major benefit these organisations deliver to members. They are advocates for city tourism and culture, helping to build greater public understanding of the size, scope and impacts of the sector in urban areas.

Why is a book on world tourism cities needed?

If you are already reading this book, you will no doubt understand why it is needed. Earlier, it was argued that cities have heretofore been relatively neglected as tourism destinations. There are several books about tourism in cities, although historically there was an emphasis on heritage and historic cities. More recently, books with broader perspectives have been published; however, they have tended to be edited collections of contributed chapters.

This chapter has highlighted many different systems in play that assess and rank the world's cities. Their very availability signifies great interest in the relative order of cities. However, none of the existing systems measure all of the criteria for tourism cities and world tourism cities that have been recommended.

It would have been quite easy to write this introductory chapter on world tourism cities on the topmost world tourism cities like London, Paris, Tokyo, Dubai and Singapore. However, the authors elected to give more prominence to smaller world tourism cities to signal that there is a great diversity of cities that meet the criteria.

The authors believe that a more systematic approach to urban tourism management is needed and hence set about writing this text. The specific focus selected was on world tourism cities, and those urban areas that already have achieved this status as well as those that aspire to get there. Such a book must cover the major issues and challenges that these cities face including globalisation, urbanisation, multi-faceted crises, resident quality of life, sustainability and smartness. The management, planning, development, marketing and branding of tourism cities must also be included and presented in a systematic way. The 11 chapters which follow are aimed to deliver these contents.

Summary comments

The concepts of tourism cities and world tourism cities are attracting much greater attention and deservedly so (Maitland & Newman, 2009). Cities are increasing in relative importance as destinations as the world globalises. There are certain characteristics and criteria that differentiate world tourism cities from other urban areas, and they have been documented in this chapter. These include acting as transport gateways and being influential, impactful, cosmopolitan and recognised. They must also be practitioners of sustainable tourism, launching efforts to enhance economic, socio-cultural and environmental sustainability.

World tourism cities are facing innumerable challenges and issues at the time of writing, as well as having numerous opportunities to benefit more from tourism. The COVID-19 pandemic has exacted a heavy toll on city tourism in 2020 and 2021, with recovery expected to be very slow. Globalisation, discussed in the next chapter, urbanisation covered in Chapter 3 and the increasing concerns over sustainability (Chapter 8) are three other significant future challenges for world tourism cities.

The emphasis in this chapter is on world tourism city as an aspirational term rather than a static concept. Many cities are changing, and more are becoming world tourism cities. Although this chapter has put forward 14 criteria for world tourism cities, there is a need for more work on this topic so that comprehensive measurements and evaluations can be made in the future. Overall, there is a need to elevate world tourism cities to a higher priority level in academic research and teaching, and for greater recognition of the concept among city governments and practitioners.

Thought questions

1) Why do world tourism cities deserve greater attention in the future?
2) Cosmopolitism is an important feature of world tourism cities. What are the indicators of a city being cosmopolitan?
3) What steps should a city follow to become a world tourism city?
4) Why is the support of city residents critical to the success of a tourism city?
5) Can a small city also be a world tourism city and on what basis?
6) How important is sustainable tourism development to world tourism cities?
7) This chapter has suggested 14 factors that distinguish tourism cities and world tourism cities. Which of these do you think are the most important? Are there any other factors that could be added and why?
8) How should world tourism cities utilise the various tourism and non-tourism rating systems that are available? What can be done to achieve higher rankings in these systems?
9) Several new organisations have been created that represent tourism cities. What are the potential advantages of joining and supporting these organisations?
10) There are still many cities in the world that are relatively unknown and not widely recognised. If they aspire to become world tourism cities, what are the steps that should be followed?

References

Beaverstock, J. V., Taylor, P. J., & Smith, R. G. (1999). A roster of world cities. *Cities*, 16(6), 445–458.

BestCities Global Alliance. (2020). Advancing event legacies through impact measurement. https://www.bestcities.net/impact-measurement-research/

BestCities Global Alliance. (2021). Overview. http://www.bestcities.net/about-us/

BOP Consulting. (2014). Transformational cultural projects report. In World Cities Culture Forum. http://www.worldcitiescultureforum.com/assets/others/Transformational_Cultural_Projects_Report_high.pdf

BOP Consulting. (2021). About. In World Cities Culture Forum. http://www.worldcitiescultureforum.com/about

Brookings Institute. (2018). Global Metro Monitor. https://www.brookings.edu/wp-content/uploads/2018/06/Brookings-Metro_Global-Metro-Monitor-2018.pdf

CBRE. (2021). Orlando hotel market outlook 2020 (SEOR). http://cbre.vo.llnwd.net/grgservices/secure/Hotel_SEOR2020_Orlando.pdf?e=1615097808&h=9ff0ef4b87968a621aad6607228bee28

Chen, J. (2020). Real estate market tiers. *Investopedia*. https://www.investopedia.com/terms/r/real-estate-tier-classifications-tier-1-tier-2-and-tier-3.asp

CultureTrip.com. (2021). How Orlando became the theme park capital of the world. https://theculturetrip.com/north-america/usa/florida/articles/how-orlando-became-the-theme-park-capital-of-the-world/

Destinations International. (2021). About Destinations International. https://destinationsinternational.org/about-destinations-international

Economist Intelligence Unit. The Global Liveability Index 2019. https://www.eiu.com/n/the-global-liveability-index-2019/

Euromonitor International (2020). https://go.euromonitor.com/white-paper-travel-2019-100-cities.html

European Cities Marketing. (2021). https://www.europeancitiesmarketing.com/

Fred Production Company Ltd. (2021). The iceberg legacies of business events. https://www.the-iceberg.org/jmic-case-studies/business-events-legacies-jmic-case-study-project-report/

GainingEdge. (2020a). 2020 Competitive Index offers advanced tools for destination competitive analysis. https://gainingedge.com/2020-competitive-index-offers-advanced-tools-for-destination-competitive-analysis/

GainingEdge. (2020b). Competitive Index 2020. In *International Convention Destinations*, 3rd ed. Melbourne, Australia: GainingEdge.

Global Destination Sustainability Movement. (2021). Global Destination Sustainability Index (GDSI). https://www.gds.earth/index/

Hall, P. (2009). The age of the city: The challenge for creative cities. In Ooi, G. L., & Yuen, B. (Eds.). *World Cities: Achieving Liveability and Vibrancy*, pp. 47–70. Singapore: World Scientific Publishing Company.

Harley, F. (2021). City Wealth Index 2020. Where do the wealthy want to live? Knight Frank. https://www.knightfrank.com/research/article/2021-03-01-city-wealth-index-2020-where-do-the-wealthy-want-to-live

HVS. (2020). Central Florida 2020 state of the hotel market. https://www.hvs.com/Print/HVS-Central-Florida-2020-State-of-the-Hotel-Market?id=8697#:~:text=According%20to%20STR%2C%20as%20of,end%20inventory%20of%20125%2C370%20guestrooms.

International Congress and Convention Association (ICCA). (2019). *The International Association Meetings Market 2018 ICCA Statistics Report: Public Abstract*, Amsterdam, Netherlands.

Institute for Urban Strategies. (2021). Global Power City Index (GPCI). Mori Memorial Foundation. http://www.mori-m-foundation.or.jp/english/ius2/gpci2/index.shtml

Kearney. 2020 Global Cities Index (GCI). https://www.kearney.com/global-cities/2020

Maitland, R., & Newman, P. (Eds.). (2009). *World Tourism Cities: Developing Tourism off the Beaten Track*. London: Routledge.

Marino, V. (2020). The best cities in the world: 2020 Readers' Choice Awards. *Condé Nast Traveler*. https://www.cntraveler.com/galleries/2014-10-20/top-25-cities-in-the-world-readers-choice-awards-2014.

Mastercard. (2019). Global destination cities index. https://www.mastercard.com/news/res earch-reports/2019/global-destination-cities-index-2019/

Maxim, C. (2015). Drivers of success in implementing sustainable tourism policies in urban areas. *Tourism Planning & Development*, *12*(1), 37–47.

Maxim, C. (2019). Challenges faced by world tourism cities: London's perspective. *Current Issues in Tourism*, *22*(9), 1006–1024.

Maxim, C. (2021). Challenges of world tourism cities. In Alastair M. Morrison & J. Andres Coca-Stefaniak (Eds.). *Routledge Handbook of Tourism Cities*, pp. 19–30. London: Routledge.

Mercer LLC. (2020). Quality of living city ranking, https://mobilityexchange.mercer.com/Insights/quality-of-living-rankings

Morrison, A. M. (2019). *Marketing and Managing Tourism Destinations*, 2nd ed. London: Routledge.

Morrison, A. M. (2021). Marketing and managing city tourism destinations. In Alastair M. Morrison & J. Andres Coca-Stefaniak (Eds.). *Routledge Handbook of Tourism Cities*, pp. 135–161. London: Routledge.

Morrison, A. M., & Coca-Stefaniak, J. A. (2021). Introduction: City tourism and tourism cities. In Alastair M. Morrison & J. Andres Coca-Stefaniak (Eds.). *Routledge Handbook of Tourism Cities*, pp. 1–14. London: Routledge.

Morrison, A. M., Lehto, X. Y., & Day, J. (2018). *The Tourism System*, 8th ed. Dubuque, Iowa: Kendall Hunt Publishing.

OECD. (2020). Cities in the World: A new perspective on urbanisation. http://www.oecd.org/publications/cities-in-the-world-d0efcbda-en.htm

Orange County Convention Center. (2019). *2018–2019 Annual Report*, Orlando, Florida.

Orange County Convention Center. (2021). Orange County Convention Center facts. http://occc.net/About-Us-Media-Relations-Convention-Center-Facts

Pulido-Fernández, J. I., Carrillo-Hidalgo, I., & Mudarra-Fernández, A. B. (2019). Factors that influence tourism expenditure in World Heritage Cities. *Anatolia*, *30*(4), 530–546.

Ramirez, A., Brandão, F., & Sousa, A. C. (2018). Motivation-based cluster analysis of international tourists visiting a World Heritage City: The case of Porto, Portugal. *Journal of Destination Marketing & Management*, *8*, 49–60.

Renn, A. M. (2013). What is a global city? https://www.aaronrenn.com/2013/08/04/replay-what-is-a-global-city/

Resonance. (2021). World's best cities 2021. Vancouver, BC. https://www.bestcities.org/ran kings/worlds-best-cities/

Sassen, S. (2002). *The Global City: New York, London, Tokyo*. Princeton, NJ: Princeton University Press.

Sassen, S. (2005). The global city: Introducing a concept. *The Brown Journal of World Affairs*, *11*(2), 27–43.

Scruggs, G. (2020). There are 10,000 cities on Planet Earth. Half didn't exist 40 years ago. *Nextcity.org*. https://nextcity.org/daily/entry/there-are-10000-cities-on-planet-earth-half-didnt-exist-40-years-ago

Shimasaki, C. (2015). First-, second- and third-tier cities. What do the designations really mean? *Corporate & Incentive Travel*. http://www.themeetingmagazines.com/cit/first-second-third-tier-cities/

South China Morning Post. (2016). Urban legend: China's tiered city system explained. https://multimedia.scmp.com/2016/cities

Sustainable Development Solutions Network. (2020). *World Happiness Report 2020*. New York: SDSN. https://worldhappiness.report/

TheBiggestCitiesinChina.com. (2020). Tier 1 cities in China: Definition and rankings. https://thebiggestcitiesinchina.com/tier-1-cities-in-china-definition-and-rankings/

Themed Entertainment Association (TEA)/AECOM. (2019). TEA/AECOM 2019 theme index and museum index: The global attractions attendance report. https://www.teaconnect.org/images/files/TEA_369_18301_201201.pdf

Travel + Leisure. (2020). The top 25 cities in the world. https://www.travelandleisure.com/worlds-best/cities

UNESCO. (2021a). Creative Cities Network. https://en.unesco.org/creative-cities/home

UNESCO. (2021b). World Heritage Cities Programme. https://whc.unesco.org/en/cities/

UNESCO. (2021c). World Heritage List. https://whc.unesco.org/en/list/

UNESCO Cities Platform. (2020). *Community-centred Urban Development: A Paradigm of Inclusive Growth*. UNESCO: Paris. https://en.unesco.org/sites/default/files/report_world_cities_day_2020_ucp_en.pdf

United Nations. (2021). World Urbanization Prospects 2018. https://population.un.org/wup/

United Nations Human Settlement Programme. (2021). World Urban Forum. https://unhabitat.org/world-urban-forum

UNWTO/WTCF. (2019). UNWTO/WTCF city tourism performance research. https://www.unwto.org/city-tourism-performance-research

UNWTO. (2020a). City tourism performance research. https://www.unwto.org/city-tourism-performance-research

UNWTO. (2020b). *UNWTO Recommendations on Urban Tourism*. Madrid: UNWTO. UNWTO Recommendations on Urban Tourism | World Tourism Organization (e-unwto.org)

Urban Land Institute (ULI). (2021). About ULI. https://uli.org/about/

Visit Orlando. (2021). Orlando data. https://www.visitorlando.com/media/research/orlando-data/

WorldAtlas. (2021). The most cosmopolitan cities in the world. https://www.worldatlas.com/articles/the-most-cosmopolitan-cities-in-the-world.html

World Cities Culture Forum. (2021). About. Global cities sharing a belief in the importance of culture. BOP Consulting. http://www.worldcitiescultureforum.com/about

World Cities Ranking. (2021). Best 150 cities to visit in the world. https://worldcitiesranking.com/detailed-list-150-cities/

World Conference of Mayors. (2021). https://www.worldconferenceofmayors.org/

World Travel & Tourism Council (WTTC). (2019). City travel & tourism impact. https://wttc.org/Research/Economic-Impact/Cities

Yicai Media Group. (2020). Hefei, Foshan enter China's list of emerging first-tier cities. https://www.yicaiglobal.com/news/hefei-foshan-enter-china-list-of-emerging-first-tier-cities

Yuen, & Ooi (2009). Introduction: World cities: Challenges of liveability, sustainability and vibrancy. In Ooi, G. L., & Yuen, B. (Eds.). *World Cities: Achieving Liveability and Vibrancy*, pp. 1–11. Singapore: World Scientific Publishing Company.

Chapter 2

Globalisation and world tourism cities

Abstract

This second introductory chapter highlights how the process of globalisation affects cities, tourism in general and world tourism cities in particular. Three initial dimensions of globalisation are identified and ways to measure them are examined (economic, political and social). Later, three other factors in the political, economic, social, technological, environmental, legal (PESTEL) model are added and discussed (technological, environmental and legal/regulatory), and the impacts on city residents and visitors are considered as well.

The glocalisation concept is discussed as how cities and tourism companies have adapted global concepts and ideas to better fit local circumstances. The merging of globalisation and localisation in tourism is illustrated through several good examples.

The connection of globalisation and world tourism cities is reviewed with respect to the gateway, influential, impactful, cosmopolitan and recognised features. This is followed by a detailed discussion of six dimensions of globalisation, and the effects on city residents and visitors.

The chapter closes by deriving a summary from previous materials of the advantages and disadvantages of globalisation for tourism and world tourism cities across eight dimensions and perspectives political, economic, social, technological, environmental, legal – resident, visitor (PESTEL-RV).

Keywords: Agglomeration; authenticity; climate change; cultural homogenisation; economic globalisation; globalisation; glocalisation; KOF Globalisation Index (KOFGI); multinationals; neoliberalism; political globalisation; social globalisation.

DOI: 10.4324/9781003111412-3

Learning objectives

- Define globalisation and identify its dimensions.
- Explain the KOF Globalisation Index (KOFGI).
- Pinpoint how globalisation has impacted cities.
- Elaborate on how globalisation has affected tourism.
- Describe how globalisation is influencing world tourism cities.
- Explain the PESTEL dimensions of globalisation and the PESTER-RV model.
- Summarise the advantages and disadvantages of globalisation for tourism and world tourism cities.

There is a huge debate on the pros and cons of globalisation that has raged for at least 50 years. This controversial issue, along with urbanisation, is affecting world tourism cities at several levels and is worthy of consideration in this book. The authors chose not to take a stance on either side of the debate; rather, the chapter follows a balanced treatment of globalisation and world tourism cities. The materials connect with the discussions on global cities, world cities and world tourism cities in Chapter 1. The gateway, influential, impactful, cosmopolitan and recognition features of world tourism cities are partially outcomes of globalisation. Figure 2.1 highlights the main contents of this book, with most chapters touching upon the globalisation topic. For example, Chapter 7 elaborates on quality of life, Chapter 8 deals with sustainability, Chapter 9 discusses technology, Chapter 10 reviews crises and Chapter 11 is about the rise of Asian cities (Figure 2.1).

It is well recognised that tourism is a very open system that is readily and quickly impacted by a wide range of external factors. Morrison, Lehto and Day (2018, p. 8) say that tourism is "greatly affected by external influences such as politics, demographics,

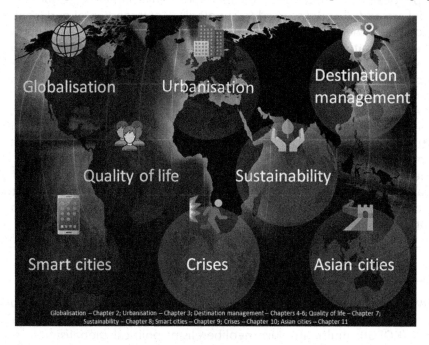

Figure 2.1 Global map of book contents.

technology, war, terrorism, crime, and disease". Therefore, the multifaceted trends arising through globalisation are hard for city tourism to resist and adapting to change is often the best strategy.

What is globalisation?

We could say that the world is getting bigger (population growth and urbanisation), but also growing smaller (globalisation). Let us start with a simple definition that "globalization is the advance of human cooperation across national boundaries" (Boudreaux, 2008, p. 1). Another definition is that globalisation is "a process that erodes national boundaries, integrates national economies, cultures, technologies and governance, and produces complex relations of mutual interdependence" (Norris, 2000, p. 155). Dreher (2006, p. 1092) approximately defined three globalisation dimensions as follows:

- Economic globalisation: The long-haul flows of products, capital and services as well as information and perceptions that accompany trading.
- Political globalisation: The spread of government policies and initiatives across countries.
- Social globalisation: The communication and diffusion of ideas, information, images and people.

Glocalisation is a term also used in this discussion and is formed by combining globalisation and localisation. Robertson (1994, p. 36) said that glocalisation was a global outlook adapted to local conditions, or we could say being global but remaining local. The example of Jollibee Food Corporation in the Philippines is a good example of glocalisation.

Sweet tweet 9

Jollibee rules fast food in the Philippines

Jollibee is the largest fast food chain brand in the Philippines, operating a network of more than 1,400 stores. A dominant market leader in the Philippines, Jollibee enjoys the lion's share of the local market that is more than all the other multinational fast food brands in the Philippines combined.

Source: Jollibee (2021).

Salazar (2005) provides another example of glocalisation from Yogyakarta, Indonesia. Here, certain local tourism guides were connected to a global network and trained in handling Western tourists. However, they conducted tours in an authentic and local way. The sale of mooncakes by Starbucks in China, Singapore and Hong Kong at Mid-Autumn Festival time is a third case showing glocalisation to fit the demands of the local market. In India, McDonald's does not have any beef or pork on its menus. Further examples of glocalisation are provided later in this chapter.

Measuring globalisation

How we measure globalisation is a question of great interest to tourism and world tourism cities. There are thought to be three dimensions of globalisation, namely economic, political and social globalisation (Keohane and Nye, 2000). One of the measurement systems available is the KOF Globalisation Index, which "measures the economic, social and political dimensions of globalisation" (KOF Swiss Economic Institute, 2021). Table 2.1 shows the 20 most globalised countries in the world according to KOFGI 2020 (based on 2018 data). Eighteen of these are in Europe, with only Canada and Singapore being the exceptions.

The KOFGI ranking criteria include several that are directly related to tourism and world tourism cities (Gygli, 2019; Potrafke, 2015). Under inter-personal globalisation, the number of international tourist arrivals is included. Migration counts the number of foreign or foreign-born residents, which relates to cosmopolitanism. Freedom to visit has the percentage of countries for which a nation requires a visa from foreign visitors.

Table 2.1 Top 20 KOFGI-ranked countries

KOFGI rank for 2020	Country	Globalisation index, overall
1	Switzerland	90.8
2	Netherlands	90.7
3	Belgium	90.5
4	Sweden	89.4
5	United Kingdom	89.4
6	Germany	88.8
7	Austria	88.6
8	Denmark	88.0
9	Finland	87.70
10	France	87.7
11	Ireland	85.5
12	Norway	85.5
13	Czech Republic	84.88
14	Portugal	84.9
15	Canada	84.2
16	Hungary	83.8
17	Spain	83.8
18	Singapore	83.5
19	Cyprus	83.1
20	Estonia	82.9

Source: KOF Swiss Economic Institute (2021).

The criterion for international airports includes the number of airports that offer at least one international flight connection. Cultural globalisation calculates the number of McDonald's and IKEA stores. It can be assumed with some degree of confidence that the major cities in the 20 countries listed in Table 2.1 are also highly globalised.

Chapter 1 reviewed several city ranking systems that could be said to be reflections of globalisation, including the Global Cities Index (GCI, AT Kearney) and Global Power City Index (GPCI, Mori Memorial Foundation). The ranking systems highlight the cities that have fared well with globalisation and are highly connected worldwide. The 2019 Global Cities Index ranked cities on business activity (30%), human capital (30%), information exchange (15%), cultural experience (15%) and political engagement (10%). The GPCI has six criteria covering the economy, research and development, cultural interaction, liveability, environment and accessibility. Mastercard's Global Destination Cities Index (GDCI) is another reflection of city tourism globalisation as it measures the number of international visitors and their expenditures.

The authors suggest that there are other dimensions of globalisation that must be measured beyond the economic, political and social. Later in the chapter, environmental, technological and legal and regulatory dimensions are examined, as well as the effects of globalisation on city residents and visitors. This provides a more holistic approach to analysing and measuring globalisation.

Globalisation and cities

It can be said without little doubt that cities have been at the frontline of globalisation. Scott (2001, pp. 817–818) said, "dramatic improvements in technologies of transportation and communication … are helping to annihilate the barriers of space by bringing all parts of the world into ever closer contact with one another". This highlights the key role of transportation and travel in spreading globalisation, as well as hinting about the similar role of information communication technologies (ICTs).

The urbanisation trend is discussed in greater detail in Chapter 3; however, the combined effects of urbanisation and globalisation are worthy of discussion here. Agglomeration (geographic and economic) is one of the outcomes of the fusion of these two trends. Generally, geographic agglomeration means the connecting of settlements or where urban areas swallow up nearby towns and rural areas (McCann and Acs, 2011). Table 1.1 in the previous chapter listed the 30 largest urban agglomerations (or megacities) in the world. Economic agglomeration is where industries or businesses cluster together in order to improve efficiency, productivity and profitability (Duranton and Kerr, 2015). California's Silicon Valley is a great example of this phenomenon, which often is based on industrial specialisation.

Globalisation and urbanisation have led to significant movements of people into cities from home and abroad. Chapter 1 argued that cities can become more cosmopolitan when they receive immigrants from other countries. However, immigration can also cause certain issues. For example, Ley and Tutchener (2001) found that immigration to Vancouver and Toronto in Canada led to significant increases in house prices and argued that this was caused by globalisation. Labour shortages in the tourism sector also cause some cities to "import" staff from other countries, and examples include Macao and several cities in the Arabian Gulf. This often is labelled as migrant labour or migrant workers.

Sweet tweet 10

Migrant workers in the hotel industry

Baum (2012) conducted an analysis of migrant workers in the hotel industry for ILO. Some of his major conclusions were:

- There is a strong consensus in the hotel industry that migrant workers are vital to the operational viability of the sector and will remain so for the foreseeable future.
- Migrant workers are seen to benefit the industry in terms of the skills and commitment they bring to the organisational culture of hotel businesses.
- Migrant workers are recognised to bring a skills profile into the industry which is frequently unavailable in the local labour market.
- Hotel businesses benefit from the culturally diverse skills which migrant workers bring to their employment.

Source: International Labour Organization (ILO) (2012).

Chapter 9 is devoted to the topic of smart tourism cities, and part of this smartness is attributed to technological innovations in urban areas. Breathnach (2000) wrote about transnational niche cities using the example of Dublin's emergence as a call centre hub.

The competition from larger international companies and the influx of foreign capital is thought to put greater pressure on small- and medium-sized businesses (SMEs) located within cities (Smeral, 1998). Some SMEs are forced to close down. However, others have prospered by adapting to the new opportunities brought by globalisation (Dana, Etemad and Wright, 1999), while also drawing upon their local advantages.

Other urban change processes that are at least partially ascribed to globalisation are the aestheticisation and gentrification of neighbourhoods and businesses (Gravari-Barbas and Guinand, 2021). Simpson (2008), for example, discussed the aestheticisation (to global standards) of traditional cafés in Macao. Third places are venues where local people go to and socialise while there and local traditional cafés are among these.

Many of the writers on globalisation discuss it in the context of the post-industrialisation of cities, and also as a post-modern phenomenon. Many cities have lost the traditional industries on which they were most dependent and have had to adjust economically as well as to deal with global forces. One good case study for such a transformation is Cape Town, South Africa, which is the topic for Short break 2.

SHORT BREAK 2

Cape Town – the adaptation of a global port

Cape Town, South Africa, is a strategic port city that has been affected by global forces for around five centuries. Although originally based on trade, its waterfront

---

has more recently been adapted for leisure and tourism purposes. Before the Suez Canal was built, Cape Town was an important port of call as ships rounded the Cape of Good Hope. It was also the debarkation port for immigrants to Southern Africa and played a significant role when diamond- and gold-mining boomed in South Africa.

There were 5.4 million arrivals into Cape Town International Airport in 2019, of which 4.1 million were domestic, 1.2 million were international and the remainder were regional (Cape Town Tourism, 2020). The major sources of international visitors for the city are the UK, Germany and the USA.

According to Ferreira and de Villiers (2014), the Victoria and Alfred Waterfront (V&AW) (Figure 2.2) in Cape Town was "transformed from a brownfields shipping wasteland to a mixed-use development boasting public spaces of distinction". This follows a global, post-industrial trend to regenerate waterfronts into lively spaces for residents and visitors. Baltimore (Maryland), Sydney (Australia) and London are just three other cities with successful waterfront regeneration projects. Ferreira and de Villiers conclude that, although considered by some as being expensive, the V&AW serves "as a reminder that Cape Town is a world-class city competing to attract affluent local and international tourists to the best 'shoppertainment' experience an African city can offer". However, Mustago (2011) found that "75.3% (of survey respondents) perceived the dining experience in the V&A Waterfront as just a copy of the Western countries".

Figure 2.2 The V&A Waterfront in Cape Town, South Africa. (Courtesy: Unsplash.com, Matthias Mullie.)

There are other bright spots of Cape Town tourism and one of the most recognised is the city's association with responsible tourism. Cape Town Tourism, the city DMO, notes that "Cape Town's tourism industry has been at the forefront of responsible tourism practices, with Cape Town Tourism signing the Responsible Tourism Charter to support the principles of sustainable development and management of tourism" (Cape Town Tourism, 2021). In 2002, the city created the *Cape Town Declaration* on *Responsible Tourism*. Booyens and Rogerson (2015) also discuss the flourishing of creative tourism in Cape Town.

Just like many world tourism cities, Cape Town is having to deal with a mixture of globalisation and locally generated issues, including safety and security concerns (George, 2003), urban gentrification (Visser and Kotze, 2008), poverty and slum-like (township) areas (Burgold and Rolfes, 2013; Rolfes, 2010), climate change (Dube, Nhamo, and Chikodzi, 2021) and a water shortage crisis.

Discussion points:

1. How has globalisation affected Cape Town in positive and negative ways?
2. What has Cape Town done to glocalise and to make its tourism offers more authentic?
3. Why are Cape Town's globalisation experiences typical of world tourism cities?

Sources: Bickford-Smith (2009); Booyens and Rogerson (2015); Burgold and Rolfes (2013); Cape Town Tourism (2020, 2021); Dube, Nhamo and Chikodzi (2021); Ferreira and de Villiers (2014); George (2003); Mustago (2011); Rolfes (2010); Visser and Kotze (2008).

Research on globalisation and tourism

The research on the interactions between globalisation and tourism reaches back to the early 1990s. Economically, tourism has benefited greatly from globalisation through the expansion of international travel. However, it could also be said that in 2020–2021, tourism suffered from de-globalisation as a result of the COVID-19 pandemic that swept the world (Niewiadomski, 2020).

The topics in the globalisation and tourism research literature have been with respect to airlines, cruise lines, food consumption, medical and dental tourism, restaurants and coffee shops and multinational tourism and hospitality companies. For example, Wood (2000) argued that globalisation affected cruise lines in several ways that included the use of flags of convenience, internationalisation and labour migration. Morley (2003) connected globalisation with the formation of airline strategic alliances. Mak, Lumbers and Eves (2012) developed a conceptual model to measure the impacts of globalisation on food consumption in destinations.

Several articles are published on how medical tourism has spread out around the globe (e.g., Chen and Wilson, 2013; Horowitz, Rosensweig and Jones, 2007). There is considerable criticism and dubiousness expressed with respect to medical, health and wellness tourism. For example, Persaud (2005) questioned the value of travelling for cosmetic surgery. With a focus on Thailand, he also lamented about the skin whitening among

Asian women. Martin (2009) picked the topic of reproductive tourism and found that national laws and regulations were lacking for this form of travel. Connell (2006), while noting the global growth of medical tourism, also highlighted that it was increasing the gap in health care for residents versus these international visitors. However, medical and dental tourism has brought benefits to poorer countries who have highly skilled doctors and dental surgeons, including Ukraine, India and Malaysia (Jaapar et al., 2017).

The impacts of multinational or transnational companies in tourism are another popular topic (Feng, 2020). Much debate has resulted from the expansion of fast food companies, coffee shop and hotel chains and theme park firms around the world. Interestingly, hospitality and tourism companies have been the direct focus of rather pejorative new expressions about globalisation including *Disneyfication*, *McDonaldisation* and *Starbuckisation*, often accompanying the word *Americanisation* (Ritzer, 2003). However, to be entirely fair to these companies, most have tried to localise their menus and service to adapt to the unique conditions in each country (Peterson, 2014). Disney is credited with glocalising its theme parks in Hong Kong and Shanghai to be more acceptable and appealing to Chinese guests (Matusitz, 2011; Yuan, 2019).

Sweet tweet 11

The man who drove McDonald's out of Iceland

McDonald's has restaurants in 118 countries and territories around the world. One of the countries that at the time of writing had no McDonald's was Iceland. The company had operated four restaurants there since 1993, which the local franchisee closed in 2009. Culture Trip ascribes McDonald's failure to local restaurateur Tommi Tómasson (who operates Tommi's Burger Joints); however, it was more the effects of globalisation that caused the stores to be shut down. A CNBC documentary video indicates that the global financial crisis of 2008–2009 caused several profitability issues for Iceland's McDonald's despite their great popularity with diners.

Sources: CNBC (2019); Culture Trip (2020, 2021); McDonald's (2021); Tommi's Burger Joint (2021).

"Casinopolitan globalism" is a term that is being used to describe the spread of casino operations and other branded entertainment globally (Luke, 2010, p. 395). In particular, the Las Vegas-like developments in Macao and elsewhere are said to be examples of diffusion of the global casino culture around the world.

Sweet tweet 12

Exporting Las Vegas

The exportation of branded entertainment and culture is a sign of the effects of globalisation on tourism development in several cities. Included are theme parks, casinos and museums.

> The casinopolitanism of Vegas and Macao are the most concentrated, complete, and concrete manifestations of more of the planet's multitudes' advances toward more urbanized living in, for, and with the material ecologies of contemporary globalism. The salience of essentially packaged, scripted, and branded experiences brings Disneyland to Japan, Europe, and Hong Kong; the Guggenheim to Spain (Figure 2.3), Romania, and Abu Dhabi; or Vegas to Atlantic City, Sun City, and Macao.
>
> Source: Luke (2010), p. 404.

Figure 2.3 The Guggenheim in Bilbao, Spain.
(Courtesy: Unsplash.com, Vitor Pinto.)

The impacts of globalisation on specific regions, countries and types of geographical areas are another area of related tourism research. Countries that are examined in these studies include Australia, China, Indonesia, Japan, Kenya, Myanmar/Thailand and South Africa (respectively by Faulkner and Walmsley, 1998; Zhang and Chiu, 2020; Sugiyarto et al., 2003; Kureha et al., 2005; Bruner, 2001; Parnwell, 1998; Heath, 2001). Globalisation's effects on tourism in the Middle East and South Asia have also been investigated (Hazbun, 2004; Mehmood et al., 2021). Islands are another focal point for globalisation and tourism research; for example, MacLeod (1999) examined the impact of tourism in globalising a Canary Island in Spain.

Several previous studies have considered the environmental impacts of globalisation through tourism (e.g., Alola et al., 2021, Aluko et al., 2021). Alola et al. (2021) concluded that an "increase in tourism arrivals and globalization is detrimental to the attainment of sustainable environmental quality in a long term". There has been a focus on the contribution of the transportation sector, and especially airlines, to greenhouse gas production (Leamon et al., 2019).

Tourism and travel are also associated with the spread of terrorism (Bianchi, 2007) and sex tourism (Clancy, 2002), and of course more recently with the transmission of COVID-19 (Chinazzi et al., 2020). The effects of globalisation through tourism have also been studied with respect to indigenous people (McLaren and Pera, 2002) and environmental quality (Alola et al., 2021). The contribution of travel and tourism to global warming and climate change is well documented.

Globalisation and world tourism cities

It has been said that "tourism is both a cause and a consequence of globalization. It accelerates the convergent tendencies in the world" (Azarya, 2004, p. 949). The increases in world tourism arrivals (up until the end of 2019) were fuelling globalisation, as people explored every corner of the planet. Also, tourism growth was spurred by numerous aspects of globalisation, including freer trade, improved transportation, visa facilitation and information communication.

Are world tourism cities a manifestation of globalisation? The answer would seem to be in the positive as world tourism cities have distinctive globalisation features. They are easily reached, well known, influential, impactful and cosmopolitan. Thus, perhaps world tourism cities as well as the open-system nature of tourism render these cities more likely to experience the latest global trends.

One global trend that has swept worldwide is the increasing power of sharing economy providers, many of whom operate within hospitality and tourism (Belarmino, 2021). She says that the sharing economy is "the single largest disrupter traditional tourist firms have ever experienced" (p. 65) and mainly due to peer-to-peer accommodation and ride-sharing (Figure 2.4).

Hjalager (2007) says that tourism is undergoing an irrevocable globalising process and suggests that this occurs in several stages. These are: (1) missionaries in markets; (2) integrating across borders; (3) fragmentation of the value chain; and (4) transcending into new value chains. She illustrates with several examples from Scandinavia that globalisation is not just a one-time effect; rather, it evolves through several stages as the private sector and governments adjust to the new realities.

Gotham (2005) raises the issue of the commodification of local traditions in the context of the Mardi Gras festival in New Orleans, Louisiana. He talks about "above" and "below" effects, the former representing the influences of globalisation and the latter being localisation as a resistance to homogenisation. Gotham describes how local groups and individuals are opposing the commercialisation of Mardi Gras. He also recognises that the expansion of Mardi Gras through tourism has created an export market for Mardi Gras floats and other aspects of this festival.

Hudson (2010) describes how international tourism has transformed the Paharganj district in New Delhi, India. The image in Figure 2.5 of Paharganj is very typical of the

Figure 2.4 The rise of sharing economy providers is a trend within globalisation. (Courtesy: Unsplash.com, taiQ.)

Figure 2.5 The neon light scene in the Paharganj district of New Delhi.
(Courtesy: Unsplash.com, Prateek Katyal.)

night-time scenes in most Asian cities where lower-priced hotels, bars, souvenir shops, convenience stores and various peddlers compete for the visitor's attention.

Sweet tweet 13

Transnational urbanism and tourism in New Delhi

Paharganj, a district of Delhi, is one of those places (a relay station in a world of flows). Like other global cities, Delhi is simultaneously anchored to the national base, yet interconnected to other cities in a shifting and unstable network of cultural, economic, and political nodes. Various categories of social actors can forge transnational relationships, operate on a multiplicity of scales, and create practices of transnational urbanism. Tourists have been identified as one of those categories instrumental for this process.

Source: Hudson (2010), p. 372.

Connecting world tourism cities with globalisation

The conception of world tourism cities in Chapter 1 was of urban areas that are globally connected and relevant. All five essential features of world tourism cities are associated with globalisation.

- Gateway: World tourism cities are conveniently linked to other parts of the world through transportation.
- Influential: World tourism cities are respected and what they do is significant nationally and internationally.
- Impactful: World tourism cities are leaders and have best practices that others follow, again in their own countries and abroad.
- Cosmopolitan: World tourism cities benefit from having residents and visitors from around the world.
- Recognised: World tourism cities are well known and recognised throughout the world.

Overall, there is significant research and on-the-ground evidence of the impacts of globalisation of tourism in general and world tourism cities specifically. Much of what has accumulated in the tourism research literature is not particularly positive, and especially with respect to the environmental and social-cultural influences of globalisation. However, there is an old saying that "there are two sides to every story", and a balanced consideration of all dimensions of globalisation is needed.

Having made the connection between world tourism cities and globalisation clearer, the dimensions of globalisation are now discussed. A PESTEL-RV framework of globalisation dimensions and perspectives is used to objectively explore the influences of globalisation on tourism and world tourism cities.

The PESTEL dimensions of globalisation

In the six sub-sections that follow, the dimensions of globalisation are expanded from three to six to follow the PESTEL model (political, economic, social, technological,

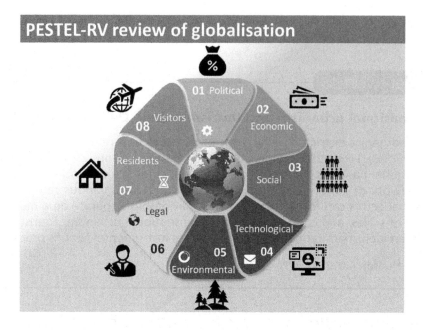

Figure 2.6 PESTEL-RV model.

environmental and legal) (Figure 2.6). The labels have been modified slightly to expand the meanings of each dimension. Thereafter, the effects of globalisation on city residents and visitors are reviewed. An attempt is made to weave into the discussions the negative and positive impacts on tourism.

Political and governmental globalisation

Political globalisation occurs when countries officially join organisations such as the United Nations, World Trade Organization, European Union, ASEAN and other inter-governmental agencies. It represents the closer integration of a country's politics and policies with other nations in the world.

On a global basis, the UN is one of the most influential of these organisations. For example, the UN Sustainable Development Goals (SDGs) for up to 2030 provide guidelines and targets in 17 specific aspects of sustainability (UN, 2021). SDG 11 is related to sustainability in cities to "make cities and human settlements inclusive, safe, resilient and sustainable". The SDGs are discussed in more detail in Chapter 8, including the *Voluntary Local Reviews* conducted by many cities related to implementation for SDG 11.

There are also several inter-governmental organisations within the UN system that exert a profound influence on tourism. For example, the UN World Tourism Organization (UNWTO, 2021b) has 159 member states. It is noteworthy that at the time of writing, Australia, Canada, New Zealand, the UK and the USA were not members of UNWTO (UNWTO, 2020). The UN agency for tourism introduces initiatives and mandates which it asks its members to support. One example is the Global Code of Ethics for Tourism (GCET).

The United Nations Educational, Scientific and Cultural Organization (UNESCO) is another UN agency that has a significant impact on global tourism. Chapter 1 mentioned UNESCO's World Heritage List (WHL) and the Creative Cities Network (UCCN). Some 194 state parties have signed the 1972 World Heritage Convention, which officially introduced the WHL (UNESCO, 2021). As the previous chapter highlights, WHL designations have increased the global recognition of several cities and caused growth in tourist arrivals.

A third UN agency is the International Civil Aviation Organization (ICAO) that "is funded and directed by 193 national governments to support their diplomacy and cooperation in air transport as signatory states to the Chicago Convention (1944)" (ICAO, 2021). ICAO's strategic objectives are aviation safety, air navigation capacity and efficiency, security and facilitation, economic development and environmental protection. The economic development of air transport includes, for example, the liberalisation of international air transport. Under environmental protection, ICAO's member states have agreed to tackle climate change and aviation emissions, aircraft noise and local air quality.

The UN Environment Programme (UNEP) is a fourth agency that plays a role that impinges on tourism. For example, UNEP is working with UNWTO and the Ellen MacArthur Foundation on initiatives to deal with and curb the disposal of plastics in tourism destinations. This situation was exacerbated in 2020 with the indiscriminate disposal of COVID-19 personal protective equipment (PPE) (UNEP, 2020; UNWTO, 2021a).

The Food and Agriculture Organization (FAO) is a fifth UN agency whose recommendations affect food consumption in tourism. For example, FAO has developed the Emergency Prevention System for Food Safety (EMPRES) Food Safety Strategic Plan (FAO, 2021). EMPRES serves as "a key international system to assist in the prevention and management of global food safety emergencies, including the three pillars of early warning, emergency prevention and rapid response".

The World Health Organization (WHO) is a sixth agency of the UN that rose greatly in visibility during COVID-19. On March 11, 2020, WHO declared the novel coronavirus (COVID-19) outbreak a global pandemic (WHO, 2021). The agency has received significant criticism for its handling of the outbreak in its early stages; however, notwithstanding the validity of these concerns, WHO had crucial impacts on travel, tourism and hospitality in cities globally in 2020–2021.

De-nationalisation (Sassen, 2003) is argued to be the other side of political globalisation, where national governments are forced to introduce fresh legislation and regulations to meet the requirements and recommendations of inter-governmental organisations.

Economic globalisation

Countries around the world are becoming more dependent on each other based on trade and flows of capital, and this is the result of economic globalisation.

Sweet tweet 14

What is economic globalisation?

Economic globalization refers to the increasing interdependence of world economies as a result of the growing scale of cross-border trade of commodities and services, flow of international capital and wide and rapid spread of technologies. It reflects the continuing expansion and mutual integration of market frontiers and is an irreversible trend for the economic development in the whole world at the turn of the millennium.

Source: Gao (2000), p. 1.

The WTO is often mentioned as an agent for economic globalisation. At the time of writing, WTO had 164 member states as well as 27 in observer status.

Sweet tweet 15

The World Trade Organization

The World Trade Organization (WTO) is the only global international organization dealing with the rules of trade between nations. At its heart are the WTO agreements, negotiated and signed by the bulk of the world's trading nations and ratified in their parliaments. The goal is to ensure that trade flows as smoothly, predictably and freely as possible.

Source: WTO (2021a).

The creation of WTO and various trade agreements among countries is said to reflect neoliberalism. This means a "new" perspective in which temporary forms of economic restructuring are more acceptable. Neoliberalism is understood to refer to "the process of opening up national economies to global actors such as multinational corporations and to global institutions such as the IMF and World Bank" (Larner, 2003).

Another phenomenon of economic integration is the regional trade agreement (RTA). According to the WTO's RTA database at the time of writing, there were 343 such agreements across the world in 2021 (WTO, 2021b). The World Bank (2018) defines an RTA as

a treaty between two or more governments that define the rules of trade for all signatories. Examples of regional trade agreements include the North American Free Trade Agreement (NAFTA), Central American-Dominican Republic Free Trade Agreement (CAFTA-DR), the European Union (EU) and Asia-Pacific Economic Cooperation (APEC).

It also needs to be mentioned that there are many bilateral agreements between specific pairs of countries, including ones relating to air transport.

The International Monetary Fund (2021) also provides information on other groupings of nations, the most well known of which might be the Group of 20 or G20, which was established in 1999 "to strengthen policy coordination between its members, promote financial stability, and modernize the international financial architecture". Some of the G20 members are China, France, Germany, Japan, the UK and the USA.

Social and cultural globalisation

The social dimension of globalisation refers to the impact of globalisation on the life and work of people, on their families and on their societies. Concerns and issues are often raised about the impact of globalisation on employment, working conditions, income and social protection. Beyond the world of work, the social dimension encompasses security, culture and identity, inclusion or exclusion and the cohesiveness of families and communities (ILO, 2003).

The introduction of tourism into cities has received much criticism from scholars and others, which more recently has had a focus on the overtourism phenomenon. Sociologists and anthropologists in particular have had a heyday in coining terms to describe the rather odious effects of greater tourism activity on local people, cultures and well-being. As previously mentioned, these have included aestheticisation and gentrification, to which can be added commercialisation, commodification, cultural contamination, cultural (or transnational) homogenisation, touristification (or tourismfication), transculturalisation and several other expressions. There is considerable validity to these adverse cultural and social impacts of tourism on cities, and they must be dealt with in an appropriate manner. The solutions are complex and must consider the needs and expectations of local citizens whose lives and work are also being reshaped by other aspects of globalisation apart from tourism.

Technological globalisation

Technological globalisation represents the diffusion of new technologies across the world and is perhaps one of the most obvious manifestations of globalisation. The rapid adoption of ICTs has affected tourism and world tourism cities in many ways. Just one example is the provision of Wi-Fi service in many cities in public areas (Figure 2.7) and within tourism businesses. This phenomenon is discussed in detail in Chapter 9 in the context of smart tourism cities.

Several cities have put great effort and investment into providing free public Wi-Fi services. These include such large cities as Paris, Moscow, New York, Seoul, Hong Kong and Tel Aviv, but also smaller ones such as Tallinn, Estonia, and Perth, Australia.

The International Telecommunication Union (ITU) is a (seventh) specialised UN agency that has a focus on ICTs. ITU is

> the inter-governmental body responsible for coordinating the shared global use of the radio spectrum, promoting international cooperation in assigning satellite orbits, improving communication infrastructure in the developing world, and establishing the worldwide standards that foster seamless interconnection of a vast range of communications systems.
>
> *(ITU, 2020a)*

It estimated that at the end of 2020, 85% of the world's population was covered by 4G mobile-broadband networks (ITU, 2020b). The same report found that in mid-2020, there were 105 mobile-cellular subscriptions per 100 inhabitants.

According to the Miniwatts Marketing Group (2021), there were 5.053 billion Internet users in the world in December 2020, equivalent to 64.2% of the total population. The largest regional Internet market is Asia, with 2.71 billion users, or 53.6% of all Internet users in the world.

Figure 2.7 Free Wi-Fi is provided in Milan. (Courtesy: Unsplash.com, Anastasia Eremina.)

The globalisation of information has created opportunities for global distribution and booking systems in travel and tourism. Global distribution systems (GDS) have developed as well as online travel agencies (OTAs) and various booking platforms. Online travel review sites, particularly Tripadvisor, have flourished and gone global.

New technologies that are being introduced globally are affecting other aspects of tourism and especially in transportation and service provision. These include greater use of augmented and virtual reality, and artificial intelligence and robotics. Electric cars, including the Teslas, are not necessarily a new trend; however, they are now much more popular. Self-driving cars, also known as autonomous vehicles, are one of the most interesting trends that could revolutionise city travel in the future. Hotel service robots are another innovation being seen much more frequently in urban hotels.

Environmental globalisation

Grainger (2012) defines environmental globalisation as increases "in global uniformity and connectedness in the language, regulations, and practices of environmental management". There are several inter-governmental and non-governmental organisations (NGOs) dedicated to the conservation and preservation of the natural environment, the International Union for Conservation of Nature (IUCN) is

> a membership Union composed of both government and civil society organisations. It harnesses the experience, resources and reach of its more than 1,400 member organisations and the input of more than 17,000 experts. This diversity and vast expertise makes IUCN the global authority on the status of the natural world and the measures needed to safeguard it.
>
> *(IUCN, 2021)*

Sweet tweet 16

The C40 network

Several world tourism cities belong to the C40 Climate Leadership Group, including Bangkok, Beijing, London, New York, Paris and Singapore. "C40 is a network of the world's megacities committed to addressing climate change. C40 supports cities to collaborate effectively, share knowledge and drive meaningful, measurable and sustainable action on climate change". It is a "global network of large cities taking action to address climate change by developing and implementing policies and programs that generate measurable reductions in both greenhouse gas emissions and climate risks".

Source: C40 (2021).

In any discussion of the environment, the influence of NGOs must be a topic. There are several powerful NGOs with an environmental orientation, including Conservation International, Greenpeace, the Nature Conservancy, Ocean Conservancy, Oxfam, Rainforest Alliance, Sierra Club and World Wildlife Fund (WWF). They conduct critical research studies, provide aid and assistance, build awareness of conservation and preservation issues and needs and lobby governments and private companies. Most of these NGOs operate membership programmes.

Sweet tweet 17

The Nature Conservancy and Hong Kong – building healthy cities

The branch of TNC in Hong Kong is deeply involved with the NGO's strategic priority to build healthier cities. They say that "by introducing nature into cities and reconnecting people to the natural world, cities can combat some of the biggest urban challenges, such as stormwater run-off, air pollution and heat islands". Their pilot cities include Hong Kong, Shanghai, Shenzhen and Melbourne, where TNC's work has a focus on:

> - Integrating nature into urban planning and design.
> - Connecting people with nature.
> - Restoring natural infrastructure and wildlife habitats.
>
> Source: The Nature Conservancy (TNC) Hong Kong (2021).

The WWF is "using tourism as a conservation tool. Ecological accommodation and nature educational trails are some of many examples of how tourism is being used to promote nature protection in the Alps" (WWF, 2021).

Several countries operate NGOs as agencies assisting lesser-developed countries, which are sometimes referred to as aid or donor agencies. These include the US Agency for International Development (USAID), Canadian International Development Agency (CIDA), Deutsche Gesellschaft für Internationale Zusammenarbeit (GIZ) and the UK Department for International Development (DFID). These development agencies are often very influential in tourism development. For example, USAID is assisting with the design, implementation and promotion of an alternative tourism development approach in the city of Esna, in the Luxor governorate of Egypt (USAID, 2021).

Another interpretation of environmental globalisation takes the negative perspective with the spread of pollution and the impacts of global warming on the earth. Climate change and other related topics are discussed in detail in Chapter 8 on sustainability in world tourism cities. It suffices to say here that there is a huge body of research about the adverse effects of tourism on natural and cultural-heritage environments.

Legal and regulatory globalisation

The globalisation of law may be defined as the worldwide progression of transnational legal structures and discourses along the dimensions of extensity, intensity, velocity and impact (Halliday and Osinsky, 2006). Regulatory globalisation is the process by which regulatory agencies extend their reach internationally (Macey, 2003). These two can best be exemplified by regional government systems such as the European Union (EU). For example, the European Parliament is vested with legislative powers that can result in new laws and supporting regulations that affect all member countries. The recent departure of the United Kingdom from the European Union (popularly known as the Brexit process) was at least partly motivated by the desire to be free from laws and regulations not established in the UK but in Brussels.

It is not only governments that regulate tourism, as private-sector companies and NGOs also play a significant role. Self-regulation on a global level is in effect for some sub-sectors of tourism. The airlines are a good example here through such organisations as the International Air Transport Association (IATA), which represents 290 airlines equivalent to 82% of total air traffic. Its key performance targets for 2021 were safety, financial resilience, industry restart and environmental sustainability (IATA, 2021). For example, one of the environmental goals of IATA in 2021 was "achieving 2.2M tons of CO_2 offset through the IATA Aviation Carbon Exchange".

Cruise Lines International Association (CLIA) represents "95% of the world's ocean-going cruise capacity, as well as 54,000 travel agents, and 15,000 of the largest travel agencies in the world" (CLIA, 2021). CLIA's articulated policies tend to be followed by its member cruise companies.

Sweet tweet 18

CLIA policies

"CLIA advances policies intended to enhance shipboard safety, security, and environmental stewardship, in some cases calling for best practices in excess of existing legal requirements".

Source: CLIA (2021).

There are numerous other industry groups that have policies, programmes and initiatives that are influencing tourism globally. Some of these were mentioned in Chapter 1, including the World Cities Cultural Forum, World Tourism Cities Federation and Destinations International. Yet other influential industry groups on a global scale are the World Travel & Tourism Council (WTTC) and the Pacific Asia Travel Association (PATA). Apart from anything else, these groups are cultivating professional standards at a global level while also building practitioner networks that spread knowledge around the world.

The city resident and visitor perspectives (RV)

It is easy just to focus on the six globalisation dimensions and to lose sight of the human aspects involved. However, it is crucial to consider the impacts, positive and negative, on city residents and visitors. The impact of tourism on local residents is the topic of detailed discussion in Chapter 7, where there is a particular focus on quality of life and well-being. One of the aspects reviewed in Chapter 7 is the overtourism phenomenon. The overcrowding and disturbance of the daily lives of residents are at the core of this problem, which appears to have been exacerbated by new spikes in tourist arrivals due to the growing capacity and use of sharing economy accommodation (P2P). The combined effects of overtourism and the COVID-19 pandemic have heightened the recognition that greater attention within cities must be paid to visitor management.

Visitors have also been greatly affected by globalisation in a variety of different ways. Many of them themselves are residents of other cities and so they share similar influences with those living in destination cities. The rapid development of ICTs has flooded people with online information on destinations. They can travel the world virtually without getting off of their sofas. Moreover, they can reach places more quickly and safely than ever before and have many more choices of places to visit and activities to be experienced. However, globalisation has introduced novel threats for visitors, including increasing crimes and scams, and a growth in terrorism aimed at them.

The loss of authenticity as perceived by visitors within destinations and a creeping sameness of places is said to be a consequence of tourism globalisation. However, authenticity is a contested concept in tourism, and a debate is being had about whether it is objective or subjective, or a combination of both. Wang (1999), in one of the most cited works, suggests that authenticity has intra- and inter-personal dimensions, and that it is not only an objective concept.

Other people affected by globalisation are the tourism stakeholders within world tourism cities. Previously, the impacts on SMEs were highlighted, as were the adaptations made by multinational firms in tourism in glocalising. Table 2.2 elaborates on how tourism and tourism stakeholders are impacted through the PESTEL-RV dimensions.

Table 2.2 Advantages and disadvantages of globalisation according to the PESTEL-RV framework

Dimensions and perspectives	Advantages	Disadvantages
Political and governmental	• Greater freedom of movement across borders (e.g., visa facilitation, visa-on-arrival) • Freer trade among countries • Increased priority and emphasis on transport and food safety	• De-nationalisation • Increase in terrorism • Refugee crises • Trade disputes • Loss of national identities
Economic	• Growth in tourist arrivals including business/MICE • More foreign direct investment (FDI) • New markets for tourism sector • Greater alliances and cooperation among companies and organisations • Professionalisation of destination management • Availability of migrant workers • Reductions in poverty	• Overcrowding and disruption of resident daily lives (overtourism) • Pressure on SMEs for survival • Global financial crises • Disruption of supply chains • Shortages of domestic labour pool • Sharing economy issues • Increased economic disparities • Economic leakage (repatriation of profits)
Social and cultural	• Increasing cosmopolitanism • Greater cultural understanding and acceptance • Enhanced diversity and tolerance • Greater harmony • Enhanced knowledge of other peoples	• Cultural homogenisation or contamination • Loss of authenticity • Commodification of local traditions • Increases in undesirable activities (e.g., sex tourism, drunk tourism, etc.) • More crime and drug trafficking

Category		
Technological	• Introduction of ICTs with global communication • More information available through the Internet and mobile telephony • Faster and more convenient transportation • Power of social media (e.g., free promotion globally)	• Information overload • Fake news/false claims • Personal security concerns • Over-reliance on technology • Need for "digital detox"
Environmental	• Greater concern for conservation and preservation • Stronger global environmental lobbying (e.g., NGOs) • More guidelines for sustainable, responsible and ethical tourism and travel • Increased importance of corporate social responsibility (CSR)	• Contribution to climate change and global warming • Demolition of heritage buildings and districts • Pollution of oceans and other bodies of water • Wildlife disturbance and land degradation • Water shortages • Indiscriminate disposal of plastic
Legal and regulatory	• More standardisation in tourism • Potential enhancement of quality and service	• Addition of more legislation and regulations • More formality and bureaucracy
City residents	• Improvements in infrastructure and amenities • Potential to enliven neighbourhoods and districts • More leisure and entertainment options • More income and employment opportunities	• Loss of third places • Gentrification and aestheticisation • Commercialisation of traditions • Overcrowding • Threats of disease spread • Housing shortages and inflated real estate prices
Visitors	• Greater choice of destinations • More availability of information • Faster and more convenient transport • Sharing economy benefits • Improved service quality • More varied experiences, activities and attractions • Improved safety and security	• Crimes and scams • Racial, ethnic and gender discrimination • Overcrowding • Overcommercialisation • Sameness of places

Advantages and disadvantages of globalisation for world tourism cities

It is rather obvious from the foregoing that globalisation brings many good things to cities; however, in its wake also flow many serious issues and challenges for urban areas and city tourism. Now, it is crucial to pinpoint and itemise these advantages and disadvantages of globalisation for world tourism cities by deducing them from the foregoing materials. Some previous authors have written on this topic in the context of tourism in general (e.g., Theuns, 2008; Zmyślony, 2011). However, the authors introduce a new and more comprehensive framework for this identification through PESTEL-RV (Table 2.2).

While acknowledging that Table 2.2 is not necessarily complete, the classification of pros and cons therein highlights the complexity of globalisation for tourism and world tourism cities. The impacts of globalisation in cities are likely to be the earliest and the most profound, with the effects gradually spreading out to peri-urban and rural areas. With many cities also dealing with rapid urbanisation (Chapter 3), this is accentuating the need for specialised and more professional city destination management, which is the focus in Chapters 4–6.

Summary comments

The world is globalising, and tourism is a powerful force in the process. Globalisation has been of benefit to city destinations around the world; however, most have had to pay a price in the transaction. The erosion of unique city identities and authenticity is a common criticism of the spread of globalisation. However, it is a main premise in this book that there are already world tourism cities and others that aspire to be world tourism cities. These cities have the vision to be on the world tourism stage and thus globalisation is both a facilitator and a challenge.

Globalisation should be viewed from at least six perspectives – political and governmental, economic, social and cultural, technological, environmental and legal and regulatory. Through the lens of these six factors globalisation has brought benefits to tourism cities; not the least has been economic growth. However, novel problems and issues have also been carried by successive waves of globalisation. These negatives include greater terrorism and pollution, and an increasing sameness of place. In addition, the perspectives of city residents and visitors must also be taken into consideration when weighing up the pros and cons of globalisation. It is crucial to objectively consider the impacts of globalisation on the lives of city residents and visitors.

Post-COVID, the increasing influence of globalisation on world tourism cities seems to be inevitable and the glocalisation route is one of the solutions. This will require a delicate balancing of what local residents expect and want, and what visitors are seeking in the blend of familiarity and novelty.

There are many who say that globalisation is a blessing while others deem it a curse; then there are those who call it a mixed blessing. However, notwithstanding these characterisations, it can be said that for world tourism cities it is a reality and part of their fabric. The trick is how to distil the benefits from globalisation while minimising the negative side-effects.

Thought questions

1. How has globalisation benefited tourism and world tourism cities?
2. Are authenticity and globalisation at two different ends of a spectrum? How can a tourism city simultaneously derive benefits from both?
3. How has globalisation negatively affected tourism cities?
4. How have multinational companies glocalised their products and service cultures to be more successful with international expansion?
5. In which ways will the COVID-19 pandemic alter globalisation in the future?
6. How do global issues and trends affect the behaviour of tourists when they are visiting cities?
7. There are often two sides to the effects of globalisation. Critics say that urban gentrification due to leisure and tourism demand harms local residents of the affected districts; others argue that this cleans up and beautifies undesirable and dilapidated parts of cities. What is your opinion on gentrification?
8. To lessen the globalisation impacts through tourism, should destinations, including cities, more tightly control visitor numbers? Why or why not, and how can visitor volumes be controlled?
9. As Asia's power increases in the world, in what ways will the East influence the West?
10. Are people in general better off as a result of globalisation and why or why not?

References

Alola, A. A., Eluwole, K. K., Lasisi, T. T., & Alola, U. V. (2021). Perspectives of globalization and tourism as drivers of ecological footprint in top 10 destination economies. *Environmental Science and Pollution Research, 28*, 31607–31617, https://doi.org/10.1 007/s11356-021-12871-4.

Aluko, O. A., Opoku, E. E. O., & Ibrahim, M. (2021). Investigating the environmental effect of globalization: Insights from selected industrialized countries. *Journal of Environmental Management, 281*, 111892, https://doi.org/10.1016/j.jenvman.2020.111892.

Azarya, V. (2004). Globalization and international tourism in developing countries: Marginality as a commercial commodity. *Current Sociology, 52*(6), 949–967.

Baum, T. (2012). *Migrant Workers in the Hotel Industry*. Geneva, Switzerland: International Labour Organization.

Belarmino, A. (2021). The sharing economy in tourism cities. In Alastair M. Morrison, & J. Andres Coca-Stefaniak (Eds.). *Routledge Handbook of Tourism Cities*, pp. 65–75. London: Routledge.

Bianchi, R. (2007). Tourism and the globalisation of fear: Analysing the politics of risk and (in)security in global travel. *Tourism and Hospitality Research, 7*(1), 64–74.

Bickford-Smith, V. (2009). Creating a city of the tourist imagination: The case of Cape Town, 'The fairest cape of them all'. *Urban Studies, 46*(9), 1763–1785.

Booyens, I., & Rogerson, C. M. (2015). Creative tourism in Cape Town: An innovation perspective. *Urban Forum, 26*, 405–424, https://doi.org/10.1007/s12132-015-9251-y.

Boudreaux, D. J. (2008). *Globalization: Yesterday and Today*. Westport, CT: Greenwood Press.

Breathnach, P. (2000). Globalisation, information technology and the emergence of niche transnational cities: The growth of the call centre sector in Dublin. *Geoforum 31*, 477–485.

Bruner, E. M. (2001). The Maasai and the Lion King: Authenticity, nationalism, and globalization in African tourism. *American Ethnologist, 28*(4), 881–908.

Burgold, J., & Rolfes, M. (2013). Of voyeuristic safari tours and responsible tourism with educational value: Observing moral communication in slum and township tourism in Cape Town and Mumbai. *Journal of the Geographical Society of Berlin, 144*(2), 161–174.

C40 Cities. (2021). *About.* https://www.c40.org/about

Cape Town Tourism. (2020). *Annual AGM Report, 2018–2019.* Cape Town, South Africa: Cape Town Tourism.

Cape Town Tourism. (2021). Cape Town as a sustainable destination. https://trade-media.capetown.travel/sustainable-cape-town/

Chen, L. H., & Wilson, M. E. (2013). The globalization of healthcare: Implications of medical tourism for the infectious disease clinician. *Clinical Infectious Diseases, 57*(12), 1752–1759.

Chinazzi et al. (2020). The effect of travel restrictions on the spread of the 2019 novel coronavirus (COVID-19) outbreak. *Science, 368*, 395–400.

Clancy, M. (2002). The globalization of sex tourism and Cuba: A commodity chains approach. *Studies in Comparative International Development, 36*(4), 63–88.

CNBC. (2019). Why McDonald's failed in Iceland. https://www.youtube.com/watch?v=AT-E_eMiwgk

Connell, J. (2006). Medical tourism: Sea, sun, sand and ... surgery. *Tourism Management, 27*, 1093-1100.

Cruise Lines International Association (CLIA). (2021). About the industry. About CLIA. https://cruising.org/en/about-the-industry/about-clia

Culture Trip. (2020). *The man who drove McDonald's out of Iceland.* Hungerlust S2. https://www.youtube.com/watch?v=zOfYZSIJRjQ

Culture Trip. (2021). Hungerlust: The man who brought the burger to Iceland. https://theculturetrip.com/europe/iceland/articles/hungerlust-the-man-who-brought-the-burger-to-iceland/

Dana, L. P., Etemad, H., & Wright, R. W. (1999). The impact of globalization on SMEs. *Global Focus, 11*(4), 93–105.

Dreher, A. (2006). Does globalization affect growth? Evidence from a new index of globalization. *Applied Economics, 38*(10), 1091–1110.

Dube, K., Nhamo, G., & Chikodzi, D. (2021). Rising sea level and its implications on coastal tourism development in Cape Town, South Africa. *Journal of Outdoor Recreation and Tourism, 33*, 100346, https://www.iata.org/en/about/priorities/

Duranton, G., & Kerr, W. R. (2015). The logic of agglomeration. *Harvard Business School*, Working Paper 16-037.

Faulkner, H. W., & Walmsley, D. J. (1998). Globalisation and the pattern of inbound tourism in Australia. *The Australian Geographer, 29*(1), 91–106.

Feng, X., Derudder, B., Wang, F., & Shao, R. (2020). Geography and location selection of multinational tourism firms: Strategies for globalization. *Tourism Review*, http://dx.doi.org/10.1108/TR-04-2020-0163.

Ferreira, S., & de Villiers, R. (2014). The Victoria and Alfred Waterfront as playground for Capetonians. *Urbani Izziv, 25*, S63–S80.

Food and Agriculture Organization (FAO). (2021). EMPRES Food Safety Strategic Plan. http://www.fao.org/3/i1646e/i1646e.pdf

Gao, S. (2000). *Economic Globalization: Trends, Risks and Risk Prevention.* New York: United Nations Development Policy and Analysis Division.

George, R. (2003). Tourist's perceptions of safety and security while visiting Cape Town. *Tourism Management*, 24, 575–585.

Gotham, K. F. (2005). Tourism from above and below: Globalization, localization and New Orleans's Mardi Gras. *International Journal of Urban and Regional Research*, 29(2), 309–326.

Grainger, A. (2012). Environmental globalization. In *The Wiley-Blackwell Encyclopedia of Globalization*. Hoboken, NJ: Wiley.

Gravari-Barbas, M., & Guinand, S. (2021). Tourism and gentrification. In Alastair M. Morrison, & J. Andres Coca-Stefaniak (Eds.). *Routledge Handbook of Tourism Cities*, pp. 88–100. London: Routledge.

Gygli, S., Haelg, F., Potrafke, N., & Sturm, J.-E. (2019). The KOF Globalisation Index: Revisited. *The Review of International Organizations*, 14, 543–574.

Halliday, T. C., & Osinsky, P. (2006). Globalization of law. *Annual Review of Sociology*, 32, 447–470.

Hazbun, W. (2004). Globalisation, reterritorialisation and the political economy of tourism development in the Middle East. *Geopolitics*, 9(2), 310–341.

Heath, E. (2001). Globalisation of the tourism industry: Future trends and challenges for South Africa. *South African Journal of Economic and Management Sciences*, 4(3), 542–569.

Hjalager, A.-M. (2007). Stages in the economic globalization of tourism. *Annals of Tourism Research*, 34(2), 437–457.

Horowitz, M. D., Rosensweig, J. A., & Jones, C. A. (2007). Medical tourism: Globalization of the healthcare marketplace. *MedGenMed Medscape General Medicine*, 9(4), 33.

Hudson, C. (2010). Delhi: Global mobilities, identity, and the postmodern consumption of place. *Globalizations*, 7(3), 371–381.

International Air Transport Association. (IATA). (2021). IATA's industry priorities. https:// www.iata.org/en/about/priorities/

International Civil Aviation Organization (ICAO). (2021). About ICAO. https://www.icao .int/about-icao/Pages/default.aspx

International Labour Organization (ILO). (2003). The social dimension of globalization. https://www.ilo.org/public/english/wcsdg/globali/globali.htm

International Monetary Fund (IMF). (2021). A guide to committees, groups, and clubs. https ://www.imf.org/en/About/Factsheets/A-Guide-to-Committees-Groups-and-Clubs

International Telecommunication Union (ITU). (2020a). *Measuring Digital Development Facts and Figures 2020*. Geneva, Switzerland: ITU.

ITU. (2020b). *Report on the Implementation of the Strategic Plan and Activities of the Union, April 2019–April 2020*. Geneva, Switzerland: ITU.

International Union for Conservation of Nature (IUCN). (2021). About. https://www.iucn .org/about

Jaapar, M., Musa, G., Moghavvemi, S., and Saub, R. (2017). Dental tourism: Examining tourist profiles, motivation and satisfaction. *Tourism Management*, 61, 538–552.

Jollibee. (2021). About us. Jollibee Foods Corporation. https://www.jollibee.com.ph/about -us/

Keohane, R. O., & Nye, J. S. (2000) Introduction. In J. D. Nye, & J. D. Donahue (Eds.). *Governance in a Globalizing World*, pp. 1–44. Washington, DC: Brookings Institution Press.

KOF Swiss Economic Institute. (2021). KOF globalisation index. https://kof.ethz.ch/en/fo recasts-and-indicators/indicators/kof-globalisation-index.html

Kureha, M., Asamizu, M., Sato, D., Saito, I., Ikenaga, M., and Funck, C. (2005). The globalization of Japanese tourism. *Geographical Review of Japan*, 78(5), 325–328.

Larner, W. (2003). Neoliberalism? *Environment and Planning D: Society and Space*, 21, 509–512.

Leamon, M. A., Rincon, E. J., Robillard, N. M., & Sutherland, J. J. (2019). Sustainable skies: How the airline industry is addressing climate change. *Journal of Strategic Innovation and Sustainability*, 14(2), 85–112.

Ley, D., & Tutchener, J. (2001). Immigration, globalisation and house prices in Canada's gateway cities. *Housing Studies*, 16(2), 199–223.

Luke, T. W. (2010). Gaming space: Casinopolitan globalism from Las Vegas to Macau. *Globalizations*, 7(3), 395–405.

Macey, J. R. (2003). Regulatory globalization as a response to regulatory competition. *Emery Law Journal*, 52, 1353–1379.

Macleod, D. V. L. (1999). Tourism and the globalization of a Canary Island. *The Journal of the Royal Anthropological Institute*, 5(3), 443–456.

Mak, A. H. N., Lumbers, M., & Eves, A. (2012). Globalisation and food consumption in tourism. *Annals of Tourism Research*, 39(1), 171–196.

Martin, L. J. (2009). Reproductive tourism in the age of globalization. *Globalizations*, 6(2), 249–263.

Matusitz, J. (2011). Disney's successful adaptation in Hong Kong: A glocalization perspective. *Asia Pacific Journal of Management*, 28, 667–681.

McCann, P., & Acs, Z. J. (2011). Globalization: Countries, cities and multinationals. *Regional Studies*, 45(1), 17–32.

McDonald's. (2021). What countries does McDonald's operate in? https://www.mcdonalds.com/gb/en-gb/help/faq/18525-what-countries-does-mcdonalds-operate-in.html

McLaren, D., & Pera, L. (2002). Globalization, indigenous peoples, and tourism. *Biodiversity*, 3(3), 16–17.

Mehmood, U., Mansoor, A., Tariq, S., & Ul-Haq, Z. (2021). The interactional role of globalization in tourism-CO2 nexus in South Asian countries. *Environmental Science and Pollution Research*, 28, 26441–26448, https://doi.org/10.1007/s11356-021-12473-0.

Miniwatts Marketing Group. (2021). World Internet users and 2021 population stats. https://www.internetworldstats.com/stats.htm

Morley, C. L. (2003). Globalisation, airline alliances and tourism: A strategic perspective. *Asia Pacific Journal of Tourism Research*, 8(1), 15–25.

Morrison, A. M., Lehto, X. Y., & Day, J. (2018). *The Tourism System*, 8th ed. Dubuque, IA: Kendall Hunt Publishing.

Mustago, T. W. (2011). In search of an African dining experience: International visitors views on service at V&A Waterfront restaurants in Cape Town. *African Journal of Hospitality, Tourism and Leisure*, 1(3), 1–10.

Niewiadomski, P. (2020). COVID-19: From temporary deglobalisation to a re-discovery of tourism? *Tourism Geographies*, 22(3), 651–656.

Norris, P. (2000). Global governance and cosmopolitan citizens. In J. S. Nye, & J. D. Donahue (Eds.). *Governance in a Globalizing World*, pp. 155–177. Washington, DC: Brookings Institution Press.

Parnwell, M. J. G. (1998). Tourism, globalisation and critical security in Myanmar and Thailand. *Singapore Journal of Tropical Geography*, 19(2), 212–231.

Persaud, W. H. (2005). Gender, race and global modernity: A perspective from Thailand. *Globalizations*, 2(2), 210–227.

Peterson, H. (2014). 18 awesome fast food items you can't get in the US. *Business Insider.* https://www.businessinsider.com/fast-food-from-around-the-world-2014-4

Potrafke, N. (2015). The evidence on globalisation. *The World Economy, 38*(3), 509–552.

Ritzer, G. (2003). The globalization of nothing. *SAIS Review, 23*(2), 189–200.

Robertson, R. (1994). Globalisation or glocalisation? *Journal of International Communication, 1*(1), 33–52.

Rolfes, M. (2010). Poverty tourism: Theoretical reflections and empirical findings regarding an extraordinary form of tourism. *GeoJournal, 75,* 421–442.

Salazar, N. (2005). Tourism and glocalization. "Local" tour guiding. *Annals of Tourism Research, 32*(3), 628–646.

Sassen, S. (2003). Globalization or denationalization? *Review of International Political Economy, 10*(1), 1–22.

Scott, A. J. (2001). Globalization and the rise of city-regions. *European Planning Studies, 9*(7), 813–826.

Simpson, T. (2008). The commercialization of Macau's cafés. *Ethnography, 9*(2), 197–234.

Smeral, E. (1998). The impact of globalization on small and medium enterprises: New challenges for tourism policies in European countries. *Tourism Management, 19*(4), 371–380.

Sugiyarto, G., Blake, A., and Sinclair, M. T. (2003). Tourism and globalization. Economic Impact in Indonesia. *Annals of Tourism Research, 30*(3), 683–701.

The Nature Conservancy (TNC) Hong Kong. (2021). Our priorities. Build healthy cities. https://www.tnc.org.hk/en-hk/what-we-do/our-priorities/build-healthy-cities/

Theuns, H. L. (2008). Globalization and tourism: Pros and cons. *Tourism Recreation Research, 33*(1), 99–105.

Tommi's Burger Joint. Tommi's Burger Joint. (2021) https://tommis.is/

United Nations (UN). (2021). The 17 goals. https://sdgs.un.org/goals

United Nations Educational, Scientific and Cultural Organisation (UNESCO). (2021). States parties ratification status. https://whc.unesco.org/en/statesparties/

United Nations Environment Programme (UNEP). (2020). Global tourism sector should continue fight against plastic pollution during and after COVID-19: New UN recommendations. https://www.unep.org/news-and-stories/press-release/global-tourism -sector-should-continue-fight-against-plastic

United Nations World Tourism Organization (UNWTO). (2020). Global code of ethics for tourism. https://www.unwto.org/global-code-of-ethics-for-tourism

UNWTO. (2021a). Global tourism plastics initiative. https://www.unwto.org/sustainable-d evelopment/global-tourism-plastics-initiative

UNWTO. (2021b). Member states. https://www.unwto.org/member-states

US Agency for International Development. (2021). Rediscovering Esna's cultural heritage. https://www.usaid.gov/egypt/economic-growth-and-tourism/rediscovering-esna-cultural -heritage

Visser, G., & Kotze, N. (2008). The state and new-build gentrification in Central Cape Town, South Africa. *Urban Studies, 45*(12) 2565–2593.

Wang, N. (1999). Rethinking authenticity in tourism experience. *Annals of Tourism Research, 26*(2), 349–370.

Wood, R. E. (2000). Caribbean cruise tourism: Globalization at sea. *Annals of Tourism Research, 27*(2), 345–370.

World Bank. (2018). Regional trade agreements. https://www.worldbank.org/en/topic/regio nal-integration/brief/regional-trade-agreements

World Health Organization. (2021). Timeline: WHO's COVID-19 response. https://www
.who.int/emergencies/diseases/novel-coronavirus-2019/interactive-timeline#event-71

World Trade Organization (WTO). (2021a). Regional trade agreements database. http://rta
is.wto.org/UI/PublicMaintainRTAHome.aspx

WTO. (2021b). The WTO. https://www.wto.org/english/thewto_e/thewto_e.htm

World Wildlife Fund (WWF). (2021). Sustainable tourism. https://wwf.panda.org/discover/
knowledge_hub/where_we_work/alps/our_solutions22222/tourism/?

Yuan, W. (2019). Disney's glocalization in Shanghai: The emotional branding strategy.
Advances in Social Science, Education and Humanities Research, *344*, 3rd International
Conference on Education, Culture and Social Development (ICECSD 2019), 95–102.

Zhang, W. W., & Chiu, Y.-B. (2020). Globalization, country risks, and trade in tourism
services: Evidence from China. *Sustainability*, *12*(14), https://www.mdpi.com/2071-1050
/12/14/5870#.

Zmyślony, P. (2011). Globalization, tourism and cities: Pros and cons. *Folia Turistica*, *25*(1),
299–312.

Chapter 3

The growth of the urban tourism phenomenon

Abstract

The number of people living in cities and towns has rapidly increased over the past century, with more than half of the 7.8 billion total global population choosing to reside in urban settlements. Considering that urban areas represent less than 1% of the Earth's surface, this leads to a remarkable concentration of population in such environments. Worth noting is that many of the cities that exist now were not there only a few decades ago. This shows the rapid changes that urban environments have undergone over a relatively short period of time, with cities and towns growing not only in number but also in size, and thus becoming more influential on the global stage. It is therefore no surprise that industrial and commercial activities are nowadays primarily located in urban areas; for many countries these environments become the most important contributor to their gross domestic product.

With this context in mind, this chapter initially focuses on the phenomenon of urbanisation and how it contributed to the development of towns and cities around the world. It then turns the attention to urban tourism, one of the oldest forms of tourism that has been largely neglected by researchers and academics until only a few decades ago. It will also discuss the complex nature of urban tourism and the evolution of this field of study, while providing examples to guide the reader.

Keywords: Urbanisation; urban tourism; growth of city tourism; double neglect; attractiveness of urban areas.

DOI: 10.4324/9781003111412-4

Learning objectives

Having read this chapter, you should be able to:

- Discuss how urbanisation and other factors have contributed to the growth of city tourism.
- Analyse the complex nature of urban tourism.
- Review the progress made in the study of the urban tourism phenomenon.

Urbanisation and the growth of city tourism

Urbanisation is one of the four demographic mega-trends identified by the United Nations in its recent report "World Urbanisation Prospects 2018", with the other three trends being the global population growth, ageing population and international migration. Urbanisation is perceived by many as a positive force that contributes to economic growth and poverty reduction, but it also creates major structural changes in the economic activities of a region and can have negative effects such as an increase in the cost of living, pollution and higher crime levels. This phenomenon has been defined as

> a complex socio-economic process that transforms the built environment, converting formerly rural into urban settlements, while also shifting the spatial distribution of a population from rural to urban areas. It includes changes in dominant occupations, lifestyle, culture and behaviour, and thus alters the demographic and social structure of both urban and rural areas.
>
> *(UN, 2019, p. iii)*

The growing level of urbanisation has contributed to a substantial rise in the number of people living in towns and cities, with recent statistics showing that the urban population worldwide has rapidly increased from an estimate of 0.8 billion in 1950, or 30% of the global population at that time, to 4.2 billion in 2018, representing 55% of the world population (Figure 3.1). To put this figure into perspective and help better understand the rate of growth, let us consider some historic data. The world urban population reached for the first time one billion people in 1959, and it then took 26 years – until 1985 – to become double that (two billion). After another 17 years, by 2002, another billion people were added to the world's urban population, which continued to grow, reaching four billion in 2015 (after only another 13 years) and is expected to reach to five billion by 2028. At the same time, the global rural population reached two billion in 1960, and it took almost 40 years – by 1989 – for another billion to be added, pushing the total to three billion people. However, according to current projections, it is expected to never reach four billion as the global trend towards urbanisation is expected to continue (UN, 2019).

Urban areas are places where innovation takes place, wealth is created and complex skills are developed. They are also places where people live, shop or enjoy leisure activities, making cities engines of growth for the regions where they are located, or even for entire countries. This is in particular true for capital cities such as Seoul, Athens, Tokyo, Paris, London or Metro Manila.

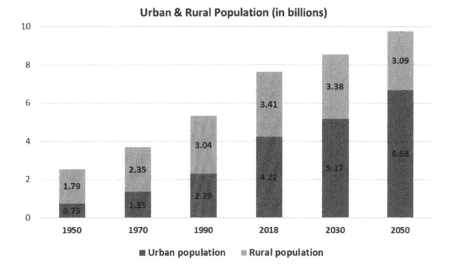

Figure 3.1 Evolution of the urban and rural population worldwide. (Source: Based on the data from the United Nations (UN, 2019).)

Sweet tweet 19

Capital cities significantly contribute to the country's GDP

Capital cities are important contributors to the economy of many countries, and some examples are given below.

> In many of Asia's economic powerhouses, the effect of the capital is felt more strongly. For example, Seoul accounts for nearly half of South Korean GDP while Tokyo's contribution in Japan is 32.3 percent. The capital is also crucial to many European economies with Athens a notable example which accounted for 47.9 percent of Greek GDP in 2016.

Source: McCarthy (2018).

Large cities in particular serve as hubs for development as they are places where businesses concentrate, and accommodation and transportation facilities are developed, thus providing an excellent infrastructure for tourism activities. Despite this, urban environments were recognised as an important setting for tourism only a few decades ago. Yet, towns and cities have always attracted people interested in visiting and experiencing a variety of activities, including iconic attractions, culture and arts events, shopping facilities and cuisine, as well as people who are interested in experiencing the vivacity, excitement and diversity of these environments.

One of the researchers who has highlighted the long existence of the phenomenon of urban tourism is Karski (1990, p. 15), who notes that

> Urban tourism has, in one form or other, been with us since Mesopotamia and Sumeria were spawning the phenomenon of urbanization. People with the means and inclination to do so have been drawn to towns and cities just to visit and experience a multiplicity of things to see and do.

He goes further and gives some more examples, noting that forms of urban tourism could be traced back to the 14th century, when pilgrims used to visit towns such as Canterbury in the UK. Another example is the Grand Tour from the 17th and 18th centuries, which was a rite of passage for young wealthy people who travelled for a couple of years to important European towns and cities and engaged in cultural activities or admired the great architecture of these places. Later, in the mid-19th century, the rapid development of railway systems in Europe allowed a large number of people to attend events such as the World Expositions, which usually took place in important capital cities.

In the second half of the 20th century, during the 1970s and 1980s in particular, industrial cities from the Western world (such as Glasgow in Scotland, UK, or Pittsburgh in Pennsylvania, US) (Figure 3.2) went through a period of economic restructuring that involved a change from industrial and manufacturing activities, towards a service-oriented economy (Wise, 2016). Tourism became an attractive option for those cities, which saw an opportunity to boost their economy and enhance their facilities through this activity. By the early 21st century, policy makers in most cities became aware of the potential of urban tourism as a means of regenerating the historic town centres, these environments being now perceived as important tourist attractions by many visitors.

Figure 3.2 The Duquesne Incline (funicular) and the Point in Pittsburgh (Courtesy: Unsplash.com, Vidar Nordli).

Sweet tweet 20

The transformation of the city of Pittsburgh

The city of Pittsburgh in Pennsylvania, United States, has undergone a massive transformation from an industrial hub for coal mining and steel production to a city destination that attracts millions of visitors.

Even though Pittsburgh faced rough times in the 1970s and 80s when steel production all but disappeared from its landscape, it has since reinvented itself as a hub for education, medicine, small manufacturing and research … Today Pittsburgh welcomes visitors from around the globe.

Source: VisitPITTSBURGH (2020).

Figure 3.3 The City of London, UK (author photo).

Over the past few decades, towns and cities worldwide found themselves in competition with each other, actively trying to attract and accommodate more visitors. Therefore, many cities recorded significant increases in visitor numbers, and these were not only the traditional tourist cities such as Paris, London (Figure 3.3), Rome or Venice that have long attracted important numbers of visitors, but also other lesser-known cities that were hardly in the minds of tourists before the 1990s (Novy and Colomb, 2019). In an effort to understand the importance of tourism in cities, Mastercard produces an annual report titled the "Global Destination Cities Index" that shows the evolution of the international visitor numbers for the top destination cities worldwide. Table 3.1 presents a synthesis of these figures for the past ten years. When looking at these data, it can be observed that there is a consistent and steady increase in the number of international tourists that visit cities, with some urban

Table 3.1 Number of international overnight visitors attracted by the top 10 destination cities worldwide, from 2010 to 2018

City	International overnight visitors (in millions)								
	2010	2011	2012	2013	2014	2015	2016	2017	2018
Bangkok, Thailand	10.44	13.8	15.82	17.47	17.03	19.59	19.41	21.09	22.78
Paris, France	13.27	13.88	15.76	17.20	17.19	16.99	15.45	17.41	19.10
London, UK	14.71	15.29	15.46	16.81	17.40	18.58	19.06	19.83	19.09
Dubai, UAE	8.41	9.20	10.95	12.19	13.21	14.20	14.87	15.79	15.93
Singapore	8.80	10.14	11.1	11.90	11.86	12.05	13.11	13.90	14.67
Kuala Lumpur, Malaysia	8.90	8.99	9.63	9.89	11.69	11.14	11.28	12.58	13.79
New York, US	9.43	10.27	10.92	11.38	12.02	12.30	12.70	13.13	13.60
Istanbul, Turkey	6.45	7.51	8.82	9.87	11.27	11.91	9.16	10.70	13.40
Tokyo, Japan	4.47	2.94	4.89	5.40	7.68	10.35	11.15	11.93	12.93
Seoul, South Korea	6.06	6.56	8.36	8.60	10.14	9.34	12.39	9.54	11.25

Source: Based on data from the Mastercard index (2014, 2017, 2019).

destinations attracting in 2018 twice as many such visitors as they did eight years before (e.g., Bangkok, Seoul and Istanbul). It should be noted however that at the time of writing, the data for 2019 and 2020 were not yet available, with figures for 2020 expected to be much lower due to the COVID-19 pandemic and the related travel restrictions put in place in many countries around the globe, which affected destinations worldwide.

When looking at how the ranking of the top 20 destination cities worldwide changed over the years (Table 3.2), it can be noted that major cities tend to dominate the top 10 positions, with Bangkok, London and Paris sharing the first three places in terms of international overnight visitors for the past decade. However, there are significant changes in the number of international visitors attracted by smaller cities such as Vienna and Amsterdam, cities that used to be in the top 20 most visited urban destinations 10 years ago, but which have been overtaken by Asian cities such as Phuket and Pattaya. Cities from the Asia-Pacific region have seen the largest increase in the number of international tourists over the past decade, this region being indeed recognised among the fastest growing travel and tourism regions in the world.

Besides the increased level of urbanisation, which played an important part in the growth of city tourism, there are other important factors that contributed to the development of urban destinations. The gradual airline liberalisation and the birth of the low-cost airlines (LCCs) in the late 20th century made it not only easier and more affordable for people to travel, but also helped bring onto the market new city destinations from emerging economies (e.g., Ljubljana in Slovenia, Budapest in Hungary, Baku in Azerbaijan, Phuket in Thailand and Nairobi in Kenya). It thus positively contributed to the growth of tourism in many destinations, with short city-breaks becoming increasingly popular among the younger generation. The low-cost revolution and the rapid increase in the number of visitors had implications for the airports as well, which were

Table 3.2 Top 20 destination cities worldwide by number of international overnight visitors – 2010 to 2018

Ranking	2010	2012	2014	2016	2018
1.	London	Bangkok	London	Bangkok	Bangkok
2.	Paris	Paris	Paris	London	Paris
3.	Bangkok	London	Bangkok	Paris	London
4.	New York	Singapore	Dubai	Dubai	Dubai
5.	Kuala Lumpur	Dubai	New York	Singapore	Singapore
6.	Singapore	New York	Singapore	New York	Kuala Lumpur
7.	Dubai	Kuala Lumpur	Kuala Lumpur	Seoul	New York
8.	Hong Kong	Istanbul	Istanbul	Kuala Lumpur	Istanbul
9.	Shanghai	Hong Kong	Seoul	Tokyo	Tokyo
10.	Rome	Seoul	Hong Kong	Istanbul	Antalya
11.	Istanbul	Barcelona	Tokyo	Hong Kong	Seoul
12.	Barcelona	Milan	Barcelona	Barcelona	Osaka
13.	Seoul	Rome	Amsterdam	Amsterdam	Makkah
14.	Amsterdam	Amsterdam	Milan	Milan	Phuket
15.	Milan	Shanghai	Rome	Taipei	Pattaya
16.	Vienna	Vienna	Taipei	Rome	Milan
17.	Tokyo	Prague	Shanghai	Osaka	Barcelona
18.	Taipei	Tokyo	Vienna	Vienna	Palma de Mallorca
19.	Lima	Taipei	Prague	Shanghai	Bali
20.	Riyadh	Los Angeles	Los Angeles	Prague	Hong Kong

Source: Based on data from the Mastercard index (2014, 2017, 2019).

transformed from simple landing strips with small size terminals, into destinations in their own right that offer shopping facilities, events and conference facilities, high-tech industrial parks and hotels.

Other factors that contributed to tourism development in cities include the development of new technologies and the proliferation of the ICTs, which changed the way visitors experience cities. Nowadays information can easily be accessed through the Internet via a mobile phone, tablet or mobile computer, or even through a smart watch. This has made travel booking increasingly simpler and more accessible, as well as making it possible to retrieve information on a destination instantly, thus saving the time and effort previously needed for such activities before and after travelling. This has contributed to a change in visitor behaviour, as the rapid progress in ICTs made it possible for visitors to find the information they needed, when they needed it and thus offered them more options with regard to the types of activities they could do in a destination, which is particularly beneficial for short city trips when time is limited.

> ### Sweet tweet 21
>
> **New technologies and tourism in cities**
>
> This example highlights the changes in the way visitors are adopting and using new technologies for their holidays.
>
> > While in the past travellers used ICTs for pre-travel and post-travel arrangements, there has been a general shift to using mobile technologies during the travel experience as many travellers are nowadays connected to the Internet during all stages of the travel cycle.
>
> Source: Bock (2015)

Many other factors have contributed over the years to the growth of tourism in general, and are also relevant for city tourism, such as higher disposable incomes and changes in working patterns allowing people to take more holidays, increased life expectancy, a more diverse offer, infrastructure improvements, changes in political regimes and the relaxation of visa restrictions (examples include the opening of a number of countries to international tourists, such as Cuba and Vietnam in the 1990s, and the expansion of the European Union in the early to mid-2000s). These factors have been discussed at length in the tourism literature to date and thus will not be developed further here. However, to offer the reader some insight into these aspects, two examples from different destinations around the world are included.

The first such example is China, which is home to a number of popular city destination such as Beijing, Shanghai, Hangzhou, Guilin and Xi'an, and is one of the emerging countries that recorded one of the highest increased rates in the number of tourists over the past few decades. According to Yang et al. (2014), tourism development in China was initially based on economic and political considerations, being stimulated by the opening of the country and the reforms promoted in the early 1980s. Although the initial focus was on international visitors, over the years the attention turned to the domestic market as well. The rapid economic growth seen by China contributed to a notable improvement in living conditions and a growth of income for its citizens. This made it possible for more Chinese people to travel abroad and domestically, making China the world's fastest growing tourism market. To stimulate domestic travel, in 2000 the government introduced long public holidays around the National Day, the Labour Day and the Spring Festival, also known as the Golden Weeks. This proved to be a very successful programme, with hundreds of millions of people travelling during these holidays. Therefore, an increase of the (affluent) middle-class population, a relaxation of visa regulations, additional holidays and significant investment in infrastructure, among other factors, have contributed to the rapid growth of (urban) tourism in this country.

The other example is Iran, which according to the latest UNWTO report was the third fastest growing tourism destination in 2019, with an increase in the number of visitors of almost 28% when compared to the previous year (Tehran Times, 2020). This rapid growth was not a surprise, as the previous year the country was ranked as the second fastest growing tourist destination worldwide, with an increase of roughly 50% in international tourist arrivals year on year. The capital Tehran and the city of Shiraz are among the leading tourist destinations in the country, which attract important numbers of visitors interested in culture and heritage. It should be noted that Iran became an attractive destination since the signing of the Iran nuclear agreement in 2015 and the subsequent softening of the international sanctions that were previously in place. As a result, a number of European and regional airlines (e.g., Lufthansa, British Airways, Air France, Air Asia) resumed their direct flights to the country. In addition, the Iranian government relaxed their visa requirements and ordered new airplanes to renew their ageing fleet (Seyfi and Hall, 2018). Other measures promoted by the Iranian authorities that contributed to the significant growth in the number of visitors and a thriving tourism industry relate to: Improving tourism infrastructure supported by proper funding and funds attracted from foreign investors, in particular in two areas – accommodation facilities and the rail transport infrastructure; diversifying the tourism offer and designing attractive packages with interesting activities and competitive prices; and a relaxation of visa regulations (e.g., 90-day visa on arrival or visa waiver).

This section has so far familiarised the reader with the importance of urban tourism and looked at a number of factors that have contributed to its growth. In the next section the attention is turned to the complex nature of urban tourism, discussing its characteristics and the attractiveness of cities as tourist destinations, as well as reviewing a number of definitions proposed by different researchers and organisations to describe this concept.

Urban tourism: A complex phenomenon

As discussed in the previous section, urban tourism is among the fastest growing tourism sectors worldwide and, as a result, it has attracted increased attention from academics and policy makers over the past few decades. Many researchers have highlighted the complex nature of this phenomenon, which for many years was only "imprecisely defined and vaguely demarcated" (Ashworth and Page, 2011, p. 1). This section therefore discusses the nature of urban tourism and its complex characteristics, followed by a review of the main definitions given for this form of tourism.

Large cities are multifunctional centres that attract international business, accommodate important cultural assets, historic monuments and iconic buildings and attract important numbers of visitors. Therefore, tourism represents only one of the many activities embedded in the economy of these cities, making tourism less visible in urban environments when compared to other forms of tourism such as rural or coastal. In addition, the distinction between visitors and locals is not very clear in cities, as tourists use in many cases the same facilities and infrastructure that are used by local people, such as museums, restaurants, shopping facilities and public transport. As a result, it is increasingly difficult to separate tourism from the other activities taking place in a city, and to link it to certain areas and times.

Sweet tweet 22

Tourism as an inextricable part of the life of the city

It is difficult to separate tourism from the other activities in the city, a fact that contributes to the complex nature of urban tourism.

> "Tourism has become pervasive, inextricably part of the life of the city. It is no longer a separate activity, confined to particular areas or to particular times", with the "boundaries between tourism and other mobilities and between tourists and the host community ... blurring and dissolving".
>
> Source: Maitland (2013), p. 14.

Furthermore, researchers highlight that visitors in large cities not only share the space, but also compete with the locals for the facilities and services they use (Pearce, 2001). As such, the tourism industry is often in competition with other local activities for the same limited resources, which can lead to a number of conflicts such as land use, property, resource and development conflicts (Campbell, 1996). In addition, in their quest to attract more visitors, world cities find themselves in competition with each other, in particular global cities such as London, Paris, Singapore and New York. These aspects add to the complex nature of urban tourism, which makes the planning and management of this activity in cities more difficult.

Another factor that has contributed to the misunderstanding of the urban tourism phenomenon is the lack of data available and, in particular, the lack of comparable data, as different countries tend to take different approaches to defining and interpreting urban tourism. This imprecision is inherently linked to the various ways of defining urban areas, with different measurements used by countries and organisations. Two of the most popular measures used to define urban areas are by a certain population size or by the population density. Even so, the minimum population considered to define a city or town varies extensively, for example, from a few hundred in Denmark, to as much as 50,000 in Japan or 100,000 in China, with the majority of countries using a threshold of 5,000 or less (Schiavina et al., 2019). This lack of clear and comparable data made urban tourism one of the most underestimated activities for many years and contributed in the past to a lack of attention from policy makers.

Edwards et al. (2008, p. 1036), however, argue that considering only a threshold for the population size in order to define what is urban is not enough; although this provides useful boundaries, it is a somewhat arbitrary figure and it does not say much about the characteristics of these environments. Instead, they propose that *urban areas* are defined as those environments that present the following elements:

• A strong and broad economic base that is serviced from multiple cores for major business and professional activities.
• A significant public transport network that acts as a gateway to other areas.
• A significant population with a workforce that commutes to and from the multiple cores.
• Long-term planned development.

This definition therefore puts emphasis on the interconnected nature of urban settlements, where people have many social, economic, political and cultural relationships.

In an effort to distinguish between different urban areas and their significance for tourism, Page (1995) put together a typology of urban tourism destinations that include:

• *Capital cities* such as London, Bangkok and Tokyo, and *cultural capitals* such as Rome and Athens.

- *Metropolitan centres* and *walled historic towns* such as York in the UK.
- *Large historic cities* such as Venice in Italy and Cambridge in the UK.
- *Inner-city areas* such as Manchester in the UK.
- *Revitalised waterfront areas* such as Sydney Darling Harbour.
- *Industrial cities* such as Bradford in the UK in the 19th century.
- *Seaside resorts and winter sport centres.*
- *Purpose-built integrated tourist resorts.*
- *Tourist entertainment complexes* such as Las Vegas and Disneyland.
- *Cultural and arts cities* such as Florence in Italy.
- *Specialised tourist service centres* such as spas or pilgrimage destinations such as Mecca in Saudi Arabia.

To these, Maitland and Newman (2009, p. 2) add another category – *world tourism cities*, which are described by the authors as large polycentric, multifunctional cities, and centres of cultural excellence that offer a variety of attractions and a range of experiences to visitors. Examples include London, Sydney, New York, Paris, Singapore and Berlin.

In an important contribution aimed at progressing the study of urban tourism, Ashworth and Page (2011, p. 1) identify and examine a number of paradoxes that characterise urban tourism, which are presented below.

a) There is a contradiction between the importance of urban tourism and the limited attention it has received from scholars, including the lack of a clear definition.
b) There are many reasons why tourists visit cities; still, the large cities that attract most visitors are multifunctional and they have the capacity to absorb significant numbers of visitors without much notice; thus tourism may become economically and physically invisible in such environments.
c) Tourists are using many of the facilities and services a city offers; however, few of them were created specifically for the use of tourists.
d) Tourism can bring an important contribution to a city's economy; however, those cities most relying on tourism are likely to see the least benefits.
e) Tourism relies on the variety and flexibility of the tourism product offered by cities, but it is not so clear whether cities need tourism.

Nevertheless, since those statements were made ten years ago, some progress has been made, with more scholars and policy makers paying attention to this phenomenon and researching urban tourism (see next section for a discussion on the latest developments and the evolution of this field of study). Although many cities are still accommodating large numbers of visitors without much effort, "overtourism" (Koens et al., 2018) has recently become a recognised issue that attracted the attention of researchers and policy makers in many popular European cities such as Venice, Barcelona, Amsterdam and Berlin.

So far, this section has focused on the complex nature of urban tourism and its characteristics. Next, the discussion is on the definitions proposed for this concept and the attractiveness of cities as tourist destinations. It should be noted that, as with many other complex concepts, authors propose different definitions for urban tourism – Table 3.3 for a selection of definitions for this phenomenon. Law (2002), for example, describes this concept simply as tourism that takes place in urban areas. This approach is criticised by some authors, who argue that only adding the term "urban" next to tourism is not

Table 3.3 Selection of "urban tourism" definitions

"Urban tourism is the set of tourist resources or activities located in towns and cities and offered to visitors from elsewhere" (European Commission, 2000, p. 21).

"The term urban tourism simply denotes tourism in urban areas" (Law, 2002, p. 4).

"One among many social and economic forces in the urban environment. It encompasses an industry that manages and markets a variety of products and experiences to people who have a wide range of motivations, preferences and cultural perspectives and are involved in a dialectic engagement with the host community" (Edwards et al., 2008, p. 1038).

"Trips taken by travellers to cities or places of high population density. The duration of these trips is usually short (one to three days) therefore it can be said that urban tourism is closely linked to the short – breaks market" (UNWTO, 2012, p. 8).

"A type of tourism activity which takes place in an urban space with its inherent attributes characterized by non-agricultural based economy such as administration, manufacturing, trade and services and by being nodal points of transport. Urban/city destinations offer a broad and heterogeneous range of cultural, architectural, technological, social and natural experiences and products for leisure and business" (World Tourism Organization & World Tourism Cities Federation, 2018).

enough as it only places the activity in a spatial setting but does little to delimitate this form of tourism from others. Morrison and Coca-Stefaniak (2021a) also emphasise that urban tourism is a system that involves more than a visit to the city, identifying four different interconnected parts which contribute to it, i.e., destination, demand, marketing and travel.

A more comprehensive definition is put forward by Edwards et al. (2008, p. 1038), who define urban tourism as:

> One among many social and economic forces in the urban environment. It encompasses an industry that manages and markets a variety of products and experiences to people who have a wide range of motivations, preferences and cultural perspectives and are involved in a dialectic engagement with the host community.

In addition, highlighting its complex nature, the European Commission (2000) states that this form of tourism depends on a number of factors, such as the size of the town or city, the history of the place and its heritage, the location and its environment and its image.

In a recent review paper conducted by Romero-García et al. (2019), the authors found that many works published on this topic do not actually include a definition for urban tourism. They point out the different approaches taken when discussing this phenomenon, with scholars understanding it either as a social phenomenon, an economic activity, a system or just referring to it as short trips taken to cities. The authors thus emphasise the multifunctional, multidimensional and multipurpose nature of urban tourism that contributes to the difficulty in delimitating and setting boundaries for this form of tourism, which in turns makes it more difficult to define.

When it comes to the attractiveness of urban areas as tourist destinations, these environments present a number of advantages that contribute to the large volume of visitors they lure. These include easier accessibility due to better connectivity (e.g., airports, rail connections); better developed attractions, including world-class attractions such as the Eiffel Tower in Paris; large number of accommodation facilities to serve the business travellers, and shopping venues. Cities are centres for business and cultural excellence with a diverse entertainment offer; they attract major sporting events and offer a vibrant nightlife with bars, clubs and restaurants. Cities also attract visiting friends and relatives

---

Table 3.4 The tourism product of Port Louis, Mauritius

Primary elements (attractions)

Cultural facilities:

- Museums: Such as Mauritius Postal Museum, Port-Louis Historic Museum, Armed Forces Museum, Blue Penny Museum, Windmill Museum, Photographic Museum
- Theatres: Théâtre de Port-Louis
- Cinemas: Star Cinema, Cine Classic, Cinecity
- Festivals: Cavadee, Diwali, Mahashivratree, Holi, fire walking, Eid-Ul-Fitr, Spring Festival

Amusement facilities:

- Le Caudan Casino, Champ-De-Mars race course

Physical characteristics:

- Historic street pattern: Pierre Poivre Street, Sir William Newton Street, Labourdonnais Street, Sir Seewoosagur Ramgoolam Street
- Interesting buildings: Le Caserne Central, Government House, Central Post Office, Supreme Court Building, Treasury Building, Bulk Sugar Terminal, Colonial House
- Ancient monument: Place D'Arme, Marie Reine De La Paix, La Citadelle, Fort Adelaide, Aapravasi Ghat, Tombeau Malartic
- Parks and green areas: Domaine Les Pailles, Jardin De La Compagnie
- Water, canals and riverfronts: GRNW river, Le Caudan and Port-Louis Waterfront
- Harbour: Port-Louis Harbour
- Socio-cultural features: Language, friendliness, local customs, mosques, temples, pagodas, churches, gastronomy, Quartier Chinois

Secondary elements (services)

- *Hotels*: Labourdonnais Hotel, Le Sufren
- *Catering facilities*: Restaurants and hotels
- *Shopping centres*: Le Caudan Shopping Centre, Happy World House, Art Gallery
- *Markets*: Central Market, on-street markets

Additional elements (infrastructure)

- *Accessibility*: The city is easily accessible by car, public transport and other modes of transport
- *Internal transport, parking and tourist facilities*: The National Transport Corporation, United Bus Service and other private bus owners; rental cars and taxis are also available in the city. The Mauritius Tourism Promotion Authority is the destination marketing organisation and provides information to tourists

Source: Based on the work of Nunkoo and Ramkissoon (2010, p. 46).

(VFR) due to the large number of people living in these environments, many of whom may not originally be from the city itself.

Jansen-Verbeke (1988) groups the features that contribute to the attractiveness of urban areas into three types of elements, as listed below:

- *Primary elements*. Represent the main reason why tourists visit a city, and include cultural facilities such as museums, art galleries, theatres and concert venues; amusement and sport facilities; the physical characteristics of the destination – including historic buildings, parks and urban landscapes.
- *Secondary elements*. Such as accommodation, shopping facilities, bars and restaurants, transportation and tourism agencies that enhance the primary attractions.
- *Additional elements*. Such as parking facilities, guides, maps, information offices, signposts and websites.

Table 3.4 presents an application of Jansen-Verbeke's model to Port Louis, which is the capital city of Mauritius, a small island country in the Indian Ocean.

Moreover, cities and towns could be either the main focus of a visit, where people spend their holiday, or places where people stop only for a while on their way to their final destinations, with Singapore and Dubai being two examples often used in the literature as stopover destinations. Therefore, they may have multiple and sometimes overlapping roles, as gateways for domestic and international visitors, key nodes of transport, staging posts, the final destination or they can be themselves a source for tourists as most visitors originate from cities.

Short break 3 briefly presents how Dubai became one of the top world tourism destinations, and the main attractions offered by the city.

SHORT BREAK 3

Dubai – from fishing village to global city

Dubai used to be in the 19th century a fishing village in the Middle East but has evolved rapidly to become the first global city in the region by the early 21st century. The city is also considered to be one of the fastest growing tourism destinations in the world, managing to double both its population and the number of international visitors over the past decade. This case study provides some insight into the factors that contributed to its rapid growth and the transformation of the city into one of the leading world tourism destinations.

Dubai is the second largest sheikhdom within the United Arab Emirates, covering only 4,114 square kilometres of land (including some land reclaimed from the sea) and with a total population of 3.19 million. The city used to rely on the oil and gas industry, but in the late 1980s it changed its strategy and diversified its economy. When the ruling king, Sheikh Rashid bin Saeed Al Maktoum, realised that the oil supplies would not last for long, he turned his attention towards the service sector, and in particular towards the tourism industry. Dubai thus started to invest heavily in the infrastructure and the facilities needed to accommodate international visitors, including air and maritime transport, iconic hotels and resorts and large shopping venues. This strategy proved to be successful and the number of international tourists to the city increased significantly in the 1990s, with the tourism industry overtaking the oil industry by 2002 and becoming one of the main contributors to the city's GDP.

The rapid expansion of the visitor economy in Dubai has continued over the past two decades, with the city being currently listed among the top five global destination cities and attracting almost 17 million international visitors in 2019, which represents more than twice the number of visitors attracted a decade earlier. This is in spite of the unfriendly climatic conditions it faces, with the city surrounded by desert and temperatures rising above 40 degrees during the summer months. This was achieved with the help of the Dubai Commerce and Tourism Promotion Board, an organisation established in 1989 with the aim of promoting the city as a luxury destination. This organisation was replaced in 1997 with the Department of Tourism and Commerce Marketing, which is the government authority under the direct supervision of the Crown Prince that is in charge of managing tourism in the city.

Dubai has a relatively short history and few historic sites survived the massive transformation undergone by the city over the years. Many of its iconic attractions are therefore built recently, with a focus on grandeur and the luxury market in mind. The most popular attractions offered by the city include:

- Burj al Arab Jumeirah, which opened in December 1999, considered one of the world's most luxurious hotels (Figure 3.4).
- Burj Khalifa, which opened in 2010, has been for more than ten years the tallest building in the world.
- The Palm Islands, the largest offshore artificial islands, built in the early 21st century entirely from sand and rocks.
- High-end shopping malls such as the Dubai Mall, the second largest mall in the world.
- The Mall of the Emirates, home to a 400-metre-long indoor ski slope.
- High-tech trade and convention centres.

The city also hosts important festivals and events, in particular during the off-peak season, such as the Dubai Shopping Festival, the Dubai Summer Surprises and Dubai Fitness Challenge. In addition, Dubai was meant to host in 2020 the World Expo Trade Convention, but the event was postponed for the following year due to the COVID-19 pandemic, which affected destinations worldwide. Yet, in spite of the diverse offer, the city is struggling to convince visitors to stay longer, being perceived by many tourists as a stopover destination (the average length of stay is 3.7 days).

Discussion points:

1. What are the most important factors that have contributed to the growth of tourism in Dubai?

Figure 3.4 Dubai shoreline with Burj Al Arab Jumeirah hotel in foreground (Courtesy: Unsplash.com, Christopher Schulz).

2. Do you think it is important for Dubai to maintain its status as one of the top world tourism cities? Why?
3. Can you see any challenges that the city of Dubai may face as a result of this rapid growth of tourism?

Researchers have identified a number of overlapping areas or functions within cities, such as the historic city, the business city, the cultural city, the tourist city, the sport city, the nightlife city and the leisure shopping city (Page and Hall, 2003). As highlighted by the authors, although relatively easy to identify, the tourist city is not easy to demarcate from the other activities within a city, an aspect also mentioned earlier in this chapter.

As seen so far in this section, urban tourism is a complex phenomenon, presenting specific characteristics that contribute to the attractiveness of those environments. The next section looks at how this field of study has evolved over the years, highlighting a number of important contributions to the research on the topic of urban tourism.

Evolution of the field of study

As mentioned earlier, urban tourism was largely neglected by academics until the 1980s, but it gradually attracted more attention from researchers and policy makers due to its growing importance.

Sweet tweet 23

Urban tourism – an under-researched area

An illustrative example of recent authors who have called for more research in the area of urban tourism.

> It is somewhat ironic that urban tourism is one of the most important forms of tourism in terms of volume and economic impact, but among its least researched phenomena … Indeed, the call for more and better research is a common theme of much of the literature written over the years.

Source: Shoval (2018), p. 372.

Ashworth (1989) was among the first academics to point out the significance of cities as spaces for tourism development, and emphasised a double neglect. Tourism researchers overlooked cities, although many tourist activities took place in these areas, and urbanists neglected the field of tourism, despite the rapid increase in numbers of visitors to these areas and the implications this had for cities. This neglect was reiterated by the same author more than ten years later in his paper "Urban tourism: Still an imbalance in attention?" (Ashworth, 2003), and was again investigated another decade later. In this latest study, "Urban tourism research: Recent progress and current paradoxes" (Ashworth and Page, 2011), the authors note that there has been some progress towards understanding the complex phenomenon of urban tourism, yet they suggest that more research is still needed in order to better grasp the inter-relationship between cities and tourism. This section therefore offers an overview of the progress recorded to date and discusses a number of important works that have contributed to the development of urban tourism as a field of study.

To begin with, it should be noted that some of the earliest works that touch on urban tourism are mainly focused on the urban geography of seaside resorts. These include, among others, the work of Gilbert (1939) on the growth of seaside health resorts in England; Barrett (1958) on seaside resort towns in England and Wales; Lavery (1972) on recreational geography; Pigram (1977) on beach resort morphology; and Pearce (1978) on form and function in French resorts.

During the 1990s, a number of other studies emerged that looked at different aspects related to urban tourism, with some of the most important contributions presented further. Ashworth and Tunbridge (1990, 2000) published a book that focuses on tourist historic cities, in particular on the importance of heritage to cities and the contribution of cities to the creation of heritage products. Mullins (1991) looks at tourism urbanisation and proposes a conceptual framework for studying this phenomenon. Law's (1992) paper discusses the contribution of urban tourism to economic regeneration by looking at a number of themes such as attractions, special events, arts, sports, conferences and exhibitions. Weaver (1993) proposes a model for urban tourism in small islands, focusing on the Caribbean region. Page (1995) published a book on urban tourism as a system, and examined a number of important aspects related to this phenomenon. This list is by no means exhaustive and may be expanded with other studies published during that time, such as Getz (1993) on tourism business districts; Zukin (1995) on how culture is shaping urban places; Chang et al. (1996) on urban heritage tourism; Hinch (1996) on sustainable urban tourism; Mazanec and Wöber (1997) on city tourism management; Hannigan (1998) on the fantasy city; Dear and Flusty (1999) who discuss postmodern urbanism; and Castells (2000) who looks at the network city.

One of the criticisms brought to the early studies in the area of urban tourism is the fragmented nature and the lack of an integrated approach towards researching this topic, with many papers limited in scope. Pearce (2001) was among the scholars who attempted to address this issue, and proposed an integrative framework for a more systematic approach to urban tourism research. This analytical framework consists of subject cells within a matrix that looks at both spatial scale (vertically) and specific themes (horizontally). The scale is defined at site, district, city-wide, regional, national and international levels, while the themes include important topics such as demand, supply, development, marketing, planning, organisation, operation and impact assessment. The author argues that placing the existing research in the cells formed by the linkages across the two axes – themes and scale – would offer a better overview of the current understanding of urban tourism and could help identify gaps in the literature. Seven years later, Edwards et al. (2008) reviewed the existing literature at the time and proposed a strategic framework for urban tourism research. The framework grouped the research issues identified in the literature around a number of themes such as the experience and behaviour of visitors to cities, impact of tourism, linkages and policy and governance. The intention was for the framework to assist in prioritising the issues identified and thus help develop a research agenda for the field of urban tourism. Although a useful contribution in the field, it should be noted that the study is mainly focused on Australia.

Other important works published in the early 2000s include Law (2002) on the visitor economy in large cities; Page and Hall (2003) on managing urban tourism; Mommaas (2004) who explores the phenomenon of cultural clustering in cities; Beedie (2005) on the adventure of urban tourism; Connelly (2007) on urban governance and tourism competitiveness; Pearce (2007) on capital city tourism; Mordue (2007) on the relationships among tourism, urban governance and public space; McNeill (2008) who examines the relationship between hotels and cities; Timur and Getz (2008) who look at managing stakeholders in urban destinations; McKercher (2008) on the transformation of market segments with distance, in urban destinations; Maitland and Ritchie (2009) who contribute to expanding the knowledge on national capital tourism; and Maitland and Newman (2009) who brought to attention the concept of world tourism cities.

Over the past decade, urban tourism has attracted increased attention from academics, with studies looking into different current trends and issues that urban tourism destinations are facing. In an influential study on urban tourism, Ashworth and Page (2011) review the state of research and identify a number of paradoxes that characterise the study of urban tourism, and which were discussed earlier. They highlight the growing scale of the literature on this topic, and identify several sub-themes that have emerged since the 1990s – i.e., management and planning, marketing, cultural agendas, impacts of tourism, sustainability, visitor perception and satisfaction, urban regeneration, typologies of tourism cities, city case studies, models, social theory, transport and infrastructure. The authors acknowledge the multidisciplinary nature of many studies, but note that these are still "weakly connected by theoretical and conceptual constructs" (Ashworth and Page, 2011, p. 2). They argue that a better understanding of the phenomenon of urban tourism will only be achieved by adopting a broader approach and integrating the academic debates from the wider domain of social sciences such as the field of urban studies.

More recently, Romero-García et al. (2019) conducted a systematic literature review on the use of the systems approach in urban tourism research, and identified three main themes trending in the literature. The first one, the development of urban tourism and its territories, includes topics such as the increase in the use of technology, increase in tourist demand and the search for memorable experiences, space conflict, changes in hotel spatial location and enhancing the vitality and viability of urban destinations. The second theme refers to globalisation and the homogenisation or diversification of destinations, and their effects on cities, while the last one focuses on stakeholder involvement. They also highlight areas for future research, such as the involvement of local communities in tourism development in cities and gaining a better understanding of tourist behaviour. They conclude that few advances have taken place in progressing the urban tourism agenda, with more interdisciplinary and transdisciplinary approaches needed to better understand this complex phenomenon.

Other works published in the past decade that contributed to expanding the urban tourism literature include a study by Nunkoo and Ramkissoon (2010) on urban tourism in small islands, with a focus on the residents' attitudes towards tourism; Castillo-Manzano et al. (2011) on the low-cost carrier phenomenon and urban tourism; a review article by Richards (2014) on creativity and tourism in cities; Miller et al. (2015) on sustainable urban tourism and pro-environmental behaviour; a special issue coordinated by Gretzel et al. (2016) on the application of smart tourism to cities; Maxim (2016) on sustainable tourism implementation in urban areas; Gutiérrez et al. (2017) on the effects of Airbnb in tourist cities; Wearing and Foley (2017) on how tourists explore and experience cities; Su et al. (2018) on expanding the knowledge on urban heritage tourism, with a focus on cultural political economy; tom Dieck and Jung (2018) who propose a theoretical framework for mobile augmented reality in urban heritage tourism; Koens et al. (2018) on overtourism and the impact of tourism in cities; Boivin and Tanguay (2019) on urban tourism attractiveness; Cohen and Hopkins (2019) on autonomous vehicles and urban tourism; Zheng et al. (2020) on personalised urban tourism itineraries.

The growing importance of urban tourism and the increased attention it has lately received from scholars led to the emergence in 2015 of the *International Journal of Tourism Cities*, a peer-reviewed interdisciplinary journal that provides a forum for the study of urban tourism and tourism cities. Another important contribution to the field is the recently published *Routledge Handbook of Tourism Cities*, edited by Morrison and Coca-Stefaniak (2021b), which explores contemporary issues, challenges and trends in urban tourism destinations worldwide.

This is by no means an exhaustive list of the studies in urban tourism published over the past years – a search of the ScienceDirect database returned many more, with over 130 results only for the past 10 years. Instead, this is only an attempt to give the reader an indication of how the topics have expanded and of the new themes researched in the field of urban tourism. It shows that over the years the attention has moved from understanding urban tourism and the importance of this phenomenon, to current debates and trends in tourism such as smart cities, sustainability, sharing economy, overtourism, autonomous vehicles and other new technologies such as mobile augmented reality.

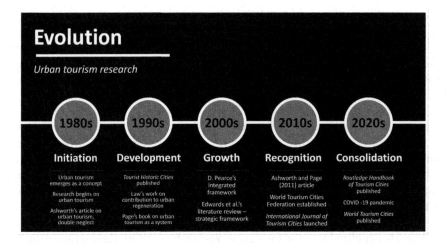

Figure 3.5 shows an approximate timeline of the evolution of urban tourism research from the 1980s to the 2020s.

Summary comments

This chapter introduces the reader to the phenomenon of urbanisation and highlights the rapid increase in the number of people who live in towns and cities over the past decades. It reveals that nowadays over half of the global population reside in urban areas and this trend is expected to continue in the near future. It then turns its attention to the phenomenon of urban tourism, which is the main focus of this book, and shows how urbanisation, together with other factors, has contributed to the growth of this form of tourism. The authors note that although urban tourism has been only relatively recently recognised as an important form of tourism by scholars and policy makers, it has a long existence, with examples dating back to the pilgrimages of the 14th century or the Grand Tour experiences of the 17th and 18th centuries.

The next section of the chapter is then focused on the complex nature of urban tourism, which is discussed in detail, with an emphasis on the multifunctional, multidimensional and multipurpose nature of this form of tourism. To better understand this concept, a number of definitions that were proposed by different researchers and organisations are reviewed and their particularities are discussed. The attractiveness of urban destinations is the next topic covered, this chapter highlighting the advantages offered by these environments, which contribute to the large number of visitors they attract. The last part of the chapter provides the reader with an overview of the latest developments in this field of study, highlighting the most important works published on this topic and their contribution to the advancement of knowledge in this particular area of research. Examples are used throughout the chapter, as well as a detailed case study of Dubai, to show how the aspects discussed apply to different city destinations around the world.

Part II of the book progresses the discussion and looks at the management, planning and marketing of world tourism cities.

Thought questions

1) What are the effects of urbanisation and how does it influence destinations worldwide?
2) What are the specific characteristics of urban areas that appeal to visitors and differentiate cities from other destinations?
3) Why do you think certain city destinations are more popular than others?
4) What factors contribute to the complex nature of urban tourism?
5) Why do you think scholars and organisations were late in recognising and studying the phenomenon of urban tourism, although this type of tourism has been around for centuries?

References

Ashworth, G. J. (1989). Urban tourism: An imbalance in attention. In C. P. Cooper (Ed.). *Progress in Tourism, Recreation and Hospitality Research*, pp. 33–54. London: Bellhaven Press .

Ashworth, G. J. (2003). Urban tourism: Still an imbalance in attention? In C. Cooper (Ed.). *Classic Reviews in Tourism*, pp. 143–163. Bristol: Channel View Publications.

Ashworth, G. J., & Page, S. J. (2011). Urban Tourism Research: Recent Progress and Current Paradoxes. *Tourism Management, 32*(1), 1–15.

Ashworth, G. J., & Tunbridge, J. E. (1990). *The Tourist-Historic City*. London: Bellhaven Press .

Ashworth, G. J., & Tunbridge, J. E. (2000). *The Tourist-Historic City*. London: Routledge.

Barrett, J. A. (1958). *The Seaside Resort Towns of England and Wales* [Thesis, University of London]. https://qmro.qmul.ac.uk/xmlui/handle/123456789/1380

Beedie, P. (2005). The adventure of Urban tourism. *Journal of Travel & Tourism Marketing, 18*(3), 37–48. https://doi.org/10.1300/J073v18n03_04

Bock, K. (2015). The changing nature of city tourism and its possible implications for the future of cities. *European Journal of Futures Research, 3*(1), 1–8. http://dx.doi.org/10.1007/s40309-015-0078-5

Boivin, M., & Tanguay, G. A. (2019). Analysis of the determinants of urban tourism attractiveness: The case of Québec City and Bordeaux. *Journal of Destination Marketing & Management, 11*, 67–79. https://doi.org/10.1016/j.jdmm.2018.11.002

Campbell, S. (1996). Green Cities, Growing Cities, Just Cities?: Urban Planning and the Contradictions of Sustainable Development. *Journal of the American Planning Association, 62*(3), 296–312.

Castells, M. (2000). *The Rise of the Network Society*, 2nd ed. Oxford: Blackwell Publishers, Inc.

Castillo-Manzano, J. I., López-Valpuesta, L., & González-Laxe, F. (2011). The effects of the LCC boom on the urban tourism fabric: The viewpoint of tourism managers. *Tourism Management, 32*(5), 1085–1095. https://doi.org/10.1016/j.tourman.2010.09.008

Chang, T. C., Milne, S., Fallon, D., & Pohlmann, C. (1996). Urban heritage tourism. *Annals of Tourism Research, 23*(2), 284–305. https://doi.org/10.1016/0160-7383(95)00064-X

Cohen, S. A., & Hopkins, D. (2019). Autonomous vehicles and the future of urban tourism. *Annals of Tourism Research, 74*, 33–42. https://doi.org/10.1016/j.annals.2018.10.009

Connelly, G. (2007). Testing Governance: A research agenda for exploring urban tourism competitiveness policy: The case of Liverpool 1980–2000. *Tourism Geographies, 9*(1), 84–114. https://doi.org/10.1080/14616680601092931

Dear, M., & Flusty, S. (1999). Engaging postmodern urbanism. *Urban Geography*, 20(5), 412–416. https://doi.org/10.2747/0272-3638.20.5.412

Edwards, D., Griffin, T., & Hayllar, B. (2008). Urban tourism research: Developing an agenda. *Annals of Tourism Research*, 35(4), 1032–1052. https://doi.org/10.1016/j.annals.2008.09.002

European Commission. (2000). Towards quality urban tourism: Integrated quality management (IQM) of urban tourist destinations. https://ec.europa.eu/growth/content/towards-quality-urban-tourism-integrated-quality-management-iqm-urban-tourist-destinations-0_en

Getz, D. (1993). Planning for tourism business districts. *Annals of Tourism Research*, 20(3), 583–600. https://doi.org/10.1016/0160-7383(93)90011-Q

Gilbert, E. W. (1939). The growth of Inland and seaside health resorts in England1. *Scottish Geographical Magazine*, 55(1), 16–35. https://doi.org/10.1080/00369223908735100

Gretzel, U., Zhong, L., & Koo, C. (2016). Application of smart tourism to cities. *International Journal of Tourism Cities*, 2(2). https://doi.org/10.1108/IJTC-04-2016-0007

Gutiérrez, J., García-Palomares, J. C., Romanillos, G., & Salas-Olmedo, M. H. (2017). The eruption of Airbnb in tourist cities: Comparing spatial patterns of hotels and peer-to-peer accommodation in Barcelona. *Tourism Management*, 62, 278–291.

Hannigan, J. (1998). *Fantasy City: Pleasure and Profit in the Postmodern Metropolis*. London: Routledge.

Hinch, T. D. (1996). Urban tourism: Perspectives on sustainability. *Journal of Sustainable Tourism*, 4(2), 95–110.

Jansen-Verbeke, M. (1988). Leisure, recreation and tourism in inner cities. *Netherlands Geographical Studies* No . 58. https://repository.ubn.ru.nl/bitstream/handle/2066/113512/mmubn000001_064292460.pdf

Karski, A. (1990). Urban tourism: A key to urban regeneration. *The Planner*, 76(13), 15–17.

Koens, K., Postma, A., & Papp, B. (2018). Is overtourism overused? Understanding the impact of tourism in a city context. *Sustainability*, 10(12), 4384. https://doi.org/10.3390/su10124384

Lavery, P. (1972). *Recreational Geography*. Pynes Hill: David & Charles.

Law, C. M. (1992). Urban tourism and its contribution to economic regeneration. *Urban Studies*, 29(3–4), 599–618.

Law, C. M. (2002). *Urban Tourism: The Visitor Economy and the Growth of Large Cities*. Andover: Cengage Learning EMEA.

Maitland, R. (2013). Backstage behaviour in the global city: Tourists and the search for the 'Real London'. *Procedia - Social and Behavioral Sciences*, 105(3), 12–19.

Maitland, R., & Newman, P. (Eds.). (2009). *World Tourism Cities: Developing Tourism Off the Beaten Track*. London: Routledge.

Maitland, R., & Ritchie, B. W. (Eds.). (2009). *City Tourism: National Capital Perspectives*. Wallingford: CABI Publishing.

Mastercard. (2014). *Global Destination Cities Index 2014*. https://newsroom.mastercard.com/documents/mastercard-2014-global-destination-cities-index/

Mastercard. (2017). *Global Destination Cities Index 2017*. https://newsroom.mastercard.com/wp-content/uploads/2017/10/Mastercard-Destination-Cities-Index-Deck.pdf

Mastercard. (2019). *Global Destination Cities Index 2019*. https://newsroom.mastercard.com/wp-content/uploads/2019/09/GDCI-Global-Report-FINAL-1.pdf

Maxim, C. (2016). Sustainable tourism implementation in urban areas: A case study of London. *Journal of Sustainable Tourism*, 24(7), 971–989.

Mazanec, J. A., & Wöber, K. W. (Eds.). (1997). *Analysing International City Tourism*, 1st ed. London: Cassell.

McCarthy, N. (2018). *Where Capital Cities Have The Most Economic Clout*. Statista. https ://www.statista.com/chart/15738/the-contribution-of-selected-capital-cities-to-their-countries-gdp/

McKercher, B. (2008). Segment transformation in urban tourism. *Tourism Management, 29*(6), 1215–1225. https://doi.org/10.1016/j.tourman.2008.03.005

McNeill, D. (2008). The hotel and the city. *Progress in Human Geography, 32*, 383–398.

Miller, D., Merrilees, B., & Coghlan, A. (2015). Sustainable urban tourism: Understanding and developing visitor pro-environmental behaviours. *Journal of Sustainable Tourism, 23*(1), 26–46.

Mommaas, H. (2004). Cultural clusters and the post-industrial city: Towards the remapping of urban cultural policy. *Urban Studies, 41*(3), 507–532. https://doi.org/10.1080/004209 8042000178663

Mordue, T. (2007). Tourism, urban governance and public space. *Leisure Studies, 26*(4), 447–462. https://doi.org/10.1080/02614360601121413

Morrison, A. M., & Coca-Stefaniak, J. A. (2021a). Introduction: City tourism and tourism cities. In A. M. Morrison & J. A. Coca-Stefaniak (Eds.). *Routledge Handbook of Tourism Cities*, pp. 1–14. London: Routledge.

Morrison, A. M., & Coca-Stefaniak, J. A. (Eds.). (2021b). *Routledge Handbook of Tourism Cities*. Routledge.

Mullins, P. (1991). Tourism urbanization. *International Journal of Urban and Regional Research, 15*(3), 326–342. https://doi.org/10.1111/j.1468-2427.1991.tb00642.x

Novy, J., & Colomb, C. (2019). Urban tourism as a source of contention and social mobilisations: A critical review. *Tourism Planning & Development, 16*(4), 358–375. https://doi.org/10.1080/21568316.2019.1577293

Nunkoo, R., & Ramkissoon, H. (2010). Small island urban tourism: A residents' perspective. *Current Issues in Tourism, 13*(1), 37–60. https://doi.org/10.1080/13683500802499414

Page, S. J. (1995). *Urban Tourism*. London: Routledge.

Page, S. J., & Hall, C. M. (2003). *Managing Urban Tourism*. London: Pearson Education Limited.

Pearce, D. (1978). Form and function in French resorts. *Annals of Tourism Research, 5*(1), 142–156. https://doi.org/10.1016/0160-7383(78)90008-7

Pearce, D. (2001). An integrative framework for urban tourism research. *Annals of Tourism Research, 28*(4), 926–946.

Pearce, D. (2007). Capital city tourism. *Journal of Travel & Tourism Marketing, 22*(3–4), 7–20. https://doi.org/10.1300/J073v22n03_02

Pigram, J. J. (1977). Beach resort morphology. *Habitat International, 2*(5), 525–541. https://doi.org/10.1016/0197-3975(77)90024-8

Richards, G. (2014). Creativity and tourism in the city. *Current Issues in Tourism, 17*(2), 119–144. https://doi.org/10.1080/13683500.2013.783794

Romero-García, L. E., Aguilar-Gallegos, N., Morales-Matamoros, O., Badillo-Piña, I., & Tejeida-Padilla, R. (2019). Urban tourism: A systems approach: State of the art. *Tourism Review, 74*(3), 679–693. https://doi.org/10.1108/TR-06-2018-0085

Schiavina, M., Melchiorri, M., Corbane, C., Florczyk, A. J., Freire, S., Pesaresi, M., & Kemper, T. (2019). Multi-scale estimation of land use efficiency (SDG 11.3.1) across 25 years using global open and free data. *Sustainability, 11*, 5674; doi:10.3390/su11205674

Seyfi, S., & Hall, C. M. (2018). *Tourism in Iran: Challenges, Development and Issues*. London: Routledge.

Shoval, N. (2018). Urban planning and tourism in European cities. *Tourism Geographies, 20*(3), 371–376. https://doi.org/10.1080/14616688.2018.1457078

Su, R., Bramwell, B., & Whalley, P. A. (2018). Cultural political economy and urban heritage tourism. *Annals of Tourism Research*, *68*, 30–40. https://doi.org/10.1016/j.annals.2017.11.004

Tehran Times. (2020, February 4). Iran third fastest growing tourism destination in 2019: UNWTO. *Tehran Times*. https://www.tehrantimes.com/news/444849/Iran-third-fastest-growing-tourism-destination-in-2019-UNWTO

Timur, S., & Getz, D. (2008). A network perspective on managing stakeholders for sustainable urban tourism. *International Journal of Contemporary Hospitality Management*, *20*(4), 445–461. https://doi.org/10.1108/09596110810873543

tom Dieck, M. C., & Jung, T. (2018). A theoretical model of mobile augmented reality acceptance in urban heritage tourism. *Current Issues in Tourism*, *21*(2), 154–174. https://doi.org/10.1080/13683500.2015.1070801

UN. (2019). *World Urbanization Prospects 2018*. https://www.un.org/development/desa/publications/2018-revision-of-world-urbanization-prospects.html

UNWTO. (2012). *Global Report on City Tourism*. https://www.e-unwto.org/doi/epdf/10.18111/9789284415300

VisitPITTSBURGH. (2020). *The History of Pittsburgh, Pennsylvania*. Visit Pittsburgh. https://www.visitpittsburgh.com/things-to-do/arts-culture/history/

Wearing, S. L., & Foley, C. (2017). Understanding the tourist experience of cities. *Annals of Tourism Research*, *65*, 97–107. https://doi.org/10.1016/j.annals.2017.05.007

Weaver, D. B. (1993). Model of Urban Tourism for Small Caribbean Islands. *Geographical Review*, *83*(2), 134. https://doi.org/10.2307/215251

Wise, N. (2016). Outlining triple bottom line contexts in urban tourism regeneration. *Cities*, *53*, 30–34. https://doi.org/10.1016/j.cities.2016.01.003

World Tourism Organization, & World Tourism Cities Federation. (2018). *UNWTO/WTCF City Tourism Performance Research*. UNWTO. https://doi.org/10.18111/9789284419616

Yang, Y., Liu, Z.-H., & Qi, Q. (2014). Domestic tourism demand of urban and rural residents in China: Does relative income matter? *Tourism Management*, *40*, 193–202. https://doi.org/10.1016/j.tourman.2013.05.005

Zheng, W., Ji, H., Lin, C., Wang, W., & Yu, B. (2020). Using a heuristic approach to design personalized urban tourism itineraries with hotel selection. *Tourism Management*, *76*, 103956. https://doi.org/10.1016/j.tourman.2019.103956

Zukin, S. (1995). *The Cultures of Cities*. Wiley-Blackwell. https://www.wiley.com/en-gb/The+Cultures+of+Cities-p-9781557864376

Management, planning, development and marketing of world tourism cities

Part II recognises that more cities around the world are getting involved in tourism for several reasons. The complexity of tourism in already complicated urban areas requires a highly professional approach to management, planning, development and marketing, and Part II reviews these in detail while drawing upon successful practices from around the world.

Chapter 4 introduces the concept of professional destination management for cities. The recommended roles for city destination management organisations (CDMOs) are identified and discussed. The eight roles present a much broader view of what needs to be accomplished in a city for tourism to be effective and successful. In particular, the key role of tourism leadership and coordination is highlighted, as is the need for crisis management planning in tourism.

Chapter 5 reviews tourism planning processes and tourism development for cities. A systematic approach to preparing tourism plans is described, and appropriate best practice examples are included. It is noted that there are many more city tourism plans and strategies than there were five to ten years ago. The chapter calls for an objective assessment of the positive and negative impacts of tourism on cities, their businesses and local citizens.

Chapter 6 explains the procedures for the marketing and branding of tourism in cities. The perspective of marketing stretches well beyond the traditional narrow view that it just involves sales and advertising. A structured approach is presented revolving around addressing five key questions. Chapters 5 and 6 recognise the interrelationships among planning, development, marketing and branding, and the vital need for cities to adopt "un-siloed" approaches to the four practices.

The three chapters when taken together provide a solid foundation for considering the contents, issues and challenges presented in the six chapters that follow in Part III.

The authors believe that the future scenarios will be more positive if informed and supported by professional and systematic approaches in management, planning, development and marketing.

DOI: 10.4324/9781003111412-5

Unique concepts in Part II:

Seven-plus-one DM roles (Chapter 4)
Seven-step tourism planning process (Chapter 5)
10 As of city tourism development (Chapter 5)
Seventeen types of tourism developments and themes (Chapter 5)
Five questions for systematic city destination marketing

Short breaks: Part II

4. London
5. Copenhagen
6. Calgary

Sweet tweets: Part II

24. City of Sydney (Australia) leading by example with sustainability
25. NYC & Company is a non-profit organisation
26. Las Vegas Visitor Profile Study
27. Residents are important to Singapore's tourism
28. Residents in Bali oppose large-scale tourism development project
29. Tokyo wants to provide more authentic experiences
30. Improving supporting amenities in Ciudad de México
31. Chicago promotes tourism partnerships
32. Prague wants to curb drunk tourism
33. Macao has a tourism crisis management committee
34. Auckland plots a tourism recovery
35. Richmond envisions a liveable, lovable future
36. What the master planners say about development
37. Tourism development master plan for Qiddiya, Saudi Arabia
38. Are you Instagrammable?
39. Austin is a creative city
40. Funds for neighbourhood tourism development in Kansas City
41. The tourism development "growth paradox"
42. Portland's opportunities and challenges
43. The tourism DNA of Tel Aviv
44. Berlin promotes its health tourism assets
45. Bruges chooses not to encourage "excursionism"
46. Helsinki involves local citizens in brand development process
47. Do not overemphasise a slogan!
48. Málaga is a smart trail-maker
49. City tourism marketing budgets under siege in 2020
50. Tourism city success stories
51. Don't take all the credit unless you can prove it!

Chapter 4

City destination management

Abstract

This chapter adopts a destination management perspective and reviews all of the roles involved in urban destination management. Destination management is a systematic and coordinated effort to manage all aspects of tourism in a city. The roles and responsibilities of city destination management organisations (CDMOs) are expanding and the reasons for this trend are identified. These roles are leadership, coordination and governance, planning and research, community and stakeholder relationships and involvement, product development, marketing and promotion, partnership and team building, and visitor management. It is suggested that the leadership and coordination of diverse stakeholders in city destinations is a core role. The heightened importance of crisis management in the COVID-19 era is explained, resulting in the recommended "seven-plus-one" roles model for CDMOs. A varied set of management approaches and skills is required to fulfil these roles. Examples of best practice in city destination management from across the world are cited.

Keywords: Seven-plus-one roles; community and stakeholder relationships and involvement; crisis management; leadership and coordination; marketing and promotion; visitor management; partnership and team building; planning and research; product development.

DOI: 10.4324/9781003111412-6

Learning objectives

Having read this chapter, you should be able to:

- Explain the city destination management concept.
- Describe the seven-plus-one roles.
- Justify why leadership and coordination of city tourism is a core role.
- Explain governance and identify its dimensions.
- Elaborate on the importance of crisis management for city tourism.

Destination management

Destination management is a systematic and coordinated effort to manage all aspects of tourism in a city. This practice undoubtedly needs to be evident in world tourism cities. City destination managers are professionals who perform multiple roles to achieve the visions and goals for tourism in urban areas.

The need for destination management arises from the existence of several stakeholders in cities who are directly or indirectly involved in or affected by tourism. The coordination of these stakeholders is vital to successful urban tourism. The most obvious stakeholders are the visitors themselves, the tourism operators who serve them and those marketing city tourism. However, there are many more stakeholders, including local residents, city government, various local groups and NGOs and the environment. Destination management must address the particular needs, expectations and requirements of all these stakeholders. Various stakeholders have different priorities and concerns and so it is challenging for CDMOs to balance all of these.

Various economic, societal, technological and environmental issues and trends have exacerbated the necessity for having professional destination management. Globalisation and the worldwide competition in tourism are creating more pressure on cities to maintain their market standing. Inclusiveness, gender equality and freedom from discrimination are just three of the societal trends impacting upon city tourism. Technology is yielding new opportunities for communications and "smart" options for enabling and managing visitor flows. The need for more sustainable and responsible tourism is drawing greater attention to environmental protection and the conservation of cultural and heritage resources (Figure 4.1).

The advent of the COVID-19 pandemic in 2020 and 2021 heralded a new era for global tourism. Not only was the long-term worldwide tourism growth bubble burst, but also cities discovered first-hand about the need to deal with major crises. Many cities were caught unprepared for this disastrous public health event as a result of paying lip service to the need for tourism crisis management planning. They had not prepared tourism crisis management plans and appointed crisis management teams or instituted other best practices for crisis management.

One core notion of the current view of destination management is that there must be a specific organisation in a city that is assigned this responsibility. The CDMO may be administered by the government or be a public-private partnership (PPP). It can be said that there is a gradual trend towards more PPPs; however, there is no template that can be given for organising and structuring a CDMO, as these vary widely from place to place. However, there is a set of roles that all CDMOs should fulfil, and these are described in the following materials.

Figure 4.1 Gyeongbokgung Palace, Seoul, South Korea. (Photo: Courtesy, Unsplash.com, Brady Bellini.)

City destination management roles

Professional destination management within cities embraces several roles. "Selling the city" is no longer sufficient as urban tourism and visitors continuously grow in sophistication. The roles of CDMOs are now multifaceted and require a varied set of management skills.

One of the authors was involved in developing and facilitating the Certified Destination Management Executive (CDME) programme for Destinations International (known as the IACVB – International Association of Convention and Visitors Bureaus – when CDME was initiated). Over the ensuing 15 years in training sessions with CDMO leaders and through experience with other DMOs worldwide, destination management roles were defined and validated by practitioners. Based on this work, seven distinct city destination management roles and the need for greater attention to be given to crisis management (seven-plus-one) are described. These are not in order of priority.

Leadership, coordination and governance

A core role of city destination managers is leadership for the tourism sector, which given its complexity requires a high level of coordination. Many CDMOs are run by government agencies that one might axiomatically think are vested with leadership powers and authority. However, even governmental CDMOs must exhibit leadership qualities and coordinate the efforts of the many players in tourism.

CDMOs are entities created to lead the tourism sector by setting a vision and coordinating the efforts of stakeholders to attain that vision. In fact, the fulcrum for leadership and coordination is the establishment of a tourism vision for a city. The vision expresses a long-term goal and desired future situation for tourism in an urban area. Short break 4 describes the tourism vision for London.

SHORT BREAK 4

The London tourism vision

London is one of the world's topmost tourism cities and a magnet for domestic and international visitors. Its CDMO, London & Partners, developed a tourism vision for the UK capital in 2018. The vision statement in the official document was as follows:

> Our vision is that visitors will be able to unlock the best version of London for them by tailoring their experience. They will be provided with better online and offline information to help them navigate the city more effectively and make more informed choices. They will be encouraged to do and see more of London, which will increase their satisfaction and likelihood of returning. The tourism industry will work together to manage the expected significant visitor growth in a sustainable way. And we will achieve our vision by balancing the needs of Londoners and visitors, with more Londoners recognising the importance of the visitor economy and benefiting from its social and economic impact.

Noteworthy in this vision statement are the mentions of experiences, visitor satisfaction, sustainability and the needs of Londoners. It also expresses the desire to have visitors to see more of London and as a result to return more often. Also, London & Partners wants local residents to be more aware of the benefits and importance of tourism in their city.

Discussion points:

1. How well does this vision encapsulate the unique characteristics of London?
2. Are there other trends, issues and opportunities that should have been incorporated in the vision and, if so, what are they?
3. With the onset of COVID-19, does London need to alter its tourism vision and, if so, in what way?

Source: London & Partners (2018).

Leadership is thus partly about getting stakeholders to imagine the future of tourism, but that is certainly not all it encompasses. "Leading by example" is a phrase often used to characterise organisations and individuals who are role models that inspire others. CDMOs must demonstrate their leadership "on the ground" by modelling the behaviour and actions they expect from stakeholders. Thus, if the CDMO leaders advocate a research-based planning approach, the CDMO itself must have a tourism plan and strategy and be active in gathering primary research data. A good example of leading by example follows with the Sydney city government demonstrating its modelling for sustainable development.

> **Sweet tweet 24**
>
> ## City of Sydney leading by example with sustainability
>
> The city of Sydney, Australia, has a strong commitment to sustainable tourism development as evidenced by this statement in its tourism plan:
>
> Developing sustainably
> The City will lead by example and drive demand by reviewing its own policies and procedures including green event guidelines, accommodation and business event procurement, sponsorship and venue operating standards.
>
> Source: City of Sydney (2013).

Leadership is not only demonstrated by CDMOs as entities, but also through the styles adopted by their executives and managers. Here, it is worthwhile noting that CDMO executives must demonstrate their leadership capabilities and styles within their own organisations and outside of them. Several leadership styles have been identified, including adaptive, authentic, servant and transformational leadership (Northouse, 2018). While there is no data on which of these styles work best for tourism, and that will be determined on a case-by-case basis, it can be said that the command-and-control authoritarian leadership as found in the military is unlikely to work in city destinations. CDMOs must also have excellent human resource management capabilities, as their staff members are the key to the services that they provide and the tasks that are performed.

Effective leadership is dependent on excellent coordination. However, coordination is a much-used word but rather elusive to define in a tourism context. CDMOs encourage groups and individuals to work together harmoniously in an organised way to achieve visions, goals or objectives. Mainly, this involves CDMOs working as the coordinator of tourism stakeholders within their destinations. Coordination of parties outside of the destination is also needed. To put the concept in more active terms, coordination involves: (1) informing and communicating; (2) engaging and involving; and (3) seeking and receiving feedback.

Coordination is required across all the other seven destination management roles as well as to support leadership. CDMOs must keep stakeholders informed about what they are doing and maintain two-way communications. Where and whenever possible and appropriate, stakeholders should be engaged in the activities of the CDMO. Feedback from stakeholders should always be welcomed and actively sought.

There is another aspect of coordination that needs to be mentioned and that is between CDMOs and more senior levels of government as well as in the larger geographic areas that surround cities. Typically, national tourism organisations within countries set tourism policies and cities, as well as states, provinces, territories and regions, should abide by these guidelines. Often the implementation of programmes and activities requires coordination and cooperation among two or three levels of DMOs (e.g., national, state/provincial and city). External coordination is also required with organisations such as travel agencies and tour operators, associations and other entities.

The concept of destination governance is associated with leadership and coordination. Governance refers to how a CDMO is administered and who does the administering.

Governance involves the policies, systems and processes to ensure that all stakeholders are involved and that the CDMO is accountable for its results and resource use and has transparency in its operations. CDMOs are either governmental or are administered by boards of directors. As an example of the latter, NYC & Company is the CDMO for New York City.

Sweet tweet 25

NYC & Company is a non-profit organisation

New York City's CDMO is an example of a public-private partnership. It is also a membership organisation.

> NYC & Company is the official destination marketing organization (DMO) and convention and visitors bureau (CVB) for the five boroughs of New York City. Our mission is to maximize travel and tourism opportunities throughout the City, build economic prosperity and spread the dynamic image of New York City around the world. A 501(c) 6 private corporation, NYC & Company represents the interests of nearly 2,000 member organizations across the spectrum of businesses and organizations in the City.

Source: NYC & Company (2020).

Governance has several dimensions including accountability, transparency, involvement, structure, effectiveness and power.

- *Accountability*. This is the obligation of a CDMO to justify and account for its programmes and activities and to accept responsibility for results. The CDMO must disclose these results in a transparent way and take responsibility for the use of all resources with which it is entrusted.
- *Transparency*. There must be openness in the CDMO's operations and communications. Tourism stakeholders and others in the destination should be able to see what the CDMO is doing and understand its decision-making.
- *Involvement*. This could be termed the opportunity to participate. Every stakeholder group and type of individual should have an opportunity to participate in the CDMO's activities and programmes.
- *Structure*. This is how CDMOs are organised and governed. There are many different ways to organise CDMOs and no single uniform structure can be recommended based upon actual practice.
- *Effectiveness*. There is a need to measure the performance results of the CDMO and the adequacy of the performance against goals and objectives. Having specific performance metrics or key performance indicators (KPIs) is critical for measurement.
- *Power*. This refers to the ways in which power is exercised within the CDMO and among those with which the CDMO is involved, especially its stakeholders. Generally, it appears to be accepted in tourism that the exercise of "collective" rather than authoritarian power tends to be more effective. The shared ownership of the city destination vision, tourism plans and branding approaches facilitates this "collective" power.

Although some might argue that governance and leadership are equivalents, the view in this text is that they are associated concepts and not exactly the same. Governance gives CDMOs power and authority; however, power and authority are not sufficient for effective leadership. City tourism requires great coordination among multiple stakeholders and often means the sharing of responsibilities and tasks. Being a "governor" does not automatically imply that one is accepted as a "leader".

A final note is that governance does not necessarily equal government with respect to CDMOs. In fact, there is an ongoing debate as to whether government agencies are the best option for governing tourism organisations given the known tendencies to bureaucracy and the often frequent changes in political leadership. Moreover, extensive approval and deliberative processes result in slowness in decision-making when compared with the private sector. However, city governments are involved in urban planning and policy making and have the power to enforce standards of various types. They may also have greater access to research information. The creativity and innovativeness along with the speedier decision-making of private enterprises are qualities that match the dynamic nature of tourism. Also, coordination and liaison with tourism operators may be facilitated by involving the private sector in tourism governance. An approach that blends the advantages of government with those of industry, as in public-private partnerships, would appear to be an ideal model for tourism.

Leadership in tourism is well demonstrated when CDMOs initiate and coordinate efforts to prepare tourism plans and strategies, and that is the next role to be discussed.

Planning and research

Research-based planning is the hallmark of professional city destination management. Although not all cities have tourism plans or strategies, these are instrumental in providing longer-term guidance for the sector. Research is also needed to inform decisions for all of the destination management roles. Chapter 5 is devoted to tourism planning in this text, and it emphasises the need for a participative and inclusive process.

Research is fundamental in developing tourism plans and strategies and should be regarded as an investment rather than an expense item. The following example from Las Vegas highlights the importance of research data for informing future planning.

Sweet tweet 26

Vegas Visitor Profile Study

The Las Vegas Convention and Visitors Authority has a very active research programme and department. Its Visitor Profile Study is an excellent model for other CDMOs.

"Nationwide, research studies such as our monthly Executive Summary of key tourism statistics and our annual visitor profile help inform and support our overall marketing strategy as well as the efforts of our resort partners".

Source: LVCVA (2020).

The Hong Kong Tourism Bureau (HKTB) is another CDMO that values the power of research for decision-making. It conducts extensive research on visitor profiles and preferences (Hong Kong Tourism Board, 2020a).

Research completed in world tourism cities should not be random; rather, it should be ongoing and well-planned. At a very minimum, as in the case of Las Vegas, a visitor profile study should be conducted each year. CDMOs also need to do research annually to measure their performance against predetermined metrics or key performance indicators (KPIs). WellingtonNZ, for example, has four KPIs that it measures, the first of which is the direct economic impact of its activities and interventions (WellingtonNZ, 2020). Other research projects that can be done by CDMOs include those on potential visitors, economic impact, resident attitudes and opinions, destination image and competitors. They may also have destination audits completed which assess city destination quality levels. With respect to resident surveys, the city of Buenos Aires in Argentina polled the residents of its barrios (neighbourhoods) in the "Mi Barrio" project to get their insights and opinions on involving and positioning each neighbourhood for tourism (Future Places, 2020).

It is well accepted that there are two categories of research data and information – primary and secondary. Here it is noticeable that many cities are relying on secondary (previously published) sources rather than gathering first-hand and original research about their own destinations. For example, there is a considerable reliance on the Mastercard *Global Destination Cities Index* for ranking purposes (Mastercard, 2019). This is an excellent secondary source of data about leading world tourism cities; however, it does have certain limitations. First, only 20 cities are included and so there are scores of other cities with no data or rankings. Second, only two data points are measured in volumes of international overnight visitors and their expenditure levels. These are undoubtedly important indicators for determining world tourism cities, but they do not reflect city tourism product characteristics, nor do they pay attention to the consumer's voice. The main point being made here is that CDMOs should not rely only on secondary data and information as these can be misleading and lacking in relevance and applicability to all cities. The bottom line here is that CDMOs should be gathering their own primary research.

CDMOs should develop annual research agendas and plans to meet them. These will include ongoing research, such as gathering visitor profile data, that is conducted each year. Other research initiatives will be repeated every three to five years and might include surveying community resident attitudes and opinions on tourism. *Ad hoc* research projects, although unpredictable at the time of planning, will also need to be done. An annual budget for research should be established.

Planning and research efforts of CDMOs should feature community and other stakeholder engagement and involvement. The following section includes ideas on how to accomplish this.

Community and stakeholder relationships and involvement

There are multiple stakeholders in city tourism. City destination management requires that attention be given to internal stakeholders as well as to external markets and partners. The overtourism phenomenon was an indicator in several cities that inadequate attention was being paid to the needs of community residents (Dodds and Butler, 2019). CDMOs must show a concern for the quality of life and well-being of local citizens, principally by not over-developing tourism beyond its capacity.

Tourism can be beneficial to communities and local people; however, past experience worldwide shows that tourism also can have harmful impacts on communities. Therefore, it is highly advisable to adopt a community perspective in destination management, and this is especially so for places that are developing tourism and where there is sensitivity to environmental and socio-cultural impacts. While DMOs and tourism stakeholders tend to stress the positive economic impacts of tourism, a wider and more holistic view needs to be taken of tourism development, its community impacts and sustainability.

There are two parts to the community and stakeholder relationship and involvement role, and these are relationship maintenance and involvement. Continuous two-way communications are the heart of relationship maintenance and professional destinations plan ahead for these efforts as they do in preparing an annual marketing plan. For example, Louisville Tourism includes a Community Awareness Overview section in its marketing plan. The strategy is to "empower residents and local business owners to become ambassadors and stewards of Louisville's brand" (Louisville Tourism, 2019). Another example of recognising the importance of resident involvement in tourism is from the Singapore Tourism Board, which emphasises the value of garnering their ideas and energy.

Sweet tweet 27

Residents are important to Singapore's tourism

With its branding of *SG Passion made possible*, the Singapore Tourism Board highlights the creativity and diversity among its local residents.

Strong support and active participation from Singapore residents are also imperative to the tourism sector as they are an integral part of Singapore's identity and appeal. STB will continue to work with tourism industry partners to nurture public engagement as part of its tourism development efforts; every local resident is a potential advocate for tourism and together, their collective ideas and energies can contribute to the sustainable development of the tourism sector.

Source: Singapore Tourism Board (2020).

Before leaving the Singapore example, it is worthwhile to note that its destination branding approach is built around the characteristics of its people. Specifically, it builds upon the passion of Singaporeans for what they do in diverse areas of endeavour. This surely must contribute to building a greater sense of community and pride.

Specific examples of establishing and maintaining ongoing relationships with communities and stakeholders are given below:

- Providing information on CDMO plans, programmes and activities.
- Educating residents and other stakeholders about tourism.
- Sharing CDMO performance data.
- Gathering data on resident and stakeholder attitudes towards tourism.
- Encouraging protection of local culture and heritage, and the natural environment.

The "be a tourist in your own city" movement is a great example for the second point above. The annual Visit York Residents Festival in England is an outstanding case study of such an event (Visit York, 2020).

Involvement or engagement means more active participation for community residents and other tourism stakeholders. Examples include engaging local communities in tourism policy and plan preparation and involving them in the delivery of CDMO programmes and activities. Some CDMOs operate ambassador or greeter programmes with teams of local residents; others engage local people as spokespersons in marketing and promotions; and there are CDMOs that have staff members work with residents and stakeholders in periodic "clean-up" efforts to beautify their cities and protect the environment. Travel Portland is one of the CDMOs that organise these volunteering efforts (Travel Portland, 2020). Additionally, several CDMOs operate award programmes that recognise residents and other stakeholders for outstanding service to visitors and for other accomplishments.

Building and maintaining community and stakeholder relationships is an essential role for CDMOs and central to their leadership and coordination. In fact, as stated earlier, this could be one of the most salient reasons for establishing CDMOs. Of course, there are different ways to tick this box; however, a cautionary note needs to be added. This role is not to be treated as an exercise in public relations, nor can it just be done online; it must involve two-way communication and real and authentic engagement and involvement. Community residents and other stakeholders, for example, should be counselled on proposed new tourism developments, and especially those that will have significant impacts on their quality of life and well-being. Product development is the next topic; however, an example from Bali here provides a very meaningful linkage between these two roles.

Sweet tweet 28

Residents in Bali oppose large-scale tourism development project

It is important to listen to the voices of residents and to get their views on tourism development initiatives. While new projects might boost tourism, they may also disrupt the lifestyles and traditions of local people.

Indonesia's maritime ministry has designated Bali's Benoa Bay a conservation zone for religious and cultural activities, and traditional and sustainable fisheries. The decision effectively kills a $2 billion plan to reclaim land in the mangrove-rich bay for a tourism development featuring hotels, restaurants, entertainment venues and a convention center … Indonesians in Bali and other cities have since opposed every proposed development project in the bay.

Source: Conservation News (2020).

Product development

The city destination product is an interdependent combination of tangible and intangible elements, including physical products, people, packages and programmes. The interactions among guests, hosts and local residents within cities is an important dimension of the urban tourism product.

Given the dynamic nature of tourism, there is a constant need to refresh the products, services and experiences offered to visitors. Cities also need to spend more time and effort nowadays on providing greater authenticity and uniqueness, as is evidenced in the example which follows from Tokyo.

Sweet tweet 29

Tokyo wants to provide more authentic experiences

One of Tokyo's six strategies for tourism was a focus on increasing revenues and an initiative included was as follows:

"Develop the ryokan brand to promote the unique charms of Japanese-style inns to overseas visitors".

Source: Tokyo Metropolitan Government (2018).

The Tokyo government recognises that ryokans express the authentic culture and traditions of Japan. As such, they deliver unique and memorable experiences for foreign visitors to the city.

The term product tends to connote physical resources such as built attractions, hotels and infrastructure; however, there are also intangible ("soft product") aspects of city tourism. These include service and service quality, the sense of welcome and the experiences to be enjoyed within a city. Tourism as a "people" business is built on the interactions between hosts and guests, and among guests and others within a city. In its Tourism Strategy 2020, Vienna Tourism stated that

> Top-end services and commitment to internationality and diversity are of outstanding importance for the attractiveness of a city that wants to lure people from all over the world. Widespread language skills are undoubtedly part and parcel of this internationality and high service quality.
>
> *(Vienna Tourism, 2017)*

Despite its top ranking among tourism cities, Vienna accepted the need to improve English language skills in enhancing service encounters.

It is much better for a CDMO to articulate a specific product development strategy rather than a more haphazard or case-by-case approach. Such strategies, for example, can be based on various categories of tourism products. The following is a set of tourism product categories that can be used by CDMOs as a framework for their product development strategies.

- *Flagships*. These are the principal attractions and tourism icons of cities. World tourism cities all have these flagships and most people, whether tourists or not, can associate them with their host cities. Some of the best known of these are the Opera House in Sydney, Australia, the Taj Mahal in Agra, India, the Guggenheim Museum in Bilbao, Spain, the Burj Al Arab Hotel in Dubai, and the CN Tower in Toronto. Today, one might think of these as the most Instagrammable sites or places within cities, and they may also be the most visited.

- *Hubs*. Like the hubs in car wheels, urban tourism hubs are anchors of activity which draw visitors and from which they disperse or radiate. These can be transportation hubs such as the Hongqiao Hub in Shanghai or they can be places where people tend to congregate, such as city centres, parks, lakes, squares and plazas.
- *Clusters*. Groupings of like products are often found in urban areas, and these can be viewed as clusters. For example, the high streets of the UK and the main streets of the USA group together many shops and retail experiences. The districts within many cities for culture, art, history, heritage, restaurants and ethnicities and national origins are another example of product clustering. Indoor and outdoor markets in cities are venues that showcase the products of many vendors, again relying on the benefits of clustering.
- *Circuits*. These are routes and walking trails developed within cities that link places of interest. The Macao Heritage Trail is a great example here that links together the UNESCO World Heritage List sites in the city's historic centre. The Freedom Trail in Boston, Massachusetts, is another outstanding circuit case.
- *Events and festivals*. Cities are hosts to many festivals and events and are often closely associated with them. For example, think of Munich and most will recall that Oktoberfest takes place there. Perhaps not as well-known globally yet, the Mitsura Food Festival in Lima, Peru, is an event that highlights the tremendous gastronomic experiences that are available in this Latin American capital city. The colourful Holi Festival is most associated with Jaipur in Rajasthan, India. Edinburgh in Scotland is another place that has recently built its reputation as being the "Festival City".
- *Supporting products*. Attractions and events require supporting products, services and amenities. These include hotels and other forms of accommodation, restaurants and dining, entertainment and shopping facilities (Figure 4.2), located within cities. CDMOs traditionally did not involve themselves in accommodation development;

Figure 4.2 Souk (market) in Casablanca, Morocco.
(Courtesy: Shutterstock.com, ShutterDivision.)

rather, this was left to private-sector developers and hotel companies. However, the entrance of sharing economy providers such as Airbnb has led to novel issues that have to be resolved and have caused some CDMOs to get involved.

- *Supporting services and amenities*. Just above, mention was made of the need for "soft products" as tourism at its roots is a people business. Vienna, it was said, had accepted the need to improve English language capabilities. Supporting amenities include such items as signage programmes and wayfinding systems, as well as tourism information centres.
- *Accessibility*. Cities and their tourism attractions need to be accessible to all people. The same goes for their tourism websites and promotional materials. The European Commission operates the Access City Award scheme and Warsaw, Poland, was awarded the Access City Award for 2020.

Sweet tweet 30

Improving supporting amenities in Ciudad de México

Enhancing and renovating public areas in cities benefits both citizens and visitors.

> Mexico City has increased its touristic attractiveness in recent years because the capital has been able to successfully recuperate public spaces, pedestrian streets, parks, plazas and boardwalks, among others, which now serve a vibrant and attractive social life for tourists to enjoy.

Source: Oxford Business Group (2020).

Undoubtedly, the top world tourism cities have extensive portfolios of these eight product development categories; nevertheless, competitive pressures as well as citizen needs are constantly putting pressure on CDMOs to be innovative and to add to these portfolios. It must also be said that CDMOs are unlikely to be operating on their own when it comes to product development. Other city planning and infrastructure agencies, community groups and private developers are often partnering in development. The extent of the product development mandate assigned to a CDMO dictates its involvement. As Morrison (2019) suggested DMOs range from bystanders to partners in tourism product development.

CDMOs are sometimes also expected to operate physical facilities to serve visitors, including tourism information centres. The I amsterdam Visitor Centres are a great example of this with one being located in Schiphol Airport (Amsterdam and Partners, 2020). Tourism information centres (TICs) perform multiple roles for cities and tourism stakeholders, including:

- *Encouraging higher per capita spending*. TICs try to up-sell their cities, encouraging tourists to spend more money during their visits.
- *Handling requests for pre-visit information*. Often people contact TICs for information prior to leaving for the city. The TIC responds to information requests received by phone, e-mail, social media platforms, online messaging services and mail.
- *Interpreting local history, culture and nature*. TICs include displays or show videos that interpret the most important tourism-related resources of the city.

- *Making bookings*. Many TICs make bookings for accommodations, attractions, entertainment shows, local tours and transportation. Typically, but not always, the TIC earns a commission on these bookings.
- *Merchandising hub for tourism* stakeholders. TICs are a place where tourism stakeholders can publicise their products and services.
- *Providing information during visits*. This is the traditional role of TICs and tourists expect them to provide accurate, detailed and up-to-date information on all aspects of the city.
- *Recommending itineraries*. TIC staff recommend customised itineraries based on people's particular interests and time constraints.
- *Selling travel-related literature and local souvenirs*. Many TICs include retail operations where tourists can buy maps, guidebooks, DVDs, clothing and local souvenirs.

Pine and Gilmore (1999) introduced the concept of the "experience economy", and they used many examples from tourism to illustrate that people were not just interested in consuming products and services; they wanted to be entertained and be active participants in consumption. Twenty-one-plus years on from Pine and Gilmore's work, many CDMOs have realised that experiences motivate people to choose and recommend urban destinations. Therefore, a CDMO must be involved in experience development and not just in the encouragement of new physical tourism products. CDMOs should work with local tourism stakeholders and travel trade companies to design and implement new and improved visitor experiences within their cities. For example, with the growing interest in craft beer visits to where they are brewed can be arranged, tastings, and there can be short talks by the brew masters. Adding new experiences not only adds to visitor participation and satisfaction, but often increases per capita spending and lengths of stay within cities.

Quality assurance is another aspect of product development in which some CDMOs become involved, and this activity was accentuated during COVID-19. The Hong Kong Tourism Board operates the Quality Tourism Services (QTS) Scheme that assures visitors of the quality standards in the businesses that carry QTS approval (Hong Kong Tourism Board, 2020b). QTS covers restaurants and retail shops. The SG Clean campaign introduced in early 2020 in Singapore is a second example of assuring people of certain quality standards (SG Clean, 2020). Owners of premises, including those providing food services, can apply for the SG Clean quality mark which will be awarded after they have passed an assessment of their sanitation and hygiene.

The extent of product development in cities depends on the priority levels attached to tourism by senior levels of government as well as to the particular city's maturity level in tourism. For example, China and Saudi Arabia are two countries that are placing a very high priority on new tourism developments and as such city governments are more proactive. In Saudi Arabia, a number of "giga projects" for tourism have been identified, including the Diriyah Gate cultural and lifestyle project in Riyadh (Diriyah Gate Development Authority, 2020) (Figure 4.3).

Increased attention in world tourism cities is now being given to sustainable tourism development and its principles. Here, the "triple bottom line" is a guiding framework, consisting of social, environmental and economic dimensions. On the environmental side, these efforts are linked with initiatives to reduce greenhouse gas emissions and pollution. Barcelona is one of the leading tourism cities that has committed to sustainable development (Meet Barcelona, 2020). Cape Town, South Africa, is another city that has been a leader in the responsible tourism movement (City of Cape Town, n.d.). Vancouver

Figure 4.3 Diriyah, Riyadh, Saudi Arabia. (Courtesy: Diriyah Gate Development Authority.)

in British Columbia, Canada, is a third city with a strong emphasis on sustainable tourism (Tourism Vancouver, 2020). Although the COVID-19 pandemic has had a disastrous impact on tourism, it has created an interlude within which city tourism planners could contemplate "new normal scenarios" that would be more sustainable.

Communicating the increasing importance of sustainable tourism development and sharing the news about new city tourism products and services can be considered part of the CDMO's marketing and promotion role, which is the next role to be discussed.

Marketing and promotion

Most cities recognise the importance of tourism marketing and promotion. This could be termed a "legacy" role for city tourism as it has existed since the late 1800s. Chapter 6 is wholly devoted to marketing and branding; however, it suffices to say here that a well-planned and systematic approach is required, especially in portraying the unique features of a city's tourism.

It must also be made clear that city marketing is affected by and influences other destination management roles, and it is not a process to be implemented in isolation. Product development, for example, can impact marketing by providing new offers to be communicated with potential visitors. The several new football stadiums in and around Doha have given the Qatari city a new range of products to promote to sport tourism markets. Nearby Dubai is consistently adding to its array of exciting tourism offers. Marketing communications also have a role to play in community relationships and involvement, as you saw in the case of Louisville. Moreover, a high level of partnership and team building is required in marketing and promotion. The co-creation of marketing contents is an overlapping between the visitor management and marketing and promotion roles.

Before leaving the topic of marketing and branding, and as a segue into the next role of partnership and team building, it is important to signal that there are allied economic sectors to tourism. One of these is film development which is known to induce tourism to destinations (VisitScotland, 2020). Another connection is with educational institutions in the city which draw students on a full- or part-time basis. A report by the Australian Government Department of Education and Training (2016) determined that international students had significant impacts on city and regional tourism through their own spending as well as by their visiting friends and relatives. A third sector overlap is the connection between business events and industry within cities. This is sometimes referred to as the "beyond tourism" effect of business tourism and has led to a partnership between the International Congress and Convention Association (ICCA) and the BestCities Global Alliance. Together they created the *Incredible Impacts* grant programme, which rewards international associations whose events have "legacy" effects on cities long after they end (International Congress and Convention Association, 2020). Yet another connection is between tourism and agriculture, with city eateries increasingly sourcing locally grown produce to enhance dining authenticity and uniqueness. These four opportunity areas – with film production, education, industry and agriculture – then highlight the need for CDMOs to seek out partnerships, which is the next role for discussion.

Partnership and team building

There are numerous opportunities in city tourism for cooperation and collaboration at many levels, internally and externally. CDMOs should view partnering as an ongoing activity and be proactive in spotting new potential cooperative relationships. Partnering can span all the seven other destination management roles and is not just limited to marketing and promotion.

Synergy is a somewhat overused word; however, it is the outcome of successful city tourism destination partnerships. The BestCities Global Alliance provides an excellent case study on city partnership formation (BestCities Global Alliance, 2020). There are 11 partner cities – Berlin, Bogotà, Cape Town, Copenhagen, Dubai, Houston, Madrid, Melbourne, Singapore, Tokyo and Vancouver. All of these cities have an interest in the planning of international conferences. They share information amongst the partners and promote professionalism in this field of business event tourism.

As the diagram in Figure 4.4 shows, CDMOs have many types of potential partners and there are multiple benefits from partnering.

It is important to acknowledge here that some CDMOs operate membership pro-grammes and call their members "partners". Membership dues are normally charged; thus, the members represent a source of revenue for a CDMO as well. However, membership programmes seldom, if ever, represent a major source of funding for DMOs. Chicago has created a Partnership department within its CDMO, Choose Chicago.

Sweet tweet 31

Chicago promotes tourism partnerships

Choose Chicago stresses the partnership benefits of belonging to its member-ship programme.

> The Choose Chicago Partnership team helps partner businesses lever-age a variety of marketing platforms, programs, and opportunities that

---

connect them with millions of annual visitors, achieving heightened exposure for their organizations. Comprising meeting and event suppliers, restaurants, tours and attractions, retail, cultural institutions, and more, our 1,600 partners are the foundation of our success.

Source: Choose Chicago (2020).

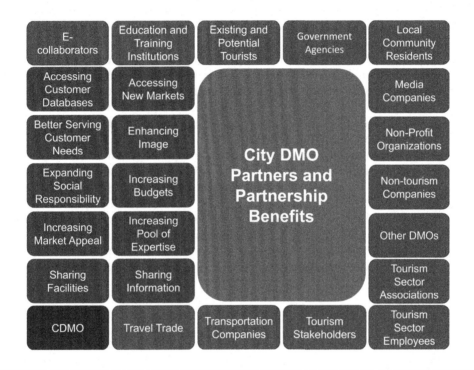

Figure 4.4 Partnership benefits and potential partners. (Adapted from Morrison, 2019.)

There are several ways for CDMOs to identify potential partners and these include: (1) similarity in resources; (2) similarity in markets; (3) geographic location; and (4) shared challenges, issues, problems and opportunities. The BestCities Alliance is an example of destinations that have a similar market in the form of international conferences; they also have similar venues and resources that accommodate such events. European Cities Marketing (ECM) is another great example of ongoing cooperation among cities. ECM is a non-profit organisation improving the competitiveness and performance of the leading cities of Europe and has approximately 120 members (European Cities Marketing, 2020). It is an example of cities that share a common geographic location.

There are many avenues for city tourism partnerships, and they include cooperative advertising and promotions, shared websites and social media platforms, CDMO partnership groups (e.g., ECM and the BestCities Global Alliance), themed routes and circuits and jointly sponsored research studies, just to name a few. Professional education and tourism advocacy are two other areas in which cities can cooperate to their mutual benefit. For example, many CDMO executives participate in the Certified Destination Management Executive (CDME) professional education programme being offered by Destinations International. Its four core courses are Strategic Issues in Destination Management, Destination Leadership, Destination Marketing and Sales and Destination Advocacy and Community Relations, and there are also several elective courses (Destinations International, 2020).

Tourism advocacy is another fertile area for CDMO cooperation. Essentially, this means that CDMOs are proponents or "champions" for tourism, while also being leaders in safeguarding the natural and heritage-cultural resources on which it is based, and the quality of life of local residents.

At the individual city level, the availability of cards that offer reduced prices of attraction admissions and public transport is another example of partnering. The Copenhagen card, for example, covers 87 attractions and museums and offers free public transport in the Copenhagen region (Wonderful Copenhagen, 2020). The Passlib' (Paris Official City Pass) is another good example, which can be purchased for one, two, three or five days (Paris Convention and Visitors Bureau, 2020).

Team building is another part of this role which supports the maintenance of partnerships as well as the achievement of the other seven CDMO roles. Teams can either be temporary (*ad hoc*) or permanent depending on the needs and requirements. Later in this chapter, the need to set up a crisis management team is highlighted. Others include advisory groups, and teams for festival and events, planning, research, sales, special promotions, tourism advocacy and tourism ambassador and welcoming teams.

Partnering and team building are often initiated in order to better serve city visitors and that also falls under the visitor management role that is covered next.

Visitor management

Historically, most of the attention in city tourism has been given to attracting visitors and it was assumed that operators would take care of their needs within destinations. This assumption no longer holds as there are mounting pressures to manage the impacts and experiences of visitors within cities. Assuring safety and security is another aspect of visitor management, and it is receiving much greater prominence during the COVID-19 pandemic. The following is a more comprehensive list of the various aspects of visitor management:

- *Visitor safety and security.* Visitor management systems and procedures need to assure the safety and security of visitors within urban destinations and at individual sites and attractions. Visitors should be protected from physical dangers as well as from scams, criminal and terrorist threats.
- *Visitor expectations, experiences, enjoyment and satisfaction.* CDMOs should be proactive in determining visitor expectations and their desired urban experiences. Visitor enjoyment should be enhanced without compromising the integrity of resources. Overcrowding and visitor incompatibility are two factors that often need to be addressed in city tourism. Visitor enjoyment can be negatively influenced by the behaviour of other tourists and in some cases by local vendors and other local residents.
- *Visitor interpretation, education and information.* The delivery of visitor interpretation, education and information is an important role of city visitor management,

although it has to be recognised that many visitors do not want or expect to be educated while on holiday or business trips. With the trend towards more responsible tourism and special-interest travel, however, the educational role of city tourism destinations requires greater attention. The earlier materials on London's tourism vision highlighted the increasing importance of information provision in world tourism cities.

- *Visitor behaviour.* While city destinations are not to be treated like school playgrounds, there are adequate reasons worldwide for concerns about some tourists' behaviours. The behaviour of individual visitors and of groups of visitors is a significant concern for certain urban destinations. Visitors may misbehave in ways that offend local residents and other visitors, or cause harm to natural and heritage resources. For example, they may engage in excessive drinking or in illegal activities such as drug use, sex tourism and shoplifting. Borderline ethical activities such as "forced shopping" may also cause problems for cities as has been witnessed in Hong Kong.
- *Visitor monitoring and management.* Monitoring and managing visitor flows is a visitor management activity that is being enhanced through the use of various ICTs.
- *Resource protection and conservation.* The traditional reason for visitor management was to protect environments, and it was a term that originated from protected area management. The experiences with tourism demonstrate that visitors can cause damage to natural and cultural-heritage resources and globalise traditional lifestyles.
- *Yield management.* This refers to the customer mix that cities desire to achieve based on maximising economic yield. For example, cities may prefer to attract high-yielding luxury travellers and discourage low-yielding markets such as backpackers.
- *Co-creation with visitors.* The notion of customer co-creation is relatively recent and is being enabled by social media platforms as well as by broader societal trends. There are at least two ways for co-creation to function. The first is for cities and visitors to create content that can be used for marketing and promotion, such as stories, photos and videos. The second is in co-creating experiences.

Sweet tweet 32

Prague wants to curb drunk tourism

The Czech capital has a reputation for "pub crawl" tourism and attracts many visitors because of this notoriety. However, the drunkenness and noise that result are annoying to city residents and may be tarnishing Prague's overall destination image.

> Now the authorities – alarmed at that possibility and the city's growing reputation as a location of cheap booze and easy fun – are pledging a harder line with miscreant visitors, some of whom stand accused of disrespecting Prague and its inhabitants.

Source: Tait (2019).

From the description of these eight aspects, it is clear that visitor management has demand and supply dimensions. From the visitor perspective, CDMOs strive to maximise the enjoyment and deepen the experiences of the people who choose to come to their cities. Sometimes cities and their CDMOs have to exercise powers on the supply side to enhance overall experiences, while at the same time limiting demand. Rome, for example, banned souvenir stalls from being set up close to its most visited tourism sites (Squires, 2020).

As mentioned earlier, ensuring visitor safety, security and comfort is a responsibility within visitor management. Some countries have introduced special police units to protect tourists and for example they can be found in Bangkok, Pattaya and Phuket, Thailand. Tourists are popular targets for a variety of scams, and police forces can be helpful in curtailing and investigating these unsavoury incidents within cities. Also, during the COVID-19 pandemic several cities took steps to assure visitors and residents of safety, as demonstrated earlier by the SG Clean campaign introduced by Singapore in February 2020.

Managing the levels and flows of tourists within cities is a supply-side concern. Resource protection and conservation are key issues here. Also, the overcrowding of certain spaces and the antagonising of locals are two situations to be avoided. Smart tourism solutions are aiding cities with real-time data on the disposition of visitors that can be used for dispersion strategies. Cities including Barcelona, New York and Tel Aviv are introducing digital signage programmes that promote wayfinding and encourage walking throughout the cities. Walk NYC is the wayfinding programme supported by digital technology that has been introduced in New York City (City of New York, 2020).

Then there is the idea of yield management, which implies attracting visitors to cities who spend the most on a per capita daily basis. Borrowed from the airlines and hotels, this idea stresses capacity utilisation and the economic returns from specific groups of customers.

A CDMO can demonstrate great performance for these above-mentioned seven destination management roles; however, unforeseen events occur that disrupt their plans, programmes and activities. This was starkly demonstrated in 2020 and 2021 when the urgent need for crisis management was felt. So, the complete set of city destination management roles can be described as "seven-plus-one" with the plus-one being crisis management.

Crisis management

The process of crisis management could be tucked into several of the above seven roles. It is certainly a demonstration of leadership and requires significant coordination. Also, it is very much related to visitor management and community and stakeholder relationships and involvement. It requires that partnerships and teams be built and there is a strong media and communication component. Moreover, crisis management requires planning and research. Finally, it may require that new services and amenities are developed, as well as physical facilities.

A crisis is an event or set of circumstances which may compromise or damage the marketability and reputation of a city tourism destination. The types of crisis events include natural disasters, security, economic and financial crises, health safety crises, environmental safety crises, accidents and calamities and public opinion crises (Duan et al., 2021). Chapter 10 takes up the topic of crises in cities and discusses the phenomenon in detail.

City tourism crisis management involves the development of strategies and plans that assist CDMOs and their partners to deal with unpredictable, significant negative events. Crisis management is not a short-term activity; rather, it is a continuous process in which CDMOs engage. The four Rs are often recommended as a basic structure for crisis management and they are reduction, readiness, response and recovery.

- *Reduction.* Identifying and taking steps to reduce the risks associated with crises and the damage they can potentially cause to city tourism.
- *Readiness.* Being better prepared for potential crises or disasters.
- *Response.* Being more ready to respond to crises when they occur. Taking action immediately when crises are encountered.
- *Recovery.* Taking immediate and appropriate actions to recover from crises.

Another "R" that can be added to these four is the concept of resilience in tourism. Essentially, this means the ability of city tourism to cope with and recover from crisis events or disasters. The COVID-19 pandemic severely tested tourism destination and business resilience worldwide. Several DMOs prepared specific recovery and resilience plans. One of the cities to do so was Edinburgh, Scotland, where the Edinburgh Tourism Action Group (ETAG) produced the Edinburgh Tourism Resilience, Reboot and Recovery Plan (ETAG, 2020). Another example from Auckland, New Zealand, is mentioned below.

Despite their potential catastrophic effects on city tourism, crises and disasters are often ignored in tourism strategies and plans. However, tourism development planning should be conducted with prevention in mind so that future crises and disasters can be avoided, e.g., master planning for beachfront areas that are prone to typhoons and tsunamis, mountain areas that can be affected by earthquakes and volcanoes, health care precautions and so on.

Most expert sources recommend that CDMOs develop crisis management plans for tourism and also set up a specific group or committee to deal with crisis management. As an example of the latter, Macao has created a special office to handle emergency situations from crises that affect tourism.

Sweet tweet 33

Macao has a tourism crisis management committee

Proactively establishing a tourism crisis management committee is a very good practice and helps cities to reduce risk and be more ready for crisis events.

> The Tourism Crisis Management Office (GGCT) is a Strategic Coordination Committee with the mission to guarantee immediate and effective operational measures to be taken when Macao SAR residents are involved in emergency situations resulting from serious accidents, catastrophes or calamities abroad, as well as tourists that are involved in similar situations when in the Macao SAR.

Source: Tourism Crisis Management Office (2014).

Another best practice in CDMO crisis management is in the recognition of actual or potential risks to tourism performance. WellingtonNZ, the CDMO for the capital city of New Zealand, noted in its plans for 2020–2023 the risks posed by COVID-19 and how these might adversely impact on the achievement of its KPIs (WellingtonNZ, 2020). Furthermore, some CDMOs prepare crisis recovery plans or strategies, as is evidenced by another New Zealand city's initiative in June 2020. Destination AKL, the CDMO for Auckland, prepared a recovery plan for the city's tourism to compensate for the negative tourism impacts of COVID-19 (Destination AKL, 2020).

The development of a crisis communications plan is another must-do task for a CDMO in responding to a crisis. These must provide accurate, clear and timely information on the crisis (Destinations International Foundation, 2020). New Orleans is a city whose tourism sector was devastated as a result of a natural disaster and its CDMO, New Orleans & Company, has developed a Crisis Communication Plan for New Orleans Tourism (New Orleans & Company, 2018). The document presents "a comprehensive and effective citywide emergency communications plan for the Greater New Orleans tourism industry".

Summary comments

The movement towards destination management is accelerating as more cities are realising the need to go beyond just the selling and promotion of tourism. This chapter has reviewed the "seven-plus-one" roles of city destination management (Figure 4.5) and featured many snippets about cities that are adopting them. There is no doubt that a professional field of city destination management is arising with multifaceted roles and responsibilities being attached to CDMOs. With the happenings of 2020 and 2021, the crisis management and resilience building roles of CDMOs also came into clearer focus.

It would be too simplistic to leave readers with the impression that every CDMO performs the seven-plus-one destination management roles or to imply that every city

Figure 4.5 The "seven-plus-one" roles of city destination management. (Authors with background template from PresentationPro .com.)

government vests these responsibilities solely with a tourism unit. Rather, what you have read is a best practice scenario for city destination management that is used by the most professional and sophisticated DMOs across the world. It also must be said that there are rivalries and "silo effects" (Tett, 2015) within city governments that preclude the effective implementation of these best practices.

Another warning label that the authors need to add is that, at least in some circles, destination management remains a fledgling concept. Whilst leading organisations such as UNWTO and Destinations International have fully embraced destination management, many academic institutions have yet to fully recognise this professional field.

Above all, this chapter has highlighted the need for a systematic and professional approach to city tourism destination management. This approach requires a set of management skills, including leadership, human resource management, planning, research, marketing and communications, project management and finance and economics. The numerous outstanding examples quoted are evidence that many cities already have embraced the destination management concept.

The following two chapters cover planning, marketing and branding of city tourism destinations.

Thought questions

1) What are the potential benefits to cities of adopting the destination management approach advocated in this chapter?
2) What are the likely reasons that some cities do not have tourism plans or strategies? What are the dangers of not having these?
3) Will the COVID-19 pandemic make more cities adopt crisis management best practices? Why or why not?
4) If local citizens are not really interested in tourism, what is the point of communicating and involving them?
5) The authors suggest that universities and colleges have been slow to integrate destination management into their curricula. What are the reasons for this lack of attention to the profession of destination management?
6) How can cities balance and harmonise the interests and behaviours of different groupings of visitors?
7) It is suggested that CDMOs must do primary research and they should not just rely on secondary data and information. Do you agree or disagree with this and why or why not?
8) The "silo effect" is mentioned as a potential barrier to fully implementing the destination management concept in urban areas. What steps can city governments take to ensure coordination and cooperation among various city departments?

References

Amsterdam & Partners. (2020). Visitor information centres. https://www.iamsterdam.com/en/plan-your-trip/visitor-information-centres

Australian Department of Education and Training. (2016). *The Value of International Education to Australia*. Canberra: Australian Government.

BestCities Global Alliance. (2020). About us. http://www.bestcities.net/

Choose Chicago. (2020). Partnership team. https://www.choosechicago.com/about-us/staff/partnership-department/

City of Cape Town (n.d.). Responsible tourism in Cape Town. http://resource.capetown.gov.za/documentcentre/Documents/Graphics%20and%20educational%20material/Responsible_tourism_bro_web.pdf

City of New York. (2020). Walk NYC. https://www1.nyc.gov/html/dot/html/pedestrians/walknyc.shtml

City of Sydney. (2013). *Tourism Action Plan*. Sydney, Australia: City of Sydney.

Conservation News. (2020). Bali mangrove bay is now a conservation zone, nixing reclamation plan. https://news.mongabay.com/2019/10/bali-benoa-bay-mangroves-conservation-reclamation/

Destination AKL. (2020). *Destination AKL Recovery Plan. Auckland Visitor Economy's Response to COVID-19*. Auckland, NZ: Auckland Tourism, Events and Economic Development.

Destinations International. (2020). Certified Destination Management Executive (CDME) credential. https://destinationsinternational.org/cdme

Destinations International Foundation. (2020). *Crisis Response Handbook*. Washington, DC: Destinations International.

Diriyah Gate Development Authority. (2020). Welcome to Diriyah. https://dgda.gov.sa/Home.aspx?lang=en-us

Dodds, R. & Butler, R. (2019). The phenomena of overtourism: A review. *International Journal of Tourism Cities*, 5(4), pp. 519–528.

Duan, J., Xie, C., & Morrison, A. M. (2021). Tourism crises and impacts on destinations: A systematic review of the tourism and hospitality literature. *Journal of Hospitality & Tourism Research*, in press.

Edinburgh Tourism Action Group (ETAG). (2020). Edinburgh tourism resilience, reboot & recovery plan. Edinburgh Tourism Action Group. https://www.etag.org.uk/2020/06/edinburgh-tourism-resilience-reboot-recovery-plan/

European Cities Marketing. (2020). European Cities Marketing. https://www.europeancitiesmarketing.com/

Future Places. (2020). "Mi barrio" district tourism promotion strategies in Buenos Aires. http://futureplaces.com/portfolio/mi-barrio-district-tourism-promotion-strategies-in-buenos-aires/

Hong Kong Tourism Board. (2020a). Corporate information. https://www.discoverhongkong.com/eng/hktb/about/corporateinfo.html

Hong Kong Tourism Board. (2020b). Quality Tourism Services (QTS) Scheme. https://www.discoverhongkong.com/uk/plan/qts.html

International Congress and Convention Association. (2020). ICCA and BestCities extend partnership for Incredible Impacts 'beyond tourism' programme. https://www.iccaworld.org/newsarchives/archivedetails.cfm?id=3054775

Las Vegas Convention and Visitors Authority. (2020). Trends and research. https://www.lvcva.com/research/

London & Partners. (2018). *A Tourism Vision for London*. London, UK: London & Partners.

Louisville Tourism. (2019). *Building on Momentum. Louisville Tourism 2019–2020 Destination Sales & Marketing Plan*. Louisville, Kentucky: Louisville Tourism.

Mastercard. (2019). Global Destination Cities Index 2019. https://newsroom.mastercard.com/wp-content/uploads/2019/09/GDCI-Global-Report-FINAL-1.pdf

Meet Barcelona. (2020). Responsible and sustainable tourism. https://meet.barcelona.cat/en/discover-barcelona/barcelona-today/responsible-and-sustainable-tourism

Morrison, A. M. (2019). *Marketing and Managing Tourism Destinations*, 2nd ed. London: Routledge.

New Orleans & Company. (2018). *Crisis Communication Plan for New Orleans Tourism*. New Orleans, Louisiana: New Orleans & Company.

Northouse, P. (2018). *Leadership: Theory and Practice*, 8th ed. Thousand Oaks, CA: Sage.

NYC & Company. (2020). About NYC & Company. https://business.nycgo.com/about-us/who-we-are/

Oxford Business Group. (2020). Mexico plans for long-term tourism growth. https://oxfordbusinessgroup.com/overview/looking-ahead-authorities-are-laying-foundation-long-term-growth

Paris Convention and Visitors Bureau. (2020). Passlib'. https://booking.parisinfo.com/il4-offer_i147-paris-passlib-paris-pass.aspx

Pine, B. J. II, & Gilmore, J. H. (1999). *The Experience Economy. Work is Theatre & Every Business a Stage*. Boston: Harvard Business School Press.

SG Clean. (2020). About SG Clean. https://www.sgclean.gov.sg/about/

Singapore Tourism Board. (2020). About STB: Overview. https://www.stb.gov.sg/content/stb/en/about-stb/overview.html

Squires, N. (2020). Rome bans souvenir stalls to ease overcrowding and 'protect' the city's image. *The Telegraph*, January 8. https://www.telegraph.co.uk/travel/destinations/europe/italy/articles/rome-bans-souvenir-stalls/

Tait, R. (2019). The fall of Prague: 'Drunk tourists are acting like they.ve conquered our city', Special report. *Observer*, August 25, https://www.theguardian.com/world/2019/aug/25/prague-drunk-tourists-conquer-our-city

Tett, G. (2015). *The Silo Effect: Why Putting Everything in Its Place Isn't such a Bright Idea*. London: Virago Press Ltd.

Tokyo Metropolitan Government. (2018). *PRIME Tourist Destination City Tokyo: Tokyo Tourism Strategy Action Plan 2018*. Tokyo: Tokyo Metropolitan Government.

Tourism Crisis Management Office (Macao). (2014). Tourism Crisis Management Office. https://www.ggct.gov.mo/en/

Tourism Vancouver. (2020). Sustainable tourism. https://www.tourismvancouver.com/about/destination-development/sustainable-tourism/#

Travel Portland. (2020). Downtown hotels organize SOLVE clean-up, https://www.travelportland.com/about-us/solve-clean-up/

Vienna Tourism. (2017). Tourism strategy 2020. http://www.tourismstrategy2020.vienna.info/downloads/wt-tourismusstrategie-2020_en.pdf

VisitScotland (2020). The Outlander effect & tourism. https://www.visitscotland.org/research-insights/about-our-visitors/interests-activities/film-tv

Visit York. (2020). Visit York residents festival 2020. https://www.visityork.org/whats-on/residents-festival

WellingtonNZ. (2020). *Statement of Intent 2020–2023*. Wellington, NZ: Wellington Regional Economic Development Agency.

Wonderful Copenhagen. (2020). Copenhagen card. www.copenhagencard.com

Chapter 5

Planning and development of world tourism cities

Abstract

Planning is a vital endeavour that contributes to managing destinations, playing an essential role in the development of tourism in world cities. This chapter describes the tourism planning process, focusing on the particularities of planning for tourism in world cities. The authors emphasise having the right process to prepare the plan and to ensure that it is participative. The participants in tourism planning are identified. A seven-step tourism planning process is described in detail. Actual tourism planning practices from several countries are highlighted to demonstrate how planning is carried out on the ground.

The factors to be considered in city tourism development are reviewed in detail through using the 10 As model. Several trends and "movements" in that development are discussed, including creative and eventful cities, smart tourism, liveable cities, experience design, authenticity, sustainable and green tourism development and the promotion of tourism in city neighbourhoods. The negative effects of tourism development in urban areas are also highlighted.

Keywords: 10 As model; participants; process; strategic planning; tourism development; tourism plan.

Learning objectives

Having read this chapter, you should be able to:

- Describe a systematic process for preparing a tourism plan.

DOI: 10.4324/9781003111412-7

- Elaborate on the participants that should be involved in city tourism planning.
- Outline a table of contents for a tourism plan.
- Review the factors to be considered when developing tourism in cities.
- Pinpoint the types and themes of tourism development in cities.
- Identify and explain the negative impacts of tourism development on urban areas.

Following on from Chapter 4 on city destination management, Chapter 5 merges two of the roles of planning and research with product development. The two main topics are tourism planning and tourism development.

Tourism planning

It is pointless to have goals without a plan to achieve them. Planning and research are identified as one of the roles of city destination management in the previous chapter. Every city destination needs to have chosen a long-term direction for tourism, a shared path for all stakeholders to follow for the next five to ten years. Creating this multi-year track to the future and the process used in city tourism planning are hugely important and particularly the people and organisations that are involved and how planning is conducted.

Tourism vision, plan or strategy?

It is confusing to look at all the tourism planning documents that have been prepared in recent years as they tend to have different labels. Some are called tourism visions, while others are plans or strategies, and some have quite unique titles. In Chapter 4, the document *A Tourism Vision for London* was a topic (London & Partners, 2018); while in Chapter 6 there is mention of the *Portland Tourism Master Plan* (Travel Portland, 2018); and Vienna produced a "Tourism strategy 2020" (Vienna Tourism, 2017). What are the actual differences among these plans and are the differences of practical significance? The answer is that they are all forms of tourism planning; however, they vary in their levels of detail. Generally, those called plans or master plans are in the most depth, while visions and strategies tend to be broader statements of future intent. The distinctions are further clarified in this chapter through inspection of several plans from throughout the world. What is most important to cities in accomplishing this task is the tourism planning process to be used.

Tourism planning process

Catalysts for tourism planning

What tells a city that it is time for a new tourism plan? This is a really good question; alas it is not much explored. However, it can be said with some confidence that tourism plans are often inspired by change and crises. The COVID-19 pandemic stirred many cities into developing new plans, some of which were called recovery plans as was the case in Auckland (Auckland Tourism, Events and Economic Development, 2020).

Sweet tweet 34

Auckland plots a tourism recovery

The development of this recovery plan was initiated by Auckland Tourism, Events & Economic Development (ATEED) – Auckland's economic development agency – on behalf of Auckland's destination industry. The plan has been overseen and endorsed by the Destination AKL 2025 Industry Leaders Group (ILG), which continues to meet regularly. ATEED sees its role as a facilitator and partner with industry and government to drive the re-activation of our visitor economy.

Source: ATEED (2020).

Plans also find their origins in opportunities, and not just because of issues and problems. For example, the *Macao Tourism Industry Development Master Plan* was instigated to build upon the destination's prior successes in tourism (Macao Government Office of Tourism, 2017). A third reason can be that new government policies require further specification and articulation through tourism planning.

Participants in tourism planning

A CDMO can demonstrate its leadership and coordination role by initiating and supervising tourism planning. After the decision is made to prepare a new tourism plan for the city, the next decision is on the planning process to be followed. There is not one single template available for such a process and in actual practice there are numerous approaches that have been used by cities based upon the many plans that the authors analysed in preparing this chapter. The diagram in Figure 5.1 shows a suggested six Ps process as well as the tourism planning participants. The beginning and end points of the process are tourism policy and the tourism plan itself, respectively. The three main parties involved are the principals, participants and planners. The principals are the organisations and people that coordinate the long-term planning process for tourism in the city. The individuals invited to participate in the long-term planning process for tourism are the participants. It is essential that all tourism stakeholders participate in the tourism planning process, including representatives of local community residents. Planners are the specialist experts in tourism planning who are hired to prepare the tourism plan. These planning companies typically facilitate the planning process and prepare the plan documents.

Planning processes usually extend across several months and may even go beyond one year to complete.

Tourism planning process

In general, the process of planning ahead in organisations for the long term is known as strategic planning (Bryson, 1988). It is considered to be an element of strategic management (Rothaermel, 2020). Normally, this requires organisations to define their missions, goals and values, and a strengths, weaknesses, opportunities, threats (SWOT) analysis triggers the steps to follow.

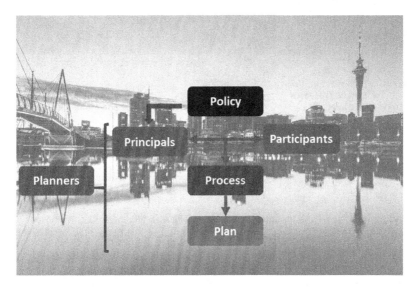

Figure 5.1 Six Ps in tourism planning process. (Author adaptation from Morrison, 2019.) Background photo of Auckland, New Zealand. (Courtesy: Unsplash.com, Dan Freeman.)

Tourism planning is a specialised form of strategic (long-term) planning that is based on a destination rather than a specific organisation. It is somewhat more complex since multiple participants and organisations (stakeholders) must be involved in the planning process. Experts have suggested different strategic planning processes and procedures for preparing tourism plans and the one suggested by Morrison et al. (2018) is a good example (Figure 5.2). This was originally developed based on tourism planning in Ontario and other parts of Canada by one of the authors. It consists of the seven steps described below.

1. *Background analysis*

This comprises an analysis of the existing city products and services, target markets, and previous and existing tourism policies, plans and strategies and programmes. The main outcome is an assessment of the strengths, weaknesses, problems and issues of city tourism. This is a process similar to the situation analysis that is described in Chapter 6. For this background analysis step reviewing secondary (previously published) data and information can be sufficient; however, primary research may also be conducted (as in the case of Copenhagen that follows).

- *Products and services*. A realistic and objective evaluation of city tourism products and services is a key component of the background analysis. This is because the plan may envisage improvements or additions to the existing inventory of products and services. In other words, development opportunities will be identified.
- *Markets*. This consists of an assessment of current and past target markets and their visitor profiles. It is particularly important here to detect the visitor volume shares, growth patterns, demand seasonality, economic yield and the portfolio compatibility of each target market.

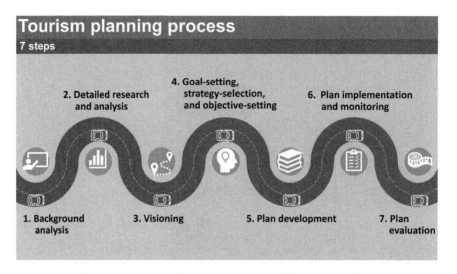

Figure 5.2 Seven-step tourism planning process.

- *Community residents and other stakeholders*. Local residents must be given careful attention in all tourism planning exercises, as too should be other stakeholders directly and indirectly involved in or affected by tourism.
- *Positioning and image*. There are two aspects here, which are described in more detail in Chapter 6 on marketing. Positioning is how the city has been attempting to communicate its image to visitors, as well as the adjustments that were made in products and services to match the desired image. The second aspect represents the actual images that visitors have of the city and its tourism.
- *Past tourism policies and planning*. The city's previous tourism policies and plans are critiqued to determine what was achieved and where they fell short in attaining their expressed goals and objectives. It is critical to learn from the strengths and weaknesses of the previous tourism planning processes to inform future planning.
- *Competitors*. The city's primary competitors are identified along with their perceived tourism strengths and weaknesses. The tourism plan will, among other initiatives, strive to better utilise the competitive advantages of the city against these other destinations.

Sometimes when taken together the analysis of these factors is called a destination audit or a destination assessment. A wonderful example of this is from Copenhagen and its 10xCopenhagen project.

SHORT BREAK 5

A destination assessment of Copenhagen

10xCopenhagen was a project conducted by Wonderful Copenhagen, the CDMO for the capital city of Denmark, to find out what visitors and residents thought of

Figure 5.3 Copenhagen is a bikeable city according to residents and visitors. (Courtesy: Unsplash.com, febiyan.)

Copenhagen. This corresponds with two of the factors in the background analysis step (market and community residents). The research also asked previous visitors about competitive cities and so competitors were addressed as well. Also, previous visitors provided their opinions on aspects of Copenhagen's tourism products and services, including accommodation, food, culture, transport and accessibility and meeting venue quality (business visitors).

The surveys that were conducted asked previous visitors and residents some of the same questions making comparisons possible. One of these was – "In your opinion what are the most characteristic aspects of Copenhagen?" The most cited aspect by residents and visitors was that Copenhagen was "bikeable" (easy to get around by bicycle) (Figure 5.3).

Some 865 previous visitors provided responses on Copenhagen's city competitors and these competitors were divided into three "leagues". The strongest competitor (League 1) was Stockholm in Sweden. There were three cities in League 2 (Oslo, Berlin and Amsterdam). Eleven cities were placed in League 3 (Helsinki, Rome, London, Prague, Paris, Dublin, Malmö, Vienna, Brussels, Lisbon and Reykjavík).

The resident survey determined that 67% of locals had not experienced any problems with city tourism and overall were positive about welcoming visitors to Copenhagen in the future.

Discussion points:

1. What are the strengths of Wonderful Copenhagen's destination assessment?
2. Do you think there would have been added value with also asking tourism stakeholders similar questions? Why or why not?
3. Is it realistic to position a city like Copenhagen against 15 competitive cities or should a smaller set be used? Why or why not?

Source: Wonderful Copenhagen (2020).

The Copenhagen case study shows how rich data can be gathered about city tourism from visitors and residents. In fact, the background analysis is the first step in building up the rationale for the eventual tourism plan, and this can be thought of as the justification for the plan's proposed initiatives for city tourism. For example, the *Tourism Master Plan 2015–2025* for Kuala Lumpur, Malaysia, considered five factors: The performance of KL tourism, overall tourist perceptions of KL, KL's offerings, supporting infrastructure and enablers for tourism and potential opportunities for KL tourism (Kuala Lumpur City Hall, 2015). These five factors were analysed using secondary research only.

2. *Detailed research and analysis*

The second step is a more in-depth analysis of markets, activities and experiences, resources and competitors, and this should preferably involve the gathering of primary research data. The background analysis in the first step highlights where additional research is needed and from whom this should be collected. This may involve qualitative research (e.g., focus groups with potential visitors or case studies of exemplary tourism elsewhere) or quantitative (e.g., surveys with potential visitors, residents or other stakeholders). As an example of the latter, one of the authors directed a series of surveys in China and abroad to guide the preparation of a plan for the city of Shaoxing in Zhejiang Province. It was discovered that Shaoxing yellow rice wine and writer, Lu Xun, were the best known of the city's assets. Another good example is the *Richmond Region 2030* tourism planning process that was facilitated by Resonance, a tourism planning company. They conducted interviews with 115 stakeholders and completed surveys with 1,000 visitors and 2,100 residents, as well as facilitating visioning workshops (Richmond Region Tourism, 2019; RVAHub, 2019).

Before moving on to the third step, there are other considerations that may have to be taken into account before developing the tourism vision for the city. The first of these are strategic issues or challenges faced by the community that must be addressed. These can be in the broader external environment or within a specific city. To exemplify this with a real case, Barcelona found five strategic challenges in governance, tourism management, territorial strategy, work and business and promotion and marketing (Barcelona City Council Tourism Department, 2017). Liverpool (UK) identified funding, governance, brand, investment, events and business tourism as challenges to its visitor economy (Liverpool City Region Local Enterprise Partnership, 2014).

In fact, many tourism plans devote attention to tourism trends, issues and challenges, and the authors believe readers need to have these terms defined now:

- *Trend*. A new development or a change in tourism, for which the trend line can be increasing or decreasing. The change may be considered positive, negative or neutral. Trends can be measurable (quantitative) or non-measurable (qualitative) and can be short, medium or long term. The intensity of the trend may vary from city to city.
- *Issue*. An important topic or problem that people are discussing or talking or writing about. The topic or problem is unresolved, and people have differing opinions on it. Issues often have proponents (advocates) and opponents (critics) and can be short-, medium- or long-term.
- *Challenge*. A new or difficult task or situation facing city tourism that tests the sector's and stakeholders' capabilities, skills and resources. Challenges often result from trends and issues (Morrison, 2021b).

The second consideration is the guiding principles and core values to be respected in the remainder of the planning process. For example, Visit Indy (Indianapolis, Indiana) articulated the five guiding principles of "community aligned, regionally embraced, diverse, big and bold, and sustainable" for its tourism master plan (Visit Indy, 2020). Macao identified three guiding principles for its tourism planning in *business environment for the tourism and leisure industries, quality tourism* and *cultural tourism* (Macao Government Office of Tourism, 2017).

Core values are what the people of a city perceive as the key identifying factors of their city that should be reflected in the tourism vision. This notion is similar to organisational culture and reflects shared beliefs among citizens. In Chapter 6, "community spirit" is the core value identified by the people of Calgary, Alberta.

3. *Visioning*

The data and information from the first two steps, and their subsequent analysis and synthesis, lay the foundation for a process of visioning. What specifically do the authors mean by a city tourism vision? – the answer follows:

A tourism vision is a clear and succinct description of what the city will be and look like after it successfully implements the tourism plan and achieves its full potential. It is an expression by the stakeholders and community about what they want their city to be – a preferred future, a "word picture" of city tourism they want to create.

For example, the *Tourism Strategy 2020* for Vienna envisioned three "qualities" to be enhanced during a five-year span – *Global Vienna, Smart Vienna* and *Premium Vienna*. Essentially the vision was to make Vienna even more international (*global*); increase the city's smartness (*smart*); and to make visitor experiences higher quality and luxurious (*premium*). Another great example is from the previously mentioned tourism master planning process from Richmond, Virginia.

Sweet tweet 35

Richmond envisions a liveable, lovable future

Objective

Create a ten-year Tourism Master Plan which builds a clear vision for our aspirational future for tourism and its impact on the region as a whole.

> **Vision**
>
> A more livable, lovable and prosperous Richmond Region through responsibly grown tourism for the benefit of all in our community.
>
> Source: Richmond Region Tourism (2019).

VisitCOS (2018) said, "Colorado Springs & the Pikes Peak Region will be the leading U.S. destination for experiential travel, inspired by the majesty of Pikes Peak; iconic, accessible natural wonders; and the Olympic spirit".

The visioning process can be followed up with the development of position (or "white") papers on product development, marketing and promotion, community and stakeholder relationships and involvement, planning and research, partnerships and visitor management. Also, as highlighted in Chapter 4, attention must be given to crisis management planning for tourism.

4. Goal-setting, strategy-selection and objective-setting

The fourth step involves setting long-term tourism goals, strategies to achieve these goals and specific objectives for each strategy. An obvious question that arises here is as to how many years a plan should cover. In practice, it appears that five or ten years are the most popular choices. Some planning periods are longer; for example, the San Diego destination master plan covered 20 years to 2040 (San Diego Tourism Marketing District, 2017).

Here are the definitions of goal, strategy and objective:

- *Goal*. A result to be achieved in tourism within three to five years that can be measured.
- **Strategy**. An approach selected to achieve a tourism goal.
- *Objective*. A result to be achieved in tourism within one to two years that can be measured.

Often these three terms are interchanged for each other; nevertheless, it is worth looking at some real examples. First, Tucson, Arizona, set goals for visitor experience, quality of life, investment, growth, seasonality, employment, education, environment and distribution (VisitTucson.org, 2019). These do not fit with the authors' goal definition of measurability; however, they are valuable strategic focus areas or outcomes for the tourism master plan.

5. Plan development

This step includes the design and writing of a planning document that details how each goal, strategy and objective will be achieved, as well as the programmes, activities, role responsibilities and funding needs. Often two or more versions of the tourism plan will be assembled, with one being a shorter, summary report and the other being a more detailed technical report. How long does a tourism plan have to be in terms of the number of pages? Typically, the summary report is around 50–60 pages or slightly more, and the technical reports are over 100 pages in length. There can also be shorter "executive" summary reports or action plans of less than 24 pages.

There are now some further nomenclature issues to clear up for readers. Quite often the plans are called master plans and it is useful to clarify what that terminology infers. Here it is important to recognise that city governments through their urban planning units often sponsor comprehensive master plans. These types of plans specify the land uses for various parts of cities. AECOM provide this definition, "a master plan is an overarching planning document and spatial layout which is used to structure land use and development" (AECOM, undated). Basically, this is a plan for future land use in an urban area. A tourism master plan is not the same.

One major tourism planning company explains that "A tourism master plan is the roadmap for destination success. It is a crucial first step that will address three important questions: 'Where are we?' 'Where do we want to go?' 'How do we get there?'" (Solimar International, 2020). Another tourism planning firm says,

> a tourism master plan will identify, innovate and articulate potential products, amenities, programming and experiences—along with corresponding policies and protocols—that will guide the long-term, sustainable planning and design of a city, state or country as a tourism destination.
>
> *(Resonance, 2020)*

Another term for tourism planning that is particularly evident in the UK and Australia is the destination management plan. Also, in the UK, the term visitor economy is used instead of tourism. For example, Marketing Manchester developed a strategy for the visitor economy (2013) and then a destination management plan (2017).

Before leaving this discussion of tourism plans and their contents, readers should know that the planning processes and plan documents vary according to the country in question, with China being a particular example. Wu et al. (2021) stated that the present tourism planning system in China was borrowed from urban planning. Unlike recent Western tourism plans, the Chinese plans are more physical in nature and depict proposed tourism land use patterns. The plans in Western countries tend to be more about destination management and marketing.

6. *Plan implementation and monitoring*

This is putting the plan into action and monitoring progress against the attainment of goals and objectives. Communicating about the tourism plan within the city should not be an afterthought and needs to be well planned in advance. Since stakeholders are varied and have dissimilar interests, using multiple forms of communication is likely to be most effective. Disseminating copies of the plan document needs to be a first priority.

Several cities developed videos to introduce their tourism planning processes or to explain the plans once developed. For the former, Vancouver and Halifax in Canada produced such videos (PLANifax, 2020; Resonance, 2013). Halifax in Nova Scotia, Canada, initiated a tourism master planning exercise in 2019 that was carried into 2020. The completion of the master plan was postponed due to the COVID-19 pandemic (Discover Halifax, 2020). For the latter, Kuala Lumpur and Colorado Springs, Colorado, prepared videos profiling their tourism master plans (VisitCOS, 2018; VisitKLOfficial, 2015).

7. *Plan evaluation*

The final step of the planning process is an assessment of the extent to which the plan's city tourism vision, goals, strategies and objectives were achieved. This can be both formative (progress checks) and summative (final) evaluations. For example, Vienna Tourism (2019) prepared a Status Report on its Tourism 2020 Strategy.

Tourism development

Planning is often followed by development (see Sweet tweet below), although development is continuous in most city destinations. Chapter 4 addresses the product development role within destination management, while Chapter 6 approaches product from the marketing and branding perspective. Here in Chapter 5, a broader view on tourism development in cities is taken. Again, it must be remembered that development has tangible (hard development) and intangible (soft development) dimensions with respect to tourism. Consider for a moment the vision for tourism in Paris for 2022. It is,

> In 2022, Paris is the city that hosts the most visitors in the world, but also the city that ensures the best welcome in the world, through its high-quality, sustainable tourism that creates jobs, and is a source of international influence.
>
> *(Mayor of Paris, 2019)*

Noteworthy in this vision statement is the mention of "the best welcome" in Paris, which has built a reputation for a lack of friendliness and courtesy towards visitors. Another "soft development" initiative is in Zagreb, Croatia, providing ten language versions of its visitor website.

Sweet tweet 36

What the master planners say about development

A tourism master plan will identify, innovate and articulate potential products, amenities, programming and experiences – along with corresponding policies and protocols – that will guide the long-term, sustainable planning and design of a city, state or country as a tourism destination.

Source: Resonance (2020).

In fact, some tourism plans offer very specific recommendations on proposed tourism developments for their cities. For example, the City of Gold Coast (2014) in Queensland, Australia, identified several "catalyst projects" including a proposed Gold Coast Cultural Precinct and an integrated resort development for the Broadwater area.

Tourism development in world tourism cities has economic, socio-cultural and environmental impacts (the "triple-bottom-line" effects). Chapter 8 is devoted to the topic of sustainability in world tourism cities. Briefly, here it can be confidently stated that sustainability and sustainable tourism development are becoming much more serious concerns for urban areas. From the destination management perspective, the goal is to maximise the economic impacts without causing harm to the environment, culture and society. As with tourism planning, there are multiple stakeholders who have an interest in tourism development in their cities, some who are supportive and others who oppose development. City governments themselves are often in the pro-development camp as they want to attract investment, boost GDP, create jobs and generate new sources of tax revenues. This, however, must be tempered by several considerations, including higher-level government policy, resident quality of life, infrastructure and transportation system capacities, zoning regulations, master plans and policies and other constraints and limitations. Tourism development in cities is affected by national government policies and priorities with respect to tourism. Where countries put a high priority on economic development and diversification, tourism development tends to be encouraged as in the cases of China and Saudi Arabia.

Sweet tweet 37

Tourism development master plan for Qiddiya, Saudi Arabia

The Kingdom of Saudi Arabia (KSA) through its Vision 2030 has set out an ambitious plan for tourism development. One of these is the "giga project" for Qiddiya which is adjoining the city of Riyadh.

> "Qiddiya is set to become the Kingdom's capital of entertainment, sports and the arts to meet and satisfy the recreational, social and cultural needs of current and future generations".

Another of the "giga projects" is the Red Sea development project.

Sources: Qiddiya Development Corporation (2020); the Red Sea Development Company (2020).

China has experienced rapid tourism development as it is considered as a pillar industry by the national government. Two of the largest projects have been the construction of Shanghai Disneyland and the Chimelong Ocean Kingdom in Zhuhai, Guangdong, close to Macao. Indonesia is another nation that has ambitious plans for future development, having announced plans for the "10 new Balis" project (Indonesia Investment Coordinating Board, 2017).

The concept of product positioning is very relevant to city tourism development, and it is insufficient to consider only market positioning (which is discussed in Chapter 6). Here, it is critical for cities to think about their destination images, city branding and the future tourism vision and to determine which types of tourism development projects fit best. In this respect, there is a wide assortment of potential tourism developments and themes, including the following (in alphabetic order):

- *Accommodation.* All major cities have an assortment of accommodation ranging from hotels to hostels. Fewer have iconic properties such as the Peninsula in Hong Kong, the Siam in Bangkok and the Burj Al Arab in Dubai. There is a trend in several cities of adding smaller boutique hotels and in adding design features that reflect the surrounding local communities. Other newer developments include pod hotels and the introduction of hotel service robots.

- *Architecture and landmarks*. Some cities are known for their architecture, whether classic or modern. There are many forms and eras of architecture that are evident in world tourism cities and that attract visitors. For example, cities such as Dubai and Shanghai are known for contemporary architecture, Florence is famous for Renaissance structures, and Miami for art deco.
- *Arts, culture and creativity*. The Cerro Bellavista in Valparaiso, Chile, and Embajadores, Madrid, are two great examples of city neighbourhoods renowned for art and culture. Creative districts have sprung up in many other cities in the world, for example, Pier 2 in Kaohsiung, Taiwan, and 798 in Beijing.
- *Built contemporary leisure attractions*. These include zoos, theme parks, water parks and family recreation centres. The San Diego Zoo in California has often been rated as the best in the world. Genting Highlands in Malaysia and Sentosa Island in Singapore are two integrated resort developments in or close to cities that offer a range of contemporary leisure attractions.
- *Business tourism and events*. Convention and exhibition centres are associated with business events and are usually found in most major cities. Being expensive to build and operate, these facilities have often been topics of controversy in cities due to the requirement for local government funding support.
- *Dining*. Culinary, gastronomic and food tourism are trending upward in popularity with city visitors. Some cities are almost synonymous with food such as New Orleans, Louisiana, Paris and Lima, Peru.
- *Education, science and technology*. Aquariums and science and technology centres belong in this category, and some would include zoos as well. The City of Science and Industry in Paris, the Ontario Science Centre in Toronto and the Miraikan in Tokyo are three of the best science centres in the world. The Chimelong Ocean World (Zhuhai) and Cube Oceanarium (Chengdu) in China are rated among the largest and best aquariums in the world. The Chengdu Research Base of Giant Panda Breeding is another highly popular tourist attraction in the capital city of Sichuan Province.
- *Entertainment*. There are of course many forms of entertainment and some might be placed under culture and others within the built contemporary attractions category. Gaming is a form of entertainment around which a few world tourism cities have been built, including Macao and Las Vegas. There are other forms of entertainment associated with certain cities, such as Akihabara in Tokyo with anime and the tango with Buenos Aires.
- *Ethnicity and diasporas*. Many cities enjoy great cultural and ethnic diversity, and this can be employed in tourism development. Chinatown in San Francisco is perhaps one of the most famous of these attractions; however, almost every city has an area or district like this.
- *Events and festivals*. Certain cities have earned a deserved reputation for the quality and variety of their events and these include Edinburgh, Scotland, and Melbourne, Australia.
- *History and heritage*. There are numerous cities that are rich in historical and heritage resources. They have historical museums, castles and forts, ports and harbours, cathedrals, mosques and churches, historic districts and buildings.
- *Industrial tourism*. There are cities that offer visitors access to their industries, and these include Dublin and Copenhagen with their world-famous breweries.
- *Nature, gardens, parks and other green spaces*. Nature should not be an afterthought for cities, and indeed some cities have nature-oriented venues as flagship attractions. They include Vancouver and Singapore with Butchart Gardens and the

Botanic Gardens, respectively. Famous parks are also a strong attraction to visitors such as Central Park in New York City and several of the parks in London.

- *Shopping*. This is a mainstay attraction for many cities and some cities "go to town on it". Of course, centres of fashion including Paris, Milan and London are famous for their shopping, while others such as Kuala Lumpur and Bangkok are building their reputations as shopping havens. The increasing popularity of outlet shopping has increased the tourism appeal of certain urban areas as well.
- *Sightseeing towers, observatories and wheels*. The Oriental Pearl Tower in Shanghai, the London Eye and the Peak in Hong Kong belong here. These venues allow visitors to get a bird's-eye view of the cities.
- *Sport*. Many major cities are homes to professional sports teams that require stadiums or arenas. Some cities put a greater emphasis on amateur sport; for example, Indianapolis, Indiana, successfully positioned itself as the "Amateur Sports Capital of the World".
- *Transportation*. Funicular railways, tramcars and overhead gondola systems are three modes of transport that add a difference to some cities. To this can be added various unique forms of water transport such as in Venice and Shaoxing, Zhejiang, China.

The authors do not suggest that this list of potential tourism development projects and themes is fully complete (Figure 5.4). The main point of including the list was to demonstrate that there are a variety of development strategies available to cities and that choices should be consistent with city images and branding. It also needs to be said that world tourism cities often strive to have a broad portfolio of these 17 tourism developments and themes in order to attract diverse sets of target markets. In fact, it is often the breadth and depth of the tourism attractions and features of world tourism cities that make them so appealing to visitors. To these considerations now must be added the "Instagram appeal" or "Instagrammability" of cities and their attractions and sites.

Sweet tweet 38

Are you Instagrammable?

There are several polls that show the places, cities and attractions where most photos are taken and posted on Instagram. The Travel Channel has the top five as Disneyland (Anaheim), the Eiffel Tower in Paris, Walt Disney World in Florida, South Beach in Miami and the Berlin Wall as its top five. TravelPulse offers another perspective by ranking the countries that are Instagrammed most and their top five for 2019 was Australia, Hong Kong, Canada, Indonesia and South Africa. The *Daily Mail*, reporting on the most Instagrammed cities in the world, cited London, Paris, New York City, Dubai, Istanbul, Jakarta, Los Angeles, Barcelona, Moscow and Tokyo as having the most hashtags.

Sources: *Daily Mail* (2019); TravelPulse (2019); Travel Channel (2020).

Since this book advocates systematic approaches to destination management, planning and marketing, the authors wished to also frame city tourism development within an organised model. Asked in 2003 during a tourism master planning exercise in Hangzhou,

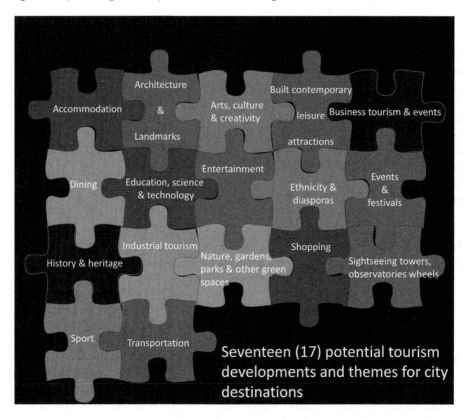

Figure 5.4 Urban tourism development projects and themes.

China (Figure 5.5) about how to transform the city into a world-class destination, one of the authors suggested a model based on several criteria, all starting with the letter "A". This was later developed into the 10 As model (Figure 5.6).

The following is a short description of the 10 A factors for city tourism development:

- *Awareness*. This factor is related to the levels of knowledge among visitors about the city destination and its major attractions. Some destinations like Bali, Indonesia, have very high levels of awareness and are on many people's travel "bucket lists" (Figure 5.7). Awareness is influenced by the amount and characteristics of the information visitors receive from and about the city, and through word of mouth. Without awareness, cities have little chance of being considered as potential destinations for trips. For example, Liverpool cited "persistent low awareness of broader product offering" as one of its major visitor economy challenges (Liverpool City Region Local Enterprise Partnership, 2014).
- *Attractiveness*. This factor is influenced by the number and geographic scope of appeal of a city destination's attractions for visitors. Cities can have top-of-mind awareness but lack a sufficient critical mass of attractions and events to draw visitors from far afield. Also, these attractions may not be perceived by visitors as significantly different from those at competitive destinations.

Figure 5.5 West Lake (Xi Hu) is Hangzhou's flagship attraction. (Courtesy: Unsplash.com, Alessio Lin.)

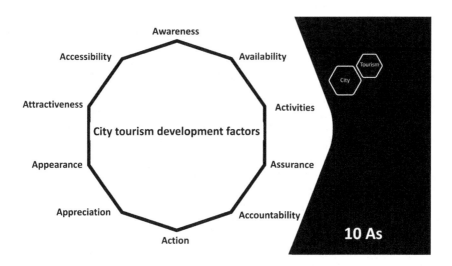

Figure 5.6 The 10 As model for city tourism development factors. (Authors, adapted from Morrison, 2021a.)

- *Activities.* Attractions in themselves are often not enough as potential visitors are now more interested in what they can see themselves doing in a city. Therefore, this factor is the extent of the array of activities and experiences available to tourists within a city. Increasingly now people want to be assured that a city offers authentic

Figure 5.7 Balinese dance performances are popular with visitors to Denpasar and other parts of Bali. (Courtesy: Shutterstock.com, Natanael Ginting.)

experiences that are of interest to them and in which they can actively participate. Many of the previously mentioned tourism plans list city experience development as a future priority.

- *Availability*. This factor reflects the ease with which bookings and reservations can be made for a city and the number of booking and reservation channels available. Online travel agencies (OTAs) and social media platforms (such as Tripadvisor) have greatly increased availability; however, some cities are also dependent on the extent to which travel trade channels (such as tour operators) have included them in tours and packages.
- *Accessibility*. This is a critical factor and has two dimensions. The first is the convenience of getting to and from a city; the second is the city's accessibility or ease of moving around within the destination. Some cities have consciously attempted to become transportation hubs with convenient international access, and these include Amsterdam, Dubai, Shanghai and Singapore. The second dimension is the degree to which cities have designed public places, transport facilities, attractions and accommodation to be accessible for all people.
- *Appearance*. This factor is comprised of the impressions that a city makes on visitors, when they first arrive and throughout their stays. Here there are two key questions to be answered: Does the city make a good first impression, and does the city make a positive, lasting impression? The significant urban improvements that have been made in Mexico were mentioned in Chapter 4 and are a good example of how a city is beautifying its appearance.
- *Assurance*. This factor is the perceived levels of safety and security within a city. Most visitors wish to be confident that a city is clean, safe and secure. Some cities, including New Delhi in India, are notorious for high levels of air pollution; others

have evoked concerns for public safety, such as Cape Town and Johannesburg in South Africa; and overcrowding is another negative perception, as for the *umrah* in Makkah (Mecca), Saudi Arabia.

- *Appreciation*. This is one of the "soft development" aspects mentioned earlier. It reflects visitor perceptions of the feelings of the levels of welcome and hospitality that they will encounter in a city. The quality of service in tourism operations and multilingual information and communication are other factors that reflect appreciation. Berlin has emphasised friendliness in this way, "Developing campaigns to create greater awareness of such topics as friendliness and consideration in public space, willingness to help others using public transport, respecting the customs of other cultures, paying more attention to the needs of others, etc." (Senate Department for Economics, Energy and Public Enterprises, 2018).
- *Action*. This factor is the pre-planning actions by a city for tourism. These actions include the preparation of a city tourism plan and destination marketing plan. Not all cities have both of these and that is a reality; however, many cities with such plans are cited in this chapter and Chapter 6. This preparedness is also reflected in overall city planning and landscaping, and in the attention given to the design of city entry points.
- *Accountability*. This factor is related to performance evaluation with respect to tourism planning and development by a city. It can be achieved through return-on-investment (ROI) measurement, for example. In addition, with greater attention now being given to resident quality of life and the neighbourhoods within cities, other KPIs are being used in addition to the economic measurements.

Some of these 10 As are closely linked with others and so what follows is a further discussion of concepts and examples that show the relationships among them. The materials also highlight certain development trends or "movements" in city tourism development.

Awareness, attractiveness and activities

The awareness of city destinations is closely related to tourism marketing efforts and that is the focus of Chapter 6. Attractiveness as the second-listed A requires significant attention from CDMOs. Almost all the tourism plans mentioned in this chapter have advocated that their cities put a higher priority on cultural tourism and its development. Of course, if done appropriately, this benefits residents as well as visitors. Certain cities go one step further and produce cultural tourism development plans or strategies. Montréal, Québec, is one of these cities, as is Austin, Texas. Montréal prepared a plan entitled *Cultural Tourism Development in Montréal: Strategies and Actions 2014–2017* (Tourisme Montréal, 2014). The City of Austin produced a *Cultural Tourism Plan* (City of Austin, 2015).

Sweet tweet 39

Austin is a creative city

Austin, Texas is an example of the "creative city" concept. The city attracts creative people and their talents cluster to form a major cultural tourism attraction.

Austin is known as a creative city with an established cultural brand. Because musicians, artists, writers, chefs, filmmakers and all sorts of interesting and talented people choose to and can live and create in Austin, the city and its community benefits. And yet more can be done to support the cultural ecosystem that enables art, culture and creativity to thrive.

Source: City of Austin (2015).

Montréal set a cultural tourism vision as "Montréal is a tourist destination recognized for the richness and diversity of its cultural offer which is constantly renewed". Austin and Montréal thus tick three of the 10 A boxes for city tourism development. They are building greater *awareness* of their cultural tourism offers, they are enhancing their tourism *attractiveness* (and differences from other cities), and they are augmenting cultural tourism *activities* and experiences. They also have taken *action* by developing specialised cultural tourism plans.

Creative cities is a movement that has drawn great attention in relation to city cultural resources (Scott, 2006; Pratt, 2008). UNESCO has established a Creative Cities Network (UCCN) whose members "commit to place culture and creativity at the core of their sustainable development strategies, policies, and initiatives" (UNESCO, 2020).

Eventful cities is another concept that relates to city tourism development as it is about the staging of events and festivals in urban areas (Richards and Palmer, 2012). Gorchakova and Antchak (2021) discuss how Melbourne, Australia, has enhanced its standing as an eventful city.

Some cities have chosen to build their awareness and reputations around other types of entertainment attractions, and Orlando, Florida, is a prime example. Others include Tokyo and Shenzhen, China. These cities are placing more emphasis on family and regional markets.

Yet another city development "movement" is the idea of liveable (or livable) cities and this has a definite effect on tourism. Adelaide in South Australia is one of the cities that has picked up on this trend and built it into its visitor economy action plan (City of Adelaide, 2017). Adelaide chose four themes for its tourism plan, including liveable, green, smart and creative. Liveability was explained as, "actions that will meet the needs of local and potential residents, actions that will increase the accessibility of the City and ensure the provision of quality infrastructure". Jones and Newsome (2016) offered a perspective on the liveability of another Australian city, Perth, by examining how various green spaces were contributing to environmental sustainability and ecotourism.

The *Global Liveability Index* published each year by the Economist Intelligence Unit is a popular source of rankings on city liveability. Vienna, Austria, garnered the top ranking in 2019 (Economist Intelligence Unit, 2020). Australia (Adelaide, Melbourne and Sydney) and Canada (Calgary, Toronto and Vancouver) each had three of the top ten liveable cities in 2019 and Japan had two (Osaka and Tokyo); Copenhagen was the second European city in the top ten. EIU uses five criteria (stability, education, health care, infrastructure and culture and entertainment) to rank 140 cities. The EIU ranks also include the most "unliveable" cities, which may have some difficulties in attracting tourists from afar.

Availability

Availability is a topic that requires greater attention from cities. It is often assumed that there are enough channels available for bookings and reservations within cities;

however, this might not be the case. CDMOs need to do much more to determine their prominence in major platforms such as Booking.com, Tripadvisor and Expedia. The information is readily available online; however, cities are not adequately analysing these "big data" sources.

Accessibility and appearance

Inclusion or inclusiveness is assigned a priority in several of the plans reviewed for this chapter. Some cities have done exceptionally well in providing accessibility for all visitors. Warsaw, Poland, is mentioned as one of these cities in Chapter 4; others are Oslo, Washington DC, Berlin and Vienna (TravelPulse, 2018).

How cities appear to visitors requires more attention. Information is readily available online in several social media platforms where the user-generated content in text, photos and videos reflects visitor impressions of the cities that they have visited. As was the case with availability, city tourism practitioners appear to not be making adequate use of this valuable information.

Appreciation and assurance

Returning to the 10 As again, there are some cities that are striving to be friendly to visitors as well as safe places to visit and happy places in which to reside. Of course, there are world rankings for this as well and these relate to *assurance* and *appreciation*. Singapore topped the list in 2017, followed by Stockholm and Helsinki (The Courier, 2020).

Action and accountability

CDMOs should be involved in planning, research and product development, and should be leaders and coordinators for these efforts. Leadership can be demonstrated by initiating and coordinating tourism planning processes. Guidance in tourism development is also required. Good governance principles suggest that CDMOs must be accountable for the resources that they are given. This includes the evaluation of planning and development processes and initiatives.

Other factors

There are other factors that can be added to the 10 As model, and one of these would be the sustainability of tourism development within the city and the sustainable development practices of the CDMO and the city government. Also, it has been suggested that accommodation might be an 11th A that is important for every city. With the entry of sharing economy providers into the accommodation supply of every city, this factor is becoming a greater city development issue. Attachment, as in place attachment, is another factor that could be added to the model; and authenticity is yet an additional one. While the model may be incomplete, the message it delivers remains intact – be sure to consider the factors that influence the success (or lack thereof) of tourism development in the city.

The tendency in the past has been for planners to focus on tourism development for cities as a whole; however, recent events have necessitated a more fine-grained approach.

There has been a distinct trend in the last decade for cities to promote neighbourhood tourism. Two reasons can be offered for this change in focus, one being that the distribution of visitors within cities is uneven. Some districts and neighbourhoods are overcrowded with tourists, while others have very few. The second reason is that the relatively "undiscovered" neighbourhoods or districts have good potential for future tourism development. The example of the neighbourhood tourism trend was mentioned in the form of the barrios in Buenos Aires in Chapter 4. Madrid and New York City are two other prominent cities that are promoting neighbourhood tourism (Destination Madrid, 2020; NYC & Company, 2020). Berlin is a fourth city that has announced its intention to manage tourism on a neighbourhood level (Senate Department for Economics, Energy and Public Enterprises, 2018). Kansas City, Missouri, is one city that proactively encouraged neighbourhood tourism development.

Sweet tweet 40

Funds for neighbourhood tourism development in Kansas City

The Neighborhood Tourist Development Fund (NTDF) program provides support to non-profit organizations through contracts for services, established by State law in 1989 to help promote Kansas City's distinct and diverse neighborhoods through cultural, social, ethnic, historic, educational and recreational activities in conjunction with promoting the city as a premier convention, visitor and tourist center.

Source: City of Kansas City, Missouri (2020).

With respect to neighbourhoods, slum and ghetto tourism has drawn the attention of scholars, often with negative accounts on the phenomenon. The slums of Mumbai and the favellas of Rio de Janeiro are the most discussed examples. The argument is made that this exploits the poverty and poor living conditions of people living in these areas, while not putting much money in their pockets.

Negative impacts of city tourism development

CDMOs and other city planners and officials must be aware of the negative effects that tourism can cause in urban areas. The *Routledge Handbook of Tourism Cities* identified some of the major of these, including overtourism (Gowreesunkar and Gavinolla, 2021), gentrification (Gravari-Barbas and Guinand, 2021), environmental and heritage damage (Day, 2021), adverse impacts of sharing economy providers (Belarmino, 2021), urbanisation (Luo and Lam, 2021), terrorism (Seabra and Paiva, 2021) and civil disputes and unrest (Webster and Hji-Avgoustis, 2021). Also, Maxim (2021) highlighted the major challenges facing world tourism cities. She mentions the added congestion that tourism brings to already busy cities and conflicts between residents and visitors. There are undoubtedly other undesirable aspects that tourism can bring to cities, including anti-social tourism behaviours of some visitors, including sex tourism, partying, drunkenness and nude photo-taking. Adding to crimes and scamming is another criticism levelled at tourism. The desirability or undesirability of slum tourism was mentioned above as well. The low-paying perceptions about jobs in tourism is an added factor to ponder, if there are other viable alternatives to consider. A "growth paradox" for city tourism has emerged that argues the positive and negative impacts sides of the argument.

Sweet tweet 41

The tourism development "growth paradox"

Tourism development is deemed paradoxical by several observers. The World Economic Forum describes the paradox in this way:

> The net result is that the places served by ministries of tourism, destination marketing organizations and convention and visitors bureau are often victims of their own success. Travellers tend to arrive in increasing numbers and flock to the same locations, resulting in issues such as overcrowding, increased stress on public services and infrastructure, cultural homogenization and growing dissatisfaction from local residents.

Social media influencer Nomadic Matt describes the paradox as follows:

> Development is good, but unfettered development is bad and, unfortunately, there's too much unfettered development in tourism today.

Sources: Nomadic Matt (2019); World Economic Forum (2018).

It must be said that there is a long list of potential negatives associated with city tourism development. When added to the mix of problems and issues that cities already face without considering tourism – including traffic congestion and pollution, rapid growth due to urbanisation, crime rates, racial and ethnic discrimination – the tasks of city planners are daunting, to say the least. A balanced approach, therefore, to assessing tourism developments is needed, which cannot be assured with just economic feasibility analysis. As highlighted on several occasions in the discussion on tourism planning processes, the gathering of opinions from all stakeholders and especially local residents is also required for tourism developments. Additionally, the visitor management role of CDMOs, as described in Chapter 4, must be given a much higher priority in the future.

Summary comments

Were this book to have been written only five years before, there would have been far fewer tourism plans to talk about. This is a positive trend in city tourism planning and development. It indicates that more cities are embracing the idea that planning for tourism is critical for the future. Moreover, it signals that an ever-increasing number of cities are treating tourism more seriously as a vital economic activity. Whilst the names and contents of these plans vary widely, the two most important considerations are the planning processes and participants. How the plans are communicated and implemented, however, is eventually of greater import.

Tourism development is accelerating at a rapid pace in many cities around the globe. Certain movements are evident here, including creative and eventful cities, smart tourism, liveability, experience design, authenticity, neighbourhood tourism, green cities and sustainable tourism development. No matter the focus chosen, it is advisable for cities to follow a systematic approach to tourism development by considering all of the critical factors and stakeholders involved. All the options in terms of alternative development projects and themes need to be on the table for discussion.

In addition, it is essential that cities ponder the potentially negative effects of tourism development, and do not just focus on the benefits, especially the economic ones. Just prior to the COVID-19 pandemic, great attention was being given to the overtourism phenomenon; however, that was not the only issue that tourism growth was raising. Gentrification, various forms of pollution, heritage relic damage and the anti-social behaviour of some tourists were other issues. A more balanced approach to tourism development is required in the future, where the advantages and disadvantages are identified and compared, and the voices of all stakeholders are heard.

The decisions that cities make based upon their planning processes and tourism developments affect marketing and branding, and that is the topic of the next chapter.

Thought questions

1) Not every city destination has a tourism plan. What are the likely reasons for this lack of planning? What are the disadvantages of not having a tourism plan?
2) How necessary is it for primary research to be collected for tourism planning? What types of data and information are the most critical for tourism planning?
3) Why is the communication about a tourism plan important?
4) Some destinations have produced videos to support tourism planning. What are the advantages of videos over printed versions of plans?
5) Tourism plans are either kept confidential or made widely available in digital and print versions. What are the pros and cons of these two different plan distribution approaches?
6) What are the advantages for an urban area in positioning itself as a creative or eventful city?
7) The lists of most liveable cities and top global destination cities are quite different. Why do you feel these rankings are not the same?
8) Several CDMOs have begun to promote city districts and neighbourhoods. This has spurred a debate about whether tourism is good for all parts of cities. How do you view this apparent dilemma?
9) There has been a discussion of a "growth paradox" with respect to tourism development in cities. Simply put, this means that tourism is not all good and not all bad for cities. How can CDMOs and other city planners ensure a balanced approach to city tourism development?
10) Convention and exhibition centres are expensive to build and operate. How can a city justify the investment and funding required for such a facility?

References

AECOM. (n.d.). Water. People. Places. In *A Guide for Master Planning Sustainable Drainage into Developments*, https://www.surreycc.gov.uk/__data/assets/pdf_file/0020/201944/Sustainable-drainage-systems-SuDS-planning-advice.pdf

Auckland Tourism, Events and Economic Development. (2020). Destination 2025. Destination AKL recovery plan. In *Auckland visitor economy's response to COVID-19*. Auckland: ATEED.

Barcelona City Council Tourism Department. (2017). Barcelona tourism for 2020. A collective strategy for sustainable tourism. https://ajuntament.barcelona.cat/turisme/sites/default/files/barcelona_tourism_for_2020_0.pdf

Belarmino, A. (2021). The sharing economy in tourism cities. In Alastair M. Morrison & J. Andres Coca-Stefaniak (Eds.). *Routledge Handbook of Tourism Cities*, pp. 65–75. London: Routledge.

Bryson, J. M. (1988). A strategic planning process for public and non-profit organizations. *Long Range Planning, 21*(1), 73–81.

City of Adelaide. (2017). Visitor economy action plan 2018–2020. https://d31atr86jnqrq2.cloudfront.net/docs/visitor-economy-action-plan.pdf?mtime=20191104153405

City of Austin. (2015). Cultural tourism plan. https://austintexas.gov/sites/default/files/files/CT_Plan_Final.pdf

City of Gold Coast. (2014). Gold coast destination tourism management plan 2014–2020. https://www.goldcoast.qld.gov.au/destination-tourism-management-plan-22034.html

City of Kansas City, Missouri. (2020). Neighborhood Tourist Development Fund (NTDF) Program. https://www.kcmo.gov/city-hall/departments/city-manager-s-office/neighborhood-tourist-development-fund-ntdf

The Courier. (2020). The 50 friendliest cities in the world. https://wcfcourier.com/travel/the-50-friendliest-cities-in-the-world/collection_b2061044-9289-11e9-913a-fb220fc3fbd5.html#49

Daily Mail. (2019). The top 50 most Instagrammed destinations in the world for 2019 revealed: London takes the No1 spot, knocking Paris into second and New York into third. https://www.dailymail.co.uk/travel/travel_news/article-7015391/The-50-Instagrammed-destinations-world-2019-revealed.html

Day, J. (2021). Sustainable tourism in cities. In Alastair M. Morrison & J. Andres Coca-Stefaniak (Eds.). *Routledge handbook of tourism cities*, pp. 52–64 . London: Routledge.

Destination Madrid. (2020). 21 destinations in Madrid. https://www.esmadrid.com/en/21-destinations-madrid

Discover Halifax. (2020). Tourism master plan. https://discoverhalifaxns.com/tourism-master-plan/

Economist Intelligence Unit. (2020). The global liveability index. https://www.eiu.com/topic/liveability

Gorchakova, V., & Antchak, V. (2021). An eventful tourism city. Hosting major international exhibitions in Melbourne. In Alastair M. Morrison & J. Andres Coca-Stefaniak (Eds.). *Routledge Handbook of Tourism Cities*, pp. 174–186. London: Routledge.

Gowreesunkar, G. V., & Gavinolla, M. R. (2021). Urbanism and overtourism: Impacts and implications for the city of Hyderabad. In Alastair M. Morrison & J. Andres Coca-Stefaniak, *Routledge Handbook of Tourism Cities*, pp. 101–120. London: Routledge.

Gravari-Barbas, M., & Guinand, S. (2021). Tourism and gentrification. In Alastair M. Morrison & J. Andres Coca-Stefaniak (Eds.). *Routledge Handbook of Tourism Cities*, pp. 88–100. London: Routledge.

Indonesia Investment Coordinating Board. (2017). All you need to know about the 10 new Bali project in Indonesia. https://www2.investindonesia.go.id/en/article-investment/detail/all-you-need-to-know-about-the-10-new-bali-project-in-indonesia

Jones, C., & Newsome, D. (2016). Perth (Australia) as one of the world's most liveable cities: A perspective on society, sustainability and environment. *International Journal of Tourism Cities, 1*(1), 18–35.

Kuala Lumpur City Hall. (2015). *Kuala Lumpur Tourism Master Plan 2015–2025*. Kuala Lumpur, Malaysia: Kuala Lumpur City Hall.

Liverpool City Region Local Enterprise Partnership. (2014). Visitor economy strategy and destination management plan. https://www.liverpoollep.org/growth-sectors/visitor-economy/dmp/

London & Partners. (2018). *A Tourism Vision for London*. London, UK: London & Partners.

Luo, J. M., & Lam, C. F. (2021). Urbanisation and its effects on city tourism in China. In Alastair M. Morrison & J. Andres Coca-Stefaniak (Eds.). *Routledge Handbook of Tourism Cities*, pp. 76–87. London: Routledge.

Macao Government Office of Tourism. (2017). Macao tourism industry development master plan. https://masterplan.macaotourism.gov.mo/Summary_Report_en.pdf

Marketing Manchester. (2013). The Greater Manchester strategy for the Visitor economy 2014–2020. https://www.marketingmanchester.com/wp-content/uploads/2017/02/tourism-strategy-2013.pdf

Marketing Manchester. (2017). Greater Manchester destination management plan 2017–2020. https://www.marketingmanchester.com/wp-content/uploads/2017/02/DMP-2017_2020-FINAL.pdf

Maxim, C. (2021). Challenges of world tourism cities. In Alastair M. Morrison & J. Andres Coca-Stefaniak (Eds.) *Routledge Handbook of Tourism Cities*, pp. 19–30. London: Routledge.

Mayor of Paris. (2019). 2022 tourism strategy: Development plan. https://cdn.paris.fr/paris/2019/07/24/692c9af6216b29354e5259511b697725.pdf

Morrison, A. M. (2019). *Marketing and Managing Tourism Destinations*, 2nd ed. London: Routledge.

Morrison, A. M. (2021a). Marketing and managing city tourism destinations. In Alastair M. Morrison & J. Andres Coca-Stefaniak (Eds.). *Routledge Handbook of Tourism Cities*, pp. 133–160. Routledge: London.

Morrison, A. M. (2021b). Reflections on trends and issues in global tourism. In P. U. C. Dieke, B. King, & R. Sharpley (Eds.). *Tourism in Development: Reflective Essays*, pp. 218–232. Wallingford. UK: CABI Publishing.

Morrison, A. M., Lehto, X. Y., & Day, J. (2018). *The Tourism System*, 8th ed. Dubuque, Iowa: Kendall Hunt Publishing.

Nomadic Matt. (2019). Why tourists ruin the places they visit. https://www.nomadicmatt.com/travel-blogs/why-tourists-ruin-the-places-they-love/

NYC & Company. (2020). Neighborhood getaways. https://www.nycgo.com/

PLANifax. (2020). Discover Halifax's tourism master plan. https://www.youtube.com/watch?v=w974eEOnVis

Pratt, A. C. (2008). Creative cities: The cultural industries and the creative class. *Geografiska Annaler: Series B, Human Geography*, 90(2), 107–117.

Qiddiya Investment Company. (2020). Master plan: Qiddiya. https://qiddiya.com/en/about-qiddiya/master-plan/

The Red Sea Development Company. (2020). The project. https://www.theredsea.sa/en/project#

Resonance. (2013). Participate in the Vancouver tourism master plan survey. https://www.youtube.com/watch?v=UoevZaH5Jq8

Resonance. (2020). Tourism master plan handbook. https://resonanceco.com/reports/the-tourism-master-plan-handbook/

Richards, G., & Palmer, R. (2012). *Eventful Cities: Cultural Management and Urban Revitalisation*. Oxford, UK: Taylor and Francis.

Richmond Region Tourism. (2019). Richmond Region 2030. A strategic direction for the Richmond Region's visitor economy. https://www.visitrichmondva.com/partners/tourism-master-plan/

Rothaermel, F. T. (2020). *Strategic Management: Concepts*, 5th ed. New York: McGraw-Hill.

RVAHub. (2019). Richmond Region Tourism launches Tourism Master Plan during annual meeting. https://rvahub.com/2020/09/30/richmond-region-tourism-launches-tourism-master-plan-during-annual-meeting/

San Diego Tourism Marketing District. (2017). San Diego tourism 20-Year master plan. https://experiencesandiego.com/20-year-master-plan/

Scott, A. J. (2006). Creative cities: Conceptual issues and policy questions. *Journal of Urban Affairs*, 28(1), 1–17.

Seabra, C., & Paiva, O. (2021). Global terrorism in tourism cities: The case of World Heritage Sites. In Alastair M. Morrison & J. Andres Coca-Stefaniak (Eds.). *Routledge Handbook of Tourism Cities*, pp. 31–51. London: Routledge.

Senate Department for Economics, Energy and Public Enterprises. (2018). Sustainable and city-compatible Berlin tourism plan 2018+. https://about.visitberlin.de/sites/default/files/2018-07/Berlin%20Tourism%20Plan%202018%2B_summary_EN.pdf

Solimar International. (2020). Tourism master plans. https://www.solimarinternational.com/what-we-do/strategic-planning/tourism-master-plans/

Tourisme Montréal. (2014). *Développement du tourisme culturel à Montréal stratégies et actions 2014–2017*. Montréal: Tourisme Montréal (in French).

Travel Channel. (2020). The most Instagrammed places in the world. https://www.travelchannel.com/interests/arts-and-culture/photos/the-most-instagrammed-destinations-around-the-world

Travel Portland. (2018). *Portland Tourism Master Plan*. Vancouver: Resonance.

TravelPulse. (2018). 25 of the world's most disability-friendly cities. https://www.travelpulse.com/gallery/destinations/25-of-the-worlds-most-disability-friendly-cities-4.html?image=11

TravelPulse. (2019). The 50 most 'Instagrammable' places in the world. https://www.travelpulse.com/gallery/destinations/the-50-most-instagrammable-places-in-the-world.html?image=5

UNESCO. (2020). Creative cities network. https://en.unesco.org/creative-cities/

Vienna Tourism. (2017). Tourism strategy 2020. http://www.tourismstrategy2020.vienna.info/downloads/wt-tourismusstrategie-2020_en.pdf

Vienna Tourism. (2019). Tourism 2020 strategy status report. http://tourismusstrategie2020.wien.info/downloads/Tourismusstrategie_2020_Statusbericht.pdf

VisitCOS. (2018). Colorado Springs' destination master plan. https://www.youtube.com/watch?v=PNcM43Y5UEA

Visit Indy. (2020). Tourism master vision. https://www.visitindy.com/indianapolis-tourism-master-plan

VisitKLOfficial. (2015). KL tourism master plan 2015–2025. https://www.youtube.com/watch?v=3X70QCTKqtI

VisitTucson.org. (2019). Visit Tucson. Metro Tucson 10-year tourism master plan. https://www.visittucson.org/tourism-master-plan

Webster, C., & Hji-Avgoustis, S. (2021). *Routledge Handbook of Tourism Cities* (Alastair M. Morrison and J. Andres Coca-Stefaniak, Eds.), pp. 121–130. London: Routledge.

Wonderful Copenhagen. (2020). 10Xcopenhagen. https://10xcopenhagen.com/

World Economic Forum. (2018). The growth paradox: Can tourism ever be sustainable? https://www.weforum.org/agenda/2017/08/the-growth-paradox-can-tourism-ever-be-su stainable/

Wu, B., Li, Q., Ma, F., & Wang, T. (2021). Tourism cities in China. In Alastair M. Morrison & J. Andres Coca-Stefaniak (Eds.). *Routledge Handbook of Tourism Cities*, pp. 508– 519. London: Routledge.

Chapter 6

Marketing and branding of world tourism cities

Abstract

This chapter reviews a prominent and long-standing role of CDMOs. It describes systematic approaches to city tourism marketing and branding that are supported with successful examples from around the globe. A marketing planning process developed by the authors provides the major framework for the chapter. The process addresses five questions, and how each one is answered by city tourism marketers is explained – these are: Where are we now? Where would we like to be? How do we get there? How do we make sure we get there? How do we know if we got there?

Particular attention is paid to the development of marketing strategies and plans. Examples of these are given through a variety of city tourism best practices. A major point is made that city tourism branding is not an exercise in developing slogans or designing logos. Rather it is a step-by-step and systematic process that requires research and the participation of stakeholders.

The critical roles for marketing objectives and marketing plans are highlighted, as is the need for marketing performance evaluation. Marketing budgets and sources of funding are reviewed, and these vary greatly from place to place. Marketing performance criteria are suggested.

Keywords: 8 Ps; branding; destination marketing; image; marketing plan; marketing strategy; marketing objectives; performance evaluation; positioning.

DOI: 10.4324/9781003111412-8

Learning objectives

Having read this chapter, you should be able to:

- Identify five questions to be answered in city tourism marketing.
- Describe the contents of a city tourism marketing strategy.
- Explain how unique selling propositions (USPs) are used in positioning a city's tourism.
- Explain the city tourism brand development process.
- Elaborate on the major parts of a marketing plan.
- Detail performance evaluation criteria and approaches for the marketing of city tourism.

Chapter 3 highlighted that urban tourism did not receive much academic attention until recently. City tourism marketing was not starved by a lack of attention from researchers; in fact, it was thriving and growing in the world of practitioners. Indeed, Chapter 4 described marketing and promotion as the "legacy" role of CDMOs since it has been a mainstay activity for many decades. However, as the 2020s advance, city marketing and branding have undergone some fundamental changes and the COVID-19 pandemic necessitated even more recalibrations to these practices. Venice went from "overtourism" to "no tourism" during COVID-19 and wild animals even roamed the streets of cities that were normally thronged by visitors. It was an interlude for great self-reflection among city tourism marketers.

In the uncharted territory of COVID-19, tourism experts are divided into two camps. The first one, which we can call the "new normal" group, argues that tourism will fundamentally change and become more sustainable. Hence, the tone of marketing and branding should be quite different in the future. The second camp, let us call them "business as usual", are projecting a return to the pre-COVID-19 situation, with very few changes needed in how tourism operates and is marketed. Rather than using their crystal ball, the authors believe that fundamentally the systematic approach to marketing and branding has not been altered by this unprecedented public health and economic crisis. Indeed, the need for such an approach has been accentuated by the chaos of 2020 and 2021.

Destination marketing and branding

Many world tourism cities excel at tourism marketing and branding; however, what do the two concepts mean and how are they connected? The authors define city tourism destination marketing as follows:

> City tourism destination marketing is a continuous, sequential process through which CDMOs plan, research, implement, control and evaluate activities and pro-grammes designed to satisfy visitor needs and wants and their cities' visions, goals and objectives for tourism in a sustainable way and taking into account the needs and requirements of all stakeholders including local residents.

This chapter explains how this definition is articulated in a professional destination marketing approach. How about branding now? You have probably heard of "*I love New York*" and "*Incredible India*". Are they within the scope of marketing or are they just destination brands? The answer is that they belong to marketing and branding as there is an overlap between the two concepts. What then is branding with respect to city tourism? The authors define it as *the steps taken by CDMOs to develop and communicate particular identities and personalities for city tourism that are different from those of all competitors.*

Branding approaches are designed as part of marketing strategy development and are typically implemented over a number of years. Not all branding approaches work for cities and they may be replaced or modified; the effective ones can survive and prosper for many years.

No matter the circumstances, city tourism marketing and branding need to follow a systematic planning process, and this is now discussed.

Marketing planning process

Chapter 5 details a step-by-step and sequenced process for developing a city tourism plan or strategy. Marketing should also be planned to use a logical process and the authors suggest that this process involves answering five questions (Figure 6.1):

- Where are we now?
- Where would we like to be?
- How do we get there?

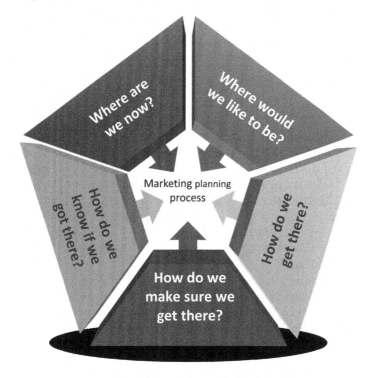

Figure 6.1 Marketing planning process (authors).

- How do we make sure we get there?
- How do we know if we got there?

Now, each of these questions is addressed in order.

1. Where are we now?

World tourism cities must first take stock of the existing situation with respect to their market standing and past marketing programmes and activities. They must also gauge recent trends, issues, challenges and opportunities affecting their city's tourism. The following five chapters are devoted to the examination of world tourism city trends, issues and challenges. However, a good example is now cited from Portland, Oregon, on building future opportunities into tourism plans.

Sweet tweet 42

Portland's opportunities and challenges

To realize the vision for Portland tourism, we narrowed down some 40 opportunities and challenges to 10, then gathered those into three areas of focus: ● Experiential – builds on the identity of Portland as a city and a destination; ● Development/Investment – enables the creation of places and projects that make our tourism industry more sustainable and create more offerings to enjoy; ● Advocacy – works toward promoting quality of life issues important to all Portlanders, residents or visitors alike.

Source: Travel Portland (2018).

One of the trends and opportunities that the Portland plan highlighted was in attracting more international visitors to the city. Others included the sustainability and smart city movements, and the trend to more visitors wanting to participate in authentic urban experiences. The plan also mentions the quality of life of residents.

The authors recommend that the situation analysis approach be implemented at this point to directly answer the "Where are we now?" question. The six factors to be analysed are: (1) product; (2) visitors; (3) community and stakeholders; (4) position and image; (5) past marketing; and (6) competitors. Some might recognise this as being the "SW" part of a SWOT analysis.

A technique known as an environmental scan can also be used to determine the opportunities and threats (the "OT" of SWOT) for city tourism posed by external environments. The PESTEL model suggests scanning six external environment factors (political, economic, social, technological, environmental, legal).

The final output in answering the "Where are we now?" question is the definition of the unique selling propositions (USPs) of city tourism. These USPs are features that make a city different from competitors and they must meet these criteria:

- Be valuable to visitors.
- Be rare among current and potential competitors.

- Be imperfectly imitable (cannot be easily copied).
- Have no strategically equivalent substitutes for the resources, assets or skills reflected in the USP.

Some cities refer to this uniqueness as their DNA, and Tel Aviv is one city that uses this expression, as does Calgary as you will see later. Basically, this means what makes cities different from all others.

Sweet tweet 43

The tourism DNA of Tel Aviv

The city's tourism DNA

Tel Aviv's distinctiveness as a tourist destination rests on a unique mix of three pillars:

Jaffa – one of the most ancient port cities in the world which, according to various surveys and research projects is the city's main attraction.

Vibrant urbanism – Tel Aviv is a pluralistic and spirited urban space with unique characteristics: culture, art, nightlife, superb food, and a safe and inviting public space.

Beaches – 14 km of golden beaches land are enhanced by beach facilities that are tightly managed by the Municipality, business establishments that dot the coast, and a boardwalk that extends from one end to the other. (Figure 6.2)

Source: Tel Aviv Municipality (2017).

In another example, the Regional Council of Tourism of Marrakech (*Conseil Regional du Tourisme de Marrakech – CRT Marrakech*) in North Africa identifies four stark contrasts of the city as its DNA: (1) history and cultural heritage vs. trendy and chic; (2) all budget destination vs. luxury collection; (3) mountains and snow vs. palm grove and camels; and (4) proximity to Europe vs. change of scenery (UNWTO/WTCF, 2019).

The identified USPs are used later in creating a marketing strategy and especially in city tourism positioning and branding.

2. Where would we like to be?

The first question took stock of the existing situation in city tourism; the second is about imagining and planning where and what it wants to be in the future. The main output from the "Where are we now?" question is the expression of USPs. The "Where would we like to be?" question produces a marketing strategy and marketing objectives. Developing strategies and objectives in a best practice mode begins with doing marketing research.

Marketing research

Data and information gathered by a CDMO to assist it in making more effective decisions comes from marketing research. It is foolish to assume that things are not constantly changing in tourism markets and in the environments surrounding them.

Figure 6.2 The shorefront and beach areas of Tel Aviv
(Courtesy: Unsplash.com, Shai Pal).

Marketing research can ensure that cities are connected to the current realities in markets and among competitors. This is research done to inform marketing and to help cities make better marketing decisions. Often the data collection involves surveys of past and potential visitors; however, information from stakeholders can also be very insightful. For example, Rotterdam Partners (2019) invited businesses and entrepreneurs to provide input for a new city tourism vision that would influence future marketing and branding. Chapter 4 cited Las Vegas as a city that surveys existing visitors on a monthly basis to inform its marketing efforts. For Vancouver, stakeholders were interviewed and then surveyed in greater detail about their priorities for city tourism (Tourism Vancouver, 2019).

Marketing strategy

A marketing strategy is the selection of a course of action from among several alternatives that involves specific visitor groups (target markets) and a positioning-image-branding (PIB) approach for city tourism. This strategy is longer-term and normally covers three to five years. The two major parts of a marketing strategy are market segmentation and targeting, and positioning-image-branding.

Market segmentation and targeting
Market segmentation analysis and target market selection are the two stages to be completed here by CDMOs.

Market segmentation analysis: This involves dividing the overall markets for city tourism into subgroups using one or more criteria. The term "markets" is used here as there are different categories of visitors and these are for business tourism, leisure tourism (also known as pleasure, holiday or vacation travel), VFR and personal travel. Although these do overlap to some extent, for example, with the "bleisure" combination, they should be treated separately in market segmentation analysis. The overlap point is reflected in the reporting of visitor statistics for Paris, which say that 66% come for leisure purposes and the remaining 34% are bleisure visitors (business + leisure) (Paris Region Tourist Board, 2020).

There are nine types of segmentation criteria that can be applied in market segmentation analysis for city tourism, based on the observed practices among destinations.

- *Trip purpose*. The four main trip-purpose divisions are leisure or pleasure travel (also holiday and vacation), VFR travel, business travel and personal travel.
- *Geographic*. Geographic markets are defined by place of residence or source of origin, and this is one of the most common ways to define the markets for urban tourism (Figure 6.3).
- *Length of stay*. The period of time spent in the city often divided into day trips (excursionists) and overnight stays (residential tourists).
- *Socio-demographic*. Characteristics such as age, education, occupation, income and household composition.
- *Psychographic*. Dividing up people by their psychological orientations, lifestyles or activities-interests-opinions (AIOs).
- *Behavioural*. Classifying visitors into groups based upon their past purchasing and travel behaviours or future travel purchase intentions. Repeat versus first-time visitors is an example.

Figure 6.3 Antalya, Turkey, receives most of its tourists from Russia, Germany and Ukraine (Courtesy: Shutterstock.com, muratart).

- *Product-related*. Having certain products that will focus attention on specific segments with the highest interest levels in using these products. For example, cultural-heritage tourism and gastronomic tourism.
- *Channel of distribution (B2B)*. This type of segmentation is used in business travel and in marketing to travel trade intermediaries. Separating travel agencies into OTAs and traditional is an example.
- *Stakeholder groups*. The specific stakeholders to be targeted including visitors, local community residents, tourism operators, media channels and others.

Trip-purpose segmentation is often used with city tourism and the leisure and business tourism markets get the greatest attention from CDMOs. However, the VFR and personal travel markets often go under the radar of city tourism marketers. This is rather surprising as well as a missed opportunity, since these two together often account for more than 50% of the visitors to cities. However, some cities are paying attention to these markets, and Berlin is one of them.

Sweet tweet 44

Berlin promotes its health tourism assets

Travel for health and medical reasons should be classified as personal rather than leisure travel. Berlin is one prominent world tourism city that is actively promoting its health tourism facilities and services.

> Guests from abroad are increasingly investing in their health during their stay in the German capital. Berlin provides medical experts of all disciplines as well as internationally renowned hospitals such as the Deutsche Herzzentrum (The German Heart Centre) or the Universitätsklinik Charité (The Charité Clinical Centre). These clinics and numerous other hospitals have international facilities offering top-class medical treatment for patients from abroad. Apart from the excellent quality of medicine, foreign patients enjoy a unique choice of health coaching, relaxation packages, city spas, and beauty treatments.

Source: VisitBerlin (2020).

Target market selection: From the market segments identified in the market segmentation analysis, the CDMO must pick out its target markets. No city can appeal to and attract all tourists, and choices have to be made about upon which markets budgets should be spent. A few examples are now provided to illustrate cities' target market selections.

A strategy report commissioned by the City of London Corporation (2018) identified four priority ("tier one") target markets as overseas sightseers, day-trip families, London adults and business visitors. Kuala Lumpur took a different tack and defined its nine target markets according to tourism product categories available in the Malaysian capital city (culture, heritage and places of interest; shopping; entertainment; nature and adventure; luxury travel; sports; business and MICE; medical and wellness; and education) (Kuala Lumpur City Hall, 2015). Newport Beach in California pinpoints the leisure traveller, meeting planner and the local community as its customers (Newport Beach &

Company, 2019). Freemantle, Western Australia, selected leisure tourism, business tourism, major events and cruise ships as its four target markets (City of Freemantle, 2018). These are four quite different approaches and apply dissimilar segmentation criteria.

There are selection criteria to be applied in selecting target markets. Their use depends on the particular situation with a city's tourism. Ten potential criteria are described below:

- *Measurable*. Selecting target markets that can be measured with a reasonable degree of accuracy.
- *Substantial*. Choosing target markets that are large enough; avoiding markets with small numbers.
- *Accessible*. Being able to reach specific groups through some form of communication, online and offline.
- *Defensible*. Justifying whether the target market should be treated separately or if it should be combined with other target markets.
- *Durable*. Ensuring the target market will be sustainable and available for the long term.
- *Competitive*. Having a distinct competitive advantage with respect to the target market. This ideally is expressed through a USP.
- *Homogenous*. Being satisfied that the customers in the target market are very like each other.
- *Compatible*. Being reasonably certain that the target market is compatible with other target markets and consistent with the city tourism vision, positioning and branding.
- *Profitable*. Determining that the target market will produce sufficient economic yield for the city.
- *Risk level*. Being assured that the return on investment (ROI) from the target market will be high enough.

Sometimes circumstances force tough choices on CDMO target market selections. Bruges, the World Heritage List city in Belgium, has traditionally been flooded by day-trippers many of whom are on organised group tours. It is a highly accessible city and can easily be visited in one day from major European capitals. However, those on day trips – the excursionists – are not entirely compatible with those staying overnight (residential tourists) as they cause overcrowding at popular sites and raise other issues as well. Yield is a second issue with the day-trip market for a city like Bruges since excursionists may not spend as much as overnight visitors.

Sweet tweet 45

Bruges chooses not to encourage "excursionism"

The following strategy was articulated in the vision for Bruges until 2024.

> Overnight tourism is a priority
> Everyone is welcome in Bruges, but no specific actions focused on day tourism will be undertaken. The growth of excursionism is being curbed,

> while multi-day residential tourism is being encouraged. Within the recreational stay segment, we are focusing proactively on the individual visitor, while the group market is only being facilitated. Within the business segment, the focus is placed on attracting residential congresses, meetings and incentives.
>
> Source: City of Bruges (2019).

Positioning, image and branding (PIB)

Positioning, image and branding are closely connected, and all three concepts are considered when selecting a city tourism marketing strategy. City marketers must decide on the desired images (positioning) and the identity and personality (branding) for their urban areas. They must also understand through research the existing images among past and potential visitors.

Positioning represents the steps taken by a CDMO to identify and communicate a unique image to people within its target markets. Therefore, positioning is how the CDMO decides to make itself unique among its competitors from the visitor perspective. Images are the mental pictures people have in their minds of specific cities as tourism destinations. These images are formed from multiple sources of information. It is known that city images are difficult to change in the short term.

An easy way to remember the steps required for effective city tourism positioning is to think of them as the five Ds of positioning:

- *Documenting*. Identifying the benefits that are most important to the specific groups of visitors to the city.
- *Deciding*. Deciding on the image that the city desires to have within its selected target markets.
- *Differentiating*. Pinpointing the competitors the city wants to appear different from and the things that make it different from them.
- *Designing*. Providing product or service differences and communicating these in city tourism positioning statements.
- *Delivering*. Making good on the promises that the city has made to visitors (this is also reflected in the city's brand promise).

Documenting requires that research be done on a city's destination image. This requires that a research study be completed with past and potential visitors, and stakeholders can also be asked to voice their opinions on city image. Chapter 4 recommended that CDMOs must engage in collecting primary data that applies directly to their cities. Sometimes, however, there are good and credible secondary data related to city images. For example, in the case of Brazil a study was conducted by Embratur, the national tourism organisation, to assess the profile of international visitors and collect opinions on their visits to destinations within the country. It was determined through this survey that the most sought-after destinations for 2018 were Rio de Janeiro, Florianopolis and Foz do Iguaçu (Hyland, 2019).

As an example for deciding, Bogotá, Colombia's CDMO, Instituto Distrital de Turismo (IDT), desires to position itself as the event capital of Latin America (UNWTO/WTCF, 2019). Glasgow decided to position itself around six core themes: Heritage, contemporary art, music, Charles Rennie Mackintosh, events and the city's capability as a world-class sporting destination (Invest Glasgow, 2019).

There should be a direct connection between the benefits mentioned for documenting with the city's USPs, as a USP must be valuable to visitors. The earlier example from Tel Aviv cited the city's DNA, which is similar to the USP concept although not exactly the same.

City destination branding

City tourism branding represents the steps taken by a CDMO, in collaboration with its stakeholders, to develop and communicate an identity and personality for the city different from those of all competitors and that benefit visitors. This has become a very hot topic in practice and among academics. Morrison (2021) suggests that tourism researchers tend to put more focus on the branding of countries, states and provinces; however, there are now also many articles and books written about city destination branding.

There is a brand development process to be followed that can be divided into six sequential steps. Before describing each of these steps, it must be emphasised that the best results in brand development come from a research-based approach and the involvement of city tourism stakeholders. Also, this is not a process of sloganeering or producing cute logos. While slogans (or straplines) and logos may be among the outputs, they are just expressions of the identity and personality chosen for city tourism; other factors such as the brand promise and brand socialisation are more critical to longer-term branding success.

- *Background analysis*. This is similar to the process used to conduct a situation analysis as it focuses on identifying the principal city tourism strengths and weaknesses.
- *Stakeholder consultations and inputs*. City tourism branding is much more likely to be successful with stakeholder input where stakeholders are encouraged to develop a sense of ownership in the branding process and its outcomes. The example discussed below for Helsinki, Finland, is a great case study, as is the example from Calgary.
- *USP confirmation*. Based upon the first two steps, the city tourism USPs are reconfirmed (or adjusted) especially with respect to visitor benefits and competitive advantages.
- *City brand development and launch*. This is the most creative part of the process as well as being the one with the greatest detail. The components are brand strategy development, brand identity development, brand launch and introduction and brand implementation.

  Isaac and Wichnewski (2021) in analysing Vancouver's new tourism branding stressed the importance for the brand promise to be matched with the actual brand experiences of the city's visitors. The brand promise can be defined as "a statement describing the intended promised experience of a brand" (Light and Kiddon, 2009, p. 78).
- *Brand socialisation and culturalisation*. This step involves introducing the brand to city tourism stakeholders and visitors. Also, it is called "embedding" the brand in the community.
- *Brand monitoring, maintenance and evaluation*. There should be an expectation that a city tourism brand will last for several years. However, a brand's longevity depends on how well it is monitored, maintained and evaluated.

Sweet tweet 46

Helsinki involves local citizens in the brand development process

The Finnish capital is a very good case study in the application of the first two steps in the brand development process, particularly in involving local stakeholders.

> Developed in 2015–2016, this concept is based on an extensive process of interaction with city residents and other local stakeholders. The process consisted, among other things, of identifying the strengths and weaknesses of Helsinki. The citizens were now brought into focus as the main content and makers of the city's brand and reputation.

Source: City of Helsinki (2018).

Brand socialisation and brand culturalisation involve steps taken by the CDMO to embed the city tourism brand within its community. This is especially important to accomplish with tourism operators and others who will integrate the brand in their own marketing and promotions. Tourism Calgary, for example, held *Living the brand* workshops to assist partners to align with the city's new destination brand (Tourism Calgary, 2020). The Singapore Tourism Board selected *"Passion Ambassadors"* to exemplify and spread its branding approach, *Passion made possible* (Singapore Tourism Board, 2020).

Before leaving the topic of branding, the place branding concept needs to be mentioned. So far, the discussion has mainly had a focus on tourism destination branding; however, many cities are engaged in broader branding initiatives that encompass tourism and other economic sectors. Balch (2019), for example, describes the successful city branding for Porto, Portugal (Figure 6.4).

City destination branding is not easy; in fact, it is replete with challenges. Also, it cannot be done quickly and sometimes takes several months or even years to get right. Destinations represent a mix of different products and services, and they are complex and variable. Cities are not single products but rather a composite of products and services under different ownership. CDMOs do not have total control over all that is to be branded; they do not own or manage the products and services that are covered under the city destination brand. Effective branding requires a team effort and CDMOs should not do destination branding just on their own. City destination branding needs a long-term commitment as it may not produce immediate results. Tourism is an "experience good" since the quality of destinations cannot truly be observed and assessed in advance; destinations must be experienced to determine their real quality. Finally, there is often a lack of sufficient funding to support destination branding efforts with CDMOs not having sufficient funds to hire branding consultants and to pay for the approaches that they recommend.

City politicians are very sensitive about the images of the places within their jurisdictions. Moreover, brands and destination advertising are subject to public scrutiny, discussion and criticism. Because almost everybody travels and becomes a tourist themselves, they all have opinions about how to put across the images of the places where they live.

Figure 6.4 The blue and white tile patterns were an inspiration for Porto's tourism logo (Courtesy: Unsplash.com, Nathalia Segato).

Sweet tweet 47

Do not overemphasise a slogan!

It seems that newspaper, magazine and online content reporters love to critique the slogans for tourism destinations. Slogans, with so few words at their disposal, attract a host of "armchair experts" who immediately take on the role of tourism marketing gurus. Often these critiques are framed as "best and worst" lists, which place New York City and Amsterdam in the positive side. Other slogans are ridiculed for being facile or pretentious or just not believable. So, the lesson for CDMO marketers is a simple one – do not overemphasise a slogan!

Sources: Coldwell (2013); Curator (2019); Haines (2016).

Given the challenges to city destination branding and the various traps that brand developers often fall into, how can a CDMO get it right? This is not an easy feat, as has just been highlighted; however Short break 6 from Western Canada provides a best practice case study for an effective brand development process.

SHORT BREAK 6

The tourism brand evolution of Calgary, Alberta

The brand development process for Calgary began in 2017 and was based on the vision to position it as the "ultimate host city". To support the achievement of this vision the CDMO, Tourism Calgary, sensed the need to articulate and attach an emotional touch to communicate Calgary's unique personality. The brand evolution project was initiated with four specific targets in mind – visitors, residents, post-secondary students and businesses. It was to extend the city's "*be part of the energy*" brand which reflects Calgary's historic and contemporary association with the oil and gas industry.

Tourism Calgary describes three phases of the brand evolution process that were applied.

Phase 1: Research was conducted to define Calgary's DNA as a place and destination. This included a local resident survey, a two-year analysis of online comments about Calgary and interviews with community leaders and workshops. The main conclusion was that "Calgary is a city with an undeniable, remarkable community spirit".

Phase 2: The objective here was to further articulate the concept of Calgary's community spirit that emerged from Phase 1. A series of so-called ideation workshops were held with city partners, people from various industry sectors, local influencers and business community members. A brand model was developed based on the feedback received from these sessions.

Phase 3: The staging of *Living the brand* workshops in Calgary was designed to introduce and embed the new branding approach.

After three years of effort, Tourism Calgary launched its new brand promise, *Eager to share*, in December 2019. This was supported during 2019 by two videos explaining the branding in more detail.

This is an outstanding case study that demonstrates the application of the steps in the brand development process. It is especially excellent in the approach to stakeholder consultations and inputs, and in brand socialisation and culturalisation (*Living the brand*). Also, the brand promise (*Eager to share*) is very clear and actionable. The support from a large amount of research data and information is commendable as well. The reader can see that the emphasis here was not on coming up with a fancy slogan and logo; rather, it was on finding out about the city's DNA. Moreover, building a groundswell of support for the new brand will give it greater longevity as the Calgary community feels a sense of ownership through involvement in the brand development process.

Discussion points:

1. What are the strengths of the brand development approach used by Tourism Calgary?

2. The brand development process in Calgary lasted for three years. Is this a reasonable timeframe or should cities try to accelerate the process? Why or why not?
3. How could more data and information on visitors and competitors have been used to improve this branding process?

Sources: Tourism Calgary (2019, 2020); Tourism Calgary (2019); Calgary brand model; Tourism Calgary (2019); Eager to share brand promise.

Marketing objectives

Marketing objectives are set for each selected target market, and they are the foundation for subsequent steps in city tourism marketing (Figure 6.5). Experts suggest that marketing objectives need to be SMART, which means:

- *Specific*. The objective applies to a specific target market that the CDMO has selected.
- *Measurable*. The results for the achievement of the objective can be measured by the CDMO.
- *Attainable*. There is a reasonable probability of achieving the marketing objective.
- *Relevant*. The objective reflects the relative priority given to the specific target market and current conditions.
- *Timely*. The objective incorporates a timeframe for its achievement.

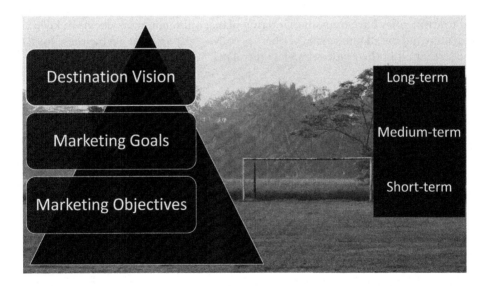

Figure 6.5 Hierarchy of marketing goals and objectives (Courtesy: Unsplash.com, Utsman media).

In actual practice, marketing objectives for city tourism are very diverse in their focus and contents. Prague City Tourism (2020) lists its marketing objectives as being the following:

- Increase average spend per visitor.
- Increase overnights.
- Increase arrivals or, in some markets, recover declining arrivals.
- Motivate repeat visits.
- Improve off-season arrivals in some target groups.
- Bolster interest in visiting areas outside of the immediate historical centre.
- Improve Prague's image with domestic visitors, combat negative stereotypes.
- Promote Prague as a convention destination via partnership with the Prague Convention Bureau.

These are good objectives, although they are lacking in specific measurement yardsticks. Several target markets are specified, including conventions and domestic tourists. Portsmouth on the south coast of England is more specific in targeting an increase in overall visitor numbers by 5% (target 9.7 million visitors) by 2019 and increasing the number of overnight stays by 8% by 2019 (Portsmouth City Council, 2018). The more specific and quantified marketing objectives can be, the better.

3. How do we get there?

Answering the third question requires deciding on how the CDMO will achieve the marketing objectives and the main tool here is a written marketing plan. It seems that most world tourism cities have tourism marketing plans, although many decide to keep these confidential and out of public view. Others perceive great value in having these displayed online so that all in their cities can view the plans.

Marketing plan

A city tourism marketing plan is a written plan of action used to guide a CDMO's marketing activities usually for the year ahead. The three parts of a city tourism marketing plan are the executive summary, marketing plan rationale and implementation plan. The executive summary is a short summary of the key highlights of the marketing plan. The marketing plan rationale explains all the research and assumptions on which the marketing plan's programmes and activities have been based. The implementation plan provides a detailed description of the action steps proposed to achieve the marketing objectives.

Just as a footnote and to avoid possible confusion, not every CDMO calls a marketing plan a marketing plan. Some include the marketing plan in a broader-scope business plan, as was the case earlier cited for Newport Beach, California. London & Partners also puts together an annual business plan (London & Partners, 2019). In addition, there are DMOs that assemble longer-term marketing perspective documents, often under the name of destination marketing strategies or strategic marketing plans.

Marketing mix (8 Ps)

The activities and programmes specified in a marketing plan are traditionally referred to as the marketing mix. The traditional "4 Ps of marketing" were product, price, place and promotion as suggested by McCarthy (1960). To these, Morrison (2019) added packaging, programming, partnership and people to better reflect the situation in tourism.

- *Product.* Product development was identified as one of the city destination management roles in Chapter 4.
- *Price.* CDMOs usually do not set prices; however, they are concerned with the value for money that visitors receive within their cities. They may work with other stakeholders to offer visitors better value such as with the issuance of city cards (European Cities Marketing, 2020a).
- *Place.* This is the distribution channels that are used, online and offline. Some also associate this with the location of the city as in the earlier example of Marrakech.
- *Promotion.* This is now commonly referred to as integrated marketing communication (IMC) and includes digital marketing, advertising, sales, sales promotion and merchandising and public relations and publicity.
- *Packaging.* This is offering facilities and services in combinations at a single price. The bed and breakfast offer is an example, as are city tours that can be purchased at a single price.
- *Programming.* This involves arranging activities, experiences and events in which visitors participate (Figure 6.6 has an example).
- *Partnership.* Partnership and team building is one of the city destination management roles and it was discussed in Chapter 4.

Figure 6.6 Visiting mosques in the GCC, Abu Dhabi, in the United Arab Emirates (Courtesy: Unsplash.com, David Rodrigo).

- *People*. This is the human factor in city tourism, including visitors (guests), those who serve them (hosts) and local residents.

Undoubtedly promotion is the most visible of these 8 Ps and also usually the most expensive. During 2020 and 2021, CDMOs were forced to rethink their target markets and promotional campaigns due to the impacts of COVID-19. For example, Hong Kong started its first-ever promotional campaign aimed at local residents (Pantaleon, 2020), called "*Holiday at home*". Shanghai held a promotional event on World Tourism Day 2020 for expatriates residing in the city (Hu, 2020). The Shanghai Administration of Culture and Tourism hosted expatriates from countries including Japan, South Korea, Thailand, Hungary and Croatia to experience five touring routes covering the Baoshan, Jinshan, Chongming, Fengxian districts and the Pudong New Area. Prague in its "*Prague unlocked*" campaign offered free admissions to numerous tourist attractions in order to stimulate more travel during the summer of 2020 (Outlook Traveller, 2020).

Many DMOs put a high priority on participating at travel and tourism exhibitions and shows, of which there are many on a global basis. Among these, two of the largest are the ITB in Berlin and the World Travel Market in London. The ITB was cancelled for the first time in its history in 2020 as a result of the impacts of the COVID-19 pandemic. The World Travel Market (WTM) has taken place each year since 1980 (WTM, 2020) and; however, in 2020 it was held in a completely virtual format. Typically, for these larger shows, CDMOs will exhibit along with their national and state/provincial tourism organisations and not on their own. Exhibiting at these shows can be classified as a mixture of promotion and place since CDMOs interact with travel trade partners (tour operators and travel agencies) at these events.

Digital marketing is fast becoming the major promotional mode for CDMOs and traditional media advertising is declining in relative importance. The use of major social media platforms is essential, including Facebook, Instagram, Twitter and YouTube. For those CDMOs with a strong emphasis on MICE markets, sales forces are normally employed to develop and maintain relationships with event planners. CDMOs also frequently have communications offices that handle press and media relations and publicity.

As discussed in Chapter 4, product development is an ongoing proposition for world tourism cities. Traditionally, product initiatives have been considered to be within the purview of marketing. Some cities are still trying to introduce flagship tourism projects that will be the icons for their urban areas. One of these is Muscat, Oman, that is indicating a desire to build a one-of-a-kind landmark (Zawya, 2020).

The concept of an eventful city (Richards and Palmer, 2010) is related to both the product and programming elements of the 8 Ps. Gorchakova and Antchak (2021) explained how Melbourne, Australia, had enhanced its standing as an eventful city through a programme of hosting major international cultural exhibitions.

Possibly straddling a number of the 8 Ps is the idea of smartness and creating smart tourism destinations. Boes et al. (2016, p. 110) suggested that smartness had become a vital component of destination management and marketing. Smartness affects the experiences of visitors to cities, improves information availability and encourages co-creation. The European Union (2020) classified smartness in tourism destinations into the four categories of accessibility, cultural heritage and creativity, digitalisation and sustainability. A competition is held by the EU among cities and awards are given for best practices in specific sub-categories of the four main smart tourism categories. For example, Brussels was recognised for its "Mixity Walks" programme (Visit Brussels,

2020). Málaga in Spain was another winner with its creativity in assembling trails for visitors.

Sweet tweet 48

Málaga is a smart trail-maker

Smart tourist trails, Málaga

> Málaga's tourism authority has cooperated with local businesses, to provide innovative itineraries for visitors. This includes the Cicerones Málaga Confraternity Trails, which guide tourists through the most significant spaces and events involving confraternities; culinary trails, which lead visitors through the city's gastronomic highlights; the espeto trails, which allow visitors to experience life in the traditional fishing quarter and of course, the Picasso trail, which introduces visitors to the city's most famous son.

Source: European Union (2020).

CDMOs may be involved in a host of activities and programmes related to the people element of the marketing mix. This can be in the form of training and education programmes, and other efforts to engage with stakeholders, including local community residents. For example, NYC & Company in 2010 introduced an online training programme for domestic US travel agencies (NYC & Company, 2010). Wonderful Copenhagen (2020) provides several online courses about the city and its neighbourhoods in the *Copenhagen Academy*. Also, Chapter 4 described the visitor management role for CDMOs, and that can involve enhancing visitor enjoyment as well as various forms of "de-marketing" as in the Bruges and Prague cases. A rather amusing example of this occurred in Rome in 2019 as reported by *The Guardian*. The city banned "men who dress up in tunics and leather breastplates, wielding plastic swords – and make money by posing for photos" (Giuffrida, 2019).

Marketing budgeting

City tourism marketing budgets are usually drawn up on an annual basis. The European Cities Marketing survey mentioned below indicated that many city tourism marketing budgets were cut in 2020.

Sweet tweet 49

City tourism marketing budgets under siege in 2020

European City Marketing (ECM) did a survey of its members in 2020 on the status of their budgets.

> The immediate observation is that few DMOs are left unaffected by the crisis – almost 75% of the 67 DMOs in the survey have had their 2020 budgets reduced and almost a third of these have seen severe reductions of more than 50%.
>
> Source: European Cities Marketing (2020b).

There is not much written about what CDMOs should spend on marketing, although budget information is shared among the members of Destinations International and European Cities Marketing. Given this situation and the absence of benchmarks, it is best for a CDMO to apply the objective-and-task approach to estimating a marketing budget. This involves enumerating the tasks to achieve each marketing objective and then putting a price tag on achieving each task. This is also known a zero-based budgeting process.

Readers might be curious about the actual budgets of some world tourism cities. These data can be difficult to find although the budgets should be public records. One figure that can be found quite easily is the budget for London & Partners, the CDMO for the UK capital. According to the Greater London Authority, London & Partners requested a budget of £13.1 million for 2019–2020 (Greater London Authority, 2020). The size of marketing and overall CDMO budgets is, of course, dependent on the funding arrangements. CDMOs generally do not earn revenues unless they operate convention and exhibition centres. The "bed tax" formula used to support DMOs in the USA can yield significant budgets, while elsewhere CDMOs have to get their operating funds from various levels of government. Possibly the largest CDMO budget in the world is for Las Vegas. LVCVA, the CDMO, projected $357.8 million in revenues for 2019–2020. Of this total amount, it budgeted $161.4 million (45%) for marketing. Some 81.7% of LVCVA's revenues were to be from room taxes and gaming fees, and 18.2% from facility and services (it runs the Las Vegas Convention Center) (Las Vegas Convention and Visitors Authority, 2019). A note needs to be tagged onto this information in that LVCVA's income was drastically cut during 2020 as a result of travel restrictions, lockdowns and social distancing. A cut of 43% was approved (Velotta, 2020). This shows the risk of funding programmes for CDMOs that are mainly based on "user-pay taxes" such as the room tax and gaming fees in Las Vegas. These are great when tourism business is good; however, they also can be catastrophic when there is a sharp downturn.

Marketing responsibility assignment

Marketing plans assign responsibilities for specific activities and programmes. Here, it should be realised that CDMOs seldom do everything by themselves and cooperative marketing partnerships with members and other stakeholders are a very common initiative. For example, Destination Perth (2019) in Australia publishes a *Cooperative Marketing Handbook* that informs local tourism partners about how they can work together on marketing.

DMOs typically divide marketing responsibilities among different departments or divisions. These can include sales, communications and content creation, product development and research. Each will be assigned specific marketing plan activities and programmes to coordinate and control.

Marketing timetable

A month-by-month timetable is included in most city tourism marketing plans. Since many CDMOs participate in travel and tourism exhibitions and shows, their dates are included in the schedules. CDMOs should also incorporate major events and festivals in their cities in the timetable.

Marketing plan implementation

Next, marketing plans are actioned by CDMOs and partners may also be involved in their implementation.

Marketing plans, and the objectives, programmes and activities therein are the benchmarks for the fourth question.

4. How do we make sure we get there?

The fourth question is intended to stress the importance of the continuous monitoring of a city tourism marketing plan. This can also be called "formative evaluation", as it is the first step in marketing performance evaluation. It is also termed marketing control. You can think of this step as formative, meaning "in-process evaluation". One of our authors always say that "a marketing plan is printed on paper (or displayed online) but it is not cast in stone". This means that marketing plans can (and sometimes should) be modified as they are being implemented. The disruption to city tourism marketing by the COVID-19 pandemic is such a good example of an event that required marketing plans to be revised (or shelved).

Marketing implementation control

Control points ("milestones"), measurements and procedures should be inbuilt to every marketing plan. There are four items that CDMOs can measure:

- *Activities.* The activities and programmes that the CDMO initiated in the past year to achieve its marketing objectives.
- *Activity metrics.* Measures of the outputs from the CDMO's activities and programmes.
- *Productivity metrics.* The relationship of the outputs from specific activities and programmes to the resources used (financial, staff and other).
- *Performance metrics.* The results from activities and programmes in relation to marketing objectives and KPIs.

Activities and activity metrics are the two most basic measures and they are insufficient in determining a CDMO's marketing performance. Productivity and performance metrics are more reflective of what the CDMO has accomplished in its marketing given its objectives and resource usage.

As the marketing plan is being implemented the progress towards achieving each marketing objective is checked either on a monthly, bi-monthly or quarterly basis. Performance standards should be predetermined to indicate the acceptable range of deviations from expectations.

All the progress report results are added up to address the fifth and final question.

5. How do we know if we got there?

The fifth question is addressed after or just before a marketing plan ends. The task is basically to determine if the marketing objectives were achieved. In addition, the successes and failures in the plan must be used to inform the next marketing plan. This process can be thought of as "summative evaluation". In other words, it sums up the results from the implementation of a marketing plan.

Marketing performance evaluation

The UNWTO and the World Tourism Cities Federation analysed the performance of 15 cities around the world (Antwerp, Beijing, Berlin, Bogota, Buenos Aires, Cape Town, Copenhagen, Hangzhou, Linz, Marrakech, Sapporo, Seoul, Tianjin, Tokyo and Turin) (UNWTO/WTCF, 2019). Each city was asked how they measured tourism performance. The analysis produced ten success factors for city destinations. While these factors went beyond marketing, several of them had marketing implications. They were: (1) long-term vision and strategic planning; (2) public- and private-sector involvement; (3) economic support; (4) authenticity; (5) community engagement; (6) cultural-heritage investments; (7) product development; (8) events; (9) policy for sustainable development and management; and (10) technology.

Sweet tweet 50

Tourism city success stories

"The UNWTO/WTCF City Tourism Performance Research brings forward the success stories of 15 different cities worldwide with the objective of enabling other cities to observe and learn from them".

Source: UNWTO/WTCF (2019).

These success factors, as the report's sponsors say, can be of great value to other cities in their marketing activities and programmes. For example, placing a great emphasis on authentic experiences is a very fine recommendation. Also, this chapter has emphasised the requirement for and value of community engagement in CDMO marketing.

As mentioned above for the fourth question, evaluation is based upon measures of activities, activity metrics, productivity metrics and performance metrics. These metrics are built into the marketing objectives and are sometimes referred to as key performance indicators (KPIs). The measurement is part of the CDMO governance mentioned in Chapter 4 as well as being a best practice of professional destination marketing.

As an example of a statement of metrics, Visit Canberra in Australia specified these in its *Destination Marketing Strategy 2015–2020* (Visit Canberra, 2015):

- Increased exposure to and awareness of the destination and key experience pillars.
- Year-on-year growth in engagement and visitation to visitcanberra.com.au and other key digital channels.

- Increase in quality and integrity of content on owned channels, specifically on Australian Tourism Data Warehouse (ATDW) and visitcanberra.com.au.
- Year-on-year growth in national and international overnight visitor expenditure from key markets.

Although this example is a longer-term strategy rather than a one-year marketing plan, it shows that awareness, visitor volumes, visitor expenditures and content quality and integrity were the items being measured by Canberra.

The authors wish to add another warning label here for CDMOs, and it is to not take all of the credit for the tourism results in their urban areas. Why? This is because many entities are responsible for attracting visitors and their spending, not just the CDMO. A prominent association of DMOs also advises against assuming that all visitors to a city arrive solely due to the CDMO's efforts.

Sweet tweet 51

Don't take all the credit unless you can prove it!

An international association of DMOs provides this warning about the quoting of performance related to metrics:

> In practice, when addressing the issue of visitors generated, DMOs can, at the very least, set into place monitoring and research programs that identify visitors and visitor spending that were clearly and significantly generated by its efforts. The sections on the Marketing & Communications function, the Visitor Information Center and DMO Return on Investment expand on this issue. DMAI strongly encourages DMOs to take a conservative approach when determining the number of visitors generated by its efforts in order to ensure that its stated DMO Return on Investment is credible and can stand up to external scrutiny.

Source: Destination Marketing Association International (now Destinations International) (2011).

As a postscript to the above, CDMO marketers should remember that many city visitors come for VFR and personal travel. They are invited by their friends and relatives or have individual reasons for being there, such as for medical care. Also, business travellers arrive at their companies' or clients' requests. Generally, CDMOs have little influence on these travellers' decisions. It is also worth bearing in mind that many people choose to visit cities mainly through word of mouth recommendations and increasingly as a result of eWoM (electronic word of mouth) via shared content on social media platforms.

CDMOs are recommended to measure results and outputs for which they are clearly responsible. In this respect, Destinations International (then DMAI) produced a landmark set of measures for DMO marketing and sales performance evaluation (Destinations International, 2011). These measures were in five areas of activity: DMO convention sales performance reporting, DMO travel trade sales performance reporting, marketing and communications performance reporting, DMO membership performance reporting and DMO visitor information centre reporting. For each of the five areas, activity measures, productivity measures and performance measures were detailed.

Summary comments

The marketing and promotion role of CDMOs attracts much attention due to its public visibility and often is where CDMOs receive the most criticism. Everybody thinks they are a marketing expert; actually, few really are. However, destination marketing is a profession that requires training, education and actual experience for proficiency. While the systematic approach described in this chapter does not provide a suit of armour against all criticism, it is a reflection of a best practice and professional approach to destination marketing.

CDMOs are experiencing unprecedented difficulties and challenges at the start of the 2020s. Navigating these uncharted waters requires resilience and is accentuating the need for certain parts of the marketing planning process. Performance evaluation is particularly critical for CDMOs, as is the gathering of data to support performance measurement. Overall, a greater (rather than lesser) investment in research is required. Third, a reassessment of city target markets is needed, and closer-to-home segments may be worthy of more priority.

Now there has never been a better time for city tourism marketers to "think outside of the box" and to pursue markets and ideas that they did not contemplate in the past. VFRs and local people are two of these obviously neglected markets, as are the people arriving in cities for personal reasons.

There is a need to expunge the myth that city destination branding is simply coming up with a catchy slogan. Sloganeering is unscientific and a dangerous practice if it is adopted by CDMOs. Also, the branding process is not only about coming up with a beautiful and eye-catching logo. After all, logos seldom benefit visitors despite their good looks. City destination branding is a step-by-step process that ideally involves all stakeholders. The case study of Calgary presented in this chapter truly reflects this process.

The following chapters address some of the most important challenges that CDMOs face now and into the future. Although the changing trends in markets could not be fit into this chapter, they will definitely be a factor affecting the target markets of the future. Therefore, city tourism marketing approaches must be flexible and adaptable to the changes among visitors and the external environment. A marketing plan might look beautiful – in its design and contents too – however, even beautiful things often require attention.

Thought questions

1) What are the dangers of sloganeering for CDMOs?
2) Should CDMOs set their marketing budgets at levels close to their competitors? Why or why not?
3) What are the advantages and disadvantages for a CDMO in having a tourism branding approach that is not exactly the same as the overall branding of their cities?
4) Should CDMOs put aside a specific amount for marketing research each year? Why or why not?

5) Some critics say that cities like Paris and London market themselves and there is no need to spend money on promoting them. Do you agree or disagree and why?

6) Why are CDMOs in jeopardy if they do not monitor and evaluate the performance of their marketing plans?

7) How long should a city destination brand last for in years, in your opinion? Why do you suggest this figure?

8) Do you feel that cities spend too much time and effort on marketing and branding? If yes, to what should they be giving more attention? If you disagree, how is the marketing and branding emphasis to be justified?

9) The authors state that some CDMOs make their marketing plans very readily available online, while others do not reveal them publicly. What are the pros and cons of these two practices?

10) This chapter strongly warns against the dangers that CDMOs can face with taking too much of the credit for the visitor numbers and spending in their communities. Do you think this is good advice and why or why not?

References

Balch, O. (2019). Porto. A masterclass in city branding. https://www.raconteur.net/tech nology/future-cities-2019/eduardo-aires-city-branding

Boes, K., Buhalis, D., & Inversini, A. (2016). Smart tourism destinations: Ecosystems for tourism destination competitiveness. *International Journal of Tourism Cities*, 2(2), 108–124.

City of Bruges. (2019). *A Four-leafed Clover for Tourism in Bruges. Strategic Vision Memorandum Tourism 2019–2024*. Bruges, Belgium: City of Bruges.

City of Freemantle. (2018). Destination marketing strategic plan 2018–2022. https://ww w.fremantle.wa.gov.au/sites/default/files/Destination%20Marketing%20Strategic%20 Plan%202018-2022.pdf

City of Helsinki. (2018). Helsinki's city brand and tourism image has evolved through various stages of history. https://www.hel.fi/uutiset/en/kaupunginkanslia/helsinkis-city -brand-and-tourism-image-has-evolved

City of London Corporation. (2018). *Discover the City. The City of London Visitor Destination Strategy (2019-2023)*.

Coldwell, W. (2013). Tourism slogans from around the world. *The Guardian*, 21 November. https://www.theguardian.com/travel/2013/nov/21/tourism-slogans-around-the-world

Curator. (2019). The best & worst tourism slogans: From unforgettable tag lines to those that are best forgotten. https://citi.io/2019/04/09/the-best-worst-tourism-slogans-from -unforgettable-tag-lines-to-those-that-are-best-forgotten/

Destination Marketing Association International (Destinations International). 2011. *Standard DMO Performance Reporting a Handbook for Destination Marketing Organizations (DMOs)*. Washington, DC: Destinations International.

Destination Perth. (2019). *Cooperative Marketing Handbook*. https://www.experienceper th.com/sites/ep/files/2019-07/Destination%20Perth%20Cooperative%20Marketing %20Handbook.pdf

European Cities Marketing. (2020a). City cards project. https://www.europeancitiesmark eting.com/city-cards-project/

European Cities Marketing. (2020b). Urban tourism organisations hit hard by crisis. https:/ /www.europeancitiesmarketing.com/tourism-hit-hard-by-crisis/

European Union. (2020). Compendium of best practices '2019 & 2020 European Capital of Smart Tourism competitions'. https://smarttourismcapital.eu/wp-content/uploads/2020/03/Compendium_2020_FINAL.pdf

Giuffrida, A. (2019). When in Rome, don't dress as a centurion, say city authorities. *The Guardian*, 7 June. https://www.theguardian.com/world/2019/jun/07/rome-clamps-down-on-tourists-uncouth-behaviour

Gorchakova, V., & Antchak, V. (2021). An eventful tourism city. Hosting major international exhibitions in Melbourne. In Alastair M. Morrison & J. Andres Coca-Stefaniak (Eds.). *Routledge Handbook of Tourism Cities*, pp. 174–186. London: Routledge.

Greater London Authority. (2020). MD2449 London & Partners 2019/20 business plan. https://www.london.gov.uk/decisions/md2449-london-partners-201920-business-plan

Haines, G. (2016). Mapped: The world's best (and worst) tourism slogans. *The Telegraph*, 22 December. https://www.telegraph.co.uk/travel/maps-and- graphics/mapped-the-worlds-best-and-worst-tourism-slogans/

Hu, M. (2020). Expats take virtual tour of city's suburban splendours. https://www.shine.cn/news/metro/2009276916/

Hyland, P. (2019). Brazilian tourism numbers stagnating. *Tourism Review News*. https://www.tourism-review.com/brazilian-tourism-reported-stable-results-news11100

Invest Glasgow. (2019). Glasgow launches new Tourism and Visitor Plan to 2023. http://investglasgow.com/tourism-events/glasgow-launches-new-tourism-visitor-plan-2023/

Isaac, R. K., & Wichnewski, J. (2021). How credible is Vancouver's new destination brand? An analysis of a destination's brand promise and the tourist's brand experience. In Alastair M. Morrison & J. Andres Coca-Stefaniak (Eds.). *Routledge Handbook of Tourism Cities*, pp. 187–206. London: Routledge.

Kuala Lumpur City Hall. (2015). *Kuala Lumpur Tourism Master Plan 2015–2025*. Kuala Lumpur, Malaysia: Kuala Lumpur City Hall.

Las Vegas Convention and Visitors Authority. (2019). *Las Vegas Convention and Visitors Authority Fiscal Year Approved Annual Budget, 2019–2020*. Las Vegas, Nevada: Las Vegas Convention and Visitors Authority.

Light and Kiddon. (2009). *Brand Revitalization. Creating a Plan to Win*. Upper Saddle River, NJ: Pearson Education.

London & Partners. (2019). London & Partners' 2019/2020 business plan. https://files.londonandpartners.com/l-and-p/assets/business-plans-and-strategy/london-and-partners-business-plan-201920.pdf

McCarthy, E. J. (1960). *Basic Marketing: A Managerial Approach*, 1st ed. Homewood, IL: Richard D. Irwin.

Morrison, A. M. (2019). *Marketing and Managing Tourism Destinations*, 2nd ed. London: Routledge.

Morrison, A. M. (2021). Marketing and managing city tourism destinations. In Alastair M. Morrison and J. Andres Coca-Stefaniak (Eds.). *Routledge Handbook of Tourism Cities*, pp. 133–160. Routledge: London.

Newport Beach & Company. (2019). *Beyond 2020. Newport Beach & Company Destination Business Plan*. Newport Beach, CA: Newport Beach & Company.

NYC & Company. (2010). NYC & Company launches NYC training academy targeting U.S.-based travel agents. https://business.nycgo.com/press-and-media/press-releases/articles/post/press-release-nyc-company-launches-nyc-training-academcy-targeting-us-bas/

Outlook Traveller. (2020). Prague unlocks a campaign to boost tourism. https://www.outlookindia.com/outlooktraveller/travelnews/story/70654/prague-city-tourism-prague-unlocked-campaign-successful

Pantaleon, K. (2020). Hong Kong launches first-ever domestic tourism campaign: 'Hello Hong Kong: Holiday at Home'. https://www.brandinginasia.com/hong-kong-launches-first-ever-domestic-tourism-campaign-hello-hong-kong-holiday-at-home/

Paris Region Tourist Board. (2020). Reference documents. http://pro.visitparisregion.com/en/Tourism-figures/Reference-documents

Portsmouth City Council. (2018). *Portsmouth City Council Visitor Marketing Strategy 2017–2020.*

Prague City Tourism. (2020). Marketing objectives. https://www.praguecitytourism.cz/en/our-services/marketing-/prague-city-tourism-marketing-objectives

Richards, G., & Palmer, R. (2010). *Eventful Cities.* Oxford: Butterworth-Heineman.

Rotterdam Partners. (2019). *The Rotterdam Way. IABx 2019 on Tourism.* Rotterdam, Netherlands: Rotterdam Partners.

Singapore Tourism Board. (2020). About passion made possible. https://www.visitsingapore.com/about-passion-made-possible/

Tel Aviv Municipality. (2017). 2030 Tourism in Tel Aviv. In *Vision and Master Plan.* Tel Aviv, Israel: Tel Aviv Municipality.

Tourism Calgary. (2019). 2019 Tourism Calgary Town Hall. https://www.visitcalgary.com/industry-partners/programs-resources/news-events/2019-tourism-calgary-town-hall

Tourism Calgary. (2020). Brand evolution. https://www.visitcalgary.com/industry-partners/programs-resources/brand-evolution

Tourism Vancouver. (2019). *Tourism Vancouver 2030 Draft Scenario Report.* Vancouver, BC: Resonance.

Travel Portland. (2018). *Portland Tourism Master Plan.* Vancouver: Resonance.

UNWTO/WTCF. (2019). *UNWTO/WTCF City Tourism Performance Research.* Madrid, Spain: UN World Tourism Organization.

Velotta, R. (2020). Slimmed-down LVCVA budget 43% below last year's financial plan. *Las Vegas Review – Journal*, May 27. https://www.reviewjournal.com/business/tourism/slimmed-down-lvcva-budget-43-below-last-years-financial-plan-2037202/

VisitBerlin. (2020). Top medicine made in Berlin. https://about.visitberlin.de/en/top-medicine-made-berlin

Visit Brussels. (2020). MIXITY.brussels. https://visit.brussels/en/article/mixity.brussels

Visit Canberra. (n.d.). Destination marketing strategy 2015–2020. https://tourism.act.gov.au/wp-content/uploads/2017/05/Marketing_Strategy_15-20.pdf

Wonderful Copenhagen. (2020). Copenhagen Academy. https://www.onlinetraveltraining.com/free-courses/providers/copenhagenacademy#

World Travel Market (WTM). 2020. The history of World Travel Market. https://www.wtm.com/portfolio/en-gb/history.html

Zawya. (2020). Oman plans its own Eiffel Tower. https://www.zawya.com/mena/en/business/story/Oman_plans_its_own_Eiffel_Tower-SNG_177202724/

Trends, issues and challenges for world tourism cities

Resident quality of life, sustainability, smart tourism and smart cities, crisis events and the relative growth of Asian tourism cities are featured in the chapters in Part III.

Chapter 7 defines quality of life and explains why it must be an issue of concern in city tourism destination management. Tourism rankings are compared with their quality of life counterparts for the top world tourism cities. The twin topics of carrying capacity and overtourism are tackled, and overcrowding is pinpointed as a key disturbance for local residents. Solutions to this issue are identified, and the need for visitor management is highlighted.

Chapter 8 examines the concept of sustainability and how it applies to city destinations. It examines the impacts of tourism, both positive and negative, followed by a discussion on the sustainability measures and policies promoted by urban destinations. The contributions of world tourism cities towards achieving the Sustainable Development Goals and addressing climate change are reviewed.

Chapter 9 discusses the progress of ICTs, the Internet of Things and new technologies that impact society in general and tourism in particular. It explains what a smart city is, its dimensions and the "smart" initiatives promoted by global cities from different parts of the world, focusing on their relevance to tourism. It introduces the concepts of smart destinations and smart tourism, with an emphasis on how these apply to city destinations, and also notes a number of challenges associated with this rapid progress. The latest technologies and debates that are expected to shape the tourism ecosystem in the future are discussed.

Chapter 10 reviews different types of crises and disasters that can affect world tourism cities and discusses a number of crisis management approaches that can be adopted by these destinations to limit the impact of such events. Crisis communication is a vital part when dealing with crises and disasters, with accurate and timely data needed to be provided to those affected.

Chapter 11 identifies the factors that are contributing to this rise of Asian cities using the 10 As model. In particular transportation network improvements are reviewed, as is the expansion of culture and heritage tourism, nature, shopping and food tourism, entertainment attractions, health and medical tourism and cruises. Major growth markets for Asian city tourism are pinpointed.

DOI: 10.4324/9781003111412-9

Unique concepts in Part III:

ADVICE model (Chapter 7)
Stakeholders' roles in sustainable tourism (Chapter 8)
ICT evolution (Chapter 9)
Social-mediated crisis communication (SMCC) model (Chapter 10)
10 As applied to Asian cities (Chapter 11)

Short breaks: Part III

7. Vienna
8. Valencia
9. Santiago
10. Bangkok
11. Singapore

Sweet tweets: Part III

52. Tourism's employment of youth is important for Ireland
53. QoL is broader than standard of living and GDP
54. What Longwoods International says about the importance of residents
55. Low ranking for Paris on Mercer survey
56. Barcelona and Amsterdam take action on Airbnb
57. Paris is on a mission to improve QoL
58. Kings Park in Perth, Western Australia
59. Pandemic exposes tourism's ill effects on cities
60. Keeping the angklung culture alive in Bandung
61. The contribution that travel and tourism bring to city economies
62. Tourism cities and crime
63. Barcelona is threatening to shut out tourists
64. Bonn aiming for more sustainability
65. Challenges of sustainable tourism implementation in urban areas
66. Seoul promotes sustainable urban tourism
67. Old and New Towns of Edinburgh – Management Plan
68. The public transport system in Singapore
69. Cities are on the front line of tackling climate change
70. Building a smart city destination – Hanoi
71. Los Angeles as an example of a smart city
72. South Korea – smart governance during a global pandemic
73. Future City Glasgow – people make Glasgow
74. Bucharest on its way to becoming a smarter city
75. Smart city strategy – the Royal Borough of Greenwich, London
76. The application of IoT in Sanya, China
77. Examples of smart tourism initiatives
78. ExpATHENS Cultural Route – "The Road of Museums"
79. New trends in ICT and tourism
80. Examples of recovery time needed for different types of crisis

81. The theatre of terrorism to cities
82. 2020 – worst year in tourism history
83. Visit London website – coronavirus update: Latest information and advice
84. Action Guide on Recovery and Revitalization of City Tourism amid COVID-19
85. Examples of commonly employed tourism disaster recovery messages
86. ASEAN deepens cooperation in tourism to deal with COVID-19
87. Shopping the markets of Kuala Lumpur
88. Food as another ingredient of Asianness
89. Theme parks and attractions expand in China
90. Bangkok is a leading medical tourism destination
91. Food safety improving in Asia
92. Tourism in Asia plunges in first half of 2020
93. Is Asia seventh heaven or 7-Eleven?
94. Under the red lights of Bangkok

Chapter 7

Quality of life and resident well-being in world tourism cities

Abstract

Although not traditionally given adequate attention, the overtourism concept has shone a brighter light on tourism's impacts on city resident quality of life and well-being.

The chapter begins by defining quality of life and explains why it must be an issue of concern in city tourism destination management. A general trend is noted in public awareness of this issue in major European cities and elsewhere. The academic research on resident quality of life and well-being is reviewed.

Eurostat's "8+1" dimensions, OECD and other indicators of quality of life, well-being and liveability are used to frame the discussion on how tourism affects residents in world tourism cities. Tourism rankings are compared with their quality of life counterparts for the top world tourism cities. Several case studies where cities are taking the initiative to improve resident quality of life are provided.

The twin topics of carrying capacity and overtourism are tackled, and overcrowding is pinpointed as a key disturbance for local residents. Solutions to this issue are identified and the need for visitor management is highlighted and exemplified through the ADVICE model.

Keywords: 8 + 1 dimensions; ADVICE model; carrying capacity; overtourism; quality of life (QoL); subjective well-being.

DOI: 10.4324/9781003111412-10

Learning objectives

Having read this chapter, you should be able to:

- Define quality of life.
- Identify the dimensions or indicators of quality of life.
- Elaborate on the research about quality of life.
- Describe what cities are doing to improve resident quality of life.
- Discuss the relationship between carrying capacity and overtourism.
- Explain the ADVICE model for visitor management.

Chapters 4 to 6 in Part II discuss the management, planning, development, marketing and branding of tourism in cities. In a very broad sense, it is accurate to say that city destination management is charged with maximising the positive benefits of tourism for all stakeholders while minimising negative consequences. Although easy to say, this is not simple to accomplish in a practical way on the ground. More residents are developing negative attitudes towards visitors, and residents and visitors are two key stakeholder groups for city destination management.

Part III examines trends, issues and challenges for world tourism cities, and one of these is how to balance tourism growth and city resident quality of life. Quality of life is emerging as an increasingly important issue and concern for tourism cities. Additionally, there is a trend for more research to be done on the quality of life and tourism. The issue and trend are framed in the following ways based on the definition of issues and trends from Chapter 5:

- The resident quality of life issue is a critical topic that people are discussing and writing about. The issue within cities is unresolved, and people have differing opinions on how to deal with it. There are proponents (advocates) of maintaining tourism at current levels and opponents (critics) who wish to place greater restrictions on tourist volumes and activities. Resident quality of life is a long-term issue for cities.
- The quality of life research trend is a change in the increasing rate of publishing about the interactions of tourism and quality of life. This is considered to be a positive contribution to eventually solving quality of life issues raised by tourism. The upward trend can be measured by the number of articles and books published on the topic. This is expected to be a long-term trend. The rate of publishing on the topic seems to be higher for Europe and North America.

The quality of life issue within cities is producing challenges for city governments, many of which are already dealing with urban growth dilemmas. Resources are being channelled into new ways of handling issues of pollution, traffic congestion, significant population increases and increasing crime rates.

From the city destination management perspective, based on Chapter 4, the two roles most involved here are community relationships and involvement and visitor management. The first role relates to resident life quality; the second affects the quality of life of city visitors.

Before delving more deeply into this topic, the authors wanted to highlight one critical point – many more economic activities and other factors influence quality of life than just tourism. It is difficult to separate out the tourism effects from these other factors.

What is quality of life?

Defining quality of life (QoL) has proven to be quite difficult, and there are numerous explanations of what it means (Andereck and Nyaupane, 2011). These two authors say QoL is a person's life satisfaction and feelings of contentment or fulfilment. They also stress that QoL is partly subjective (or qualitative) and also has aspects with quantitative measures. Uysal, Sirgy, Woo and Kim (2016) term the former as subjective well-being that includes need satisfaction, life satisfaction, perceived QOL, happiness or life fulfilment.

The European Commission's Eurostat unit suggests that QoL be measured by the "8 + 1" dimensions, and these are shown in Table 7.1. They also specify 25 sub-dimensions (topics). Eurostat specifies how to measure each of the dimensions. As you can see from Table 7.1, some of the sub-dimensions are quite measurable (quantitative), such as income and quantity of employment; others, such as life satisfaction, are very subjective and qualitative. QoL can be measured at the city (or country) level and at an individual resident level. Most of the ranking schemes that are available are at the country or city level, while tourism researchers bring this down to the individual resident level. The Eurostat data is published at the country QoL level.

Sweet tweet 52

Tourism's employment of youth is important for Ireland

One of the employment benefits of tourism that is often quoted is that it provides jobs, especially for women and younger people. The latter is stressed in Ireland's policy on tourism:

> The tourism sector is an essential component of Ireland's employment base. It supports around 325,000 jobs on the island of Ireland. In addition, many third-level students are employed on a part-time or seasonal basis in the tourism industry. The income earned from this employment assists in meeting their living expenses and costs associated with third-level education.

Source: Government of Ireland (2019).

How tourism affects all the QoL dimensions and sub-dimensions is unknown as they have not yet been collectively measured. However, the proponents of tourism suggest that it positively influences 1.1, 2.1 and 5.1 (income, quantity of employment and leisure). Increased income and more employment (1.1 and 2.1) lead to increased personal consumption that improves people's material conditions. Greater availability of leisure amenities and facilities (5.1) is often cited as a benefit of tourism to communities. It can also be argued that having more leisure and recreation activities also can enhance resident health (3.1). Some of the research to be discussed later suggests that tourism creates social interactions (5.2) with visitors that some residents value. With the increased priority on safety and security (6.2) in cities from crime, scams and terrorism, this may be seen as a benefit for residents and visitors. Enhanced natural environments (8.1 to 8.3) in cities appear to be another benefit for both groups, as is well evidenced by the

Table 7.1 The "8 + 1" dimensions of quality of life

Dimensions	Topics (sub-dimensions)
1. Material living conditions	1.1. Income
	1.2. Consumption
	1.3. Material conditions
2. Productive or main capacity	2.1. Quantity of employment
	2.2. Quality of employment
	2.3. Other main activity
3. Health	3.1. Outcomes
	3.2. Drivers: healthy and unhealthy behaviours
	3.3. Access to healthcare
4. Education	4.1. Competences and skills
	4.2. Lifelong learning
	4.3. Opportunities for education
5. Leisure and social interactions	5.1. Leisure
	5.2. Social interactions
6. Economic security and physical safety	6.1 Economic security and vulnerability
	6.2. Physical and personal security
7. Governance and basic rights	7.1. Institutions and public services
	7.2. Discrimination and equal opportunities
	7.3. Active citizenship
8. Natural and living environment	8.1. Pollution (including noise)
	8.2. Access to green and recreational spaces
	8.3. Landscape and built environment
9. Overall experience of life (the +1)	9.1. Life satisfaction
	9.2. Affects
	9.3. Meaning and purpose

Source: Eurostat (2020a; 2020b). Adapted by authors.

case examples later in this chapter. The academic research studies discussed later have a focus on overall experience of life and life satisfaction (9.1) and are generally positive with respect to tourism.

On the contrary, there are critics who assert that the quality of tourism employment is relatively low. Again, on the positive side, it is often argued that tourism provides more leisure and recreation facilities and activities for local residents. There are also criticisms of tourism for negative social, cultural and environmental impacts.

Eurostat takes its overall experience of life dimension (#9 in Table 7.1) from the Organization for Economic Cooperation and Development (OECD) guidelines on measuring subjective well-being (OECD, 2013). For the life satisfaction sub-dimension, the items to be measured are work satisfaction, health satisfaction and income satisfaction. Affects include happiness, worry and anger. Eudaemonic well-being is comprised of meaning and purpose, autonomy and competence.

In addition to Eurostat, there are several other governmental agencies and private companies that have developed QoL indicator sets or their proxies and that publish rankings. OECD is one of the agencies because of its *OECD Better Lives Initiative*, and it has developed the OECD well-being framework. The indicators in the OECD framework are divided into current well-being and resources for future well-being. Current well-being has 11 indicators – income and wealth, work and job quality, housing, health, knowledge and skills, environment quality, subjective well-being, safety, work–life balance, social connections and civil engagement. The resources for future well-being are four types of capital – natural, economic, human and social.

City liveability rankings provide other representations of quality of life and the two most recognised systems are those of the Economist Intelligence Unit and Mercer. The EIU ranks are assigned based on scores for the five indicators of stability, healthcare, culture and environment, education and infrastructure. Ten categories are used in the Mercer rankings (political and social environment, economic environment, socio-cultural environment, medical and health considerations, schools and education, public services and transportation, recreation, consumer goods, housing and natural environment) (Mercer, 2019). The Numbeo scheme of quality of life rankings is discussed later.

Why study and be concerned about QoL and tourism?

Now that the meaning and indicators of quality of life have been explained, the next topic is to explore its significance for tourism within cities. Historically, the planning and development of cities, and tourism, have had a focus on the creation of economic benefits including employment and income. Whilst this economic emphasis is changing in several developing countries, there are nations that continue to put GDP at the top of their agendas.

Sweet tweet 53

QoL is broader than standard of living and GDP

The main argument for measuring QoL is that the results provide a more holistic view of how city residents are faring on factors that are important to them. Eurostat summarises this point as follows:

> Quality of life (QoL) is broader than economic output and living standards. It includes the full range of factors influencing what people value in life beyond its material aspects. Factors potentially affecting our quality of life range from job and health status to social relationships, security and governance.

This statement reflects the "social indicators movement" that emphasises measuring the broader range of factors including subjective well-being.

Sources: Eurostat (2020a, 2020b); Uysal, Sirgy, Woo and Kim (2016).

To be honest, city marketers were traditionally given a first priority of getting "heads in beds", meaning getting more people into hotel rooms. They were not charged with the responsibility of maintaining or improving resident quality of life. Because of the complaints and demonstrations against tourism in several famous European destinations, as well as a maturing of city destination management, there is an increasing recognition that quality of life – for residents and visitors – matters and must be continuously in focus. The scholarly attention in tourism to quality of life issues peaked after the overtourism concept was coined in 2016, and that research literature is the next topic of discussion.

Research on quality of life and tourism

Uysal et al. (2016) in a review of QoL and well-being research in tourism found that it was gaining momentum in terms of scholarly contributions. This was confirmed in a search of the Scopus database at the time of writing that showed 1,029 documents for a search by quality of life and tourism. The first document to appear in a tourism journal was in 1987 in *Tourism Management*. Interestingly, this short article was about urban tourism and urged cities to provide "improved quality of life" in the form of restaurants, shops, attractions and entertainment (Hall, 1987). The three most highly cited articles are Crouch and Ritchie (1999), Andereck and Nyaupane (2011) and Kim, Uysal and Sirgy (2013). With 1,029 documents and 671 cites for the most quoted, this indicates that QoL is a moderately popular theme for tourism researchers. However, it must be mentioned here that there are two "branches" of QoL and tourism research. The first concerns how travel affects visitor quality of life; the second is about how tourism influences resident quality of life. The latter is the theme for this chapter.

Uysal et al. (2016) identified three streams of research concerning tourism and resident QoL: (1) identifying the mediators between the impact of tourism and QoL; (2) comparing different types of community residents; and (3) investigating residents' QoL depending upon the level of tourism development over time. These authors importantly point out that tourism is generally assumed to have positive benefits for communities and residents; however, the assumptions about the costs and benefits to different stakeholders are rarely tested with the exception of some researchers including Chase, Amsden and Phillips (2012) and Weiermair and Peters (2012). Chase, Amsden and Philipps, while acknowledging the potential negative QoL impacts on residents in tourism-dependent destinations, urged the active engagement of local people, as critical stakeholders, in tourism planning and development. Weiermair and Peter suggested that there are many tourism stakeholders in destinations, including residents, and they do not necessarily perceive the positive and negative effects on QoL in exactly the same ways.

Crouch and Ritchie (1999, p. 139) stated that there were difficulties in measuring the impacts of tourism on resident quality of life. Andereck and Nyaupane (2011) later took up this challenge and proposed and tested a new model for measuring tourism's impact on resident QoL using a survey in Arizona. Eight tourism quality of life (TQoL) factors (domains) were identified – recreation amenities, community pride and awareness, economic strength, natural/cultural preservation, community well-being, way of life, crime and substance abuse and urban issues. They confirmed positive TQoL influences of more jobs, better shopping, more recreation opportunities, cultural exchange, better public services and more parks, and negative effects including more crime and traffic (p. 258). As in previous studies, Andereck and Nyaupane (2011) concluded that "those who have contact with tourists on a frequent basis view tourism in a much more positive light than those who do not".

Kim, Uysal and Sirgy (2013) conducted research in Virginia with residents to determine if they perceived the economic, social, cultural and environmental impacts of tourism. If they were aware of the impacts, the researchers also wanted to test how they affected resident sense of well-being. The results were that residents did, in fact, sense the impacts of tourism. A positive relationship was found between positive perceptions of tourism's economic impact and residents' sense of material well-being. Also, resident satisfaction with community well-being was positively correlated with feelings of the beneficial social impacts of tourism. The same was true in the relationship of positive cultural impacts and emotional well-being. Conversely, if the respondents perceived that tourism was negatively influencing the environment, their feelings of health and safety were adversely affected.

Woo, Kim and Uysal (2015) introduced the variable of the perceived value of tourism development and found it was a determinant of sense of material and non-material life domain satisfaction. The survey respondents were from Virginia, Las Vegas, Hawaii and Orlando in the USA. A new finding was that QoL had a positive impact on resident perceptions of future tourism development.

The results from the research by Biagi, Ladu, Meleddu and Royuela (2020) on the tourism destinations of Sitges in Spain and Alghero in Sardinia, Italy, and urban quality of life (UQoL) were not as positive as the previously mentioned researchers. They found that there was a prevailing negative effect of tourism from the resident perspective, especially in the context of the accessibility of tourism amenities. The researchers stressed that the presence of amenities was not as important to resident QoL perceptions as the actual accessibility to these amenities. This is indeed a very important observation as it reflects that it is the individual's assessment of how tourism affects them personally rather than everyone in the city as a whole that truly shows the QoL impacts.

While it is difficult to accurately reflect a consensus in this previous research on tourism's effects on resident QoL, there are findings that tend to be repeated. First, there is definite support that QoL must be measured by material (e.g., income and employment) and non-material factors (e.g., subjective well-being). Second, not all residents perceive the QoL effects in the same way. Third, it is how people perceive the personal (rather than general) impacts of tourism on their QoL that is of the greatest significance.

Research on visitor QoL

The focus of this chapter was explicitly on city resident QoL. This does not mean that visitor QoL is unimportant, nor does it imply that city destination management should ignore this phenomenon. In fact, the 10 As model discussed in Chapters 5 and 11 has criteria that are connected to visitor experiences in city destinations. Also, the visitor management role includes steps taken to measure the expectations of visitors and to enhance their enjoyment levels within cities.

Uysal et al. reviewed 35 of these research works and classified them into three groups: (1) demonstrating an effect of tourism on the QoL of individual tourists, (2) mediators between tourism experience and QoL of individual tourists and (3) personal, situational and cultural characteristics helping to explain the link between tourism experience and QoL.

The most cited research works include Gilbert and Abdullah (2004), Neal, Uysal and Sirgy (2007), Dolnicar, Yanamandram and Cliff (2012) and McCabe and Johnson (2013). Gilbert and Abdullah (2004) found that holidaymakers had a greater sense of well-being than non-holidaymakers. Neal, Uysal and Sirgy developed a model around tourism as a component of leisure life. She and her co-researchers found that satisfaction with tourism services during trips spilled over positively to other aspects of QoL. Dolnicar and her colleagues, using online panel data from Australia, also found that holidays contributed positively to QoL for the majority of people; however, the relative importance varied significantly among respondents with different circumstances (e.g., financial constraints). McCabe and Johnson examined the QoL effects of holiday breaks by social tourists, being those who are given financial support for their travel. Once again, they found that taking holidays had a beneficial impact on people's subjective well-being domain of QoL.

Resident opinion and attitude surveys about tourism

There are many research studies to determine resident attitudes and opinions about tourism. Organisations such as the Hawaii Tourism Authority (2019) regularly survey resident sentiment on tourism. UNWTO and Ipsos (2019) conducted a global survey of 12,000 online respondents in 15 countries about city resident experiences with and perceptions of tourism in their communities. Destinations International (2019) published a white paper based upon research done on *"American Resident Sentiment towards Tourism"*. Longwoods International is a research company that conducts these types of research studies on resident sentiment about tourism.

Sweet tweet 54

What Longwoods International says about the importance of residents

Longwoods thinks that economic development and QoL must be balanced.

"Increasingly, destination management must be considered a partnership between the industry and residents, to ensure that tourism development benefits both parties and contributes to the community economically while maintaining or enhancing quality of life for its residents".

Source: Longwoods International (2020).

There are those who argue that the resident surveys as they are being conducted do not measure QoL (e.g., Andereck and Nyaupane, 2011). These studies tend to ask residents for their attitudes and opinions about tourism and not question people about how it affects their personal QoL. Nevertheless, if conducted continuously these surveys are useful to CDMOs in tracking trends in resident feelings about tourism. Also, in a practical sense they indicate that CDMOs care and are concerned about resident opinions and are one method for engaging with locals.

Figure 7.1 lists some questions that could be included in a resident survey.

Overall, these two "branches" of QoL research in tourism are making a valuable contribution to our understanding of tourism's effects. The research literature is particularly useful in bringing the focus down to the individual resident level as well as indicating that the QoL impacts differ from person to person and from place to place. It is dangerous, therefore, to make broad and sweeping assumptions and assertions on how tourism affects resident QoL.

Before leaving the topic of research on QoL, it needs to be mentioned that there are several academic journals dedicated to the topic. These include *Applied Research in Quality of Life* (Springer) and the *Quality of Life Research* (Springer). There are also many books published about QoL.

Relationship between QoL and world tourism city standings

Is there a positive relationship between world tourism city standings and QoL rankings? Are the top tourism cities in the world also great places in which to live? These are interesting questions, and they can be answered by contrasting different ranking system scores. Large cities are complex and home to millions of people and several economic sectors and activities. Tourism is seldom, if ever, the sole activity that supports all urban employment and income generation.

Before making the comparisons, the case of Paris and local sentiments is previewed below:

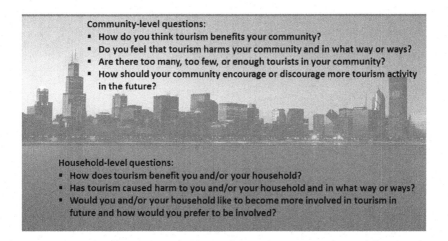

Figure 7.1 Potential questions for a resident survey (The authors, background image of Chicago from PresentationPro).

Sweet tweet 55

Low ranking for Paris on Mercer survey

As mentioned in Chapter 3 and shown in Table 3.1, Paris was the second highest ranking world tourism city in 2018 based on the number of overnight international visitors. However, it was only in 39th place in the Mercer survey of city liveability in 2018. The following quote from a local Parisian source acknowledges that this great tourism city has some QoL issues:

> One thing that Paris fell down on, according to the survey was in the category of "medical and health considerations", which is judged by a variety of factors including sewage, waste disposal and air pollution. Paris has been dogged by spikes in air pollution ... (see Figure 7.2) ... in recent years which has prompted authorities to ban the most polluting cars from the city and make public transport free.

Source: The Local (2018).

Figure 7.2 Air pollution in Paris (Courtesy: Unsplash.com, Leonard Cotte).

Table 7.2 Comparison of world tourism city, QoL and liveability rankings

City	World tourism city ranking, 2018	Numbeo quality of life ranking, 2020	Mercer liveability ranking, 2019
Bangkok, Thailand	1	227	133
Paris, France	2	174	39
London, UK	3	153	41
Dubai, UAE	4	103	74
Singapore	5	131	25
Kuala Lumpur, Malaysia	6	203	85
New York, US	7	137	44
Istanbul, Turkey	8	189	130
Tokyo, Japan	9	97	49
Seoul, South Korea	10	152	77

Sources: Mastercard (2019); Mercer (2019); Numbeo (2020).

It can be argued that comparing ranking schemes measuring different variables is rough and incomplete, and that is so. However, as the above opinions about Paris indicate, people do make these sorts of comparisons. Numbeo is a crowd-sourced cost of living database that provides extensive quality of life information (Numbeo, 2020). It publishes rankings of cities by their quality of life. Numbeo's QoL index is made up of the purchasing power, safety, health care, cost of living, property price to income ratio, traffic commute time, pollution and climate indexes.

Table 7.2 contrasts the Mastercard rankings of world tourism cities and their respective rankings by Numbeo and Mercer. The results are rather surprising if not consistent, as only one of Mastercard's top ten cities made the top 100 in QoL, and that was Tokyo scraping in at 97th. Two other Asian cities – Bangkok and Kuala Lumpur – had the poorest QoL rankings of the Mastercard top ten at 227th and 203rd, respectively. The Mercer liveability ranks are higher for world tourism cities; however, Singapore is the best at 25th and Bangkok ranks 133rd. While the results raise more questions than they provide answers, the comparisons seem to suggest that the top world tourism cities are not necessarily the best places in which to reside.

Bangkok was the first-rated world tourism city in *the Global Destination City Index* by Mastercard. However, the city is plagued with traffic congestion (Figure 7.3) and air pollution (Yuda, 2020). Again, it must be said that this is a result of rapid urbanisation.

In interpreting the results in Table 7.2, it needs to be said that medium- and small-sized cities tend to be rated higher on QoL and liveability rankings (for example, Vienna, Austria, Figure 7.4). Due to the greater size, scale and complexity of the largest cities, there are more difficulties in addressing issues that deflate QoL indicator scores. Another caveat here is that there may not be a direct, negative correlation between the numbers of tourists and QoL. That has not been universally proven to date except through anecdotal evidence, and it must also be recognised that multiple other non-tourism factors affect QoL scores.

Figure 7.3 Traffic in Bangkok (Courtesy: Unsplash.com, Tan Kaninthanon).

SHORT TRIP 7

Vienna ranks at the top for liveability

Vienna, Austria, is mentioned in several chapters of this book, and for good reason. It is rated as the top city in the world for international conferences by ICCA. It is a world leader in setting the standards for green meetings (*greater energy efficiency, waste avoidance and an environmentally friendly arrival and departure of the guests* according to Tourism Vienna, 2020a). Chapter 5 talks about its CDMO's rather innovative tourism strategy; and now in Chapter 7 the discussion is about Vienna's high quality of life and liveability ratings. However, Vienna was not among the top 20 in Mastercard's *Global Destination City Index 2019*. Vienna ranked first in the *Mercer Quality of Living Ranking* for 2019, and this was for the tenth year in succession. The next cities with the highest positive rankings were Zurich, Auckland, Munich and Vancouver. The City of Vienna summarised the 2019 Mercer top ranking as follows:

Figure 7.4 Vienna ranks highly on quality of life and liveability (Courtesy: Unsplash.com, Anna Hunko).

Vienna's excellent infrastructure, the well-structured and reliable public transport network, the first-class water supply and healthcare and the large variety of cultural facilities and leisure activities were the main reasons why the Austrian capital was again ranked 1st. The low crime rate and the availability of high-quality housing and leisure facilities also added to Vienna's top ranking.

Vienna's population of around 1.93 million in 2020 was far less than London's almost nine million. Tourism Vienna (2020b) reports approximately 6.28 million arrivals from foreign countries in 2019 and around 1.65 million domestic arrivals. The major sources of international visitors are Germany, the USA, Italy, the UK and China. As mentioned in this chapter, Vienna is one of the ten European cities that are calling for tighter government controls on sharing economy provider, Airbnb. It is a strong advocate of the smart tourism city movement.

Vienna has two World Heritage List cultural sites in the Historic Centre of Vienna and the Palace and Gardens of Schönbrunn. The centrepiece of the Historic

Centre is St. Stephen's Cathedral. The city also has several wonderful museums, splendid gardens, and is famous for its coffee house culture. Vienna prides itself as a destination of openness, tolerance and diversity, and these are attributes that directly contribute to QoL. Two prominent examples are the Life Ball held in Vienna and Tourism Vienna's LBGT initiatives (Tourism Vienna, 2020c).

Discussion points:

1. How is being a smaller city an advantage to Vienna with respect to QoL?
2. Why is Vienna such a popular destination for international conferences?
3. Will Vienna's QoL and liveability be adversely affected if its tourist arrivals increase more rapidly? Why or why not?

Sources: City of Vienna (2019); ICCA (2020); Mastercard (2019); Mercer (2019, 2020); Tourism Vienna (2020a, 2020b, 2020c).

Human Development Index (HDI)

HDI is another important yardstick that is related to standards of living and QoL. National HDI statistics are produced on a country basis by the United Nations Development Programme (UNDP). UNDP defines HDI as "a composite index measuring average achievement in three basic dimensions of human development – a long and healthy life, knowledge and a decent standard of living". The indicators measured are life expectancy at birth, expected years of schooling, mean years of schooling and gross national income (GNI) per capita. In 2018, the top ten countries in order were Norway, Switzerland, Ireland, Germany, Hong Kong SAR, Australia, Iceland, Sweden, Singapore and the Netherlands (UNDP, 2020). In terms of the ten top-ranking cities in Mastercard's Global City Destination Index 2019, some are in countries that received relatively low HDI rankings, including Bali (Indonesia at #111 in HDI), Bangkok (Thailand at #77) and Kuala Lumpur (Malaysia at #61).

There are other ranking schemes and indicators of QoL, including the city QoL rankings of Teleport (2020), the Knight Frank *City Well-Being Index* (Knight Frank, 2020) and the *World Happiness Report* (Sustainable Solutions Network, 2020). There are too many of these to review in this chapter and so their existence is just acknowledged. Several of them are oriented towards providing advice to people contemplating moves to particular cities.

City quality of life improvement cases

While QoL and liveability scores are like a still photo taken at one point in history, cities and city development are dynamic, always changing. Most cities are actively involved with initiatives to improve resident QoL, and some case studies are now reviewed.

Barcelona and Amsterdam

Sharing accommodation providers and especially Airbnb have raised several issues for cities and their residents. Amsterdam, Barcelona, Berlin, Bordeaux, Brussels, Krakow,

Munich, Paris, Valencia and Vienna are ten European cities that are advocating tighter regulation of Airbnb hosts and their premises (O'Sullivan, 2019). The primary reason is because these operations are disrupting the normal daily lives of residents.

Sweet tweet 56

Barcelona and Amsterdam take action on Airbnb

Barcelona and Amsterdam are two of the cities that have taken action to curb the growth and impacts of what some call the "grey accommodation sector".

> Barcelona is one of the most popular destinations in Spain and the world. In this city, Airbnbs must get licensed, but no new permits were issued in recent years. Hosts in Amsterdam also face Airbnb restrictions so they can only rent their properties for a limited number of days. As of January 2019, there is a 30-day limit out of the year and the city collects a 6% tourist tax on all bookings.

Source: Passive Airbnb (2018).

Copenhagen

Another city that must be mentioned here is Copenhagen in Denmark, which was the topic for Short break 5 in Chapter 5. That vignette on the Danish capital highlighted that Copenhagen was considered to be very bicycle-friendly and that is no accident. The city government has developed an integrative public transport model that includes a combination of bus stops and cycle parking facilities at metro stations (Wong, 2014).

Hong Kong

Hong Kong is often associated with high urban densities, air pollution and traffic congestion. However, perhaps not as well known is the Hong Kong Wetland Park in the northern part of Tin Shui Wai in the New Territories. The 61-hectare park is one of the very best in the Asia-Pacific region and is a popular destination for residents and visitors. The mission of the park, which was opened in 2006, is as follows (Hong Kong Wetland Park, 2020):

> The mission of the Hong Kong Wetland Park is to foster public awareness, knowledge and understanding of the inherent values of wetlands throughout the East Asian region and beyond, and to marshal public support and action for wetland conservation. The Hong Kong Wetland Park will also be a world-class ecotourism facility to serve both local residents and overseas tourists.

This is a good example of a facility that serves tourists and also enhances the QoL of local residents.

Paris

Although a rather sad photo of air pollution features in Figure 7.2 earlier, the city and its leaders are taking steps to improve the situation. The following quote summarises the intentions to make QoL improvements in the French capital.

Sweet tweet 57

Paris is on a mission to improve QoL

The Mayor of Paris is determined to improve the environmental conditions in the city. The reduction of air pollution is at the centre of this agenda.

> Paris Mayor Anne Hidalgo has been on a mission to rid the city of cars for some time, and to reduce the air pollution that kills 6,600 people in the Paris metropolitan area, the majority of them in banlieues (suburbs), every year. In June, she was handily re-elected on a platform to accelerate the ecological transformation of Paris. She has vowed to make permanent some of the changes she enacted during the lockdown and to regreen Paris with urban forests.

Source: Kamdar (2020).

One of the ways that Paris is trying to achieve its objectives is by making it more attractive to use public transportation. In September 2020, the city allowed passengers under the age of 18 to use the public transportation network for free (Bloomberg City Lab, 2020).

Perth, Western Australia

Perth ranks highly in the Mercer, EIU and Numbeo ranking schemes. Jones and Newsome (2015) argue that the accessibility to nature in Perth and its surrounds are a reason for its favourable quality of life scores. They indicate that Kings Park is one of the largest parks in Australia within the central area of a city and that it receives around six million visitors annually.

Sweet tweet 58

Kings Park in Perth, Western Australia

Overlooking the city of Perth and the Swan River is Kings Park.

> Kings Park is home to the spectacular Western Australian Botanic Garden, which displays over 3,000 species of the State's unique flora. Two thirds of the 400 hectare park is protected as bushland and provides a haven for native biological diversity.

> Kings Park is rated as the top attraction in Perth in TripAdvisor and earns a five-star rating based on more than 12,000 reviews.
>
> Source: Department of Biodiversity, Conservation and Attractions (2020).

Singapore

Like Paris, Singapore was another of the top world tourism cities not to be ranked particularly highly in the QoL and liveability rating schemes. However, there is a visionary slogan about Singapore that it is transforming *"From garden city to city in a garden"*. This means that residents are surrounded by nature everywhere although they are living in a city. The Singapore Botanic Gardens are on UNESCO's World Heritage List; however, there is much more, including the Gardens by the Bay and its Supertrees. Six initiatives are being used to realise the City in a Garden vision for Singapore:

- Establish world-class gardens.
- Rejuvenate urban parks and enliven the streetscape.
- Optimise urban spaces for greenery and recreation.
- Enrich biodiversity in the urban environment.
- Enhance competencies of the landscape and horticultural industry.
- Engage and inspire communities to co-create a greener Singapore.

In this respect, Singapore is now recognised as a world leader in biophilic design, which essentially means bringing nature into cities (Newman, 2014). Newman says that a biophilic city introduces "landscaping both into and onto buildings, walls, roads and concrete watercourses to bring nature into every element of the built environment" (Kellert, Heerwagen, and Mador, 2011; Beatley 2011).

Stockholm and others

Sustainability and smart cities are the topics for the next two chapters; however, it is appropriate here to mention what some cities are doing to deal with the twin problems of traffic congestion and air pollution. These are not necessarily caused by visitors to cities, although in many cases they do contribute to the issues. Many solutions are available and have been proposed to counter traffic congestion in cities. Smarter Cambridge Transport in the UK (2016) outlines several approaches in three categories – one-hit solutions (e.g., widen roads), low capital investment (e.g., improve perceptions of public buses), medium capital investment (e.g., using inbound flow control) and high capital investment (e.g., new light rail system).

Stockholm, capital city of Sweden, in 2006 introduced "congestion taxes" on a trial basis in 2006 and later after a referendum they were made permanent (Centre for Transport Studies, Stockholm, 2014; Wong, 2014). Although controversial when first proposed, these taxes have proven successful in reducing congestion at traditional highway bottlenecks, increasing travel speeds while reducing travel times and improving air quality.

Some cities in the UK are proposing to set up clean air zones (CAZs), including Bath, Birmingham and Manchester. Hong Kong has introduced a minibus system to relieve traffic congestion (Transport Department, 2020).

The case studies show initiatives that deal with traffic congestion, the greening of cities and making adjustments to handle sharing economy accommodation providers. Earlier chapters highlighted programmes introducing tourism police units in South Korea, Thailand and Turkey. They also demonstrate that, while it is easy to be critical of certain tourism cities due to some of their urban issues, one must also recognise the positive initiatives that their respective governments have to improve QoL and to make them better places to visit.

Carrying capacity and overtourism

These case studies have highlighted the overall efforts of some cities to improve quality of life. Now, the focus is specifically on tourism and how it sometimes can negatively affect the quality of life of residents unless visitor volumes and types are carefully managed.

Long before the overtourism term emerged the carrying capacity of tourism and recreation resources was recognised and measured (Bretlaender and Toth, 2014, p. 6). There are several different forms of capacity, and they are as follows:

- *Physical carrying capacity*: Capacity is reached when the sites/infrastructure can no longer support the number of visitors.
- *Ecological carrying capacity*: Capacity is reached when native wildlife populations are endangered due to visitor activities.
- *Economic carrying capacity*: Capacity is reached when beneficial local activities can no longer be carried out due to tourism.
- *Social carrying capacity*: Capacity is reached when visitors can no longer tolerate the behaviour of other visitors, or local people can no longer tolerate visitors.
- *Perceptual carrying capacity*: Capacity is reached when visitors no longer enjoy themselves due to observable damage caused by previous visitors.
- *Environmental carrying capacity*: Capacity is reached when environmental problems start to occur due to visitor interaction with the environment.

UNWTO (2018) stated that the perceptions of overcrowding are one of the reasons for the resident backlash against tourism. Milano, Novelli and Cheer (2019) suggest that "the excessive growth of visitors leading to overcrowding in areas where residents suffer the consequences of temporary and seasonal tourism peaks, which have caused permanent changes to their lifestyles, denied access to amenities and damaged their general well-being". So, these authors make the connection between overcrowding and well-being and quality of life. In terms of carrying capacity, it is the social carrying capacity that is most involved here and the behaviour of visitors.

In a global survey by UNWTO and Ipsos (2019), 52% of respondents believed that tourism had a large or moderate positive impact on employment and income. However, 46% felt that tourism created overcrowding in their cities. Almost half (49%) suggested that there was a need for measures to better manage city tourism.

Since around 2016, several tourism researchers have been examining the effects of overcrowding on cities, and many journal articles and books have been published on the topic. The *International Journal of Tourism Cities* produced two Special Issues on overtourism: *Overtourism and the sharing economy* (6.1 in 2020), and *Overtourism and the marketing of smart tourism destinations* (5.4 in 2019). *Tourism Planning &*

Development had a Special Issue entitled *Overtourism and tourismphobia: A journey through four decades of tourism development, planning and local concerns* (16.4 in 2019).

Some examples of specific research studies are quite revealing and suggest that overcrowding and overtourism are more complex than many people think. For example, Namberger, Jackisch, Schmude and Karl (2019) posed the research question of overcrowding, overtourism and local-level disturbance – how much can Munich handle? They found that local residents were most disturbed by crowds of people in the main shopping streets, Oktoberfest visitors and football fans on match days. They identified "crowds of tourists" (e.g., football fans) and "disturbances by small groups of tourists" (e.g., stag and hen parties) to be the two main components of local-level disturbances. Navarro-Ruiz, Casado-Díaz and Ivars-Baidal (2019) examined crowding caused by cruise shore excursions in Barcelona and Valencia, Spain. They found that both cities suffered from congestion in their port areas and also, especially Barcelona as the more established cruise port, the cruise excursionists put more pressure on the city's main tourist attractions.

While academics have been researching and writing about overtourism, destinations have been instituting practical measures to deal with the issue and particularly with overcrowding. Generally, the measures taken include: (1) demarketing; (2) closures; (3) use restrictions; and (4) pricing strategies. As an example of the first approach, Bruges in Belgium stopped advertising to the day-trip (excursionist) market (Marcus, 2019). The second approach was demonstrated when the Government of the Philippines closed the island of Boracay for six months in 2018 in order to clean up the local environment (BBC, 2018). Similarly, the Government of Thailand in 2018 closed down Maya Beach on Phi Phi Leh island until 2021 (BBC, 2019).

Various restrictions on the use of entire destinations or parts of them is the third strategy for dealing with overcrowding and overtourism. For example, Venice in 2019 banned large cruise ships from docking at its historic centre (Saraogi, 2019). Dubrovnik in Croatia decided in 2018 to limit the number of cruise ship calls to two per day and a maximum capacity of 5,000 passengers in a move to cut down on overcrowding. This is an example of using quota systems to manage usage levels. Other places to impose restrictions on cruise ship stays include Amsterdam, Barcelona, Dublin (Ireland) and Santorini, Greece.

Pricing strategies are the fourth approach to controlling visitor numbers and for avoiding overcrowding. The Himalayan country of Bhutan famously used to cap the annual number of foreign tourists. This has been changed in favour of requiring a minimum daily package price spend (Tourism Council of Bhutan, 2020). Adding taxes are another pricing strategy, as evidenced in the examples in this chapter for Amsterdam and Stockholm.

Goodwin (2019), a champion for responsible tourism, suggested 21 solutions for dealing with tourism and some of those just discussed were included. He discusses supply- and demand-side initiatives and actions that local governments should consider. One interesting idea is that of providing preferential access for local residents to tourism attractions and sites, for example, by offering them free admission. Also mentioned is requiring advance bookings or authorisations to visit, with the example of the Praia das Catedrais (Cathedrals on the Beach) on the coast of Galicia, Spain (Xunta de Galicia, 2020). Creating new itineraries and guided tours to less visited areas of cities is another suggested solution.

UNWTO (2018) outlined a number of strategies for dealing with overtourism. These included dispersing visitors within cities, promoting time-based dispersal of visitors, stimulating new visitor itineraries and attractions, reviewing and adapting regulations, enhancing visitor segmentation, ensuring local communities benefit from tourism, creating city experiences that benefit residents and visitors, improving city infrastructure and facilities and others.

The COVID-19 pandemic has had a dramatic downward impact on visitor numbers to city destinations and some, objectively as well as cynically, are asking if it is the solution to ending overtourism. Molz (2020) argues that COVID-19 illustrates the overdependence on tourism and the harm it brings to certain cities.

Sweet tweet 59

Pandemic exposes tourism's ill effects on cities

The impact of COVID-19 has been an eye-opener with all associated with tourism. The unprecedented event has led to deserted city centres and streets and produced results and photographic images that were unexpected only months earlier.

> The pandemic has thrown all of tourism's ill effects into stark relief. In Amsterdam's city center, for example, the deserted streets, shuttered souvenir shops and empty rental properties have exposed the extent to which residents have given over their public spaces, neighborhoods and livelihoods to tourism. In Amsterdam and elsewhere, more and more residents, businesspeople and local officials are now recognizing the harm mass tourism does by locking communities into a dependence on tourism dollars. Likewise, the dramatic reduction in emissions during the pandemic has made clear the harm that the travel industry does to the planet.

Source: Molz (2020).

Undoubtedly, the pandemic has exposed the dilemma of tourism development in cities as Molz (2020) observed. The pre- and post-pandemic images are dramatic indeed. Finding the right solutions for the dilemma, however, is much more difficult than pointing out its existence. There is a sentiment that in the future cities should place more emphasis on the quality of tourism and visitors, and not have such a great focus on the volumes of tourists (Buckley, 2020). There is also a belief that visitors should be spread out more, spatially within cities and temporally (arriving at different times).

There is a related concept to overtourism known as NIMBY, or not in my backyard. This is an emotional, parochial and self-serving community reaction which increases the cost of higher, more rational decision-making authorities of locating "locally unwanted land uses" (Wexler, 1996). This concept can also be interpreted as local residents not wanting tourists in their neighbourhoods (or at least not too many of them). The growth of sharing economy short-term rentals has introduced more tourists into city neighbourhoods, and this has become an annoyance for locals who are not used to their presence.

The phenomena of overtourism and overcrowding have accentuated the need for more focus on visitor management within city destinations, which is the next topic.

Visitor management and the ADVICE model

Visitor management was identified in Chapter 4 as a role of city destination manage-ment. As a basic framework model for visitor management, the ADVICE model is highly recommended (Morrison, 2019). The model identifies the main stakeholders and players in city tourism.

- *Authority*. This represents the government agencies with jurisdiction over tourism or aspects related to tourism.
- *Destination*. These are the official representatives of tourism in a destination and usually a destination management organisation.
- *Visitors*. The people who visit destinations for a variety of purposes.
- *Industry*. The companies, other organisations and individuals that serve visitors.
- *Community*. The residents who live in a destination.
- *Environment*. The natural and cultural-historic resources of a destination.

The ADVICE model diagram in Figure 7.5 places the community at the centre sur-rounded by the other five stakeholder groups. Although this representation in the diagram is just symbolic, in actual practice it should be the focus of city destination management. The community and its residents interact, directly and indirectly, with all of the other stakeholder groupings. UNWTO (2020) recommended that all stakeholders (residents, visitors, local, regional and national authorities and the private sector) needed to cooperate to meet the contemporary challenges of urban tourism.

The ADVICE model recognises that tourism does have an impact on community resi-dent quality of life, directly and indirectly. Overcrowding in CBDs may affect resident access to places and traffic congestion can restrict their everyday movements. Visitor use of recreational and tourism amenities may limit resident access to them. Property values may be pushed upward and become too expensive for locals as property developers spec-ulate and tourism companies buy up land and buildings. Traditional neighbourhoods

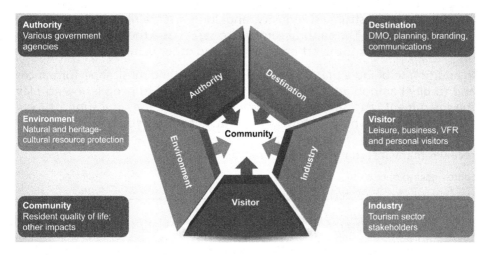

Figure 7.5 The community focused ADVICE model (Adapted from Morrison, 2019).

disappear with gentrification. However, residents also benefit in different ways from the positive economic impacts of tourism, including having better infrastructure and public amenities. The main application of the ADVICE model is to seek a more equitable balance between visitor needs and activities and those of local residents.

For example. as mentioned above in the context of overtourism, overcrowding and the behaviour of certain tourists are disruptive for local residents. Visitor monitoring and management are functions to deal with such problems and to seek solutions to them. Also, as emphasised in Chapter 5, residents must be involved in a meaningful way throughout the city tourism planning process. Since QoL should be a concern vis-à-vis residents and visitors, it should be beneficial for CDMOs to align parts of their community relationships and involvement and visitor management roles. For example, creating encounters between groups of residents and visitors who would not normally meet will be beneficial to increasing mutual understanding and discovering shared values.

While working in Bandung, Indonesia, one of the authors was invited to attend an evening musical performance in the city. It was an unexpected but totally memorable experience about how tourism can engage local people and also entertain visitors.

Sweet tweet 60

Keeping the angklung culture alive in Bandung

Saung Angklung Udjo is located in the city of Bandung, Indonesia, and it is a very good example of how tourism can benefit the QoL of community residents while also preserving important cultural traditions and promoting the arts and musical education. The angklung is a bamboo-based wind instrument that is on the World Heritage List and is associated with the province of West Java, Indonesia, and Sundanese culture. A description of the facility follows:

> Saung Angklung Udjo is one of the arts institutions engaged in the bamboo musical instrument industry, angklung arts training and traditional Sundanese art. The cultural center also serves as a tourist cultural attraction that presents the art of angklung and other bamboo art.

In addition to being a place that tourists go to attend musical performances and to buy bamboo art, Saung Angklung Udjo teaches people how to play the instrument, and this is especially important for the education of local children, some of whom feature in the shows. It was established in 1966, and the facility consists mainly of an amphitheatre, shop and dining facility. It receives many international and domestic tourists.

Source: gokayu.com (2020).

The authors deliberately chose to end the main text of Chapter 7 on a positive note with the cultural tourism facility example from Indonesia. This case exemplifies that tourism in a city has the potential to deliver on many of the "8 + 1" dimensions of QoL and especially if local residents are actively engaged. Saung Angklung Udjo is a major tourism attraction for Bandung that delivers considerable economic benefits to the community. However, the facility goes well beyond material benefits by conserving cultural traditions and providing educational opportunities for residents, as well as creating many memorable experiences for visitors. Sceptics might say that this is a wonderful and positive example of the beneficial effects of tourism; however, tourism does not always deliver on many fronts in this way. Undoubtedly, the evidence in this chapter is mixed and suggests that tourism has positive and negative effects on resident QoL.

Summary comments

How tourism affects resident quality of life is becoming an issue of growing concern for city tourism management. Tourism has been receiving greater criticism, especially in popular European city destinations, for disrupting the normal lives of local residents. Thus, resident QoL must now be elevated from afterthought to priority status. The adoption of various visitor management initiatives is crucial to protecting the interests of local residents, as is engaging residents in tourism planning, development and marketing.

QoL is multidimensional, partly measurable and partly subjective. Tourism is rather paradoxical in this respect, bringing benefits to local residents while also raising some resentment. Overcrowding and the presence of crowds of certain types of tourists tend to be what disturbs residents the most. Solutions to overcrowding issues are many, and cities need to implement them. Other specific factors affecting resident quality of life in this chapter are air pollution, traffic congestion, sharing economy accommodation providers and crime.

Cities must consider the QoL of residents as well as the QoL of visitors. Visitor management is required to accomplish both. Often, but not always, if a city improves the QoL for residents this also benefits visitors. The reverse can also be true.

The next three chapters deal with issues that are related to resident quality of life – sustainability, smart cities and smart tourism and crises. Sustainable development initiatives, for example, tend to improve the environment for residents and visitors. Technological applications in smart tourism assist with easing traffic congestion and in the dispersal of visitors. Crisis management tends to make cities safer and more secure for all.

Thought questions

1) Should CDMOs measure resident quality of life and how tourism affects QoL? If not, why not? If yes, how should resident QoL be measured?
2) The quality of life in some of the world's top tourism cities is not ranked very highly. Why do you think this happens?
3) Why is it important for cities to consider the quality of life effects of people who visit them?
4) In considering the QoL indicators or dimensions, which of these does tourism most affect and why?
5) What steps or initiatives should a CDMO take to demonstrate that it is community focused?
6) Is it fair or unfair to separate out tourism from other city economic activities in terms of its effects on resident QoL? Justify your answer.

7) How should cities deal with overcrowding and overtourism?
8) The ADVICE model is a useful framework for CDMOs. How should they apply it?
9) How should cities use the various forms of carrying capacity measurements to improve tourism for the benefit of local residents and visitors?
10) Should cities such as Venice and Barcelona return to the pre-COVID models of tourism or should they follow new tourism scenarios? Why?

References

Andereck, K. A., & Nyaupane, G. P. (2011). Exploring the nature of tourism and quality of life perceptions among residents. *Journal of Travel Research, 50*(3), 248–260.

BBC. (2018). Philippines to temporarily close popular tourist island Boracay. https://www.bbc.com/news/world-asia-43650627

BBC. (2019). Thailand: Tropical bay from 'The Beach' to close until 2021. https://www.bbc.com/news/world-asia-48222627

Beatley, T. (2011). *Biophilic CITIES: INTEGRATING NATURE into Urban Design and Planning*. Washington, DC: Island Press.

Biagi, B., Ladu, M. G., Meleddu, M.,& Royuela, V. (2020). Tourism and the city: The impact on residents' quality of life. *International Journal of Tourism Research, 22*, 168–181.

Bloomberg City Lab. (2020). Free transit for riders under 18? In Paris, it's here. https://www.bloomberg.com/news/articles/2020-09-03/why-paris-dropped-transit-fares-for-young-riders

Bretlaender, D., & Toth, P. (2014). Kwanini carrying capacity assessment. http://kwaninifoundation.org/wp-content/uploads/2018/10/Kwanini-Carrying-Capacity-Assessment-Study.pdf

Buckley, J. (2020). Venice sees a new future for tourism post-pandemic, Condé Nast Traveler. https://www.cntraveler.com/story/venice-sees-a-new-future-for-tourism-post-pandemic

Centre for Transport Studies, Stockholm. (2014). The Stockholm congestion charges: An overview. https://www.transportportal.se/swopec/cts2014-7.pdf

Chase, L. C., Amsden, B., & Phillips, R. G. (2012). Stakeholder engagement in tourism planning and development. In Uysal M., Perdue R., & Sirgy M. (Eds.). *Handbook of Tourism and Quality-of-Life Research*. Dordrecht: Springer.

City of Vienna. (2019). Quality of living: Vienna remains the number one. https://www.wien.gv.at/english/politics/international/comparison/mercer-study.html

Crouch, G. I., & Ritchie, J. R. B. (1999). Tourism, competitiveness, and societal prosperity. *Journal of Business Research, 44*, 137–152.

Department of Biodiversity, Conservation and Attractions (Western Australia). (2020). Kings Park and Botanic Garden. https://www.dbca.wa.gov.au/botanic-gardens-and-parks-authority/kings-park-and-botanic-garden

Destinations International. (2019). American resident attitudes towards tourism. https://longwoods-intl.com/sites/default/files/2019-05/WhitePaper_ResidentSentiment_FINAL.pdf

Dolnicar, S., Yanamandram, V., & Cliff, K. (2012). The contribution of vacations to quality of life. *Annals of Tourism Research, 39*(1), 59–83.

Eurostat. (2020a). Quality of life. https://ec.europa.eu/eurostat/cache/infographs/qol/index_en.html

Eurostat. (2020b). Why should quality of life be measured. https://ec.europa.eu/eurostat/web/quality-of-life/data

Gardens by the Bay. (2020). Our story. https://www.gardensbythebay.com.sg/en/the-gar dens/our-story/introduction.html

Gilbert, D., & Abdullah, J. (2004). Holidaytaking and the sense of well-being. *Annals of Tourism Research*, 31(1), 103–121.

gokayu.com. (2020). Cultural activities at Saung Angklung Udjo. https://gokayu.com/indone sia/bandung/activity/cultural-activities-at-saung-angklung-udjo

Goodwin, H. (2019). Overtourism solutions: 21 strategies to manage mass tourism. https:// responsibletourismpartnership.org/overtourism-solutions/

Government of Ireland. (2019). Policy: Tourism. https://www.gov.ie/en/policy/3fcc3a-tour ism/#

Hall, P. (1987). Urban development and the future of tourism. *Tourism Management*, 8(2), 129–130.

Hawaii Tourism Authority. (2019). HTA resident sentiment survey 2018 highlights. https:/ /www.hawaiitourismauthority.org/media/2984/resident-sentiment-presentation-to-hta-b oard-01-31-2019.pdf

Hong Kong Wetland Park. (2020). About us. https://www.wetlandpark.gov.hk/en/aboutus /index

International Congress and Convention Association. (2020). *ICCA Statistics Report Country & City Rankings: Public Abstract*. Amsterdam: ICCA.

Jones, C., & Newsome, D. (2015). Perth (Australia) as one of the world's most liveable cities: A perspective on society, sustainability and environment. *International Journal of Tourism Cities*, 1(1), 18–35.

Kamdar, M. (2020). Paris Is about to change. The city was hit hard by the pandemic, but French leaders know transformation is necessary. *The Atlantic*. https://www.theatlantic.c om/ideas/archive/2020/09/paris-not-dead/616099/

Kellert, S. R., Heerwagen, J., & Mador, M. (2011). *Biophilic Design: The Theory, Science and Practice of Bringing Buildings to Life*. Hoboken, NJ: Wiley.

Kim, K., Uysal, M., & Sirgy, J. (2013). How does tourism in a community impact the quality of life of community residents? *Tourism Management*, 36, 527–540.

Knight Frank. (2020). The City Wellbeing Index: How happy are the world's leading cities? https://www.knightfrank.com/wealthreport/article/2020-03-03-the-city-wellbeing-i ndex-how-happy-are-the-worlds-leading-cities

The Local. (2018). Quality of life: How Paris ranked in annual global survey. https://www .thelocal.fr/20180321/paris-and-lyon-drop-in-annual-quality-of-life-global-ranking

Longwoods International. (2020). Resident sentiment research. https://longwoods-intl.com /resident-sentiment-research

Marcus, L. (2019). Popular medieval Belgian town Bruges makes moves to restrict tourism. *CNN*. https://www.cnn.com/travel/article/bruges-belgium-overtourism-cruise-ship-restr ictions/index.html

McCabe, S., & Johnson, S. (2013). The happiness factor in tourism: Subjective well-being and social tourism. *Annals of Tourism Research*, 41, 42–65.

Mercer. (2019). Vienna tops Mercer's 21st quality of living ranking. https://www.mercer.com /newsroom/2019-quality-of-living-survey.html

Mercer. (2020). Quality of living city ranking. https://mobilityexchange.mercer.com/insi ghts/quality-of-living-rankings

Milano, C., Novelli, M., & Cheer, J. M. (2019). Overtourism and tourismphobia: A Journey through four decades of tourism development, planning and local concerns. *Tourism Planning & Development*, 16(4), 353–357.

Molz, J. G. (2020). Will COVID-19 bring an end to overtourism? *World Politics Review.* https://www.worldpoliticsreview.com/articles/28947/will-covid-19-bring-an-end-to-over tourism

Morrison, A. M. (2019). *Marketing and Managing Tourism Destinations*, 2nd ed. London: Routledge.

Namberger, P., Jackisch, S., Schmude, J., & Karl, M. (2019). Overcrowding, overtourism and local level disturbance: How much can Munich handle? *Tourism Planning & Development, 16*(4), 452–472.

Navarro-Ruiz, S., Casado-Díaz, A. B., & Ivars-Baidal, J. (2019). Cruise tourism: The role of shore excursions in the overcrowding of cities. *International Journal of Tourism Cities, 6*(1), 197–214.

Neal, J. D., Uysal, M., & Sirgy, M. J. (2007). The effect of tourism services on travelers' quality of life. *Journal of Travel Research, 46,* 154–163.

Newman, P. (2014). Biophilic urbanism: A case study on Singapore. *Australian Planner, 51*(1), 47–65.

OECD. (2013). *OECD Guidelines on Measuring Subjective Well-Being.* Paris: OECD Publishing.

O'Sullivan, F. (2019). European cities fear they'll lose power to regulate Airbnb. https://www.bloomberg.com/news/articles/2019-07-02/10-cities-ask-the-eu-to-help-regulate-airbnb

Passive Airbnb. (2018). Top cities (and countries) where Airbnb is illegal or restricted. https://www.passiveairbnb.com/top-cities-and-countries-where-airbnb-is-illegal-or-restricted/

Saraogi, V. (2019). Not just Venice: Six countries which have banned cruise ships. *Ship Technology.* https://www.ship-technology.com/features/cities-who-banned-cruise-ships/

Smarter Cambridge Transport. (2016). Urban congestion inquiry. https://www.smartertransport.uk/smarter-cambridge-transport-urban-congestion-enquiry/

Sustainable Solutions Network. (2020). The world happiness report. https://worldhappiness.report/

Teleport. (2020). Move to your best place to live and work. https://teleport.org/cities/

Tourism Council of Bhutan. (2020). Frequently asked questions. https://www.bhutan.travel/page/frequently-asked-questions

Tourism Vienna. (2020a). Arrivals & nights/Arrivals & bednights 2019. https://b2b.wien.info/de/statistik/daten/naechtigungen-2019

Tourism Vienna. (2020b). For LBGT. https://www.wien.info/en/vienna-for/gay-lesbian

Tourism Vienna. (2020c). Sustainability & green meetings. https://www.vienna.convention.at/en/sustainability#:~:text=In%202019%2C%2090%20events%20were,points%20which%20help%20save%20costs.

Transport Department, Government of Hong Kong SAR. (2020). Minibuses. https://www.td.gov.hk/en/transport_in_hong_kong/public_transport/minibuses/index.htm

United Nations Development Programme (UNDP). (2020). United Nations Development Programme. Human development reports. http://hdr.undp.org/en/content/table-1-human-development-index-and-its-components-1

UN World Tourism Organization (UNWTO). (2018). 'Overtourism'? Understanding and managing urban tourism growth beyond perceptions: Executive summary. https://www.e-unwto.org/doi/pdf/10.18111/9789284420070

UNWTO. (2020). UNWTO recommendations on urban tourism. https://www.e-unwto.org/doi/10.18111/9789284422012

UNWTO, & Ipsos. (2019). Global survey on the perception of residents towards city tourism: Impact and measures. https://webunwto.s3-eu-west-1.amazonaws.com/imported_images/52027/unwtoipsosglobalsurveysummary.pdf

Uysal, M. , Sirgy, J., Woo, E., & Kim, H. L. (2016). Quality of life (QOL) and well-being research in tourism. *Tourism Management, 53*, 244–261.

Weiermair K., and Peters M. (2012). Quality-of-life values among stakeholders in tourism destinations: A tale of converging and diverging interests and conflicts. In Uysal M., Perdue R., & Sirgy M. (Eds.). *Handbook of Tourism and Quality-of-Life Research.* Dordrecht: Springer.

Wexler, M. N. (1996). A sociological framing of the NIMBY (not-in-my-backyard) syndrome. *International Review of Modern Sociology, 26*(1), 91–110.

Wong, R. (2014). Seven ways cities around the world are tackling traffic. World Economic Forum. https://www.weforum.org/agenda/2014/07/seven-ways-cities-around-world-tackling-traffic/

Woo, E., Kim, H., & Uysal, M. (2015). Life satisfaction and support for tourism development. *Tourism Management, 50*, 84–97.

Xunta de Galicia. (2020). Verán 2020. https://ascatedrais.xunta.gal/monatr/inicio

Yuda, M. (2020). Smog-choked Bangkok struggles to improve air quality. *Nikkei Asia.* https://asia.nikkei.com/Spotlight/Environment/Smog-choked-Bangkok-struggles-to-improve-air-quality

Chapter 8

Sustainability in world cities

Abstract

The previous chapter focused on one of the key stakeholders in urban destinations, the local residents, and looked at how tourism growth in cities affects their quality of life. This chapter continues the discussion on trends, issues and challenges faced by world tourism cities, and examines the concept of sustainability and how it applies to these destinations.

Sustainability is an important topic that cannot be overlooked when discussing tourism development in world cities. This is even more significant in the current economic climate when urban destinations are facing many challenges as a result of the COVID-19 crisis. Chapter 8, therefore, begins by examining the impacts of tourism, both positive and negative, followed by a discussion on the sustainability measures and policies promoted by urban destinations. It acknowledges the complex nature of the two concepts, sustainable development, and sustainable tourism, which makes their implementation in practice more challenging for tourism organisations. It then identifies a number of factors that could help urban destinations apply the sustainability principles at the local level. Particular attention is given to the role played by the main stakeholders in tourism cities in sustainable tourism implementation.

Another aspect deemed important to discuss here is the contribution of world tourism cities towards achieving the Sustainable Development Goals and addressing climate change. The tourism industry plays an important part in both, in particular urban destinations that attract many visitors and are important CO_2 emitters.

Keywords: Sustainability; impact of tourism; sustainable tourism; Sustainable Development Goals (SDGs); stakeholders; climate change.

DOI: 10.4324/9781003111412-11

Learning objectives

Having read this chapter, you should be able to:

- Identify and explain the impacts of tourism in city destinations, both positive and negative.
- Explain the meaning of sustainable development and its evolution.
- Analyse the sustainable tourism concept and its applicability to city destinations.
- Elaborate on the role played by world tourism cities in tackling climate change, and in achieving the Sustainable Development Goals.
- Describe the roles played by the main stakeholders in sustainable tourism implementation.

Impacts of tourism development in cities

Researchers highlight that tourism activities can have both positive and negative impacts on a destination, and this depends on how wisely tourism is planned and managed. Chapters 4 and 5 already discussed the importance of these two processes for the success of a destination.

As noted in Chapter 5, the impacts that accompany tourism development in a destination can be grouped around three key areas – economic, social and environmental. This section expands on the topic and discusses some of the main impacts seen in world tourism cities, giving examples that highlight both positive and negative effects of tourism in urban destinations.

Among the *economic* benefits of tourism in city destinations are an increase in the local economic activities and tax revenues, job creation and an improvement in the standard of living, this activity being considered an easy source of income for many cities. A number of world tourism cities rely on a significant contribution of tourism to their GDP, which in some cases accounts even for half of their economy (WTTC, 2019). Examples include Macau (50.3%), Cancún (46.8%), Marrakech (30.6%), Las Vegas (27.4%), Orlando (19.8%), Dubrovnik (17.8%), Dubai (11.5%), Bangkok (10.6%), Antalya (10.1%) and Miami (9.2%).

Sweet tweet 61

The contribution that travel and tourism bring to city economies

The World Travel & Tourism Council (WTTC) produced a report to highlight the contribution of tourism to the economy of many large cities worldwide.

> Our new research of 73 major Travel & Tourism cities around the world reveals that the sector in these centres directly accounted for 4.4% of city GDP and 17 million jobs, or 5.7% of total employment in these cities in 2018 … These important revenues will in many cases pay for

> infrastructure projects, the provision of public workers and services that improve the quality of life for residents.
>
> Source: World Travel & Tourism Council (2019).

For the years of 2020 and 2021, however, these figures are likely to look very different due to the lockdown measures imposed in many cities around the world as a result of the COVID-19 pandemic. It is estimated that it could take a few years for tourism activities to recover to pre-pandemic levels, with world tourism cities being among the worst affected destinations. Their characteristics, discussed in Chapter 3 and which are usually seen as positive aspects (e.g., very good connectivity attracting many people to visit, study or work there), contributed to the very high number of infections recorded in these areas and led to severe travel restrictions during the crisis.

But aside from its beneficial effects, tourism development in cities can also have undesired economic impacts such as a rise in the price of land, properties and food. These are likely to negatively affect the local residents as the cost of living could see an increase in certain areas. For example, the price of renting houses in the central area of Athens went up 30% from 2016 to 2018. This is assumed to be a direct consequence of the shortage created on the residential market by the significant increase in short-term rentals in the area (Balampanidis et al., 2019). Another example is Old Québec, the historic neighbourhood of Québec City in Canada, where the housing market was impacted by the rapid growth of tourism in the area (Gravari-Barbas and Guinand, 2021). Further examples include Barcelona, Boston and London, where Airbnb is considered responsible for the increase in rental prices in those cities (Benítez-Aurioles and Tussyadiah, 2020).

From a *socio-cultural* perspective, tourism is considered to contribute to better local facilities and infrastructure and better recreational and entertainment facilities, as well as helping revitalise traditional activities and preserving the local culture. While the latter may be seen as more important for some other types of destinations (e.g., heritage and cultural sites), tourism cities have also realised the importance of preserving their local characteristics that help them differentiate from other urban destinations. This is a result of the increased interest shown by visitors lately for the authentic and unique experiences that a city may offer. Many tourists now prefer so-called "off-the-beaten-track" experiences, which generally refers to the exploration of the city as a local, away from the well-known tourist hotspots. Examples include Spitalfields, Brick Lane, Shoreditch and London Fields areas in London (Pappalepore et al., 2014); Podgórze and Nowa Huta districts in Krakow (Matoga and Pawłowska, 2018); as well as the "True York City" global tourism campaign initiated by New York City in 2017, inviting visitors to discover its lesser known attractions.

However, the interaction between tourism and hosts may contribute to the corruption of the local culture and traditions, leading to a loss of cultural identity. Other potential detrimental effects may include an increase in crime rates and antisocial behaviour, as highlighted in the sweet tweet below, as well as conflicts that can arise between locals and visitors, particularly when the increase in the number of visitors leads to the overuse of local infrastructure and facilities. In effect, this is how the concept of *overtourism* emerged, considered by some researchers to be just "a new term for an old problem" (Dodds and Butler, 2019, p. 519). The term is used to reflect the excessive number of visitors at specific destinations or sites, putting pressure on the local resources and likely to have negative impacts on the local communities. The concept was introduced in Chapter 3 and examined in Chapter 7 in relation to the concept of carrying capacity and the local residents' quality of life.

Sweet tweet 62

Tourism cities and crime

There is considerable evidence that many tourist resorts suffer higher than average crime rates, that tourists are disproportionately victimised, and that tourists often cause crime and disorder problems. This poses a dilemma for cities and towns seeking to expand their tourism industry.

Source: Mawby (2017).

The debate on the socio-economic impacts of tourism in cities has also been fuelled by the rise in the sharing economy (e.g., Airbnb, Homeaway, Uber, BlaBlaCar, EatWith, ToursByLocals). One of the most popular such platforms, Airbnb, is perceived "as a major transformative force of urban space, economy and society, which can be neither utterly condemned nor fully celebrated" (Balampanidis et al., 2019). This is because while it can contribute to upgrading and reusing existing buildings and bringing money into the local economy (if the properties are owned by local people), it may also contribute to displacement, gentrification or touristification in those areas. This has led some city governments to take action and impose restrictions. For example, in 2018 the city of Los Angeles passed a law that restricts to 120 the number of days per calendar year that a host could rent out their property through Airbnb. Similar measures were taken by other destinations, with much lower limits set by some European cities such as London (90 nights per calendar year), and Amsterdam (30 nights per calendar year), including a recently enacted total ban for three of its districts.

Moving on to the *environmental* perspective, tourism activities can contribute to maintaining and restoring attractions through the revenues they generate. However, tourism can also have notable negative impacts, such as traffic congestion, littering and increased pollution, which is already a concern in some large cities. Examples of popular tourism cities with poor air quality include Paris, Krakow, Sydney, Seoul, Hong Kong and other Chinese cities. Some cities (e.g., Amsterdam, Venice, Barcelona and Rome (Figure 8.1)) are already taking measures to try to limit the negative social and environmental impacts of tourism by limiting or reducing the number of visitors in certain areas, and an example from Barcelona is given below.

Sweet tweet 63

Barcelona is threatening to shut out tourists

Barcelona is often used as an example when discussing overtourism. The local government is looking at measures to redress the balance and focus more on the needs of local people.

Barcelona Mayor Ada Colau is working to limit the number of cruise ships that visit the city in order to reduce water and air pollution as well as curb the abundance of tourists.

Source: Lakritz (2020).

Figure 8.1 St. Peter's Square, Vatican City – located in the heart of Rome (Author photo).

Although it is largely accepted that tourism development in cities is accompanied by negative impacts, and a number of examples were given earlier, it is difficult, if not almost impossible, to accurately measure the actual contribution of tourism to those impacts. That is because tourism interacts with many other local activities, in particular in large cities where the tourism economy is formed by different sectors that offer services to both locals and visitors (e.g., entertainment, restaurants and transport facilities).

So far the discussion has covered a number of impacts that accompany tourism development in world tourism cities. Moving on, the attention will turn to the concept of sustainability and how this applies to urban destinations.

Sustainable development

Sustainable development (SD) has attracted the attention of tourism researchers and policy makers for decades. There is wide consensus that implementing this concept in practice would help destination managers to balance the negative impacts of tourism in a destination with the positive effects that it can bring to local communities. The origins of the concept can be traced back as far as the 1950s, 1960s or 1970s, depending on the author, in the debates around the conservation and management of resources in National Parks.

Sustainable development aims to bridge the gap between social and environmental concerns associated with the development of an activity (tourism in our case) and the economic development agenda of a destination. The concept evolved over the years, being the focus of a number of important international events that contributed to its advancement. Among these, the 1972 *UN Conference on the Human Environment* that took place in Stockholm is considered an important milestone, where delegates agreed that there is an inextricable link between development and the environment and called for more action to protect the environment.

Another important event was the publishing in 1987 of the report *Our Common Future* (also known as the Brundtland Report), which put forward the definition of sustainable development that became the most widely used. The concept is thus defined as "development that meets the needs of the present without compromising the ability of future generations to meet their own needs" (World Commission on Environment and Development, 1987, p. 41). Perhaps one of the most significant contributions of this report is that it promoted the issue of sustainable development on the international agenda, with the concept being subsequently adopted by a number of governments in their policy documents.

As is the case with many complex concepts, sustainable development is defined, interpreted and implemented differently by various organisations and scholars. Yet, they all share a common view in that resources should be used in a wise and balanced manner. The concept also attracted criticism, such as for being ambiguous, vague, illusive and difficult to implement. Yet, others consider its vagueness as one of its strengths as it makes it flexible and adaptable to different circumstances. This is particularly relevant for city destinations, which present different characteristics and promote in some cases a very diverse offer to their visitors.

Subsequently, several other international events were organised every five years by the United Nations to discuss the progress made by governments in implementing this concept in practice (e.g., 1992 the *Earth Summit*, Rio de Janeiro; 1997 *RIO+5*, New York; 2002 *RIO+10*, Johannesburg; 2012 *RIO+20*, once again in Rio de Janeiro). While some progress was noted during these meetings, such as the commitment showed by a number of governments towards introducing the sustainability debate into their political agenda, insufficient progress was made towards implementing sustainable development in practice and integrating the three dimensions or pillars of sustainability, i.e., economic growth, social inclusion and environmental protection (Figure 8.2).

Tourism received little attention at the Earth Summit in 1992. This however changed with the publication in 1995 of the *Agenda 21 for the Travel and Tourism Industry* by the World Tourism Organisation, the World Travel & Tourism Council and the Earth Council. Furthermore, during the UN Conference on Sustainable Development held in 2012 (*RIO+20*), sustainable tourism was identified as one of the cross-sectoral issues that contribute to the three dimensions of sustainability.

Another important event that took place more recently is the *UN Sustainable Development Summit 2015* in New York, where the 2030 Agenda for Sustainable Development was formally adopted by all UN member states. At the heart of this document is a set of 17 Sustainable Development Goals (SDGs) that are expected to guide

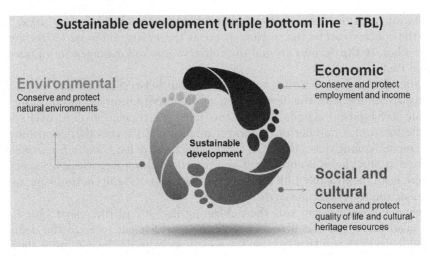

Figure 8.2 The three pillars of sustainable development ("triple bottom line").

decisions for the following 15 years (Table 8.1). The SDGs are considered by international organisations, such as the UN and UNWTO, as a useful framework to guide destinations in developing tourism sustainably. They argue that tourism has the potential to contribute, either directly or indirectly, to all 17 goals, particularly in the case of SDGs 8, 12 and 14 (Rasoolimanesh et al., 2020).

In the latest *Sustainable Development Goals Report 2020*, the United Nations recognises that although some progress was made towards achieving the SDGs, there are many areas where this is insufficient or very slow (UN, 2020b). On top of that, the COVID-19 pandemic and the ensuing crisis have disrupted even further the uneven progress towards implementing the SDGs, making it difficult, if not impossible, to meet those goals by 2030 as set initially.

Cities are expected to play a crucial role in achieving the Sustainable Development Goals, and an example from Bonn is given in the next sweet tweet. Cities are best placed to take action as they are well connected with the surrounding regions and the rest of the world; can bring together and mobilise key actors; and as hubs for innovation, they can address urban challenges such as transportation, housing and density. Recognising the key role played by urban environments towards sustainable development, a specific SDG was included for cities, also known as the Urban Goal – *Goal 11: Make cities and human settlements inclusive, safe, resilient, and sustainable.*

Sweet tweet 64

Bonn aiming for more sustainability

Bonn's first Sustainability Strategy was adopted by the City Council in February 2019. This strategy is Bonn's contribution to a systematic implementation of the United Nations 2030 Agenda with its 17 Sustainable Development Goals. The municipal Sustainability Strategy was drafted in a two-year participatory process, involving political representatives and stakeholders from civil society, academia and economy.

Source: City of Bonn (2020).

Among the cities that took action towards implementing the Sustainable Development Goals is New York City, which was the first to create a tool that provides an overview of the progress made towards achieving SDGs – the *Voluntary Local Review* (VLR). In 2018 they submitted their first VLR report directly to the United Nations. The following year more cities joined the movement and submitted their VLR reports, e.g., Buenos Aires, Los Angeles, Bristol and Helsinki (Hartley, 2019; UN, 2020a). One year

Table 8.1 Sustainable Development Goals (SDGs)

Goal 1: End poverty in all its forms everywhere

Goal 2: End hunger, achieve food security and improved nutrition and promote sustainable agriculture

Goal 3: Ensure healthy lives and promote well-being for all at all ages

Goal 4: Ensure inclusive and equitable quality education and promote lifelong learning opportunities for all

Goal 5: Achieve gender equality and empower all women and girls

Goal 6: Ensure availability and sustainable management of water and sanitation for all

Goal 7: Ensure access to affordable, reliable, sustainable and modern energy for all

Goal 8: Promote sustained, inclusive and sustainable economic growth, full and productive employment and decent work for all

Goal 9: Build resilient infrastructure, promote inclusive and sustainable industrialization and foster innovation

Goal 10: Reduce inequality within and among countries

Goal 11: Make cities and human settlements inclusive, safe, resilient and sustainable

Goal 12: Ensure sustainable consumption and production patterns

Goal 13: Take urgent action to combat climate change and its impacts

Goal 14: Conserve and sustainably use the oceans, seas and marine resources for sustainable development

Goal 15: Protect, restore and promote sustainable use of terrestrial ecosystems, sustainably manage forests, combat desertification and halt and reverse land degradation and halt biodiversity loss

Goal 16: Promote peaceful and inclusive societies for sustainable development, provide access to justice for all and build effective, accountable and inclusive institutions at all levels

Goal 17: Strengthen the means of implementation and revitalise the Global Partnership for Sustainable Development

Source: UN (2015).

later, in 2020, the European Commission published the *European Handbook for SDG Voluntary Local Reviews*, aimed at helping city policy makers and practitioners in European cities to implement the SDGs. The handbook provides examples of indicators that could help cities to monitor their progress towards the achievement of the SDGs (European Commission, 2020).

Another example is Los Angeles, which in 2019 published a new policy document – the "Green New Deal" – aligning all its chapters and initiatives with the SDGs. The measures proposed in the document include: (1) localising SDG indicators and reporting via an open-source data platform; (2) attracting both local and global partnerships using the universal language of the SDGs to mobilise new initiatives and accelerate progress on the goals; (3) working closely with regional academic partners to engage undergraduate, graduate and even high school students in SDG implementation; (4) learning from other cities that are advancing the SDGs locally (Hartley, 2019, p. 13).

This section has looked at what sustainable development represents and how the concept evolved over the years, discussing a number of important international documents and agreements adopted to help with its implementation in practice. A number of examples were also presented, showing the actions taken by world tourism cities towards implementing sustainable development measures in practice. Moving on, the next section will focus onto the tourism sector and how sustainability applies to city destinations.

Sustainable tourism development in cities

Sustainable tourism development is broadly the application of the concept of sustainability in a tourism context. It gradually gained in popularity from the mid-1990s as a response to the negative impacts that accompany tourism development in destinations, which were discussed earlier.

As was the case with sustainable development, sustainable tourism (ST) has also faced challenges with its definition and implementation, as noted in the sweet tweet below. Initially, the concept was perceived by some as a specific form of tourism, closely related to ecotourism, that focuses not only on environmental protection but also on social justice and considerations of scale (McCool, 2013).

Sweet tweet 65

Challenges of sustainable tourism implementation in urban areas

Mirroring the arguments on sustainable development … the extent to which sustainable tourism policies have been translated into practice is debatable … despite the attention lately received by this concept, there are still many gaps in our understanding of the sustainable development of tourism … particularly when it comes to its implementation.

Source: Maxim (2016).

Other interpretations of sustainable tourism focus on two opposing views: One that is *tourism centred* – where the priority is to support the tourism sector and encourage economic growth; the other is *ecologically centred* – where the main focus is on environmental protection. These two views can be found among organisations and researchers even today, with some who militate for a rapid recovery of the tourism industry, as this would help regions to recover from the devastating impacts of the COVID-19 pandemic, while others argue that the current crisis presents the world with an opportunity to reform the tourism industry and make it more "ethical, responsible and sustainable" (Higgins-Desbiolles, 2020, p. 1). Some authors go further and suggest that "the global policy of sustainable development in general should be replaced with a focus on *sustainable de-growth*" (authors' emphasis), which requires not only reducing the number of visitors to a destination but also fossil fuel-based travel on a global scale (Sharpley, 2020, p. 1941).

The United Nation World Tourism Organisation, in partnership with the United Nations Environment Programme (UNEP, 2017a) defines sustainable tourism as types of tourism that:

1) Make optimal use of environmental resources that constitute a key element in tourism development, maintaining essential ecological processes and helping to conserve natural resources and biodiversity.
2) Respect the socio-cultural authenticity of host communities, conserve their built and living cultural heritage and traditional values, and contribute to inter-cultural understanding and tolerance.
3) Ensure viable, long-term economic operations, providing socio-economic benefits to all stakeholders that are fairly distributed, including stable employment and income-earning opportunities and social services to host communities, and contributing to poverty alleviation.

(UNEP and WTO, 2005, p. 11)

This definition takes into account the impacts of tourism, looking at present as well as future activities, while also considering the needs of the main stakeholders – visitors, hosts, the industry and the environment. It also refers to all three pillars of sustainability introduced earlier, i.e., economic, social and environmental.

During the past few decades, many tourism organisations, as well as local and central governments, have made efforts to incorporate the principles of sustainable development within their tourism policy documents and strategies, as seen in the example below. Yet, researchers note that not much progress has been made towards implementing those policies in practice. As one scholar points out, policies promoted by governments "may give the appearance of a paradigm shift towards sustainable development, but in reality they are still pro-growth, and focused on traditional concerns of economic returns" (Ruhanen, 2013, p. 84). This is despite the extensive literature available on sustainable tourism, the development of various accreditation schemes, sectoral initiatives and sustainability indicators and the establishment of organisations such as the Global Sustainable Tourism Council (Sharpley, 2020). Hence, there are calls for governments and tourism organisations "to walk the talk" and put ideas into action. This is, however, not an easy task as it requires the involvement of all stakeholders in the destination and, in many cases, difficult political choices.

Sweet tweet 66

Seoul promotes sustainable urban tourism

Seoul is one of the world tourism cities that made sustainability one of its priorities with regard to its travel and tourism sector, promoting policies and initiatives such as "A Great City for Walking" and "Shared City Seoul".

Seoul's "A Great City for Walking" initiative has been used to diversify and spread tourists across the city's many districts.

The broader "Shared City Seoul" policy is focused on creating a more sustainable and liveable city, developing new economic opportunities, reducing waste, and improving the life of its residents by encouraging a concept of "sharing" into their daily lives.

Source: WTTC (2019).

The importance of considering the sustainability principles by tourism destinations is also emphasised in the Global Guidelines to Restart Tourism and the associated *Restart Tourism* campaign produced by the UNWTO (2020), which include sustainability among the priorities for the recovery of tourism post-COVID-19.

While widely used in connection with heritage destinations and natural attractions, the concept of sustainable tourism has attracted little attention from researchers and policy makers in relation to city destinations. This may be a consequence of the lack of attention received in the past by the phenomenon of urban tourism in general, an aspect discussed in Chapter 3. However, as seen in the previous section, world cities play a crucial role in the sustainable development of a region, and they are popular tourist destinations. Therefore, sustainable tourism development needs to be a priority for all tourism cities. Valencia is one of the cities that has made sustainability one of its key priorities and is working towards achieving the SDGs, as seen in Short break 8.

SHORT BREAK 8

Valencia – the first city in the world to measure the carbon footprint of tourism

Valencia is the third largest city in Spain, after Madrid and Barcelona. It is one of the oldest cities in the country, with a rich history and many attractions that entice both leisure and business tourists (e.g., World Heritage sites, City of Arts and Sciences, gardens, beaches). Tourism therefore plays a key role in the economy of the city.

According to Visit Valencia, the city's tourism board, sustainability became an important part of the tourism strategy since 2016. In an interview given in 2020 for Lonely Planet, the councillor for tourism of the Valencia City Council mentioned that:

In 2015, when the Valencia 2020 Strategic Plan began to take shape, the city made a commitment to develop a sustainable tourism model that was more integrated and more accessible for both citizens and visitors, while also generating economic wealth for the city.

The city representatives recognise the challenges posed by climate change and the implications of the COVID-19 pandemic on the tourism sector, taking measures to make tourism development in the city more sustainable. Thus, they designed a new *Sustainable Tourism Strategy 2030* and identified key stakeholders that can help in achieving their objectives. They have also created a *"sustainability roadmap"* to help Valencia become a *carbon-neutral destination by 2025*.

To achieve this ambitious target, the city recently carried out research to measure the sources of CO_2 emissions from tourism activities in ten different areas, including water management, waste, transportation, day visitors, cruise passengers and accommodation. They also identified 151 indicators to help with measuring and monitoring the progress made. These actions helped the city authorities understand where they are and what further steps they need to take in order to become one of the world's leading city destinations in sustainable tourism with zero environmental impact.

Discussion points:

1. Why do you think it is important for Valencia to measure the carbon footprint of tourism?
2. What are the strengths of the measures taken by the city of Valencia towards becoming a carbon-neutral destination?
3. What other specific measures would you propose in order for them to achieve this ambitious target?

Sources: Visit Valencia (2020); Keith (2020).

In a recent report produced by WTTC (2019), it is argued that tourism development in cities can only achieve sustainable growth if the focus extends beyond the tourism sector, into the broader urban agenda. The approach taken by WTTC, while rather tourism centred, acknowledges the importance of considering tourism within the broader context and in relation to other activities found in cities. They stress the importance of involving all key stakeholders in the planning process from an early stage, an aspect addressed in Chapter 4 and discussed in more detail later on in this chapter.

When looking at the most recent literature published on sustainable urban tourism, this includes a study by Miller et al. (2015) on understanding the pro-environmental behaviour of visitors in Melbourne; Zamfir and Corbos (2015) who discuss sustainable tourism development in Bucharest, the capital city of Romania; Maxim (2015, 2016) who analyses sustainable tourism implementation practices in London; Wise (2016) who discusses how urban tourism planning and development relate to the triple bottom line approach; Önder et al. (2017) who review existing frameworks for sustainable tourism indicators and propose a set of data for benchmarking urban tourism destinations, focusing on European cities; Lerario and Di Turi (2018) who also look at indicators for sustainable urban tourism practices, with a focus on the built environment; Aall and Koens (2019) who edited a special issue in *Sustainability* journal on the topic of sustainable urban tourism; Grah et al. (2020) who discuss sustainable urban tourism management in the case of Ljubljana, the capital city of Slovenia; Boom et al. (2020) who investigate the stakeholder perspectives on sustainable urban tourism development; Phuc and Nguyen (2020) who assess the residents' support for sustainable tourism development in urban destinations, focusing their work on Ho Chi Minh City in Vietnam; and Day (2021) who published a book chapter on sustainable tourism in cities, emphasising a number of challenges faced by city destinations as a result of the complex nature of both the urban tourism system and the sustainable tourism programmes.

It can be said that research on sustainable tourism in urban areas is still in its infancy, with many works being case study-driven and focused on understanding different aspects of sustainable tourism development in tourism cities.

Sustainable tourism objectives, principles and indicators

Over the years tourism scholars and organisations have put together different sets of objectives and principles to help with the implementation of the concept of sustainable tourism in practice. Both the objectives and principles, can be grouped around satisfying the needs of the main stakeholders in sustainable tourism, i.e., visitors, tourism industry, local community and the environment.

Examples of objectives proposed by different organisations and researchers (DCMS, 2009; Sharpley, 2009; UNEP and WTO, 2005; UNWTO, 2013) that would apply to key stakeholders include:

- *Tourists*: Offer a high-quality visitor experience; visitor fulfilment; improve the quality of holidays and make these accessible to all; optimum fulfilment of guest requirements.
- *Tourism industry*: Economic viability; benefit the local economy; improve the quality of tourism jobs; economic health.
- *Local community*: Local prosperity; social equity; local control; community quality of life; well-being; support local communities and culture.
- *Environment*: Physical integrity; biological diversity; resource efficiency; environmental purity; protect and enhance the built and natural environment of a destination; minimise the environmental impact and the use of resources; unspoiled nature and protection of resources.

To get an understanding of the aspects considered important and included within the sustainable tourism principles proposed by different researchers and organisations, two examples are included below. The first one is from two scholars, Dwyer and Edwards (2010), who propose the following guiding principles for sustainable tourism planning: (1) protect the built and natural environment; (2) commitment and leadership at all levels; (3) cooperation between the stakeholders involved in tourism development in a destination; (4) education and training to improve public understanding and professional skills; (5) social creativity and freedom.

Another set of principles is proposed by the South Australian Tourism Commission (2007), in its 'Design Guidelines for Sustainable Tourism Development', and includes: (1) minimising environmental impacts; (2) achieving conservation outcomes; (3) being different; (4) achieving authenticity; (5) reflecting community values; (6) understanding and targeting the market; (7) enhancing the experience; (8) adding value to existing attributes to achieve a richer tourism experience and help diversify the local economy; (9) having good content (telling the story); (10) enhancing the sense of place through design; (11) providing mutual benefits to visitors and hosts; (12) building local capacity.

These principles make reference to the three pillars of sustainable development – economic, social and environmental – looking to promote mutual benefits to both tourists and locals, while safeguarding the built and natural environment. They can apply to any type of destination, including cities, although some aspects may be more important to some destinations than others, depending on the characteristics they present and their priorities.

To help operationalise the objectives and principles of sustainable tourism, different sets of indicators were proposed over the years. These were, however, often perceived by the industry and policy makers as too complex and thus difficult to implement in practice. In a paper discussing sustainable tourism indicators (Tanguay et al., 2013), the authors identify no less than 507 expert-recognised indicators, which demonstrates the diversity of the potential indicators that destinations and policy makers could work with; however, the multitude of indicators may also create confusion. After going through a number of selection criteria, the authors propose a set of 20 sustainable tourism indicators (STIs) which are presented in Table 8.2.

In a recent review paper on sustainable tourism indicators in relation to the SDGs discussed earlier, the authors find that government, residents and local businesses appear to be the stakeholders that are most often acknowledged in such studies, with tourists receiving little attention. The business sector is however largely recognised as the key stakeholder in the development and implementation of sustainable tourism indicators (Rasoolimanesh et al., 2020).

The complex characteristics of urban environments (discussed in Chapter 3) and the multitude of tourism stakeholders with their different needs and interests can hamper the implementation of sustainability principles and of STIs in tourism cities. The next section therefore focuses on the key factors seen to help with putting into practice the concept of sustainable tourism.

Factors contributing to sustainable tourism implementation in cities

One of the main challenges faced by urban destinations in their efforts to become more sustainable is the implementation of sustainable tourism measures in practice. To help with that, researchers and organisations have looked at best practices and factors that contribute to implementing sustainable tourism policies at local (city) level, and some of these are presented further on.

To start with, *designing policies, strategies and plans* for (sustainable) tourism development in cities is one of the key measures that local authorities can take to help develop tourism more sustainably. Planning, in particular *long-term planning*, plays an important role in the management of tourism in world cities, as seen in Chapter 5. Without conducting research to understand the situation and designing dedicated policies to guide tourism development, it would be difficult for urban destinations to have a clear understanding of the challenges they face and to take advantage of the opportunities this activity may bring. In addition, a *clear vision and objectives* that are *shared* by the main

Table 8.2 Sustainable tourism indicators and the issues they address

Indicator	Issue
Protect natural areas	Ecosystem
Water consumption (tourism sector)	Water
Air pollution (tourism sector)	Atmosphere
Energy consumption (tourism sector)	Energy
Volume of recycled or treated waste/total volume generated	Waste
Level of satisfaction of the local population	Well-being
Environmental vulnerability	Resilience and risk
Ratio of tourists to local population at cultural events	Security and safety
Quality of bodies of water (lakes, rivers, sea)	Health
Level of tourist satisfaction	Satisfaction
Level of public participation in elections	Public participation
Level of maintenance of heritage sites	Culture
Frequency, capacity of services or level of use by existing transport modes to the destination	Accessibility
% of new real estate developments intended for tourism	Investments
Number of businesses that acquired an eco-responsible label	Promotion of ecotourism
% of income generated by tourism in the community	Economic vitality
% of new jobs in the tourism sector occupied by local residents	Employment
% of return visits	Marketing
Number of visits to heritage and cultural sites	Distinction
Volume of tourists	Tourist traffic

Source: Adapted from Tanguay et al. (2013).

players in tourism development in cities are needed, so everyone is aware of and supports the measures and works together towards achieving those objectives. Furthermore, sustainable tourism *policies need to be aligned* with policies promoted in other related sectors, such as transportation, housing and environmental conservation. This is because policies tend to be adjusted or changed during the implementation stage, and this may have implications for other sectors.

Having in place tourism policy documents is not enough, however, if *funding and other resources* (e.g., trained people) are not allocated by the local authorities to help implement them in practice. This is particularly challenging during periods of recession and crisis, as seen during the 2007–2008 global financial crisis, when urban destinations tended to focus on economic growth and recovery, with sustainability moving down on their list of priorities. For resources to be allocated, *strong leadership* and *political will* are needed to push forward the sustainability agenda. Strong political leadership can help in bringing together the key stakeholders in tourism development and trying to achieve a consensus on the measures to be taken.

Promoting legislation and regulations such as standards, incentives and penalties for sustainable tourism practices is seen by some authors as necessary in order to implement ST measures in practice. This approach is however not favoured by the tourism industry, who are usually proponents of voluntary practices such as certifications and codes of conduct.

Stakeholder cooperation and partnership is another important factor that facilitates sustainable tourism implementation in cities. This includes cooperation between local and central government, the tourism industry, as well as the other organisations and groups that have an interest in or are impacted by tourism development in urban destinations (an example from Edinburgh is given below). A list of the key stakeholders in the implementation of sustainable tourism and their roles is included in the following section. It is worth noting that cooperation between different departments within the same organisation/local authority is also important for a coordinated effort and a holistic view of the sustainable development measures promoted by a city.

Sweet tweet 67

Old and New Towns of Edinburgh – Management Plan

Edinburgh could be considered a good practice example with regard to stakeholder consultation and partnership, when producing the latest Management Plan 2017–2022. This document states that:

> It is important that the Plan not only reflects the views of the key organisations involved in its management, but those of its users, including residents, visitors to the city and broader stakeholders. With that in mind, an extensive programme of public engagement was carried out … This took the form of online public consultation in July 2016 and 2017, but it was also carried out over the same time frame using social media and public events.

Source: The City of Edinburgh Council (2018).

In addition, the *support of the local community* is essential for the sustainable development of tourism in urban destinations, residents having an important role to play in the entire process, from planning to implementation. Still, in many tourism cities, in particular in developing countries, locals are not involved at all in the decision-making processes and policy formulation. This may lead to conflicts between the needs and wants of the local communities, and those of tourists. Phuc and Nguyen (2020) identified three factors that contribute to residents' support for sustainable tourism development in urban areas, namely perception of value (benefits from tourism vs costs), collaboration and emotional solidarity (understood as local attitudes and perceptions towards tourists).

Knowledge and understanding of the tourism industry are considered to help with the adoption and implementation of ST initiatives in practice as well. There are many examples in the literature where the government and the tourism industry are operating on two different agendas, without much communication or coordination. In addition, a clear understanding is needed from all those involved in tourism of what sustainable tourism is, its importance and the benefits of implementing it in practice. This may require *awareness and education* for a number of stakeholders, including policy makers, tourism businesses and visitors. A good understanding of the concept and its principles may help those responsible for tourism development in cities to choose the most suitable approach for a specific destination, considering its characteristics and the challenges it faces (which in many cases differ from one city to another).

Good *public transport accessibility* and *transport infrastructure* are critical to world tourism cities that attract many visitors, as this will facilitate the movement of people around the city attractions. Transport is the main contributor to the carbon emissions produced by tourism activities in a destination, and it affects the residents' quality of life. Therefore, efforts should be made by policy makers and the tourism industry to make transport more environmentally friendly. An example from Singapore is included in the sweet tweet below.

Sweet tweet 68

The public transport system in Singapore

Singapore's public transport system is considered one of the best in the world as it is accessible, efficient, convenient, sustainable and affordable.

> Singapore is among the top-ranked cities for public transport, and also has among the safest and most ecologically sustainable systems. However, the city continues to evolve ... the government is improving the existing transport network by building a new terminal and runway at Changi Airport, extending and increasing the reliability of the Mass Rapid Transit (MRT) system, opening more cycling paths, and launching EV sharing and taxis, among other initiatives.

Source: Knupfer et al. (2018).

Having discussed a number of factors that can help with the implementation of sustainable tourism in practice, the focus of the next section will be the main stakeholders in urban destinations and their role in sustainable tourism implementation.

The roles of stakeholders in sustainable tourism implementation

One of the main aims of sustainable tourism is to find a balance between the different or even conflicting interests of all stakeholders in a destination. Their cooperation and partnership are essential for the sustainable development of tourism in a region, and they have been included among the guiding principles for sustainable tourism planning presented earlier. The importance of stakeholder cooperation is also acknowledged in the SDGs, in particular in Goal 17 (*Strengthen the means of implementation and revitalize the Global Partnership for Sustainable Development*).

Who are the stakeholders in a destination and how are these recognised? Hardy and Pearson (2018) propose a three-stage process in stakeholder recognition. The first step consists of *deciding who is a stakeholder* and thus may be included in the planning consultations and the management of tourism. There are two opposing approaches here, one in favour of all tourism stakeholder groups to be consulted, without prioritising them. The other approach, largely criticised by academics but often the reality in practice, is when a central organisation assesses stakeholders' interests and decides who will be consulted. The second step consists in *identifying the power and specific interests* of the stakeholders, while the third step entails *understanding the needs* of those stakeholders.

Several studies have identified the lack of cooperation among stakeholders in a destination as one of the barriers that affects the implementation of sustainable tourism policies in practice. Examples include the paper published by Dodds and Butler (2010) on the cases of Calvia in Spain and Malta, and Maxim (2015) on London. Among the factors found to hinder cooperation among stakeholders is the complex and multifaceted nature of tourism that involves many different stakeholders; stakeholders from a particular group are not necessarily homogeneous in their attitudes; the lack of a shared vision; lack of clear leadership; lack of government support; and a tendency to focus on short-term policies.

To help better understand the role that each stakeholder can play in the implementation of sustainable tourism in practice, UNWTO identified nine important stakeholders and their responsibilities (Figure 8.3). This may help destination managers to better understand the relationships among key stakeholders and thus find ways to effectively work together in the planning and management of tourism in cities.

Climate change and world tourism cities

Any discussion about sustainable tourism development in urban destinations cannot overlook the climate change debates and the associated challenges that cities are facing in the current environment. The last section of this chapter therefore looks at the implications of climate change for world tourism cities.

Climate change, while a relatively recent phenomenon, has increasingly attracted the attention of international organisations and researchers over the past few decades due to concerns that human activities and the fast-increasing CO_2 emissions may lead to global warming. One of the first actions taken by the international community to address climate change was the establishment in 1988 of the International Panel on Climate Change (IPCC), with the aim of investigating and reporting on this phenomenon. The IPCC's first report significantly contributed to the United Nations Framework Convention on Climate Change (UNFCCC), which was signed by 166 nations at the 1992 Earth Summit and included some key points which laid the foundation for the subsequent debates and events on climate change. Other important international events that advanced the climate change agenda include the 1997 Kyoto Protocol, where a number of developed countries agreed to reduce their greenhouse gas emissions by 2008–2012, and the 2009 meeting in Copenhagen where participant countries however failed to agree on specific targets.

The latest major event was the Conference of the Parties (COP) 21 that took place in December 2015, when the *Paris Agreement on Climate Change* was adopted. The Agreement was subsequently signed by 196 countries, including the United States, China and the European Union, who are among the larger emitters in the world. Since then,

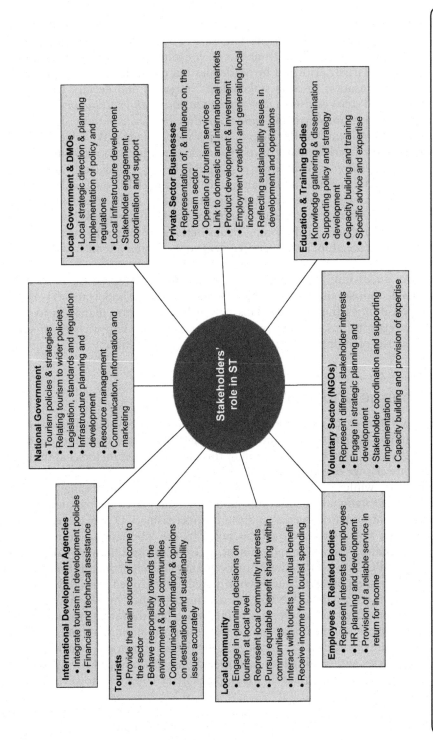

Figure 8.3 The roles of stakeholders in sustainable tourism development. (Source: Based on data from UNWTO (2013).)

the United States under the Trump presidency formally withdrew from the Agreement in November 2020, but the new president elect, Joe Biden, has pledged to re-join it. The Paris Agreement proposes an ambitious target to reduce the greenhouse gas emissions and limit global warming to a maximum of 1.5°C above pre-industrial levels. In December 2020, the virtual *Climate Ambition Summit* was co-hosted by the UN, the UK and France to mark the fifth anniversary of the Paris Agreement. The summit brought together around 70 leaders from those countries that were ready to make new commitments to tackle climate change. An important moment of the summit was when António Guterres, the UN secretary general, has called on all countries to declare a climate emergency (McGrath, 2020).

Researchers highlighted that there are very strong links between the two documents, the Paris Agreement and the 2030 Agenda promoting the SDGs introduced earlier, with the tourism industry playing an important part in both (Scott et al., 2016). As was the case with the Agenda for Sustainable Development and the SDGs, cities have an important role in implementing the Paris Agreement.

Large cities are considered a key contributor to climate change, with estimates suggesting that urban environments are responsible for 75% of the global CO_2 emissions (UNEP, 2017b). At the same time, climate change has been recognised as one of the fundamental challenges faced by cities in the coming decades (Pandy and Rogerson, 2019; UNEP, 2017), with implications for all stakeholders. Urban areas are expected to see changes in the weather and climate patterns that can lead to more frequent heat waves, natural disasters, water shortages, floods and storms. This can have implications not only for the urban infrastructure and the basic services offered by cities but could also impact cities' habitability in some parts of the world, particularly in the southern hemisphere.

Many cities are vulnerable to the negative impacts of climate change, especially in developing countries that are already facing many other challenges. Examples include the city of Lagos in Nigeria that is likely to face an increased number of hot days and droughts; Manila in the Philippines that could face an increased risk of natural disasters, including floods, tsunamis and hurricanes; Mumbai in India that is at risk of more frequent flooding; and Rio de Janeiro (Figure 8.4) in Brazil which is expected to be the most affected city in South America, being prone to flooding, landslides and water shortages. All these aspects would have significant implications for tourism development in the affected areas.

Several cities around the world, however, are already taking action towards tackling climate change and cutting carbon emissions, as can be seen in the sweet tweet below. Examples of such cities and the measures they have taken include the Hague in the Netherlands that built an additional layer of protection against flooding in a seaside resort within its boundaries; the Ultra-Low Emission Zone (ULEZ) introduced by London in 2019 to reduce pollution and improve air quality in central areas; Calgary in Canada that is building a new light rail line aimed at cutting CO_2 emissions; and Taipei in Taiwan that is working on fixing water leaks in an attempt to tackle droughts (Scott, 2019).

Sweet tweet 69

Cities are on the front line of tackling climate change

The actions taken by cities and the policies they promote could play an important role in cutting greenhouse gas emissions.

Five cities have set city-wide 100% renewable energy targets – including Paris, San Francisco and Canberra – while Reykjavik has already achieved this, thanks to Iceland's plentiful geothermal energy resources. Thirteen cities plan to be climate or carbon neutral by 2050, including the Hague, Boston and Sydney.

Source: Scott (2019).

Yet, the world is still significantly off track in terms of meeting the agreed targets, with more action needed from all stakeholders at all levels (UN, 2020b). On top of that, the level of policy integration between climate change and tourism domains was found to be limited, with researchers suggesting that in many destinations "climate change has not yet become a priority for tourism policy makers" (Becken et al., 2020).

Figure 8.4 Rio de Janeiro (Courtesy: Unsplash.com, Mariano Diaz).

Summary comments

Sustainable development and sustainable tourism are two important concepts that have attracted the attention of tourism researchers and policy makers in the past decades. Although criticised for being ambiguous, vague and difficult to implement, these concepts help policy makers in their efforts to manage tourism wisely, taking advantage of the benefits brought by this activity for the local economies and communities, while trying to minimise its negative impacts. To help with the implementation of these concepts in practice, different sets of objectives, principles and indicators were proposed, with some examples discussed in this chapter.

It has been noted that while destinations have made some progress with the adoption of strategies and measures for the sustainable development of tourism, the same cannot be said about their implementation in practice. Therefore, many organisations and researchers are calling for more action from governments and the tourism industry.

World tourism cities play a key role in the sustainable development of a region and in tackling climate change, two important objectives for many international organisations and governments. They can bring together and facilitate stakeholder cooperation and thus contribute towards finding solutions to difficult problems that are associated with the sustainable development of tourism in a region. To achieve that, a strong political will is needed to help cities commit the necessary resources to manage tourism sustainably. This however is not an easy task in the currently difficult economic climate, with most cities still dealing with the devastating impacts of the coronavirus.

Thought questions

1) How can policy makers address the negative impacts that accompany tourism development in world cities?
2) What challenges can you see in achieving a balance between the three pillars of sustainability (economic, social and environmental) in urban destinations?
3) There are voices who criticise the concept of sustainable development for being vague or imprecise, while others consider this to be one of its strengths. What is your opinion on the topic?
4) Why is it important for policy makers in world tourism cities to consider the sustainability principles when developing tourism strategies and plans?
5) What are the challenges associated with sustainable tourism implementation in urban destinations? How can these be addressed and by whom?
6) What can be done to encourage cooperation among the main stakeholders in tourism destinations?
7) There are hundreds of sustainable tourism indicators developed by different organisations and researchers. How can organisations decide which ones are the most appropriate to use for their destinations?
8) How can cities contribute to the Sustainable Development Goals? Can you give examples of urban destinations that took steps towards achieving these goals?
9) Why are cities important players in addressing climate change? What measures can they take to reduce the CO_2 emissions related to tourism activities?
10) There are voices that call for a rapid recovery of the tourism industry as this would help regions to recover from the impacts of the COVID-19 pandemic, while others call for reforming the tourism industry, making it more sustainable. What is your opinion on this?

References

Aall, C., & Koens, K. (2019). The discourse on sustainable urban tourism: The need for discussing more than overtourism. *Sustainability, 11*(15), 4228.

Balampanidis, D., Maloutas, T., Papatzani, E., & Pettas, D. (2019). Informal urban regeneration as a way out of the crisis? Airbnb in Athens and its effects on space and society. *Urban Research & Practice.* https://doi.org/10.1080/17535069.2019.1600009

Becken, S., Whittlesea, E., Loehr, J., & Scott, D. (2020). Tourism and climate change: Evaluating the extent of policy integration. *Journal of Sustainable Tourism*, 28(10), 1603–1624.

Benítez-Aurioles, B., & Tussyadiah, I. (2020). What Airbnb does to the housing market. *Annals of Tourism Research*. https://doi.org/10.1016/j.annals.2020.103108

Boom, S., Weijschede, J., Melissen, F., Koens, K., & Mayer, I. (2020). Identifying stakeholder perspectives and worldviews on sustainable urban tourism development using a Q-sort methodology. *Current Issues in Tourism*, https://doi.org/10.1080/13683500.2020.17 22076

City of Bonn. (2020). *Bonn Aiming for More Sustainability*. English Website. https://www.bonn.de/microsite/en/international-profile/sutainability-cluster/bonn-aiming-for-more-sustainability.php

Day, J. (2021). Sustainable tourism in cities. In A. M. Morrison & J. A. Coca-Stefaniak (Eds.). *Routledge Handbook of Tourism Cities*, 1st ed., pp. 52–64. London: Routledge.

Department for Digital, Culture, Media & Sport (DCMS). (2009). *Sustainable Tourism in England: A Framework for Action—Meeting the Key Challenges*. DCMS, London, UK.

Dodds, R., & Butler, R. (2019). The phenomena of overtourism: A review. *International Journal of Tourism Cities*, 5(4), 519–528.

Dwyer, L., & Edwards, D. (2010). Sustainable tourism planning. In J. J. Liburd & D. Edwards (Eds.). *Understanding the Sustainable Development of Tourism*, pp. 19–44. Oxford: Goodfellow Publisher Limited.

European Commission. (2020). *European Handbook for SDG Voluntary Local Reviews*. https://publications.jrc.ec.europa.eu/repository/bitstream/JRC118682/european_ha ndbook_for_sdg_voluntary_local_reviews_online.pdf

Grah, B., Dimovski, V., & Peterlin, J. (2020). Managing sustainable urban tourism development: The case of Ljubljana. *Sustainability*, 12(3), 792.

Gravari-Barbas, M., & Guinad, S. (2021). Tourism and gentrification. In Alastair M. Morrison & J. A. Coca-Stefaniak (Eds.). *Routledge Handbook of Tourism Cities*, pp. 88–100. London: Routledge.

Hardy, A., & Pearson, L. J. (2018). Examining stakeholder group specificity: An innovative sustainable tourism approach. *Journal of Destination Marketing & Management*, 8, 247–258.

Hartley, K. (2019). *Global Goals, Global Cities: Achieving the SDGs through Collective Local Action*, p. 40. Chicago Council. https://www.thechicagocouncil.org/sites/default/fi les/report_global-goals-global-cities_190923.pdf

Higgins-Desbiolles, F. (2020). The "war over tourism": Challenges to sustainable tourism in the tourism academy after COVID-19. *Journal of Sustainable Tourism*. 29(4): 551–569. https://doi.org/10.1080/09669582.2020.1803334

Keith, L. (2020, November). *This Spanish City Is the First to Measure Tourism's Carbon Footprint*. Lonely Planet. https://www.lonelyplanet.com/articles/valencia-carbon-emissi ons-tourists

Knupfer, S. M., Pokotilo, V., & Woetzel, J. (2018). *Elements of Success: Urban Transportation Systems of 24 Global Cities*. McKinsey & Company. https://www.mckinsey.com/~/med ia/McKinsey/Business%20Functions/Sustainability/Our%20Insights/Elements%20of %20success%20Urban%20transportation%20systems%20of%2024%20global%20ci ties/Urban-transportation-systems_e-versions.ashx

Lakritz, T. (2020, February 5). 7 places being ruined by cruise ships. *Insider*. https://www .insider.com/cruise-ships-environmental-impact-tourism-2019-9

Lerario, A., & Di Turi, S. (2018). Sustainable Urban Tourism: Reflections on the Need for Building-Related Indicators. *Sustainability*, 10(6), 1981.

Matoga, Ł., & Pawłowska, A. (2018). Off-the-beaten-track tourism: A new trend in the tourism development in historical European cities. A case study of the city of Krakow, Poland. *Current Issues in Tourism*, 21(14), 1644–1669.

Mawby, R. I. (2017). Crime and tourism: What the available statistics do or do not tell us. *International Journal of Tourism Policy*, 7(2), 81–92.

Maxim, C. (2015). Drivers of success in implementing sustainable tourism policies in urban areas. *Tourism Planning and Development*, 12(1), 37–47.

Maxim, C. (2016). Sustainable tourism implementation in urban areas: A case study of London. *Journal of Sustainable Tourism*, 24(7), 971–989.

McCool, S. (2013). Sustainable tourism: Guiding fiction, social trap or path to resilience? *Tourism Recreation Research*, 38(2), 214–221.

McGrath, M. (2020, December 12). World needs to declare 'climate emergency': UN. *BBC*. https://www.bbc.com/news/science-environment-55276769

Miller, D., Merrilees, B., & Coghlan, A. (2015). Sustainable urban tourism: Understanding and developing visitor pro-environmental behaviours. *Journal of Sustainable Tourism*, 23(1), 26–46.

Önder, I., Wöber, K., & Zekan, B. (2017). Towards a sustainable urban tourism development in Europe: The role of benchmarking and tourism management information systems: A partial model of destination competitiveness. *Tourism Economics*, 23(2), 243–259.

Pandy, W. R., & Rogerson, C. M. (2019). Urban tourism and climate change: Risk perceptions of business tourism stakeholders in Johannesburg, South Africa. *Urbani Izziv*, 30(supplement), 229–243.

Pappalepore, I., Maitland, R., & Smith, A. (2014). Prosuming creative urban areas. Evidence from East London. *Annals of Tourism Research*, 44, 227–240.

Phuc, H. N., & Nguyen, H. M. (2020). The importance of collaboration and emotional solidarity in residents' support for sustainable urban tourism: Case study Ho Chi Minh City. *Journal of Sustainable Tourism*. https://doi.org/10.1080/09669582.2020.1831520

Rasoolimanesh, S. M., Ramakrishna, S., Hall, C. M., Esfandiar, K., & Seyfi, S. (2020). A systematic scoping review of sustainable tourism indicators in relation to the sustainable development goals. *Journal of Sustainable Tourism*. https://doi.org/10.1080/09669582.2020.1775621

Ruhanen, L. (2013). Local government: Facilitator or inhibitor of sustainable tourism development? *Journal of Sustainable Tourism*, 21(1), 80–98.

Scott, D., Hall, C. M., & Gössling, S. (2016). A report on the Paris climate change agreement and its implications for tourism: Why we will always have Paris. *Journal of Sustainable Tourism*, 24(7), 933–948.

Scott, M. (2019). *Cities Are On The Front Line Of Tackling Climate Change—And They Need To Do More*. Forbes. https://www.forbes.com/sites/mikescott/2019/06/05/cities-are-on-the-front-line-of-tackling-climate-change-and-they-need-to-do-more/

Sharpley, R. (2009). *Tourism Development and the Environment: Beyond Sustainability?* London: Earthscan Ltd.

Sharpley, R. (2020). Tourism, sustainable development and the theoretical divide: 20 years on. *Journal of Sustainable Tourism*, 28(11), 1932–1946.

South Australian Tourism Commission. (2007). *Design Guidelines for Sustainable Tourism Development*. Adelaide: South Australian Tourism Commission.

Tanguay, G. A., Rajaonson, J., & Therrien, M.-C. (2013). Sustainable tourism indicators: Selection criteria for policy implementation and scientific recognition. *Journal of Sustainable Tourism, 21*(6), 862–879.

The City of Edinburgh Council. (2018). *Management Plan 2017—2022*. https://ewh.org.uk/plan/assets/Management-Plan-2018b.pdf?

UN. (2015). *Resolution Adopted by the General Assembly on 25 September 2015*. https://www.un.org/ga/search/view:doc.asp?symbol=A/RES/70/1&Lang=E

UN. (2020a). *SDG Good Practices: A Compilation of Success Stories and Lessons Learned in SDG Implementation*, 1st ed. UN. https://sdgs.un.org/sites/default/files/2020-11/SDG%20Good%20Practices%20Publication%202020.pdf

UN. (2020b). *Sustainable Development Goals Report 2020*. https://www.un.org/sustainabledevelopment/progress-report/

UN Environment Programme (UNEP). (2017a). *Sustainable Tourism*. https://www.unep.org/regions/asia-and-pacific/regional-initiatives/supporting-resource-efficiency/asia-pacific-roadmap-3

UN Environment Programme (UNEP). (2017b, September 26). *Cities and Climate Change*. UNEP – UN Environment Programme. http://www.unenvironment.org/explore-topics/resource-efficiency/what-we-do/cities/cities-and-climate-change

UNEP & World Tourism Organization (WTO). (2005). *Making Tourism More Sustainable: A Guide for Policy Makers*. Geneva: UNEP/WTO.

UNWTO (Ed.). (2013). *Sustainable Tourism for Development Guidebook: Enhancing capacities for Sustainable Tourism for development in developing countries*. World Tourism Organization (UNWTO). https://doi.org/10.18111/9789284415496

UNWTO. (2020). *Global Guidelines to Restart Tourism*. https://webunwto.s3.eu-west-1.amazonaws.com/s3fs-public/2020-05/UNWTO-Global-Guidelines-to-Restart-Tourism.pdf

Visit Valencia. (2020). *Sustainable Tourism Valencia 2030*. https://www.visitvalencia.com/en/valencia-tourism-foundation/tourism-and-city/sustainable-tourism-strategy-project-valencia-2030

Wise, N. (2016). Outlining triple bottom line contexts in urban tourism regeneration. *Cities, 53*, 30–34.

World Commission on Environment and Development. (1987). *Our Common Future*. Oxford: Oxford University Press.

World Travel & Tourism Council (WTTC). (2019). *City Travel and Tourism Impact 2019*. World Travel & Tourism Council. https://protect-eu.mimecast.com/s/IKVVCP7vnC3Gyryu1sBP4?domain=wttc.org

Zamfir, A., & Corbos, R.-A. (2015). Towards sustainable tourism development in urban areas: Case study on Bucharest as tourist destination. *Sustainability, 7*(9), 12709–12722.

Chapter 9

Smart cities and smart tourism in cities

Abstract

This chapter discusses the progress of ICTs, the Internet of Things and new technologies that impact society in general and tourism in particular. It explains what a smart city is, its dimensions and the "smart" initiatives promoted by global cities from different parts of the world, focusing on their relevance to tourism.

It then introduces the concepts of smart destinations and smart tourism, with an emphasis on how these apply to city destinations. While acknowledging the critical advantages brought by the rapid development of ICTs and the benefits they bring for tourism destinations, the chapter also notes a number of challenges associated with this rapid progress.

The last part of this chapter focuses on the latest technologies and debates that are expected to shape the tourism ecosystem in the future.

Keywords: ICTs; IoT; e-tourism; digitisation; smart city; smart destinations; smart tourism.

Learning objectives

Having read this chapter, you should be able to:

- Discuss the rapid development of ICTs and other new technologies over the past decades.
- Summarise the benefits and limitations of ICTs.
- Explain what a smart city is and discuss its key dimensions.

DOI: 10.4324/9781003111412-12

- Define smart destinations and present their characteristics.
- Describe the latest technologies that are expected to shape the tourism ecosystem and discuss the associated challenges faced by destinations.

ICTs, the Internet of Things and other new technologies

Technology innovation and ICTs had a major impact on the transformation of the tourism industry over the years by influencing business practices and strategies and consumer behaviour and affecting industry structures. The fast progress of ICTs has profoundly changed society, and ICTs have become part of the contemporary consumer culture, thus having fundamental implications for city tourism destinations.

ICTs evolved over the past decades from the central reservation systems (CRSs) used by major airlines in the 1960s, to the computer reservation systems (CRSs) used by the tourism businesses in the 1970s, to the major changes brought by global distribution systems (GDSs) in the 1980s, followed by the Internet revolution and the network era in the 1990s, to social media and user-generated content (UGC) in the 2000s and smart technologies in the 2010s. Smartphones, in particular, had major implications over the past decade for how visitors purchase holidays, experience destinations and share their experiences via social media platforms. Figure 9.1 gives a brief overview on how ICTs have evolved over the past six decades, and outlines some of the main technology innovations that have transformed city destinations.

Before looking at how ICTs and other new technologies have contributed to the transformation of cities and their transition towards smarter destinations, a number of key concepts need to be introduced first .

ICT developments

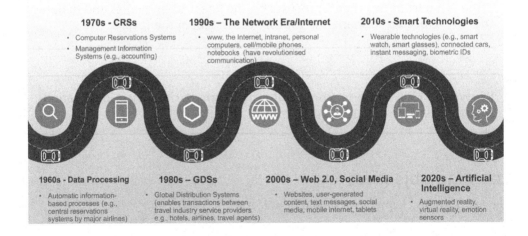

Figure 9.1 Stages of the ICT revolution.

ICTs have revolutionised the tourism sector, in particular the promotion and communication functions, and played a key role in increasing the competitiveness of tourism destinations (Buhalis and Law, 2008). ICTs help organisations to better manage their resources and improve productivity, to communicate with their stakeholders, including visitors and service providers, and to develop new partnerships. ICTs represent a large variety of communication technologies, including the Internet, email, chat apps, laptops, smartphones and mobile networks, mobile phone applications, wireless technologies and digital cameras, to name but a few.

E-tourism encompasses the "analysis, design, implementation and application of IT/e-commerce solutions in the travel and tourism industry, as well as the analysis (of the impact) of the respective technical/economic processes and market structures" (Neidhardt and Werthner, 2018, pp. 1–2). It helps tourism organisations to maximise their profits, by improving their efficiency and effectiveness (Buhalis and Law, 2008).

More recently, there has been a shift from e-tourism towards smart tourism, a concept discussed later in this chapter. This represents a move from the "digital sphere" into a combined "digital and physical sphere", with websites replaced by smartphones and sensors, a move towards big data and technology-mediated co-creation and public-private-consumer collaborations (Treiblmaier, 2020).

The **Internet of Things** (IoT) is an important concept that also needs to be introduced when discussing ICTs. It is described as a giant network that connects physical objects and virtual things, using ICTs with the aim of enabling advanced services. The IoT impacts every step in our lives, from the way we travel, to the way we do our shopping. In a tourism context, it enables the more active engagement of tourists with the places they visit.

The **Internet of Everything** (IoE) is a broader concept than the IoT, and it represents "a digital ecosystem of networks, devices and applications, interconnected through the Internet infrastructure" (Buhalis, 2022). The IoE brings together four pillars – people, processes, things and data – to help make network connections more relevant. The difference between the two concepts is that the IoT is focused on *things*, while the IoE brings together all four aspects mentioned earlier.

ICTs and other new technologies can play a number of key roles in destinations (Neuhofer et al., 2012; Sigala, 2018), as they:

- Help with the operations, structures and strategies of tourism organisations.
- Contribute to the innovation of products, processes and management.
- Enable opportunities for tourism organisations to attract and retain visitors.
- Facilitate individual expression, e.g., visitors can more easily share information about their experiences, self-constructing their social images and identities.
- Act as decision support tools for both tourism companies and visitors, e.g., in setting and comparing prices, and providing meta-search engines.
- Support market intelligence activities, e.g., collecting, analysing, sharing and interpreting data.
- Offer e-learning tools, e.g., education and knowledge management via collaborative and open learning models such as massive open online courses (MOOCs).
- Provide automation tools, e.g., substituting labour with programmable tasks such as in the case of self-driven cars.
- Enable new business models, such as the sharing economy, and new management practices, including crowdfunding and gamification.

- Transform tourism experiences, such as in the case of virtual tours and augmented experiences that are discussed later in this chapter.
- Constitute a co-creation platform, with examples including review websites and wiki-based tourism guides.

The latest developments in ICTs and other new technologies have also influenced the attitudes and behaviour of tourists. Navío-Marco, Ruiz-Gómez and Sevilla-Sevilla (2018) looked into this aspect and found that *eTourists* (those visitors who seek information and buy services online) tend to perform a number of digital activities to help with their travel and destination experiences, such as:

- Consulting and gathering information to help them design travel experiences, including through online searches and price comparison websites.
- Managing the travel and tourism services purchased via the Internet and mobile phones before they travel, such as booking hotels and attractions or purchasing airline tickets.
- Other activities needed once they travel or when they arrive at destinations, such as looking for restaurants.
- Post-trip activities, such as recommending destinations to other people or writing blogs about travel experiences.
- Getting involved themselves in tourism e-business by co-creating value with other tourists, for example, becoming an Airbnb *Superhost* and sharing services with other visitors, e.g., BlaBlacar.

While they bring many benefits to the tourism sector and in the way visitors experience destinations, ICTs also have several limitations. Table 9.1 presents some of the main benefits and limitations of ICTs in relation to tourism.

Authors have also looked at the role of ICTs in achieving the Sustainable Development Goals, which were introduced in Chapter 8. It is expected that the development of ICTs will play a significant role in achieving SDG targets as they will contribute to more efficient and effective processes through innovative solutions. Examples include investments in green technologies aimed at reducing pollution, technology development, business innovation, improved performance, resilient infrastructure and safer environments. Still, there are voices that point to the negative impacts associated with the development of ICTs and the inhibitor role they may play in achieving the SDGs. The loss of jobs as a result of automation is often cited as a negative effect, as is the fact that ICTs may widen inequalities among people, and the high energy requirements of such new technologies (Vinuesa et al., 2020).

This section offered an overview on the evolution of ICTs and looked briefly at how new technologies have transformed tourism. It also reviewed a number of key concepts and highlighted the benefits and limitations of ICTs. The next section considers how ICTs and other new technologies are contributing to the development of smart cities.

Smart cities

The ever-growing level of urbanisation and the increasing number of people who live in cities require smart solutions to help policy-makers address important issues such as mobility, energy, healthcare and infrastructure. The IoT, a concept introduced earlier,

Table 9.1 Benefits and limitations of ICTs

Benefits of ICTs

For organisations	*For consumers*
• Locate customers and/or suppliers worldwide, at reasonable cost and relatively quickly	• Can shop anywhere, anytime
• Reduce costs of information processing, storage, distribution	• Large selection to choose from a variety of channels (e.g., vendors, products, styles)
• Reduce delays and costs through supply chain improvements	• Can customise many products and/or services
• Business always open (24/7/365)	• Can compare and shop for lowest prices
• Customisation/personalisation at a reasonable cost	• Digitised products can be downloaded immediately upon payment
• Seller can specialise in a narrow field, yet make money	
• Facilitate innovation and enable unique business models	• Easy to find what is needed, with details, demos, etc.
• Short time-to-market and increased speed	• Sometimes no sales tax
• Lower communication costs	• Can socialise online in communities yet be at home
• Saves time and reduce costs by enabling e-procurement	• Can find unique products and items
• Improves customer service	
• Easier to keep distributed material up-to-date	
• E-commerce helps small companies to compete against large ones	
• Reduce distribution costs by online delivery	

Limitations of ICTs

Technological limitations	**Non-technological limitations**
• Lack of universal standards for quality, security and reliability	• Security and privacy concerns
• Telecommunications bandwidth can be sometimes insufficient, especially for m-commerce (mobile commerce)	• Lack of trust in e-commerce and unknown sellers can deter buyers
• Some systems may be inefficient and prone to failure	• Legal and public policy issues are unclear
• Software development tools are still evolving	• Online fraud is increasing
• Can be difficult to integrate e-commerce software with existing (especially legacy) applications and databases	• Digital exclusion
	• Information manipulation
	• Reduced social interaction between hosts and providers and guests/consumers
• Internet accessibility is still expensive and/or inconvenient in many parts of the world	• Threats to languages and cultures
	• Knowledge and information loss

Sources: Developed from the works of Buhalis and Jun (2011) and Buhalis (2020).

Figure 9.2 Hanoi, the capital of Vietnam, aims for smart city status (Courtesy: Unsplash.com, Minh Luu).

is perceived to offer "the most promising enabling technologies for tackling these challenges" (Alavi et al., 2018, p. 589) and being able to make a substantial contribution towards the sustainable development of smart cities.

The concepts of *smart* and *smartness* evolved over the years from a narrow technological interpretation linked to mobile devices towards a more "nuanced application" that makes reference to geographical locations, such as smart cities (Coca-Stefaniak and Seisdedos, 2021). Smart cities have been previously described as "social entities focused on human interaction", which contribute to innovation and business creation (Abella et al., 2017, p. 48). Other related terms used for smart cities are the "digital city" or the "intelligent city". These cities rely on the implementation of new ICTs and other advanced technologies, e.g., smart hardware devices, mobile networks, software applications, artificial intelligence and sensors, that are transforming the world we live in and also our behaviour. Therefore, smart cities are considered both creative and intelligent. Examples of such cities include London, Stockholm, Amsterdam, Boston (Figure 9.5), Vienna, Luxembourg City, Turku, Montpellier, Seoul and San Francisco. Many other cities around the world are working towards becoming "smart", such as Santiago in Chile (the focus of Short break 9), Athens in Greece (Figure 9.6), Jakarta in Indonesia (Figure 9.7) and Hanoi in Vietnam (Figure 9.2).

Sweet tweet 70

Building a smart city destination – Hanoi

The Director of the Hanoi Department of Information and Communications, Phan Lan Tu, has identified four key areas to lay the foundations for Hanoi's smart city transformation by 2030. These areas are health, education, transportation and tourism, with work for developing those areas having already started in 2017.

Three stages have been identified in becoming a smart city: the first one, before 2020, focused on the development of the infrastructure and the necessary technology for a smart city; the second, from 2020 to 2025, is a focus on making this technology functional and establishing the city's digital economy; in the third stage, from 2025 to 2030, the different parts of the project will be connected so that the Vietnamese capital will become a functional smart city.

Source: Ariffin (2018).

A variety of definitions are proposed for smart cities by academics and organisations, with some focusing on the characteristics of such cities, and others emphasising the key roles played by technology. According to the European Commission (2020):

> A *smart city* goes beyond the use of information and communication technologies (ICTs) for better resource use and less emissions. It means striving for sustainability through smarter urban transport networks, upgraded water supply and waste disposal facilities, and more efficient ways to light and heat buildings. It also means a more interactive and responsive city administration, safer public spaces and meeting the needs of an ageing population.

Smart cities are thus seen to help "balance social development and economic growth in a context of high urbanisation" (Ben Letaifa, 2015, p. 1414), by improving a number of services such as transportation, energy use, education and healthcare systems. An example from Los Angeles is given now.

Sweet tweet 71

Los Angeles as an example of a smart city

Los Angeles is a good example to illustrate the changes that have been taken place in many cities across the world.

> Los Angeles has a technologically proactive city government. Since 2013, Los Angeles has progressed from a moderate digital status to a leading digital city. The new mayor Eric Garcetti issued Executive Directive 3 on Open Data, which mandated that the city supply raw data to the public in easily accessible formats, leverage public information as a civic asset, promote innovation from entrepreneurs and businesses, and that each city department be required to implement open data.

Source: Samih (2019).

Another concept closely linked to smart cities is *digitisation*, which refers to the process of improving an activity or entity through the use of new technologies and that need frequent adjustments due to the rapid development of ICTs (Manfreda et al., 2021). Digitalisation and digital transformation are prerequisites for developing smart city destinations.

Smart cities represent a multidisciplinary field of study that is constantly evolving due to the rapid developments in new technologies. Different frameworks were proposed over the years to emphasise the key dimensions of smart cities, and a synthesis is presented in Figure 9.3. The most common dimensions used in those frameworks tend to be smart governance, smart people and smart infrastructure (Allam and Newman, 2018).

Smart governance has been defined as "a socio-technical approach, which aligns technological potential with novel forms of collaboration between local government and citizens with the aim of tackling urban issues based on the principles of sustainability" (Tomor et al., 2019, p. 4). The concept developed from the need to adjust the mainstream urban governance approaches to the complex nature of urban systems (discussed in Chapter 3) and to make use of new developments in ICTs and other technological innovations when responding to current societal challenges.

Traditional *governance* represents the "regime of laws, administrative rules, judicial rulings, and practices that constrain, prescribe, and enable government activity, where such activity is broadly defined as the production and delivery of publicly supported goods and services" (Lynn et al., 2000, p. 235). Smart governance, therefore, helps make this process more interactive by taking advantage of the digital technologies available to improve communication and cooperation among various state and non-state actors, promoting innovative policies and optimising urban management.

The main components of smart governance, as identified by Tomor, Meijer, Michels and Geertman (2019), are:

- *Governmental organisation*, which includes a variety of aspects such as vision and strategies, motivation, attitudes, decision-making, roles and responsibilities, process coordination, the provision of financial, regulative, technological means and human resources, knowledge management and organisational culture.
- *Citizen participation*, in particular the level of interactive citizen participation in urban governance, the capacity and willingness of citizens to engage in the process of smart governance and their motivations to take part in smart governance.

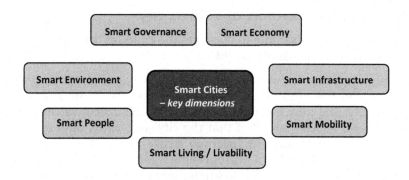

Figure 9.3 Key dimensions of smart cities.

- *Use of technology*, and in particular ICTs, consisting of a growing variety of tools, devices and technologies such as web portals, augmented and virtual reality, mobile phone apps, discussion forums, wikis, blogs and various social media tools.

In the aforementioned review paper, the authors found that despite the efforts made by governments and an increase in digital-based collaboration, smart governance is still rarely implemented successfully in practice, with the old structures and patterns being difficult to replace with new approaches. Among the reasons identified for this situation is a lack of capacity and willingness to genuinely engage in smart governance among governments and citizens. Examples of unsuccessful smart tourism initiatives include the City Data Exchange project in Copenhagen launched in 2015 and closed three years later due to lack of engagement from stakeholders; and the Rijenradar virtual queuing system launched in April 2017 in Amsterdam and designed to better manage visitor flows in the city, but which was closed two months later due to the small number of attractions that signed up to take part in the initiative (Johnson et al., 2021). This is not to say that there are no success stories, and indeed an example from South Korea is now presented.

Sweet tweet 72

South Korea – smart governance during a global pandemic

This example shows how a smart destination, South Korea, took rapid action during the COVID-19 pandemic and made use of ICTs and other smart technologies to engage in smart governance and actively communicate with citizens.

> Proactive information-sharing enabled citizens to develop a shared understanding of the situation, comply with the newly adopted rules and safety measures, and build confidence in their government's abilities to manage the crisis. The case suggests that smart governance in South Korea can help to enable a smart form of justice that involves equity and fairness in information sharing and resource allocation among its residents and visitors, mitigates discrimination and exclusion, and facilitates democracy through an informed and involved citizenry.

Source: Choi, Lee and Jamal (2021).

Smart people constitute one of the fundamental components of the smart city system, as without their active participation and involvement the system will not be able to function. Two significant goals of smart cities relate to increasing the quality of life of citizens and improving the living environment (Kirimtat et al., 2020), focusing on social and human capital. The programmes implemented by smart cities should therefore aim to foster better informed and educated, and more participatory citizens. In doing so, smart cities are expected to find new ways to empower their citizens to take an active role and contribute to the governance process with their input via various ICT tools and platforms.

Smart people can be described as the result of a cosmopolitan society, with ethnic and social diversity, showing tolerance, creativity and flexibility, as well as a willingness to participate in public life. Smart citizens are expected to contribute directly to the co-creation and co-production of public services and policies promoted by governments using the new ICTs, and thus ensuring that services are delivered in their interests. In order to improve the social capital and raise its qualification, cities can organise online courses and workshops and education programmes and offer online assistance (Ben Letaifa, 2015).

Sweet tweet 73

Future City Glasgow – people make Glasgow

The city of Glasgow in Scotland is a good example of a destination that explores new ways to harness the power of data to make the city a better place for everyone.

> From our state-of-the-art city operations centre to the creation of an innovative city data hub, Glasgow is putting people at the heart of its future … We have been exploring how we can use technology to make our streets safer, making it easier for people to get active and improve their health and understanding how we can better use, save and generate energy.
> Glasgow has unlocked hundreds of data sources and opened up access to allow smart people to do smart things. We have been involving and empowering communities, bringing people together to explore their vision for our city and inspiring future generations to make a difference.

Source: Glasgow City Council (2021).

Still, not everyone has access to the Internet, or the skills and opportunities needed to be able to participate in the smart governance process. Figure 9.4 shows how the world population and the number of Internet users have evolved over the past two decades. In 2000, less than 10% of people worldwide (about 7%) had Internet access; by 2020 more than half of the global population (58%) were Internet users. This shows the rapid development of ICTs, with access to the Internet ever-expanding and more affordable (smart) digital devices. As may be expected, Europe and North America have the highest Internet penetration rate, while Africa has the lowest.

Smart infrastructure has been defined as "the result of combining physical infrastructure with digital infrastructure, providing improved information to enable better decision making, faster and cheaper" (Cambridge Centre for Smart Infrastructure and Construction (CSIC), 2016, p. 2). Physical infrastructure includes:

- Transport
- Telecommunications
- Energy
- Water
- Waste

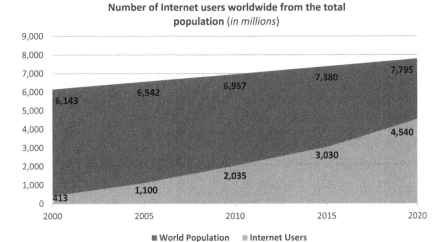

Number of Internet users worldwide from the total
population (*in millions*)

■ World Population   ▦ Internet Users

> **Figure 9.4** Number of Internet users worldwide of the total population
> (Source: Authors' work based on data from Statista (2021) and
> Worldometer (2021)).

Digital infrastructure includes:

- Sensors
- Networks
- Internet of Things
- Big data
- Machine learning

Smart infrastructure is key to smart cities, as it can help improve efficiency and save costs, minimise service failure and disruption, improve user experience, facilitate better use of resources, minimise greenhouse gas emissions and improve the quality and range of the services. These are very important aspects, considering that the number of people living in urban areas is constantly increasing (as noted in Chapters 2 and 3), which puts significant pressure on the limited resources and physical infrastructure in world cities. An example from a capital city in a developing country in Eastern Europe, Bucharest in Romania, is given here to show the efforts made by cities around the world towards implementing smart solutions.

Sweet tweet 74

Bucharest on its way to becoming a smarter city

Romania's capital has made significant progress towards becoming a smart city in recent years, yet it is far from being ready to join the league of top smart cities worldwide.

> From apps that allow you to pay for public transport online by card (B-Pay) to those that help you reach your destination more easily using overground public transportation (InfoTB), improve traffic conditions (Traffic Alert Bucharest), help you find quick parking (Parking Bucharest), notify authorities about people in need for social assistance (Social Alert Bucharest) or promote tourist attractions, the city is growing increasingly smarter.
>
> Source: Cristea (2020).

The other four dimensions of smart cities (i.e., smart mobility, smart living, smart environment and smart economy) are briefly introduced.

Smart mobility is another crucial dimension of smart cities, in particular in the context of tourism, which involves the movement of people towards and within a destination. It refers to the accessibility within and outside a city destination and requires the use of computers and other digital devices (such as transport infrastructure, mobile sensors and camera networks) to monitor, manage and control the flow of people in a city and the processes in place. It also helps gather useful data that can assist city managers to better understand the most popular locations or attractions visited by tourists and the type of activities people tend to engage in during their stays (Park et al., 2020).

Smart living or liveability refers to the use of information and communication technologies to improve the quality of life for residents, by ensuring public safety, education and access to proper healthcare. During the lockdown measures introduced by many cities around the world throughout the COVID-19 pandemic, many activities were transitioned onto smart platforms. Examples include online learning due to school closures, smart applications of delivery systems as a result of the temporary closure or suspension of businesses and the use of various virtual networks by organisations for communication during the isolation periods. This was made possible by the smart measures and infrastructures already in place in many urban destinations, but it also brought challenges as not all citizens were prepared for this rapid transition to smart services (Han and Kim, 2021).

Smart environment means employing ICTs and other smart technologies for the efficient and effective use of natural resources, including energy efficiency, quality of water, green spaces, waste management and air pollution reduction.

Smart economy refers to the use of new technologies in the production, distribution, promotion and consumption of products and services. It relies on a number of principles such as encouraging innovation; appreciating creativity; stimulating the growth of entrepreneurship; offering better economic opportunities; creating a globally powerful competitive economic sector; and thinking locally, acting regionally and competing globally.

The London Borough of Greenwich is one of the city destinations that has put together a smart city strategy to address the challenges and opportunities faced by these ever-changing environments.

Sweet tweet 75

Smart city strategy – the Royal Borough of Greenwich, London

The strategy sets out an ambitious programme of transformation in four main areas:

1) Transforming Neighbourhoods and Communities, with a focus on promoting digital skills to ensure that all citizens can take advantage of the Internet and have access to good connectivity and high-quality public services.
2) Transforming Infrastructure – a fast and affordable digital infrastructure is central to the council's objectives; enhanced transport infrastructure, developments in the physical infrastructure, energy efficiency and sustainability.
3) Transforming Public Services – the development of a shared and trusted software environment to ensure relevant information is brought to the fore, and new insights obtained from the data available.
4) Transforming the Greenwich Economy – recognising the strong visitor economy in the borough; it encourages the growth of entrepreneurial digital businesses.

Source: Digital Greenwich (2019).

The Center for Globalization and Strategy at the IESE Business School, University of Navarra, Spain, produced an index of smart cities, with the top ten smart cities in the world presented in Table 9.2. In this index, cities are ranked across nine different

---

Table 9.2 Comparison of the top ten smart cities in the world and their quality of life ranking

City	Smartest cities in the world, 2019	Numbeo quality of life ranking, 2021
London, UK	1	161
New York, US	2	144
Amsterdam, Netherlands	3	66
Paris, France	4	181
Reykjavík, Iceland	5	25
Tokyo, Japan	6	101
Singapore	7	125
Copenhagen, Denmark	8	20
Berlin, Germany	9	89
Vienna, Austria	10	14

Sources: Data from Berrone and Ricart (2019); Numbeo (2021).

Figure 9.5 Boston was one of the first cities to launch experimental smart initiatives in 2010 (Courtesy: Unsplash.com, Wenzheng Hu).

dimensions considered essential for sustainable cities: Human capital, social cohesion, economy, environment, governance, urban planning, international outreach, technology and mobility and transportation (Berrone and Ricart, 2019).

As mentioned earlier in this chapter, smart cities are considered best placed to address major challenges faced by society, such as transportation, pollution, energy, security, sustainability and health. They provide innovative and high-quality services and products and are thus expected to contribute to improving the quality of life and well-being of their citizens. Still, none of the top ten smart cities listed in Table 9.2 makes it to the top ten cities in terms of quality of life (introduced in Chapter 7 and presented in Table 9.2). This indicates that further efforts are needed from policy-makers in smart cities in finding ways to use new technologies to improve the living conditions of their residents. For this to be possible, a better understanding is needed of citizen preferences and their perceptions about the services provided by smart cities.

Short break 9 presents the case of Santiago de Chile, which is considered the "smartest" city in Latin America. It briefly introduces the city and the smart initiatives promoted by the government and points out the challenges it faces.

SHORT BREAK 9

Santiago de Chile – the "smartest" city in Latin America

Santiago, the capital of Chile, is a cosmopolitan city with a population of 5.6 million. It is situated in a valley surrounded by the Andes Mountains and the Chilean

Coast Range and is considered the safest city in Latin America. Santiago is a modern city, concentrating most of the industry in the country and having an active financial sector.

The city ranks at the top of the Latin American list of smart cities (#68), according to the Cities in Motion Index, with only one other city from this region – Buenos Aires – being ranked in the top 100 (#90).

In terms of smart city initiatives, these are considered relatively limited in scope, impact, investment and visibility. They are related to mobility projects, waste disposal, recycling and reuse, CO_2 reduction, risk and disaster prevention and security and safety issues. The smart city model in Santiago mainly focuses on two aspects, an increased use of ICTs and the constant training of human resources.

Over the past years, the government implemented two major projects related to smart cities, which are presented below:

- The *Smart Cities Unit* created in 2011 within the Ministry of Transportation and Telecommunications was initially established as a smart transportation system unit, but later broadened its scope to information coordination. The unit has thus evolved over the years from understanding the role of technology in smarter management, to network management and communication with different stakeholders. It also supports various projects in the country and participates in smart city events organised in Chile and abroad.
- *SE Santiago* (the Smart Cities Strategy for Santiago) is also focused on network management, but it has a broader scope that includes mobility, waste disposal and security and safety issues. The agency has its own budget, and although the projects implemented tend to be low-budget, they have a good visibility and are aimed at impacting public opinion. Examples of projects supported by the agency are bike-sharing systems, bike parks, cycling paths and a course on city technology design and innovation.

According to researchers, Santiago faces a number of challenges in trying to implement smart city approaches, including urban planning and governance challenges, public transportation and urban accessibility, socio-spatial inequalities and the engagement of more and diverse actors in their initiatives.

Discussion points:

1. Why is Santiago ranked as the "smartest" city in Latin America?
2. What is your opinion on the smart city initiatives promoted by the government? What other smart initiatives could they implement?
3. How can the city address the challenges it faces in its efforts to become a smarter destination?

Sources: Berrone and Ricart (2019); Irazábal and Jirón (2021); Jirón et al. (2021).

There are many research themes that fall under the topic of smart cities, including smart mobility, smart citizens, smart living, smart economy, smart environment, smart government, smart destinations and smart tourism. The next section focuses on the last two – smart destinations and smart tourism – and discusses relevant aspects related to smart tourism in cities.

Smart city destinations

The concept of a smart destination has emerged from the notion of smart cities, which was discussed in the previous section. *Smart destinations* are defined as innovative tourist destinations that are

> built on an infrastructure of state-of-the-art technology, which guarantees the sustainable development of tourist areas, facilitates the visitor's interaction with and integration into his or her surroundings, increases the quality of the experience at the destination, and improves residents' quality of life.
>
> *(Xiang et al., 2015, p. 143)*

Smart tourism destinations are thus characterised by "advanced services, a high degree of innovation and the presence of open, integrated and shared processes for enhancing the quality of life for both residents and tourists" (Vecchio et al., 2018, p. 848). They rely on the adoption of new and emerging technologies, including ICTs, mobile technologies, social media, smart devices and sensors that help with collecting and making use of the large amount of data available. This has implications for the way city destinations compete with each other, with the most successful ones considered to be those that are making the most of the available data by transforming it into competitive assets.

Smart tourism destinations combine three main components (Wang et al., 2013):

1. *Cloud services*, which are key for smart destinations as they provide convenient access to software, applications and other data via web browsers. Examples include a complex tour guide system that can be accessed by a large number of visitors, without the need to install it on their personal devices.
2. *The Internet of Things*, a concept introduced earlier in the chapter, represents various objects and things around us that interact with each other and cooperate to achieve common goals. Examples include smart mobile phones, smartwatches, wireless sensors and voice assistants (e.g., Siri and Alexa). The IoT contributes to smart destinations, helping with the information and analysis, and automation and control functions. An example from China is now given.

Sweet tweet 76

The application of IoT in Sanya, China

Sanya, in Hainan Province, used the IoT to implement a number of solutions to help with managing tourism in the city, as presented below:

- Entrance tickets are embedded with specific reader chips, so tourists' location and consumption behaviour can be tracked.
- Presence-based advertising and payments can be implemented.
- The system is designed to control the number of visitors to heritage sites in the city.
- The carrying capacity of heritage sites is monitored by a variety of sensors such as the sensors for air quality, crowdedness and electricity consumption.

- The monitoring system is automatically connected with the ticketing system to implement pricing strategies that affect visitor numbers.

Source: Wang, Li and Li (2013).

3. *The End-User Internet Service System*, which refers to the equipment and applications that support the previous two components, the IoT and cloud services, at various levels of end-users. To better understand how this works, a few examples are given. The design of the individual payment systems takes into account the devices that will be used to access them, such as smartphones and tablets. To help with providing more information to visitors, wireless connections and touchscreens are placed around the most popular attractions. The government and tourism organisations have access to portals and connections to the cloud service, to help them better monitor and manage visitor numbers.

As mentioned earlier, the advances in ICTs and other new technologies are constantly transforming tourism destinations and changing the way these are planned and managed. It has fundamental implications for the way city destinations and tourism businesses market their products and services and interact with visitors and other stakeholders. Smart city tourism can thus generate value-added experiences for visitors and locals, through an effective coordination of available data and real-time services. This has the potential to foster sustainability, by improving the efficiency of tourism services and enhancing visitor experiences. Two examples from Gothenburg in Sweden, and Málaga in Spain are given below.

Sweet tweet 77

Examples of smart tourism initiatives

The two examples given here are from the 2020 winners for the European Capital of Smart Tourism competition organised by the European Commission.

Gothenburg aspires to stay on top of digital trends

The city stands out for its digital offering that is helping improve experiences for both citizens and tourists. This includes future-oriented solutions for traffic and transport, open data, as well as sustainability measures. The water-side city works together with a wide variety of stakeholders and sectors to implement a truly integrated approach to smart tourism.

Málaga – from sun-and-sea tourism hotspot to an innovative tourism destination

After two decades of change, this city is now successfully incorporating the concepts of sustainability, accessibility, innovation and culture into its holistic smart tourism strategies and actions. The coastal city has a strong focus on using novel technologies to improve the visitor experience and boost the innovative capacity of local businesses.

Source: European Commission (2021).

While bringing many benefits, ICTs can also create new challenges for visitors and destinations, which tend to be little discussed in the literature. Gössling (2021) is one of the authors who looked into this aspect, and identified four different stages in the adoption of ICTs in tourism – opportunity, disruption, immersion and usurpation.

The first stage, *opportunity* (1985–1995), is associated with the major advances in ICTs related to connectivity and coordination, which contributed to better efficiency and a more user-friendly experience. Examples include the computer reservation systems that made bookings easier, global distribution systems that revolutionised air transportation and company websites that made it possible for visitors to access useful information and for organisations to better promote themselves.

The second stage, *disruption* (1996–2006), was characterised by the emergence of the platform economy, with global platforms such as Booking.com becoming intermediaries in the reservation process. That opened the way for "disruptive" innovations such as low-cost carriers that introduced new business models, leading to increased competition on prices, and making it easier for visitors to book holidays. Rating systems also emerged during this stage, which had major implications for the way businesses and destinations managed their reputation, and their efforts to gain the trust of customers.

The third stage, *immersion* (2007–2015), brought about the widespread use of smartphones and an immersion in social media as a result of the wider adoption of ICTs and other new technologies in the daily lives of consumers. Platforms such as Airbnb are perceived as disruptive innovation models that, while offering more choices to visitors, continue to have implications for the accommodation market. Most businesses started to collect consumer data to help them better understand visitor behaviour and their needs, which made it possible to better predict changes in demand. This stage also saw a market concentration, with established platforms becoming more interconnected and increasing their outreach.

The fourth stage, named by Gössling *usurpation* (2016–2022 and ongoing), is described as the expansion on a global scale of a limited number of dominant platforms with expanded powers. These big players collect and have access to a large amount of data about consumers and their views. The author notes that surveillance has become the norm and that there is a growing dependence of consumers on ICT and social media platforms.

Gössling (2021) also identifies a possible fifth stage, *assertion*, characterised by a reinforcement of the power structures through ICTs, with a major role envisaged for robotics, artificial intelligence and cryptocurrencies.

Sweet tweet 78

ExpATHENS Cultural Route – "The Road of Museums"

ExpATHENS is an initiative promoted in Athens, Greece, which illustrates the added value of ICT-enabled approaches, tools and technologies that can be used in promoting cultural tourism.

> A pilot ICT-enabled participatory cultural tourism planning exercise aimed at developing a cultural route in the historical centre of Athens. Taking advantage of the abundance of arts and cultural assets in the study area,

the scope of the exercise is to create a narrative or story – "The Road of Museums" …

The whole effort is based on an inclusive spatial planning approach, i.e., a cooperative and ICT-enabled spatial planning endeavour engaging the local business community in producing a pilot visual cultural tourism package.

Source: Panagiotopoulou, Somarakis and Stratigea (2020).

During the COVID-19 pandemic, discussed in Chapter 10, city destinations and tourism businesses were "pushed" even more to adopt new technologies and implement smart solutions. ICTs were widely used by destinations and businesses in their efforts to limit the transmission of the virus by putting in place measures to help in minimising human interaction and thus reducing the spread of the virus. Examples of such measures that were implemented in many major airports include:

- *Self-service check-in kiosks* that allow passengers to complete the check-in themselves by using computer terminals, without the need to interact with a staff member.
- *Automated baggage drop-off machines*, where travellers can drop off passenger-tagged bags without having to interact with staff members in the airport.
- *Self-boarding*, also known as quick boarding gates, which allow passengers to self-scan their boarding pass and proceed to the aircraft once the pass has been verified.
- *Biometric passports*, which enable the automated identification of a person when going through the airport security gates by using specific physiological characteristics such as face and fingerprints.
- *Smart wearable technologies*, such as a smartwatches, are used by passengers to alert them about gate changes and delays, or even to scan a boarding pass.

Oktadiana and Pearce (2020), however, note that while self-service technologies can play several roles in the co-creation of tourism experiences (e.g., creator, enabler, enhancer, attractor, educator), they can also turn into a "destroyer" of tourism experiences due to the lack of human interaction and social engagement. Tribe and Mkono (2017, p. 112) proposed the term *e-lienation*, a concept that refers to a form of alienation in ICT-enabled tourism. The authors define it broadly as "the negative consequences of ICT on the tourist experience". They argue that although the world is nowadays better connected than ever, visitors may feel more disconnected sometimes due to less authentic experiences and alienation.

Other examples of how ICTs were instrumental during the pandemic include museums and other attractions that opened their doors to *"virtual tourists"* (the concept of virtual reality is explained later on); visitors used social media platforms to remember their past holidays and dream about future trips; mobile apps became very popular with tourists wishing to cancel their trips due to the disruption caused by the pandemic, or to make complaints; Airbnb hosts offered virtual experiences; residents sharing their views on different forums and social media platforms about the lack of tourists in those cities that used to suffer from overtourism; and the use of technologies that were able to track and monitor visitors (Gretzel et al., 2020).

Figure 9.6 Athens, the city that won the European Capital of Innovation award in 2018 (Courtesy: Unsplash.com, Chronis Yan).

Latest technologies and debates expected to shape the tourism ecosystem

The last part of this chapter focuses on the latest technologies that are expected to shape the tourism ecosystem. According to the OECD (2020), these can be grouped around three main themes:

a) *Business management technologies*, such as mobile technologies, robotics, data analytics, blockchain and cloud computing.
b) Technologies that *produce innovative tourism products, services and experiences*, such as virtual reality, augmented reality and the Internet of Things.
c) Technologies that *assist, understand and connect with markets*, such as data analytics and artificial intelligence.

Some of these technologies were introduced earlier (e.g., IoT), while the others are covered now.

Cloud computing makes it easier for tourism organisations (in particular small ones) to implement online solutions without the potentially prohibitive costs associated with maintaining their own ICT infrastructure. Together with wireless networks, cloud technologies make it possible for tourism organisations to manage their business from anywhere as long as they have access to high-speed Internet. Furthermore, cloud computing and **mobile technologies** enable visitors to access information in real time, to do online bookings and to make mobile payments (OECD, 2020).

Big data refers to large and diverse sets of information, continuously expanding as more data is gathered, that would require extensive resources to be analysed with traditional systems. Aside from the far-reaching data it offers, big data analysis has the potential to provide new and original insights that could help tourism organisations and city destinations to better understand visitors, their views, needs, preferences and attitudes. It can also help with new product development, performance improvement, customised services and better decision-making. Social media platforms, in particular, are considered a key source of big data for tourism (so-called social big data) that offers many opportunities for destination management organisations to better understand their markets and be more efficient (Vecchio et al., 2018).

Artificial intelligence (AI) refers to the simulation of human intelligence, with machines programmed to "think and act like humans". Many tourism organisations from different sectors, such as airlines, hotels, restaurants and attractions, have implemented AI solutions. Examples include the personalisation of user experience in the airline industry; estimates of hotel rates and flight tickets; dynamic pricing; intelligent concierge services and other virtual assistants; facial recognition and voice services that are already implemented by many hotels around the world.

Virtual reality and augmented reality are two other emerging technologies aimed at providing better experiences to customers. They contribute to enhancing visitor satisfaction and building memorable experiences (before, during or after) by using stereoscopic head-mounted displays (HDM) and other upcoming technologies. They can be instrumental in promoting a city destination or attraction. Smart cities, in particular, are using such technologies in their efforts to improve the quality of life of residents and enhance visitor experience.

Virtual reality (VR) is when the users are presented with an immersive 3D simulated environment that may mimic the real world or not, using both audio and visual stimuli. The intention is to create a completely different setting that feels like a real-world environment (telepresence). This technology has been successfully used by destinations to prepare customers for what they will experience in a setting (before travelling), and also to enhance their experiences during visits. A relevant example is the Rome Reborn project on Google Earth, which allows visitors to explore the city the way it used to be centuries ago (Loureiro et al., 2020).

Augmented reality (AR) refers to a superimposition of virtual objects or content, such as text, images and videos, over the real-world surroundings. Visitors can thus see, with the help of see-through displays, including their own smartphones or digital cameras, both the real world and the overlapping virtual objects (Loureiro et al., 2020). This technology is extensively used in museums, where it helps improve visitor interaction between the actual reality and the augmented reality, and thus enhances the experience of tourists by providing additional images and information.

Autonomous vehicles (AV or CAV) or self-driven vehicles are intelligent forms of transportation that are expected to play a key role in smart cities, as they address important challenges such as energy efficiency, travel time and environmental issues related to pollution. They are expected to transform the future of transport systems, making it safer, with fewer accidents, reduced city congestion, lower environmental impacts,

Figure 9.7 Jakarta, a city that has one of the highest rates of urbanisation in the world and which is working towards becoming a smart destination (Courtesy: Unsplash.com, Sulthan Auliya).

improved energy efficiency and better time utilisation by passengers (Manfreda et al., 2021). More about this topic is covered in Chapter 12.

Personalised interactive real-time tours (PIRTs) are considered a step forward in the use of new technologies, aimed at better connecting people and settings. They allow people to experience destinations and events from home, via 5G streaming in real time, using 360-degree view cameras, webcams or drones. Such tours would have the disadvantage of not providing the "real experience", but they may appeal to those eco-friendly visitors interested in decreasing their ecological footprint, to people with disabilities and elderly people who might not have the opportunity to travel to those places due to accessibility constraints, or it may be seen as a cheaper alternative to conventional trips (Fennell, 2021).

Ambient intelligence tourism is considered the next step for machine learning and artificial intelligence, driven by several disruptive technologies such as IoT, IoE, radio frequency identification, smartphones and wearable devices, the fifth-generation mobile network (5G), cryptocurrency and blockchain technology and sensor and beacon networks. It is expected to make tourism ecosystems more flexible and adaptive to the needs of all stakeholders involved in tourism development in a destination. These technologies will allow the use of autonomous vehicles, cars and drones and robots, together with virtual and augmented reality, concepts that were introduced earlier (Buhalis, 2020).

Research on smart tourism destinations has been expanding rapidly over the past decade, with many scholars investigating this topic. In trying to understand the progress and significance of the literature published so far on ICTs and tourism, Navío-Marco, Ruiz-Gómez and Sevilla-Sevilla (2018) conducted a review study that identified several new trends. They grouped these trends around three main themes, as presented below.

Sweet tweet 79

New trends in ICT and tourism

Consumer and demand trends: Personalisation, prosumers and co-creation, trust in peers, digital natives, experiences and immersion in destination life-styles, global mobility, total connectivity and altruism.

Technological innovation trends: Everything connected, convergence between the physical and digital worlds, big data and analytics, ontology and semantics, artificial intelligence, robots and gamification.

Industry and businesses trends: Ratings, comments, rankings and reputation, the influence of social networks, from static to dynamic, pre-eminence of intermediaries, platforms peer-to-peer (P2P), new alliances and new partners, opportunities for highly skilled professionals, growing profitability and sustainability.

Source: Navío-Marco, Ruiz-Gómez and Sevilla-Sevilla (2018).

Coca-Stefaniak (2020) takes a step further into the future and introduces the notion of *"wise"* post-smart tourism cities that focus on long-term challenges faced by destinations such as overtourism (a concept discussed in Chapters 7), ageing populations, the rise in inequalities, better understanding of developing trends or the need to switch off sometimes from digital media. The author argues that while smart tools and big data are part of the solution, so could be slow tourism initiatives in some cases, a wider ecosystem approach to sustainable development and a more people-centred approach focused on the well-being of resident and visitors.

Digital well-being, linked to the well-being of visitors and locals, has become a popular topic in the public discourse lately and is considered an emerging paradigm in tourism studies. This is a result of the rising concerns regarding the effects on the mental and physical health of an overuse of ICTs. In a tourism context, it has been argued that the stress related to technology use (technostress) can impede on "one of the central roles of tourism, namely to provide hedonic, altruistic, and meaningful experiences" (Stankov and Gretzel, 2021, p. 7). Therefore, there are calls for more attention to be given to digital well-being and more actions to be taken by the tourism sector and governments. First, in adopting the digital well-being philosophy in the travel and tourism sector; second, in developing new policies to address the issue; and third, in designing new services and experiences that account for digital well-being.

Summary comments

The past few decades have brought many challenges and disruptive events for city destinations, such as the rapid evolution of new technologies, health and safety concerns, chaotic episodes in markets and economies and environmental crises (Fennell, 2021). In particular, the developments in ICTs and other innovative technologies have radically transformed tourism destinations, leading to changes in business models, in consumer behaviour and in how visitors experience city destinations, having implications for the industry structure.

City destinations were thus forced to adapt rapidly to the new realities and implement smart solutions to improve their efficiency, enhance visitor experience and remain competitive in the global market. ICTs and other new technologies brought many opportunities for destinations, but also challenges. These were presented in this chapter, together with examples from various city destinations around the globe.

The next chapter looks into another important challenge faced by world tourism cities and discusses how crises and disasters affect urban destinations.

Thought questions

1) How did ICTs and other new technologies evolve over the past decades?
2) What is the difference between ICTs, the IoT and the IoE?
3) What are the benefits and limitations of using ICTs in tourism?
4) In what ways did ICTs and other new technologies transform the travel and tourism sector?
5) What is a smart city and what are its key dimensions?
6) Why is it difficult for many urban destinations to successfully implement smart governance measures?
7) What are the characteristics of a smart tourism destination? Can you give examples of smart city destinations and explain why they are "smart"?
8) What opportunities and challenges are associated with the implementation of new technologies in the tourism sector?
9) What are the latest technologies expected to have major implications for the tourism sector?
10) How can city destinations better prepare for the digital future?

References

Abella, A., Ortiz-de-Urbina-Criado, M., & De-Pablos-Heredero, C. (2017). A model for the analysis of data-driven innovation and value generation in smart cities' ecosystems. *Cities, 64*, 47–53.

Alavi, A. H., Jiao, P., Buttlar, W. G., & Lajnef, N. (2018). Internet of things-enabled smart cities: State-of-the-art and future trends. *Measurement, 129*, 589–606.

Allam, Z., & Newman, P. (2018). Redefining the smart city: Culture, metabolism and governance. *Smart Cities, 1*(1), 4–25.

Ariffin, E. (2018). Smart city spotlight: Hanoi. *The ASEAN Post*. https://theaseanpost.com/article/smart-city-spotlight-hanoi

Ben Letaifa, S. (2015). How to strategize smart cities: Revealing the SMART model. *Journal of Business Research, 68*(7), 1414–1419.

Berrone, P., & Ricart, J. E. (2019). *IESE Cities in Motion Index 2019*. Servicio de Publicaciones de la Universidad de Navarra. Pamplona: University of Navarra. https://doi.org/10.15581/018.ST-509

Buhalis, D. (2020). Technology in tourism-from information communication technologies to eTourism and smart tourism towards ambient intelligence tourism: A perspective article. *Tourism Review*, 75(1), 267–272.

Buhalis, D. (2022). Smart tourism. In D. Buhalis (Ed.), *Encyclopedia of Tourism Management and Marketing*. Cheltenham, UK: Edward Elgar Publishing.

Buhalis, D., & Jun, S. H. (2011). E-Tourism. In C. Cooper (Ed.). *Contemporary Tourism Reviews Series*. Oxford: Goodfellow Publishers.

Buhalis, D., & Law, R. (2008). Progress in information technology and tourism management: 20 years on and 10 years after the Internet: The state of eTourism research. *Tourism Management*, 29(4), 609–623.

Cambridge Centre for Smart Infrastructure and Construction (CSIC). (2016). Smart Infrastructure: Getting More from Strategic Assets. Cambridge: CSIC. https://www-smartinfrastructure.eng.cam.ac.uk/system/files/documents/the-smart-infrastructure-paper.pdf

Choi, J., Lee, S., & Jamal, T. (2021). Smart Korea: Governance for smart justice during a global pandemic. *Journal of Sustainable Tourism*, 29(2–3), 541–550.

Coca-Stefaniak, J. A. (2020). Beyond smart tourism cities: towards a new generation of "wise" tourism destinations. *Journal of Tourism Futures*, ahead-of-print(ahead-of-print). https://doi.org/10.1108/JTF-11-2019-0130

Coca-Stefaniak, J. A., & Seisdedos, G. (2021). Smart urban tourism destinations at a crossroads. In A. M. Morrison & J. A. Coca-Stefaniak (Eds.). *Routledge Handbook of Tourism Cities*, pp. 359–373. London: Routledge.

Cristea, M. (2020, August 14). Bucharest embraces its smart city future. *Business Review*. https://business-review.eu/br-exclusive/br-cover-story-bucharest-embraces-its-smart-city-future-212423

Digital Greenwich. (2019). *Smart City Strategy*. https://www.digitalgreenwich.com/smart-city-strategy/

European Commission. (2020). *Smart Cities—Smart Living* [Text]. Shaping Europe's Digital Future: European Commission. https://ec.europa.eu/digital-single-market/en/smart-cities-smart-living

European Commission. (2021). *European Capitals of Smart Tourism-Competition winners 2020*. https://smart-tourism-capital.ec.europa.eu/competition-winners-2020_en

Fennell, D. A. (2021). Technology and the sustainable tourist in the new age of disruption. *Journal of Sustainable Tourism*, 29(5), 767–773.

Glasgow City Council. (2021). *Future City Glasgow*. https://futurecity.glasgow.gov.uk/

Gössling, S. (2021). Tourism, technology and ICT: A critical review of affordances and concessions. *Journal of Sustainable Tourism*, 29(5), 733–750.

Gretzel, U., Fuchs, M., Baggio, R., Hoepken, W., Law, R., Neidhardt, J., Pesonen, J., Zanker, M., & Xiang, Z. (2020). e-Tourism beyond COVID-19: A call for transformative research. *Information Technology & Tourism*, 22(2), 187–203.

Han, M. J. N., & Kim, M. J. (2021). A critical review of the smart city in relation to citizen adoption towards sustainable smart living. *Habitat International*, 108, 102312. https://doi.org/10.1016/j.habitatint.2021.102312

Irazábal, C., & Jirón, P. (2021). Latin American smart cities: Between worlding infatuation and crawling provincialising. *Urban Studies*, 58(3), 507–534.

Jirón, P., Imilán, W. A., Lange, C., & Mansilla, P. (2021). Placebo urban interventions: Observing smart city narratives in Santiago de Chile. *Urban Studies*, 58(3), 601–620.

Johnson, A.-G., Rickly, J. M., & McCabe, S. (2021). Smartmentality in Ljubljana. *Annals of Tourism Research, 86*, 103094. https://doi.org/10.1016/j.annals.2020.103094

Kirimtat, A., Krejcar, O., Kertesz, A., & Tasgetiren, M. F. (2020). Future trends and current state of smart city concepts: A survey. *IEEE Access, 8*, 86448–86467.

Loureiro, S. M. C., Guerreiro, J., & Ali, F. (2020). 20 years of research on virtual reality and augmented reality in tourism context: A text-mining approach. *Tourism Management, 77*, 104028.

Lynn, L. E., Heinrich, C. J., & Hill, C. J. (2000). Studying governance and public management: Challenges and prospects. *Journal of Public Administration Research and Theory, 10*(2), 233–262.

Manfreda, A., Ljubi, K., & Groznik, A. (2021). Autonomous vehicles in the smart city era: An empirical study of adoption factors important for millennials. *International Journal of Information Management, 58*, 102050.

Navío-Marco, J., Ruiz-Gómez, L. M., & Sevilla-Sevilla, C. (2018). Progress in information technology and tourism management: 30 years on and 20 years after the internet – Revisiting Buhalis & Law's landmark study about eTourism. *Tourism Management, 69*, 460–470.

Neidhardt, J., & Werthner, H. (2018). IT and tourism: Still a hot topic, but do not forget IT. *Information Technology & Tourism, 20*(1), 1–7.

Neuhofer, B., Buhalis, D., & Ladkin, A. (2012). Conceptualising technology enhanced destination experiences. *Journal of Destination Marketing & Management, 1*(1), 36–46.

Numbeo. (2021). *Quality of Life Index by City 2021*. https://www.numbeo.com/quality-of -life/rankings.jsp

OECD. (2020). *OECD Tourism Trends and Policies 2020*. Paris: OECD Publishing. https:// doi.org/10.1787/6b47b985-en.

Oktadiana, H., & Pearce, P. L. (2020). Losing touch: Uncomfortable encounters with tourism technology. *Journal of Hospitality and Tourism Management, 42*, 266–276.

Panagiotopoulou, M., Somarakis, G., & Stratigea, A. (2020). Smartening up participatory cultural tourism planning in historical city centers. *Journal of Urban Technology, 27*(4), 3–26.

Park, S., Xu, Y., Jiang, L., Chen, Z., & Huang, S. (2020). Spatial structures of tourism destinations: A trajectory data mining approach leveraging mobile big data. *Annals of Tourism Research, 84*, 102973. https://doi.org/10.1016/j.annals.2020.102973

Samih, H. (2019). Smart cities and internet of things. *Journal of Information Technology Case and Application Research, 21*(1), 3–12.

Sigala, M. (2018). New technologies in tourism: From multi-disciplinary to anti-disciplinary advances and trajectories. *Tourism Management Perspectives, 25*, 151–155.

Stankov, U., & Gretzel, U. (2021). Digital well-being in the tourism domain: Mapping new roles and responsibilities. *Information Technology & Tourism, 23*(1), 5–17.

Statista. (2021). *Number of Internet Users Worldwide*. Statista. https://www.statista.com/ statistics/273018/number-of-internet-users-worldwide/

Tomor, Z., Meijer, A., Michels, A., & Geertman, S. (2019). Smart governance for sustainable cities: Findings from a systematic literature review. *Journal of Urban Technology, 26*(4), 3–27.

Treiblmaier, H. (2020). Blockchain and tourism. In Z. Xiang, M. Fuchs, U. Gretzel, & W. Höpken (Eds.). *Handbook of e-Tourism*, pp. 1–21. Berlin: Springer.

Tribe, J., & Mkono, M. (2017). Not such smart tourism? The concept of e-lienation. *Annals of Tourism Research, 66*, 105–115.

Vecchio, P. D., Mele, G., Ndou, V., & Secundo, G. (2018). Creating value from social big data: Implications for smart tourism destinations. *Information Processing & Management, 54*(5), 847–860.

Vinuesa, R., Azizpour, H., Leite, I., Balaam, M., Dignum, V., Domisch, S., Felländer, A., Langhans, S. D., Tegmark, M., & Fuso Nerini, F. (2020). The role of artificial intelligence in achieving the Sustainable Development Goals. *Nature Communications, 11*(1), Article 1. https://doi.org/10.1038/s41467-019-14108-y

Wang, D., Li, X. (Robert), & Li, Y. (2013). China's "smart tourism destination" initiative: A taste of the service-dominant logic. *Journal of Destination Marketing & Management, 2*(2), 59–61.

Worldometer. (2021). *World Population Clock.* https://www.worldometers.info/world-population/

Xiang, Z., Tussyadiah, I., & Buhalis, D. (2015). Smart destinations: Foundations, analytics, and applications. *Journal of Destination Marketing & Management, 4*(3), 143–144.

Chapter 10

World tourism cities in crisis times

Abstract

Tourism in all destinations is highly susceptible to being influenced, often negatively, by external factors. The COVID-19 pandemic and its disastrous impacts on world travel and tourism were a stark reminder of this assertion. Chapter 10 reviews different types of crises and disasters that can affect world tourism cities and discusses a number of crisis management approaches that can be adopted by these destinations to limit the impact of such events. Special attention is given to the unprecedented situation created by the coronavirus crisis and how city destinations were affected.

An important challenge of crisis management is to ensure effective communication with all stakeholders in a destination, both internal and external. Therefore, crisis communication is a vital part when dealing with crises and disasters, with accurate and timely data needed to be provided to those affected. The new developments in technology and the social media revolution have transformed how destinations communicate and interact with their stakeholders, including visitors. This has brought many opportunities, but also significant challenges for city destination management organisations, which have had to quickly learn how to manage the influx of information posted on social media platforms. These, together with other important aspects related to crises and disasters, are discussed in this chapter, with examples provided from different parts of the world.

Keywords: Crisis; disasters; tourism crisis; crisis management; crisis communication; social media; SMCC model; COVID-19 crisis.

DOI: 10.4324/9781003111412-13

Learning objectives

Having read this chapter, you should be able to:

- Define a crisis, disaster and tourism crisis.
- Identify and describe different types of crises.
- Elaborate on the impact of the COVID-19 pandemic on world tourism cities.
- Describe the phases of the tourism disaster management framework.
- Discuss the importance of crisis communication and of managing social media during a crisis.

Crisis and disasters in tourist cities

As witnessed over the past decade, and in particular over the last few years, destinations are vulnerable to many crisis events and disasters that can have serious consequences for the tourism in a region. World cities are even more exposed to such events due to their characteristics discussed in Chapter 3, including their multifunctional nature and their high interconnectivity. Still, researchers have started to study the topic of crises in relation to tourism cities only recently, with most works published after 2000. This is in contrast to the research available on crises in tourism in general, that dates back to the 1970s, and to urban tourism studies that emerged as a research area in the 1980s. Therefore, this section looks at the concepts of a crisis and a disaster, and their implications for world tourism cities.

The concept of *crisis* can be defined as a "low-probability, high-consequence event that develops very rapidly and involves ambiguous situations with unknown causes and effects" (Roberts et al., 2007). In the context of tourism, scholars tend to define crisis from various perspectives, such as in relation to the nature of the event, that can be either external or directly linked to tourism activities, or in relation to the effects of an unexpected event on the tourism sector.

Sönmez and Allen (1994, p. 22) define a *tourism crisis* as "any occurrence which can threaten the normal operation and conduct of tourism-related businesses; damage a tourism destination's overall reputation for safety, attractiveness and comfort by negatively affecting visitors' perceptions of that destination". As may be noted, this definition focuses mainly on possible consequences of crisis events in tourism destinations.

A *disaster* has been defined as an "unpredictable catastrophic change that can normally only be responded to after the event, either by deploying contingency plans already in place or through reactive response" (Prideaux et al., 2003, p. 478). The two concepts, crisis and disaster, are often used interchangeably. Researchers, however, note that there is a difference between the two and this relates to the nature of the cause, whether this is internal or external to a destination or organisation (Ritchie and Jiang, 2019).

Scholars point out that there is an increase in the frequency of crises and disasters that affect destinations, such as natural disasters, including hurricanes, earthquakes and tsunamis; human-induced incidents; health crises; and political and economic instability (these will be discussed in more detail in the next section). Table 10.1 presents examples of crisis and disaster events that have occurred over the past 25 years in tourism cities, outlining their consequences in brief.

Table 10.1 Examples of crisis events and disasters in tourist cities

Year	Event and city	Type of crisis	Consequences
2019–2021	The COVID-19 pandemic affected most tourist cities worldwide	Health crisis	Large cities have suffered as a result of travel restrictions; international visitors dropped by 60–80% in some destinations.
2015	A series of coordinated Islamist terrorist attacks were carried out in Paris, France	Terrorist attack	130 people died and more than 400 were injured.
2012	Hurricane Sandy hit New York City	Natural disaster – hurricane	44 people died; critical infrastructure was damaged.
2010; 2011	Powerful earthquakes occurred in Christchurch, New Zealand	Natural disaster – earthquake	185 people died, with widespread damage across the city.
2007–2009	Global recession that affected many cities worldwide, including Athens, Lisbon, Rome, Macao, Hong Kong and Johannesburg	Financial and economic crisis	The demand for international tourism decreased worldwide.
2005	Suicide bombings at a hotel in Amman, Jordan	Terrorist attack	57 people died and 120 were injured.
2002–2003	SARS, Hong Kong (started in China, spreading to 29 countries)	Health crisis	Cumulative total of more than 8,000 cases and about 800 deaths.
2002	Terrorist bombings in the tourist district of Kuta, Bali, Indonesia	Terrorist attack	202 people died and 209 injured.
1997	Terrorist attack on tourists visiting an historic site at Luxor, Egypt	Terrorist attack	58 people died.
1995	Earthquake in the Japanese city of Kobe	Natural disaster – earthquake	Over 5,500 people died; disrupted transport services.

In a literature review article on tourism crises, Duan, Xie and Morrison (2021) found that the impact of crises on destinations can be grouped into three different levels: macro – relates to the impact on the destination's natural, economic and social environments; meso – refers to the impact on tourism businesses and operations; and micro – focuses on the impact on tourists, community residents and other individuals.

The ways crises affect a destination can also vary considerably, and this depends on a number of aspects, including the magnitude of the event, the scale and its nature.

As a result, the recovery can last from short periods of time, which is usually the case with terrorist attacks, to years in the case of global recessions and earthquakes that can affect infrastructure and other essential services, as seen in the sweet tweet below. Such events are most of the time accompanied by a high level of uncertainty and can cause significant damage to tourist cities. This is why it is very important for urban destinations to prepare specific strategies and plans to help them deal with crises and disasters in an effective way. This aspect was highlighted in Chapter 4, and it will be developed further later on in this chapter, in the section dedicated to crisis and disaster management frameworks.

Sweet tweet 80

Examples of recovery time needed for different types of crises

The Global Rescue and World Travel & Tourism Council analysed the impact of 90 crises between 2001 and 2018 at the national and city level. They found that:

"Travellers are seemingly becoming more resilient, with terrorist attacks having the shortest recovery time at 11.5 months on average, with a range of 2 to 42 months".

"Political instability and civil unrest cases had the longest recovery time on average at 22.2 months, with recovery ranging from 10 months to 44.9 months".

"The recovery from natural disasters took 16.2 months on average".

"Epidemics and outbreaks have become the new normal … The recovery time from disease cases took 19.4 months on average, with a range in recovery from 10 months to 34.9 months".

Source: Global Rescue and World Travel & Tourism Council (2019).

Types of crises and disasters

Researchers acknowledge that different types of crises may impact cities in dissimilar ways, having implications for the perceived safety and the confidence of tourists in the affected destinations (U and So, 2020). Crises can lead to changes in consumer patterns, in new and emerging demands, which may translate into new business models, products and services. Therefore, to better prepare destinations to deal with potential crises and disasters and to develop corresponding management strategies, organisations need to have a good understanding of these events. This section thus briefly introduces different types of crises and disasters, using examples from tourism cities in different parts of the world.

Two of the crises most researched in tourism studies are *economic and financial crises*. The tourism sector has experienced several such crises over the years, with the latest global economic crisis in 2008–2009 having severe implications for destinations. According to official data, this crisis led to the first serious decline of international tourism worldwide in decades, with figures showing a 4% decrease in international tourism arrivals and a 6% decrease in international tourism revenues for the year 2009 (UNWTO and International Labour Organisation, 2011). It took five years for Las Vegas, a city that relies on tourism for as much as 27% of its GDP, to recover from this global economic and financial crisis. At its peak, for example, the total number of visitors to the city dropped by 7% for two consecutive years, mainly from a sharp drop recorded in the number of domestic visitors (Lim and Won, 2020). Several factors contributed to the city's successful recovery, including diversification of the tourism product and a focus on new markets, such as Asia, with the city having to quickly adapt to the new realities.

Health-related crises also have important implications for tourism. As tourism plays an important role in the rapid spread of contagious diseases, travel restrictions tend to be imposed in the affected destinations, while people tend to avoid these destinations even without such measures in place. These events can thus have a dramatic impact on tourism, as seen during the current COVID-19 pandemic (a specific section on this topic is included later in the chapter). Other examples of health crises include the Ebola outbreak in West Africa between 2013 and 2016; the severe acute respiratory syndrome (SARS) outbreak in 2003 that spread to 29 countries in three world regions; and the UK foot and mouth outbreak in 2001 that impacted the country's agriculture and tourism sectors. In Hong Kong, for example, the SARS epidemic caused a 62% drop in international visitors between March and April 2003, with the industry starting to recover in June and tourist numbers returning to their previous level by August that year. The segments that recovered quickest were business tourism and visiting friends and relatives (Siu and Wong, 2004).

Political crises and *instability* often affect city destinations, yet this topic is rarely discussed in tourism studies. According to some scholars, this may be the result of a lack of awareness with regard to politics, policy formulation and agenda setting in the tourism sector (Hall, 2010). Antalya is one of the tourism cities that was severely affected by a (geo)political crisis as a result of a number of internal and external conflicts in 2015. The city's economy relies on revenues from foreign visitors, which saw a sharp drop in numbers (47%) in the year following the events, and it took a few years for the destination to recover (Terhorst and Erkuş-Öztürk, 2019). The main decline was from the Russian market, with a 95% drop recorded in 2016 when compared to the previous year, as a result of an incident that sparked a diplomatic crisis between Russia and Turkey. This is a good example of how one crisis can lead to other crisis events within a destination.

Terrorism is a human-caused disaster that, while considered to have a low probability, can have a high impact and, therefore, poses major challenges for destinations. The recent decades have seen a rapid increase in the frequency of such events in world tourism cities, these destinations being more prone to terrorism attacks due to their characteristics discussed in Chapter 3 (e.g., they attract many international visitors, host important attractions, are well connected and advanced in using communication technologies). Examples of recent terrorist events include the 2020 Vienna attacks in Austria; 2019 Christchurch shootings in New Zealand; 2019 Colombo Easter bombings in Sri Lanka; 2017 Barcelona attacks in Spain; 2016 Istanbul airport attack in Turkey; 2016 Brussels bombings in Belgium; 2015 Paris attacks in France; 2005 London bombings in the UK; 2004 Madrid train bombings in Spain; and the 2001 (9/11) attack in New York City, USA.

Research conducted on the topic shows that these events have serious negative consequences for tourism destinations and the local and national economies (as noted in the Sweet tweet below), including an immediate sharp decline in visitor numbers and negative feelings generated among the targeted populations, while the recovery can be slow (Song et al., 2019). The intensity of the effects of terrorism attacks depends on a number of factors, such as the severity of the incident, the location where it takes place and the number of casualties. Frequent terrorist incidents, in particular, can have a negative impact on the image of a destination (Seabra and Paiva, 2021). Therefore, city destination management organisations (introduced in Chapter 4) are expected to develop effective strategies to try to identify and minimise the risks associated with such events (Coca-Stefaniak and Morrison, 2018) and to have in place crisis management plans, a topic that is discussed later on in this chapter.

Sweet tweet 81

The theatre of terrorism to cities

In recent years, terror has become a global issue reaching almost every metropolis worldwide. In most cases – terror incidents occurred in capitals and holiday resort locations … According to data collected about the number of tourists visiting popular capital cities in Europe during 2016 (the year in which global terrorism was on its biggest rise in the last decade) – the number of tourists considerably decreased. The finding demonstrates an 18% drop of tourism in Brussels, after three suicide bombings in the city in March and a 14% drop in incoming tourism in Paris – after November 2015 Terror attacks.

Source: European Cities Marketing (2018).

Natural disasters are important events that affect tourism destinations and have attracted the attention of researchers over the years. They can be associated with earthquakes, tornadoes, cyclones, hurricanes, tsunamis, bushfires and floods. Scholars have observed that lately, as a result of climate change, such natural disasters tend to be more common than before. They usually create major property damage and, in many cases, even loss of life, with destinations suffering significant harm (U and So, 2020). One such example is the 2011 earthquake in Christchurch, New Zealand, which is considered to be the most destructive natural disaster to happen in this country since 1931, when another major earthquake occurred. The impact of the event was devastating for the city, with 185 lives lost and many people injured, as well as extensive damage to the built environment. As a result, the number of hotel rooms in the city was reduced by almost 80% virtually overnight, with huge implications for the tourism sector (Faisal et al., 2020). It took many years for the destination to recover, and at the time of writing pre-event tourism levels are yet to be reached. Extensive investments were needed for the reconstruction of the city centre and of the destroyed infrastructure, with the city council estimating that it may take over 20 years for the roads to be rebuilt to the expected standard.

Other ways to categorise crises are by taking into account aspects such as:

- Their *duration*: Immediate crises (with very little or no warning in advance); emerging crises (that may be stopped, or the damage limited); and sustained crises (that may last for months or even years).

- Their *geographical scale*: local, regional, national and international.
- The *scale of the damage* they can cause to people's lives and properties.

Having discussed a number of different crises and disasters, the next section looks briefly at the current coronavirus crisis (COVID-19) and its impact on world tourism cities.

COVID-19 crisis and tourism cities

The current pandemic, a highly contagious airborne illness known as COVID-19, is believed to have started in the Chinese city of Wuhan in December 2019. What was perceived at the time as a local outbreak quickly developed into a global pandemic that affected destinations worldwide, with many countries imposing travel restrictions or even closing their borders for certain periods of time (Yang et al., 2020). At the time of writing this chapter, there were more than 120 million confirmed cases worldwide and almost 2.7 million deaths (World Health Organization, 2021), with the number of cases and deaths increasing with each day. Besides the devastating effects it had on travel and tourism, the pandemic also had major social, economic and political implications.

The stay-at-home orders and the unprecedented travel restrictions imposed by many countries caused one of the most severe disruptions of global tourism since the Second World War. As a result, entire air fleets were grounded, cruise ships docked, hotels, restaurants and entertainment venues shut and important tourist attractions closed their doors. The latest figures produced by the UNWTO (2021) showed an average 74% decrease in international tourist arrivals globally when compared to the previous year (see the Sweet tweet below), with Asia and the Pacific being the most affected region.

Sweet tweet 82

2020 – worst year in tourism history

Global tourism suffered its worst year on record in 2020, with international arrivals dropping by 74% according to the latest data from the World Tourism Organization (UNWTO). Destinations worldwide welcomed one billion fewer international arrivals in 2020 than in the previous year, due to an unprecedented fall in demand and widespread travel restrictions. This compares with the 4% decline recorded during the 2009 global economic crisis.

Source: World Tourism Organization (2021).

World tourism cities were among the most affected destinations during the pandemic, with many travel restrictions put in place and with people avoiding them due to the high levels of coronavirus infections in these environments. As a result, during the year 2020 many famous landmarks, city centres and attractions in urban destinations around the world found themselves almost completely deserted, something that had never been seen before (a number of examples are given in Figure 10.1). Besides the strict travel restrictions imposed by many such popular destinations, other measures included mandatory testing, temperature checking and quarantines, all impacting on

> **Figure 10.1** Deserted city centres during the coronavirus lockdown: 7th Avenue, New York City (Courtesy: Unsplash.com, Paulo Silva); Regent Street, London (Courtesy: Unsplash.com, Joe Stubbs); Chur, Switzerland (Courtesy: Unsplash.com, Christian Regg); Ljubljana, Slovenia (Courtesy: Unsplash.com, Miha Rekar).

the international tourist arrivals. With the COVID-19 vaccine gradually rolling out in many countries, there is hope that the travel restrictions may be lifted progressively, and efforts would be made by city destinations to restore travellers' confidence.

While some tourism cities started to reopen their borders to international visitors, such as Dubai, which in July 2020 ran a marketing campaign titled "Ready when you are", others, such as London, went through a number of national lockdowns. The Sweet tweet below shows an example of a message posted in February 2021 on the website of London & Partners (formally known as VisitLondon), the official promotional agency for London. This shows how popular tourism cities had to change and retool to the new realities imposed by the coronavirus, with their marketing strategies adapted to the situation they were facing.

Sweet tweet 83

**Visit London website – coronavirus update:
Latest information and advice**

This is an example of a message posted in March 2021 on the promotional website of one of the top world tourism cities.

- London is currently subject to national lockdown restrictions.
- If you need to travel for essential reasons, plan ahead and avoid using public transport at peak times – cycle or walk where possible.
- You must wear a face covering in certain places across the city, including on public transport.
- For people already in the UK, use the 111 online coronavirus service to get further information about coronavirus and check your symptoms.
- Find the latest information on the official UK government website.

Source: London & Partners (2021).

As mentioned earlier, Asia and the Pacific was the most affected region worldwide during the coronavirus pandemic, with key tourism cities from this part of the world suffering devastating consequences for their economies. Short break 10 presents one such case study, focusing on Bangkok, and the impact of the crisis on the tourism industry in this top world tourism city. The recovery of tourism in the region is believed to be helped by a reliance on short-haul and medium-haul travel, which is expected to have a quicker rebound (Oxford Economics, 2020). Although difficult to predict, some organisations expect that it may take up to five years for the number of international visitors to reach pre-coronavirus levels in the Asian and Pacific cities.

SHORT BREAK 10

Bangkok – one of the most affected cities in the Asia Pacific region

Bangkok, the capital of Thailand, used to be the most visited city in the Asia Pacific region, ranked for a number of years prior to the pandemic as the number one city destination in the world for international overnight visitors. The city, which also serves as a gateway to other parts of the country, has a population of more than ten million people and used to attract almost 23 million international visitors before the pandemic. This capital city accommodates a number of important historic and religious attractions, including the Grand Palace and a number of temples such as Wat Phra Kaew – Temple of the Emerald Buddha, and Wat Traimit – Temple of the Golden Buddha. The city is also known for its street food markets, a colourful and vibrant atmosphere and its nightlife.

Bangkok was one of the most affected urban destinations in the region due to the coronavirus crisis, and it is forecast that it will lose its title as the most visited city in the world as a result of the international travel restrictions imposed by the government in Thailand (and other countries worldwide) in their efforts to limit the spread of the coronavirus. These measures have severely impacted the economy of the city and of the country, which relies on international visitors and tourism income.

One of the recovery measures put together by the Tourism Authority of Thailand (TAT) was its offer *"Amazing Thailand Plus"* launched in December 2020, in collaboration with a number of other organisations such as Thai Airways International (THAI), the Thai Hotels Association (THA) and the Association of Thai Travel Agents (ATTA). The offer was available for a certain period of time, from December 2020 until the end of March 2021.

According to Mr. Yuthasak Supasorn, the Governor of the Tourism Authority of Thailand,

> The Amazing Thailand Plus offer gives visitors value added benefits while ensuring safety and health for both themselves and the Thai people. Every foreign traveller to Thailand must undergo a mandatory 14-day quarantine

and follow all rules and regulations set by the Ministry of Public Health just like every Thai national returning home from overseas.

This offer, while aimed at attracting rich visitors, was criticised by the industry, as they believe that tourism promotion requiring visitors to quarantine for two weeks was destined to fail.

Discussion points:

1. Why do you think Bangkok was one of the most affected city destinations from the Asia and Pacific region?
2. What do you think about the "*Amazing Thailand Plus*" offer launched by the government of Thailand? Would such a measure be successful in attracting foreign visitors to Bangkok?
3. What other measures do you think the city could take in order to speed up its recovery?

Sources: Tourism Authority of Thailand (2020); Oxford Economics (2020); Mastercard (2019).

A number of international organisations, including the World Tourism Organization (UNWTO), the World Travel & Tourism Council (WTTC), the Organisation for Economic Co-operation and Development (OECD) and World Tourism Cities Federation (WTCF), have put together a set of measures and recommendations to help the tourism industry recover. They called for governments to support tourism businesses, so they survive this dramatic downturn, and to help the sector recover. OECD (2020), for example, put together a list of seven key policy priorities to help the tourism industry during these challenging times:

- Restoring traveller confidence.
- Supporting tourism businesses to adapt and survive.
- Promoting domestic tourism and supporting the safe return of international tourism.
- Providing clear information to travellers and businesses, and limiting uncertainty (to the extent possible).
- Developing response measures to maintain capacity in the sector and address gaps in support.
- Strengthening cooperation within and between countries.
- Building a more resilient, sustainable tourism.

In their paper, the OECD particularly emphasise that the tourism sector should become more sustainable and resilient to be able to survive future crises. The UNWTO also highlights the importance of focusing on sustainability in its #*RestartTourism* campaign. Chapter 8 already discussed the importance of sustainable development and sustainable tourism implementation in city destinations and identified some of the challenges.

Finally, although pandemics greatly impact on the tourism sector in many ways, little attention was received by this niche field of study before the COVID-19 crisis. This situation, however, has changed and many academics and organisations are currently researching this topic, with increasing numbers of academic papers, reports and other publications looking into different aspects of pandemics and tourism, such as the challenges faced by the destinations and organisations during the pandemic, impacts, responses from organisations or governments, recovery strategies, case studies and how tourism behaviours are changing, to name but a few.

Crisis and disasters management frameworks

The previous sections introduced the topic of crisis and disasters in tourism cities and looked at a number of different types of crises using relevant examples from city destinations. This section moves the discussion further and examines the importance of crisis management plans and frameworks, and how these can be used by city destinations to better prepare for crises and disasters.

The concept of crisis management was briefly introduced in Chapter 4, when discussing the roles and responsibilities of CDMOs. It was noted there that many world tourism cities were caught unprepared by the COVID-19 pandemic as they did not have crisis management plans in place to help them navigate through this unprecedented crisis. This section continues the discussion on crisis management and presents one of the most cited frameworks for tourism crisis and disaster management.

Crisis management has been defined as an

> ongoing integrated and comprehensive effort that organisations effectively put into place in an attempt to first and foremost understand and prevent crisis, and to effectively manage those that occur, taking into account in each and every step of their planning and training activities, the interest of their stakeholders.
>
> *(Santana, 2004, p. 308)*

This definition points out the importance of constantly surveying and identifying potential problems that an organisation or destination may face and trying to avoid or manage those as best as possible, through planning actions and relevant training. It also emphasises the importance of considering all stakeholders and their interests at every step.

The tourism sector has a very fragmented nature, in particular in tourism cities, with many organisations and stakeholders that often have diverse goals and interests as they deliver different products and services. In addition, as seen in one of the previous sections, there are many different types of crises, each of them with their unique characteristics. Therefore, designing and implementing successful crisis and disaster management strategies is not an easy task, with crisis management models being sometimes criticised for failing to acknowledge the complex issues associated with specific crises that destinations may face (Novelli et al., 2018).

Still, having crisis management models and frameworks is important as it can help organisations and destinations to better understand, prepare for and minimise the potential harm that such events can cause. Over the years, several different crisis management models have been proposed, such as the four Rs presented in Chapter 4 (reduction, readiness, response and recovery); the four Cs (cognition, communication, coordination and control); mitigation, preparation, response, recovery (MPRR); and prevention, preparation, response, recovery (PPRR).

This section discusses Faulkner's (2001) disaster management framework, which is considered "one of the most appropriate for systematically analysing crisis management

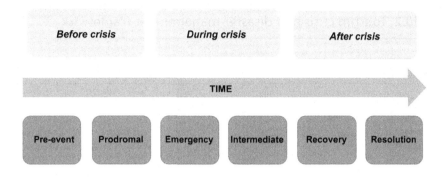

Figure 10.2 Phases of tourism crises and disasters.

processes in the tourism industry" (Pforr and Hosie, 2016). This model includes six phases, i.e., pre-event, prodromal, emergency, intermediate, recovery and resolution (Figure 10.2 and Table 10.2). Each of these phases, together with their key elements for an effective response to crises and disasters, is briefly discussed further on.

The *pre-event phase* is where actions can still be taken in order to prevent a crisis or disaster from occurring, such as identifying risks and preparing plans. Identifying and evaluating possible risks and hazards faced by destinations is an important step in crisis management and in how tourism cities can prepare to deal with such events.

Risks can be described as the chance of something unwanted happening and that will have an impact on a tourism destination. These can be associated with external and internal threats faced by organisations in relation to economic, political, socio-economic, environmental, technological and commercial domains. *Hazards*, on the other hand, are considered extreme events that are capable of causing disasters. Considering their origins, hazards can be classified into four separate groups:

- Atmospheric: e.g., cyclones, tornadoes, storms, floods.
- Geological (Earth): e.g., earthquakes, tsunamis, volcanoes, erosions.
- Biological: e.g., epidemics, pandemics, bushfires.
- Human: e.g., political conflicts, terrorism, crime, traffic accidents, industrial accidents.

A good understanding of the potential risks and hazards faced by tourism cities may help these destinations to be better prepared to cope with crises and disasters. Tourists are particularly at risk as they are usually new to the destinations and are not familiar with the threats faced by these locations.

In an effort to help organisations prepare for crisis, Paraskevas and Altinay (2013) developed a *crisis signal detection framework* that consists of three stages: Signal scanning, signal capture and signal transmission to the response centre. According to the authors, many crises do emit "warning signals", and if these are picked up early then the organisation may be able to either prevent the crisis or to take the necessary measures to help minimise its impacts. The effectiveness of identifying those signals (if any) largely depends on the ability of city destinations to scan their internal and external environments and identify any deviations or abnormal patterns that may lead to a crisis.

Table 10.2 Tourism crisis and disaster management framework

Phases in the crisis and disaster process	Actions	Principal strategies
1. *Pre-event* • Actions can still be taken to prevent or mitigate the crisis or disaster	*Reduction*	**Risk assessment** • Assess potential crises and disasters, their probability of occurrence and the potential impacts they may have • Develop contingency plans
2. *Prodromal* • When it is apparent that a disaster is imminent	*Readiness*	*Contingency plans* • Identify potential impacts and who is at risk
3. *Emergency* • The effects are felt, and actions are required to protect people and property	*Response*	• Assess the local community's and visitors' capability to cope with the impacts • Articulate the specific objectives of the contingency plans (linked to the type of crisis or disaster faced)
4. *Intermediate* • The main focus is to restore the affected services, once the short-term needs of people have been addressed		• Identify measures to be taken to avoid or minimise impacts
5. *Recovery (long-term)* • A continuation of the previous stage, with a focus on items that could not be attended to earlier	*Recovery*	• Design strategic priorities for each phase • Ongoing review and revision, taking into account the experience and the changes in the internal and external environment
6. *Resolution* • Either the routine is restored, or a new improved state is established		

Source: Adapted from Faulkner (2001), p. 144.

Furthermore, proactive planning is a necessity in crisis management as it can help destinations and organisations to return to normal quicker and potentially reduce the damage. Still, many tourism organisations and destinations fail to prepare crisis management plans and strategies (Mair et al., 2016; Ritchie and Jiang, 2019), and this could be seen during the recent COVID-19 pandemic.

Prodromal is when it is apparent that a crisis or a disaster is about to happen in a destination, and therefore the contingency plans that (hopefully) were developed in the previous phase need to be activated. In the case of certain natural disasters such as earthquakes, the pre-event and prodromal phases are very short and mostly overlapping, if not absent, which gives little time for preparation.

Once a threat or hazard has been identified, a warning is required to alert those people that might be affected. This could be done via the media, e.g., TV channels, radio, newspapers, social media platforms or even by the police and other emergency personnel. A command centre may be established for the crisis management team to coordinate the actions. The proactive approach is important in this and the previous phase, as it can help prevent or mitigate the effects of potential crises and disasters. During this phase, the tourism sector should focus on providing accurate information, rapid communication and preparing the necessary facilities and materials to protect visitors and the local community as much as possible.

During the *emergency phase*, when the effects of the crisis or disaster are felt, the actions focus on protecting the affected people and property, with rescue and evacuation procedures put in place if needed. This phase represents the immediate response to the crisis event or disaster and includes actions such as:

- Evacuation of visitors and locals from the affected area, if needed.
- Ensuring that visitors are safe, and their basic needs are addressed.
- Ensuring that staff members are safe.
- Carrying out emergency infrastructure repairs, if needed.
- Providing regular and accurate updates about the crisis (COMCEC, 2017).

During this phase, certain systems are required to monitor the situation and the impacts of the crisis. In addition, special attention needs to be paid to the emergency communications with all stakeholders, including governmental organisations, visitors, locals and the media, a topic that is discussed later in this chapter.

The *intermediate phase*, named by some authors the "emergency recovery phase", focuses on a quick return to stability through the restoration of essential services and addressing the immediate needs of local people and visitors who were affected by the crisis. During this phase, government involvement and leadership are essential to coordinate the response actions and support the tourism sector.

Examples of measures that need to be taken during the response phase include:

- A coordinated response between governmental bodies and tourism organisations.
- Repairs of the infrastructure affected by the crisis, to facilitate the return to normal operation of tourism services as quickly as possible.
- Improvements to security, if needed, in particular in the case of political unrest or terrorist attacks.
- Fiscal and monetary measures promoted by government to support the tourism sector.
- Regular communication from the tourism sector and government of the measures taken, to avoid the spread of "fake news", in particular via social media platforms (COMCEC, 2017).

The *recovery phase* represents the long-term approach to rebuilding the affected areas and the damaged infrastructure, with many studies focusing on this and the response phase discussed earlier. One of the main challenges faced by city destination managers during the recovery phase is to restore all operations to normal. In addition, strategic thinking is needed to reshape the destination offer as essential tourism infrastructure and equipment may have been affected and may need replacing, new operation processes may be required and new markets sought.

A number of strategies can be adopted by tourism organisations to facilitate an effective and quick tourism recovery, with some of the key ones listed below (Ritchie and Jiang, 2019):

- Recovery of damaged infrastructure (e.g., roads, electricity, water, accommodation) and plan for infrastructure improvements or reconstruction.
- Provision of financial assistance for tourism businesses affected by the crisis to help with business continuity (e.g., waiving taxes, low-interest loans and subsidies).
- Crisis communication – it is very important that up-to-date information about the crisis and its impacts is provided to the main stakeholders.
- Recovery marketing, including market segmentation – with a focus on existing and new markets, and recovery promotion.
- Multi-level stakeholder cooperation, including cooperation between different governmental bodies, and between the public and private sectors.
- Adaptation to the new systems and realities.
- Personnel management.

Sweet tweet 84

Action Guide on Recovery and Revitalization of City Tourism amid COVID-19

The WTCF has produced an Action Guide to help city tourism destinations to recover from the devastating impacts of the COVID-19 crisis. The eight actions included in the guide are listed below:

1. Taking comprehensive measures for pandemic prevention and control among tourism cities.
2. Coordinating the orderly resumption of city tourism activities.
3. Implementing more proactive and effective incentive policies.
4. Enhancing international cooperation on pandemic prevention and tourism recovery.
5. Establishing a service platform for pandemic information sharing.
6. Reinforcing the relief and rescue system of emergency in tourism cities.
7. Promoting innovative models for urban tourism amid COVID-19.
8. Popularising greener and healthier tourism.

Source: World Tourism Cities Federation (2020).

An important activity that can help cities during the recovery phase is *destination recovery marketing*, which is key to re-establishing tourism activities in a post-disaster environment, as it can provide economic benefits and boost tourism arrivals in the affected destinations. In certain situations, however, such as in the case of disasters that create massive infrastructure destruction and casualties, *de-marketing* strategies may be more appropriate to consider immediately after the event, in order to relieve the burden on the affected areas and allow the authorities to rebuild the destination. Therefore, timing is crucial in deciding when to start the recovery marketing efforts.

The sweet tweet below presents a number of commonly employed tourism disaster recovery messages, giving examples from destinations that adopted such messages over the years.

> ## Sweet tweet 85
>
> ### Examples of commonly employed tourism disaster recovery messages
>
> - Business as usual (e.g., *"Greece is open for business"*, a campaign promoted in the summer of 2020 to help rescue part of the tourism season, which was severely affected by the COVID-19 pandemic).
> - Community readiness (e.g., *"We are ready to welcome you"* was used extensively in Sri Lanka following the Boxing Day Tsunami in 2004).
> - Solidarity messages (e.g., *"By visiting you are helping the Maldives recover"* message proved successful in attracting visitors following the Boxing Day Tsunami).
> - Celebrity endorsement (e.g., *David Hasselhoff* was among the celebrities praising the Lake District in the UK as a holiday destination, in an effort to attract domestic visitors to the region during the COVID-19 pandemic).
> - Restore confidence and change misperceptions (e.g., *"New Orleans – Never Better"* emerged in an attempt to restore market confidence after Hurricane Katrina).
> - Curiosity enhancement (e.g., *"Come, see for yourself"*; curiosity was one of the main reasons why tourists visited the island of Phuket after the Boxing Day tsunami).
> - Using visitor testimonials (e.g., *#FijiNow* was a campaign that used social proof to help revive Fiji's tourism industry after the 2016 Cyclone Winston).
>
> Source: Developed from Walters and Mair (2012).

Resolution, the final phase of the crisis management framework, is about returning to normality or moving to an improved state. It consists of reviewing and evaluating the actions taken in the previous phases and, if needed, proposing improvements. This includes activities such as monitoring the success of short- and medium-term measures, evaluating longer-term measures needed to rebuild the tourism sector and adjusting the contingency plans in view of the lessons learned from the crisis (COMCEC, 2017). Therefore, future crisis management plans should take into account past strategies implemented successfully, as well as learning from previous mistakes.

While Faulkner's framework discussed in this section provides a useful tool to better understand the different phases of crises and disasters in tourism, the model has its limitations (Zheng, 2015). Scholars have pointed out that crises and disasters are complex events that are in many cases unpredictable in their evolution and outcomes. Therefore, it may be difficult for destinations to predict a crisis, and to have in place scenario planning and risk assessments for all possible events, as expected in the preparatory stage. Another limitation relates to the linear and prescriptive approach taken in the framework, while it is recognised that crises are often chaotic in nature and therefore they rarely follow a defined path or lifecycle. Finally, the framework takes a supply-focused view and tends to overlook the multitude and diversity of different stakeholder groups in a destination, neglecting an important stakeholder – the visitors, as their perceptions and attitudes could inform certain stages.

Crisis communication

The importance of crisis communication was mentioned a number of times in the previous section, when discussing the different crisis management phases. This reflects the key role that communication plays in crisis management at all stages, as it can either mitigate or exacerbate the impact of a crisis or disaster. These complex and, in many cases, unpredictable events generate a high demand for information from various stakeholders, including the general public, industry and governmental agencies (Park et al., 2019).

Crisis communication has been defined as "the strategic use of words and actions to manage information and meaning during a crisis" (Coombs, 2019, p. 53). As seen from this definition, there are two parts of crisis communications:

- Managing information, which refers to collecting and disseminating information related to a crisis or disaster.
- Managing meaning, which refers to how people perceive a crisis or a destination in crisis.

A more encompassing definition is provided by Frandsen and Johansen (2010, p. 431), who define crisis communication as

> a complex and dynamic configuration of communicative processes which evolve before, during, and after an event, a situation or a course of events that is seen as a crisis by an organization and/or one or more of its stakeholders. Crisis communication also includes various actors, contexts, and discourses (manifested in specific genres and specific texts) related to each other.

Crisis communication therefore comprises three important elements: Managing stakeholder relationships; narrating the crisis via media and other stakeholders' engagement, making use of various platforms of communication; and the development and implementation of a communication strategy (Diers-Lawson, 2020).

According to Diers-Lawson (2020), organisations and destinations tend to employ four common patterns in their response to crises events: (1) *defensive strategies*, characterised by a tendency to minimise the problem and a denial of responsibilities, adopting image-protective messages; (2) *accommodative strategies*, where an apology is offered and empathy shown for those affected, with a focus on solving the problem; (3) *image-oriented responses*, where the main focus is on promoting the organisation/destination but without offering an apology; and (4) *status updates*, where the critical role of providing information to stakeholders and managing communication during a crisis is recognised.

Consistency is a key element in crisis communication, and special attention should be paid to providing consistent messages to all stakeholders (Ritchie, 2004). This will help tourism organisations that are facing crises to improve their credibility and preserve their good image. To be able to do that, tourism organisations and destinations need to have a clear understanding of who the audience is and to develop goals to help them communicate effectively with those groups.

Another important factor to consider in crisis communication is *timing*, which refers to when an organisation or destination starts speaking about the crisis they face. It has been found that it is best for the managers of an organisation to be the first to speak about a crisis, as this may help reduce the damage, a method known as *steal the thunder*

(Coombs, 2019). Tourism organisations and destinations with a good reputation prior to a crisis are more likely to benefit from a stealing-thunder effect, with customers likelier to be sympathetic to the organisation and the brand attachment becoming even stronger.

In response to the travel disruptions created by crisis events, governments in many countries issue *travel advisories* to warn citizens, travellers and others about the risks and threats they may encounter if they choose to travel to certain destinations. An example is Hong Kong's Outbound Travel Alert (OTA) system that uses three symbolic colours to indicate the level of risk associated with travelling to a region, i.e., amber, red and black, with black indicating the highest risk (Tsang et al., 2018).

Traditionally, crisis communication used to be a linear top-down flow of information, from government organisations to the general public via various mass media platforms. However, more recently, the rapid developments of new communication technologies, such as social media platforms, have changed the way information is communicated during a crisis or disaster, an aspect discussed in the following section (Figure 10.3).

Managing social media in a crisis

Social media has revolutionised the way we communicate and share information in general, and during times of crisis in particular. It has created new ways of exchanging information, where millions of people can easily contribute to the flow of data. Nowadays, for example, news often breaks first on Twitter before being reported in traditional media (such as TV, radio or printed newspapers). Facebook has created an "I'm safe" button that people can use to mark themselves as safe during a major incident or disaster. These are just some examples of how social media has changed crisis communication, from the one-way system used in the past – where governmental organisations release information via traditional media platforms – towards a multi-way communication via various social media tools and between various groups. Table 10.3 presents five different types of social media platforms and how these can be used to facilitate crisis communication.

Figure 10.3 Social media platforms (Courtesy: Unsplash.com, dole777).

Table 10.3 Different types of social media platforms used in crisis communication

Type of social media	Examples of social media platforms	How the tool can be used for crisis communication
1. Social networking	Facebook Myspace Friendster	• Enhance coordination among volunteers and emergency services. • Facilitate information sharing within a community. • Provide swift updates on emergency situations.
2. Content sharing	YouTube Flickr Vimeo	• Enhance situational awareness in real time through the exchange of photos and videos. • Allow emergency services to easily launch viral campaigns about risks. • Can help identify missing individuals or victims.
3. Collaborating knowledge sharing	Wikis Forums Message boards Podcasts	• Enhance dialogue between victims and emergency services.
4. Blogging and microblogging	Blogger WordPress Twitter Tumblr	• Convey recommendations, warnings, share facts. • Twitter enables immediate information sharing with a wide reach and feedback possibilities.
5. Special crisis management platforms managed by volunteer technology communities (VTC)	Mapping collaboration: • OpenStreetMap • Crisis Mappers • Google map maker Online and onsite contribution • Ushahidi • Crisis commons • Sahana Foundation • Geeks without Bounds Public-private-people partnership • Random Hacks of Kindness (with Google, Microsoft, Yahoo, NASA, World Bank)	• Mapping of emergencies. • Community emergency response team facilitator.

Source: Adapted from the OECD Working Papers on Public Governance, produced by Wendling, Radisch and Jacobzone (2013).

To help managers better understand the viral spread of information through social media and the relationship between different stakeholders (including online and offline public, social media and traditional media and word-of-mouth communication), a number of researchers proposed the **Social-Mediated Crisis Communication (SMCC) model** presented in Figure 10.4. This identifies three groups of people who generate and consume information during different phases of a crisis:

- Influential social media creators, who actively produce information related to the crisis event for others to consume.
- Social media followers, who receive information from the creators in the previous group.
- Social media inactives, those who passively consume information related to the crisis event indirectly, through word-of-mouth communication, from followers and/or traditional media.

Social media storms (SMSs) constitute another important aspect to be taken into account by city destination managers, as they can bring both challenges and opportunities. An SMS represents a "sudden and explosive social media dissemination of negative consumer emotion towards an organization" (Rydén et al., 2020, p. 108). In an effort to help destinations better understand how SMSs work, Rydén et al. (2020) developed a conceptual framework and offered empirical evidence by applying the model to the Copenhagen Zoo. They found that while an SMS is generally perceived as a threat due to bad publicity and loss of control, it can also provide opportunities for organisations if they have a good understanding of consumer anger and social media dynamics.

The fast exchange of information facilitated by social media brings many opportunities for destinations to easily and directly communicate with the key stakeholders before, during and after crisis events. However, it also brings great *challenges* in managing the huge amount of information posted on various platforms. Therefore, the

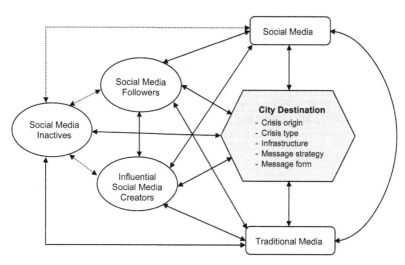

Figure 10.4 Social-mediated crisis communication model (Source: Adapted from Austin, Liu and Jin (2012)).

challenges faced by destinations when using social media platforms in crisis communication need to be considered in more detail.

To start with, having to deal with many players and a variety of communication channels, city destination managers may find it difficult to coordinate all the communication across all channels to ensure that the messages delivered are consistent and accurate. A multi-channel approach is useful, as people can check the same information from various sources; however, some of this information may be more factual than other sources, due to subjectivity. Sometimes, however, having a more centralised use of social media may help destinations eliminate multiple communication strategies from various departments and thus reduce duplication or misunderstandings.

Another challenge relates to the transparency and reliability of the circulating information, with efforts needed from destination managers to avoid the spreading and propagation of rumours or misinformation that can create situations of panic among visitors and the affected population. To address this challenge, information posted on social media platforms from official channels should be clearly labelled as such. The information posted on the official accounts can then be retweeted by other stakeholders or users, thus increasing the spread of accurate information during crisis and disaster events.

It is widely recognised that social media cannot be controlled, and therefore it may have implications for the image of a destination. People can comment, criticise or even post inaccurate information through social media platforms, which may damage the reputation and the image of a destination/organisation. Therefore, it is important that city destination management organisations have a dedicated person or unit (e.g., communication officer) to monitor the relevant information posted on social media platforms and respond to any comments and criticisms in a timely and polite fashion. This may limit the spread of inaccurate information or rumours, and thus protect the reputation of a destination.

As already mentioned, social media contributes to an increased flow of data, in particular during crisis situations. The amount of information exchanged through social media platforms during these events can be so high that it can become overwhelming, making it difficult to have a clear picture of what the situation is in reality. Therefore, efforts should be made to avoid information overload, which in extreme cases may lead to blocked systems and even bans imposed by authorities.

Lastly, the open nature of social media, where anyone can post information, could lead to *secondary crisis communication*. This has been defined as "social media users' online behaviour of commenting on, sharing, or forwarding posts about crises" (Luo and Zhai, 2017, p. 160), that can create new problems such as negative emotions, tourism boycotts and negative word-of-mouth communication that can affect the image of a destination.

Summary comments

Destinations, and in particular world tourism cities, are vulnerable to many crises and disasters, both man-made and natural, as witnessed over the past few decades. Many would say that whether a crisis will happen in a destination is not a question of if, but more of when and of what type of crisis will hit first, and how serious will be the consequences. It is therefore paramount for city destinations to be well prepared to face such events. For that, they need to be able to identify the risks they face, have a good understanding of the different types of crises and their particularities and be familiar with crisis management frameworks and other tools that can help them better deal with crisis events and disasters. Furthermore, an effective risk-management system can help destinations to prevent an issue from degenerating into a crisis, and thus resources should be invested in planning and preparing for crises and disasters.

The fragmented nature of the tourism sector, due to the many stakeholders involved in tourism development in city destinations, can lead to miscommunication and misperceptions during crisis events. Therefore, crisis communication is a vital aspect of crisis management and efforts should be made by destinations to engage proactively in communication with their stakeholders during all stages of a crisis. This is now facilitated by the recent technological advances and, in particular, by the rapid development of social media platforms, which have made it possible for destinations to easily connect and communicate with their visitors and other important stakeholders. Nevertheless, this rapid development has also brought challenges for destinations, which had to learn quickly how to communicate and effectively manage the influx of information during crises.

This chapter looked at those aspects in detail and discussed a number of examples of different crises that have affected city destinations. The next chapter takes the reader on a journey through Asian world tourism cities, discussing the factors that contributed to the rapid growth and increased prominence of these destinations, while also touching on the major challenges these environments are currently facing.

Thought questions

1) Why do you think world tourism cities are prone to crises and disasters, more so than other types of destinations?
2) The two concepts, crisis and disaster, tend to be used interchangeably. In your opinion, what is the difference between the two?
3) There are different types of crises and disasters that can affect destinations worldwide. How can tourism cities identify potential risks and predict which crises are more likely to strike their way?
4) Faulkner (2001) developed a disaster management framework to help destinations better understand and manage crisis events. What are the limitations of this model?
5) How can world tourism cities better prepare in the face of increased risks of crises and disasters?
6) In your opinion, what can city destinations do in order to recover more quickly from the devastating impacts of the coronavirus crisis? Can you propose a set of measures and mention who should be responsible with their promotion/implementation?
7) What would be the lessons to be learned from the latest pandemic, and the way city destinations and governments responded to the coronavirus crisis?
8) Crisis communication is a key element in crisis management. What can destinations do in order to improve their communication with various stakeholders during crisis events?
9) How can city destination management organisations use different social media platforms to engage with stakeholders during a crisis or disaster?
10) What challenges may be faced by destinations when managing social media within a crisis? How can they avoid secondary crises communication?

References

Austin, L., Fisher Liu, B., & Jin, Y. (2012). How audiences seek out crisis information: Exploring the social-mediated crisis communication model. *Journal of Applied Communication Research, 40*(2), 188–207.

Coca-Stefaniak, A., & Morrison, A. M. (2018). City tourism destinations and terrorism: a worrying trend for now, but could it get worse? *International Journal of Tourism Cities, 4*(4), 409–412.

COMCEC. (2017). *Risk and Crisis Management in Tourism Sector: Recovery From Crisis in the OIC Member Countries.* https://www.sbb.gov.tr/wp-content/uploads/2018/11/Ris _and_Crisis_Management_in_Tourism_Sector-.pdf

Coombs, W. T. (2019). Crisis communication: The best evidence from research. In R. P. Gephart, C. C. Miller, & K. Svedberg Helgesson (Eds.). *The Routledge Companion to Risk, Crisis and Emergency Management*, pp. 51–66. Oxfordshire, UK: Taylor & Francis.

Diers-Lawson, A. (2020). *Crisis Communication: Managing Stakeholder Relationships*, 1st ed. London: Routledge.

Duan, J., Xie, C., & Morrison, A. M. (2021). Tourism crises and impacts on destinations: A systematic review of the tourism and hospitality literature. *Journal of Hospitality & Tourism Research.* https://doi.org/10.1177/1096348021994194

European Cities Marketing. (2018). *The Theatre of Terror.* European Cities Marketing. https://www.europeancitiesmarketing.com/the-theatre-of-terror/

Faisal, A., Albrecht, J. N., & Coetzee, W. J. L. (2020). (Re)Creating spaces for tourism: Spatial effects of the 2010/ 2011 Christchurch earthquakes. *Tourism Management, 80,* 104102.

Faulkner, B. (2001). Towards a framework for tourism disaster management. *Tourism Management, 22*(2), 135–147.

Frandsen, F., & Johansen, W. (2010). Crisis communication, complexity, and the cartoon affair: A case study. In W. T. Coombs & S. J. Holladay (Eds.). *The Handbook of Crisis Communication.* Hoboken, NJ: Wiley.

Global Rescue, & World Travel & Tourism Council. (2019). *Crisis Readiness.* https://wttc .org/Research/Insights

Hall, C. M. (2010). Crisis events in tourism: Subjects of crisis in tourism. *Current Issues in Tourism, 13*(5), 401–417.

Lim, J., & Won, D. (2020). How Las Vegas' tourism could survive an economic crisis? *Cities, 100,* 102643.

London & Partners. (2021). *Coronavirus London: Latest Information and Advice.* Visitlondon.Com. https://www.visitlondon.com/coronavirus

Luo, Q., & Zhai, X. (2017). "I will never go to Hong Kong again!" How the secondary crisis communication of "Occupy Central" on Weibo shifted to a tourism boycott. *Tourism Management, 62,* 159–172.

Mair, J., Ritchie, B. W., & Walters, G. (2016). Towards a research agenda for post-disaster and post-crisis recovery strategies for tourist destinations: A narrative review. *Current Issues in Tourism, 19*(1), 1–26.

Mastercard. (2019). *Global Destination Cities Index 2019.* https://newsroom.mastercard.co m/wp-content/uploads/2019/09/GDCI-Global-Report-FINAL-1.pdf

Novelli, M., Gussing Burgess, L., Jones, A., & Ritchie, B. W. (2018). 'No Ebola…still doomed': The Ebola-induced tourism crisis. *Annals of Tourism Research, 70,* 76–87.

OECD. (2020). *Rebuilding Tourism for the Future: COVID-19 Policy Responses and Recovery.* OECD. http://www.oecd.org/coronavirus/policy-responses/rebuilding-tourism -for-the-future-covid-19-policy-responses-and-recovery-bced9859/

Oxford Economics. (2020). *City Travel Falls and Recovery: Impacts of COVID-19 on City Tourism.* http://blog.oxfordeconomics.com/content/city-travel-falls-and-recovery-impacts-of-covid-19-on-city-tourism

Paraskevas, A., & Altinay, L. (2013). Signal detection as the first line of defence in tourism crisis management. *Tourism Management, 34,* 158–171.

Park, D., Kim, W. G., & Choi, S. (2019). Application of social media analytics in tourism crisis communication. *Current Issues in Tourism, 22*(15), 1810–1824.

Pforr, C., & Hosie, P. (Eds.). (2016). *Crisis Management in the Tourism Industry: Beating the Odds?* London: Routledge.

Prideaux, B., Laws, E., & Faulkner, B. (2003). Events in Indonesia: Exploring the limits to formal tourism trends forecasting methods in complex crisis situations. *Tourism Management, 24*(4), 475–487.

Ritchie, B. W. (2004). Chaos, crises and disasters: A strategic approach to crisis management in the tourism industry. *Tourism Management, 25*(6), 669–683.

Ritchie, B. W., & Jiang, Y. (2019). A review of research on tourism risk, crisis and disaster management: Launching the annals of tourism research curated collection on tourism risk, crisis and disaster management. *Annals of Tourism Research, 79,* 102812.

Roberts, K. H., Madsen, P., & Desai, V. (2007). Organizational sensemaking during crisis. In C. M. Pearson, C. Roux-Dufort, & J. A. Clair (Eds.). *International Handbook of Organizational Crisis Management,* 1st ed., pp. 107–122). London: SAGE.

Rydén, P., Kottika, E., Hossain, M., Skare, V., & Morrison, A. M. (2020). Threat or treat for tourism organizations? The Copenhagen Zoo social media storm. *International Journal of Tourism Research, 22*(1), 108–119.

Santana, G. (2004). Crisis management and tourism. *Journal of Travel & Tourism Marketing, 15*(4), 299–321.

Seabra, C., & Paiva, O. (2021). Global terrorism in tourism cities: The case of World Heritage Sites. In A. M. Morrison & J. A. Coca-Stefaniak (Eds.). *Routledge Handbook of Tourism Cities,* pp. 31–51. London: Routledge.

Sio-Chong, U., & So, Y. C. (2020). The impacts of financial and non-financial crises on tourism: Evidence from Macao and Hong Kong. *Tourism Management Perspectives, 33,* 100628.

Siu, A., & Wong, Y. C. R. (2004). Economic impact of SARS: The case of Hong Kong. *Asian Economic Papers, 3*(1), 61–83.

Song, H., Livat, F., & Ye, S. (2019). Effects of terrorist attacks on tourist flows to France: Is wine tourism a substitute for urban tourism? *Journal of Destination Marketing & Management, 14,* 100385.

Sönmez, S. F., & Allen, L. R. (1994). *Managing Tourism Crises: A Guidebook.* South Carolina, USA: Department of Parks, Recreation and Tourism Management, Clemson University.

Terhorst, P., & Erkuş-Öztürk, H. (2019). Resilience to the Global Economic and Turkish (GEO)political crisis compared. *Tijdschrift Voor Economische En Sociale Geografie, 110*(2), 138–155.

Tourism Authority of Thailand. (2020). *TAT partners Thai tourism industry to launch 'Amazing Thailand Plus' Offers.* https://www.tourismthailand.org/Articles/amazing-thailand-plus

Tsang, N. K. F., Wong, O., & Prideaux, B. (2018). An evaluation of the effectiveness of travel advisories with a specific focus on Hong Kong's outbound travel alert system. *Journal of Vacation Marketing, 24*(4), 307–323.

UNWTO. (2021). *2020: Worst Year in Tourism History with 1 Billion Fewer International Arrivals*. https://www.unwto.org/taxonomy/term/347

UNWTO, & International Labour Organisation. (2011). *Economic Crisis, International Tourism Decline and Its Impact on the Poor*. https://assets.publishing.service.gov.uk/media/57a08ac040f0b652dd0008a0/UNWTO_29Nov11.pdf

Walters, G., & Mair, J. (2012). The effectiveness of post-disaster recovery marketing messages: The case of the 2009 Australian Bushfires. *Journal of Travel & Tourism Marketing, 29*(1), 87–103.

Wendling, C., Radisch, J., & Jacobzone, S. (2013). *The Use of Social Media in Risk and Crisis Communication* (No. 24). *OECD Working Papers on Public Governance*. https://www.oecd-ilibrary.org/governance/the-use-of-social-media-in-risk-and-crisis-communication_5k3v01fskp9s-en

World Health Organization. (2021). *WHO Coronavirus Disease (COVID-19) Dashboard*. https://covid19.who.int

World Tourism Cities Federation. (2020). *Action Guide on Recovery and Revitalization of City Tourism amid COVID-19: WTCF Academic Achievement: WTCF-Better City Life through Tourism*. WTCF. https://en.wtcf.org.cn/Research/WTCFAcademicAchievement/2020091419630.html

Yang, Y., Zhang, H., & Chen, X. (2020). Coronavirus pandemic and tourism: Dynamic stochastic general equilibrium modeling of infectious disease outbreak. *Annals of Tourism Research, 83*, 102913.

Zheng, Q. (2015). *Crisis Management, Tourism and the Three Gorges Dam, China* [PhD Dissertation]. University of Central Lancashire.

Chapter 11

The rise of the Asian world tourism cities

Abstract

Asia experienced the largest increase in the number of international visitors over the years up to and including 2018, with 12 out of the 20 top city destinations in the world located within the continent. Generally, Asian countries are increasing in travel and tourism competitiveness as well. Chapter 11 identifies the factors that are contributing to this rise of Asian cities using the 10 As model. In particular, transportation network improvements are reviewed, as is the expansion of culture and heritage tourism, nature, shopping and food tourism, entertainment attractions, health and medical tourism and cruises. Major growth markets for Asian city tourism are pinpointed, including regional, domestic, business/MICE and VFR travel. The chapter also highlights some of the particular features, positive and negative, of the tourism cities in Asia.

With the arrival of the COVID-19 pandemic, Asian cities' tourist volumes plummeted in 2020 and 2021 and the economic consequences were significant. The specific impacts are explored. Even before COVID-19, along with the tourism growth and broader external environment changes came issues and challenges for Asian cities and these are covered. Rapid urbanisation and improving income levels spurred tourism growth, but also were a source of problems within urban areas.

Keywords: Air pollution; business tourism; COVID-19 pandemic; domestic tourism; regional tourism; traffic congestion; urbanisation.

DOI: 10.4324/9781003111412-14

Learning objectives

Having read this chapter, you should be able to:

- Identify the factors that have led to the growth and competitiveness of tourism in Asian cities.
- Pinpoint the major growth markets for Asian tourism cities.
- Describe features that tend to make Asian tourism cities unique.
- Highlight the impacts of the COVID-19 pandemic on Asian city tourism.
- Explain the major issues and challenges facing Asian tourism cities at present.

Asian city tourism differs from that evident in the traditional urban tourism destinations in Europe and North America. While the historic and fashion cities of Europe have traditionally attracted the most tourists, and the urban wonders of the New World in the Americas grew in appeal, Asia's cities became increasingly alluring on a regional and global basis. Thus, Asia and the Pacific have taken market share away from Europe and North America; and yet several European cities (pre-COVID-19) were beset with overcrowding issues. It seemed that European cities were about to close their doors to visitors, while the doors were being held wide open in Asia.

This chapter commences by discussing the reasons for this growth.

Reasons for the growth of tourism in Asian cities

The World Economic Forum's *Travel and Tourism Competitiveness Report* annual series is showing that Asian destinations are becoming increasingly competitive on the world stage and therefore so are many Asian cities as well. Table 11.1 displays the ranking data for the 2019 report, with five Asian countries featuring in the top 20 overall. Japan and Mainland China were the two most competitive countries within Asia.

Mastercard's *Global Destination Cities Index 2019* rankings, using data from 2018, has 12 Asian cities in the top 20 (Bangkok, Singapore, Kuala Lumpur, Istanbul (partly in Asia), Tokyo, Antalya (as with Istanbul), Seoul, Osaka, Phuket, Pattaya, Bali (mainly Denpasar) and Hong Kong (Figure 11.1)). Chapter 3 noted that Asian cities experienced the largest increases in overnight international tourists in recent years according to these Mastercard statistics. UNWTO figures also confirm that the Asia-Pacific region was among the fastest growing in the world based on international tourist arrivals up until 2019. Whilst the People's Republic of China has been a large component of this Asian tourism growth engine, it is noteworthy that apart from Hong Kong no other of its major cities made the Mastercard top 20. The same is also true for the principal tourism cities of India.

Using different data sets to the Mastercard Index, other rankings identify additional popular Asian city destinations, including Macao, Shenzhen, Guangzhou, Taipei, Shanghai, Beijing, Ho Chi Minh City, Delhi, Mumbai, Chennai, Hangzhou, Agra, Johor Bahru and Jaipur (Ampersand Travel, 2019; Moodley, 2019). The inclusion of excursionists (day-trippers) and domestic travellers causes differences in these ratings when compared to the Mastercard data.

Chapter 3 highlighted the overall reasons for the growth in city tourism. These included increasing globalisation, visa relaxation and facilitation, airline liberalisation,

Table 11.1 Ranking of Asian countries in travel and tourism competitiveness

Country/area	Overall rating	Asia rating
Japan	4	1
China	13	2
Hong Kong SAR	14	3
South Korea	16	5
Singapore	17	6
Malaysia	29	7
Thailand	31	8
India	34	9
Taiwan	37	10
Indonesia	40	11
Turkey	43	12
Vietnam	63	13
Brunei Darussalam	72	14
Philippines	75	15
Sri Lanka	77	16
Kazakhstan	80	17
Iran	89	18
Mongolia	93	19
Lao PDR	97	20
Cambodia	98	21
Nepal	102	22
Tajikistan	104	23
Kyrgyz Republic	110	24
Bangladesh	120	25
Pakistan	121	26

Based on data from the Travel and Tourism Competitiveness Index 2019 (World Economic Forum, 2019).

low-cost airline carrier expansion, short city break holidays, ICTs, higher disposable incomes and changing work patterns, increased life expectancies, political changes, infrastructure improvements and increasing variety and enhancements to city tourism offerings. All of these have been factors fuelling urban tourism growth within Asia, and the chapter now highlights some of these and other influential trends. To better organise this discussion, the 10 As model from Chapter 5 is used as a framework.

Figure 11.1 The skyline of Hong Kong Island (Courtesy: Unsplash.com, Sébastien Goldberg).

1. *Awareness*

The levels of knowledge among visitors about city destinations and their major attractions

The world is only beginning to discover many Asian cities which points to their increased market awareness in the future. Taking India as an example, the only cities that are household names are Delhi, Mumbai (Bombay), Kolkata (Calcutta) and Chennai (Madras). Other top ten cities in terms of total GDP are Bengaluru, Hyderabad, Ahmedabad, Pune, Surat and Visakhapatnam, which have low awareness levels outside of India (Kokkranikal, Morrison and Gowreesunkar, 2020). The situation is similar for Mainland China, where many heavily populated cities are unknown to those outside of the country. Depending on whether one takes a "glass half empty" or "glass half full" perspective, the lack of awareness can be seen as a negative or as being a positive, respectively.

The volume of information on Asian city tourism and city tourism marketing has grown, particularly through heavy usage of social media platforms within Asia and elsewhere. Six of the top ten countries with the most Facebook users are within Asia, with India being the top ranked. Others include Indonesia, the Philippines, Vietnam, Thailand and Bangladesh.

The rapidly increasing review posts uploaded on Tripadvisor as well as the many vlogs and blogs about Asian cities are also increasing awareness. At the time of writing, Bali had almost three million and Bangkok had 1.97 million Tripadvisor reviews and opinions; others were Singapore (1.6 million), Tokyo (1.54 million), Istanbul (1.28 million), Phuket (1.2 million) and Hong Kong (1.16 million). As a point of reference, London had 6.51 million reviews and opinions.

The annual reports and press announcements from city DMOs in Asia indicate that they are devoting more resources to marketing as competition intensifies. Several city DMOs from Asia operate large networks of staffed and representative offices in other countries and these include Singapore, Hong Kong and Macao. The Hong Kong Tourism Board has 15 staffed offices and six representative offices abroad (HKTB, 2020). The Singapore Tourism Board has 21 staffed offices and five representative offices (Singapore Tourism Board, 2020). The Macao Government Office of Tourism has 16 representative offices (MGTO, 2020).

2. Accessibility

The convenience of getting to and from a city; and the city's accessibility or ease of moving around within its boundaries

Getting to and moving around Asian cities has greatly improved. Here, the expansion of low-cost airlines, enhanced transportation systems and facilities and visa facilitation have created more convenient access.

Growth of low-cost carriers

As mentioned in Chapter 3, the expansion of low-cost (LCC) or budget airlines is a factor that has increased the travel to many world tourism cities. LCCs have 30% of the airline capacity in the Asia-Pacific region according to CAPA (2019). The same source says they account for more than 50% of the seat capacity in seven Asian markets (India, Indonesia, Malaysia, the Philippines, South Korea, Thailand and Vietnam). The two largest LCCs in Asia are AirAsia and Lion. LCCs have relatively low penetration rates in Japan and China. It is of note that generally the growth in LCCs has accompanied the expansion of domestic tourism in several Asian countries with the notable exception of China.

Enhanced ground and maritime transportation

Improved railway networks and highways have facilitated more travel to and among Asian cities. Nowhere has this been more so than in Mainland China, where more than 25,000 kilometres of high-speed railway were built from 2008 to 2019 (World Bank, 2019). Other countries also have significant transport infrastructure projects, including Indonesia that is constructing the Trans-Java Toll Road and the Jakarta–Bandung high-speed rail link.

There have also been improvements in maritime transportation, including additions of new ferry services in the Philippines and Singapore and expanded day and overnight cruises (discussed later). New bridges have been constructed, none of which is longer or bigger than the Hong Kong–Zhuhai–Macao (HKZM) Bridge at around 42 kilometres (HZMB, 2020).

Visa facilitation

Visa facilitation by several countries has greatly enhanced access across national borders. The UNWTO in 2013 found that Southeast Asian countries were among the most open in the world in terms of visa requirements. UNWTO urged other countries to make themselves easier to visit. The introduction of visa on arrival (VOA) by several Asian countries including Indonesia has allowed their international tourism to grow more rapidly. It is noteworthy here that Asia's two most populous countries, India and China, still require most visitors to have visas in their passports.

There is a growing level of regional cooperation within Asia. This is especially evident in the Association of Southeast Asian Nations (ASEAN) and South Asian Association for Regional Cooperation (SAARC) groupings. ASEAN, for example, has established a cooperative tourism marketing effort as well as establishing professional standards for tourism. Easier cross-border movements are another benefit of closer regional market cooperation.

Sweet tweet 86

ASEAN deepens cooperation in tourism to deal with COVID-19

In April 2020, the ten Tourism Ministers of the ASEAN countries agreed to cooperate on seven new initiatives to revitalise tourism in Southeast Asia. The second one was as follows:

> Intensify ASEAN's National Tourism Organisations' (NTOs) collaboration with other relevant ASEAN sectors, especially in health, information, transport and immigration, as well as with ASEAN's external partners, relevant international organisations and the international community, to jointly implement measures and build on each other's platforms to promote a comprehensive, transparent and early response to mitigate and alleviate the impact of COVID-19 and future crises.

Source: ASEAN (2020).

---

3. Availability

The ease with which bookings and reservations can be made for a city and the number of booking and reservation channels available.

It is much more convenient to search for and book travel to Asian cities due to the many online platforms such as Booking.com and Agoda, as well as the reservation sites of carriers and hotel companies. When combined with the rapidly increasing use of the Internet, especially within Asia itself, this greater availability has been a significant facilitator of travel to Asian cities. In addition, there is now much greater access to short-break city holidays and last-minute deals through online platforms.

Asia was the region with the most Internet users in the world in July 2020, at 2.53 billion. However, Internet penetration of the total population in Asia was only at 58.8%, indicating a great future potential to expand online usage and marketing (Miniwatts Marketing Group, 2020). The expansion of Internet use in Asia is likely to be positively correlated with online travel booking, which inevitably results in increased levels of tourism.

The margins for further growth in Internet market penetration are low in developed regions of the world such as in North America (90.3% penetration) and Europe (87.2% penetration). This is not the case in Asia where there is still room to significantly increase the Internet population. This appears to be a substantial marketing and co-creation opportunity for Asian tourism cities.

4. and 5. *Attractiveness and activities*

> *The number and geographic scope of appeal of city destination attractions for visitors*
> *The extent of the array of activities and experiences available to tourists within cities*

Asian tourism cities have become more attractive to visit by expanding their attraction portfolios and creating more visitor activities and experiences.

Culture and heritage

Asia is known for its rich and varied culture and heritage, which have attracted visitors for many decades. However, more recent international designations of sites and especially by UNESCO have increased the awareness and popularity of several cultural and heritage attractions within or close to Asian cities. These include, for example, the Great Wall and the Forbidden City near and in Beijing; the Taj Mahal and Red Fort Complex in Agra; Angkor temple complex in Siem Reap, Cambodia; and Ayutthaya, Thailand, and many more. Significant areas of four cities – George Town and Melaka (Malaysia); Kyoto and Macau – are World Heritage List cultural sites. Some of the UNESCO sites are a combination of history, culture and nature, including the Chinese Classical Gardens of Suzhou in Jiangsu Province, China, and the Botanic Gardens in Singapore.

The temples, mosques, cathedrals, churches, shrines and other religious sites, relics and practices are significant cultural attractions in most Asian cities. Consider, for example, the iconic façade of St. Paul's Cathedral in Macau, the Buddhist stuppas of Bagan in Myanmar and Borobudur in Java, Indonesia, the thriving Buddhist practices at Mount Emei near Leshan in China and Luang Prabang in Laos PDR, and the Blue Mosque of Istanbul, and one can clearly see the relationships of religion and tourism in Asian cities.

There are several well-attended dark tourism sites within Asia and in or near to major cities. These include the Killing Fields near Phnom Penh, Cambodia, Hiroshima, the Nanjing Massacre site, Gallipoli and Vietnam War battlefields.

Nature and the environment

All Asian countries have significant natural attractions and resources, and these are not just in the 3S (sun, sea, sand) destinations. Many sites are on the World Heritage List or are recognised as marine protected areas or geoparks. Abundant bird and other wildlife add to the natural allure of Asia for many travellers. Some of the natural attractions are within the cities themselves, including the Batu Caves in Kuala Lumpur and the UNESCO Fangshan Global Geopark in Beijing; others are easily accessible from the cities.

Several cities in Asia function as gateways or jumping-off points for significant cultural-heritage or natural sites, and it is important to recognise this phenomenon. They include Mandalay for Bagan in Myanmar; Yogyakarta for Borobudur and Prambanan in Central Java, Indonesia; Kathmandu for Mount Everest; and Beijing for the Great Wall.

Shopping

Asian cities have long been regarded as a bargain ground for avid shoppers. Many were traditionally lured by the silk, teas and jade of China and the electronics in Hong Kong, Japan and Singapore. Nowadays, Asian cities offer the full range of shopping from the highest of fashions to the bargains in street markets.

Sweet tweet 87

Shopping the markets of Kuala Lumpur

The daytime and night markets of Asian cities are well known and attended by visitors. Kuala Lumpur is one of the cities with popular markets.

> Bazaars and night markets are a shopping category in advertising for the Malaysian capital of Kuala Lumpur and the largest is Petaling Street in Chinatown which sells clothes, food, electronic goods and fresh produce. Nearby Central Market occupies an 1888 building (Figure 11.2) and is given over to handicrafts. Markets serving Indian and Malay communities are highlighted and the city has numerous other night and flea markets (Visit KL 2018).

Source: Henderson (2021).

Not mentioned in the sweet tweet above were the popular floating markets in some cities in Thailand and Vietnam. These are a curiosity and attract many tourists.

Asia is now leading the world in shopping mall development. The three largest shopping malls in terms of area covered are in China (Dongguan, Tianjin and Beijing), one each in Thailand and Malaysia (Bangkok and Kuala Lumpur), three are in the Philippines (Manila, Quezon City and Cebu City) and two are in Iran (Isfahan and Shiraz). Additionally, several Asian cities now have large outlet shopping centres such as in Bandung and Bali, Indonesia, and in Shanghai, Beijing and Tianjin in China.

Food, culinary arts and gastronomy

While there is an absence of hard and accurate data, anecdotal evidence points to a growing popularity of food – aka culinary and gastronomic tourism – within Asia and its major cities (Park et al., 2019).

Figure 11.2 The historic Central Market in Kuala Lumpur (Courtesy: Unsplash.com, Johen Redman).

Apart from the regular food offers, some cities specialise in culinary schools and training, including Chiang Mai in Northern Thailand and Singapore. There are also a wide variety of organised food itineraries available through specialised tour operators to cities in China, Hong Kong, India, Indonesia, Japan, Malaysia, Singapore, South Korea, Sri Lanka, Taiwan, Thailand and Vietnam.

Sweet tweet 88

Food as another ingredient of Asianness

The varied cuisines from the continent are relished by many foreigners and especially Chinese, Indian, Indonesian, Japanese, Korean, Malaysian, Thai and Vietnamese food. Added to this is the appeal of the many great teas from China, Sri Lanka, Taiwan and India, and the exquisite coffees from Indonesia and Vietnam.

The unique history, background, architecture, clothing styles and cultural outlooks of Asian countries have tended to create a notion of "Asianness" in the minds of tourists from other continents. Food now adds another important layer to Asianness in the eyes of others, especially non-Asians.

Source: Lee, Kim and Yeoman (2019).

It must be noted here as well that UNESCO has designated several *Creative Cities of Gastronomy* within Asia as part of its Creative Cities Network. Hyderabad in India and Yangzhou in China were two of the cities in 2019 designated by UNESCO as *Creative Cities of Gastronomy*; Macao received this recognition in 2017 (Loi, Kong and Bandeira, 2021) and Chengdu in Sichuan and Phuket in Thailand are other notable designees (UNESCO, 2020).

Any conversation about food in Asia would not be complete without mentioning street foods. These vendors are abundant throughout Asian cities and are very much a part of their cultures and characteristics. Although highly popular with locals, many foreigners are suspicious of the food safety standards of street food vendors.

Entertainment

Another factor that has expanded tourism in Asian cities is the development of more entertainment attractions. Five of the world's most heavily attended amusement/theme parks in 2019 were in Asia (TEA/AECOM, 2019). Three were in Japan (Tokyo and Osaka) and two in China (Hengqin/Macao and Shanghai). Another seven of the top 25 parks are in Asia (Hong Kong, Japan, Mainland China and South Korea). The total attendance in 2019 at the top 20 amusement/theme parks in Asia was 143.1 million.

Seven of the 20 most attended water parks and six of the 20 most attended museums in the world were in Asia in 2019. The Palace Museum in Beijing, also known as the Forbidden City, ranked second in the world in 2019 with an attendance of 7.39 million.

Sweet tweet 89

Theme parks and attractions expand in China

China's growth in the leisure sector is a story of supply and demand: a large population with increasing income and desire for travel and leisure, across a large land mass with ever-better transportation infrastructure. These are ideal conditions for regional parks and attractions to develop and for regional chains to expand.

Source: TEA/AECOM (2019).

Several spectacular entertainment performances are available in Asian cities. Among these are the *Impression* series produced by famous Chinese film-maker, Zhang Yimou. There are seven of these and some take place in Chinese cities including Guilin, Hangzhou and Lijiang.

Festivals are very popular in many Asian tourism cities and are being used as a means to attract more domestic and international festivals. Shopping festivals or "annual sales" have been used for many years by cities including Singapore, Hong Kong and Kuala Lumpur. Firework festivals and shows, dragon boat festivals and numerous religious festivals are also quite numerous in Asia. Food festivals are a more recent addition.

The previous chapters mentioned the development of creative districts within several Asian cities, as well as the staging of more festivals. The development of gaming in several Asian cities has led to increases in tourism, and these include Macao, Singapore, Incheon and Manila.

Cruises

Asia has experienced significant growth in cruising and cruise port development. Generally, the development has focused on major cities including Shanghai, Singapore, Hong Kong, Tianjin and Qingdao, which have extensive maritime ports and trade, as well as substantial local and regional populations.

The Cruise Lines International Association (CLIA, 2019) for 2019 reported 1,917 sailings of cruise ships (two nights or more) with a total passenger capacity of 4.02 million. Japan, Mainland China, Malaysia and Thailand in that order were expected to receive the most cruise ship port calls; and Singapore, Taipei and Shanghai were the cities with the most calls.

Health and medicine

Asian cities are becoming increasingly used for medical tourism and health purposes. A report by PwC (2018) indicates that Thailand, India, Turkey, Malaysia and South Korea are among the most popular country destinations for medical tourism. In fact, Thailand was found to have the most medical tourists of any country. Lower costs of medical treatment in these countries than at home is a major reason for this growth trend.

Sweet tweet 90

Bangkok is a leading medical tourism destination

Good hospitals and medical staff, along with lower prices, attract medical tourists to Bangkok.

> Leading the list of private hospitals are the Bumrungrad International Hospital, Bangkok Hospital Group, and Samitivej Hospitals. These hospitals are widely becoming renowned globally. They are known to cater mostly to foreign patients and have been actively seeking medical tourists since the early 2000s. Around 30–50% of the patients in these hospitals are foreigners, due to the fact that, to a greater extent, they find the hospitals cheaper than their home countries. However, most Thais find the prices in these hospitals too high, as salaries in Thailand are low.

Source: Health-Tourism.com (2020).

In addition to medical treatment at hospitals, there are other aspects of Asian health and wellness that are attracting tourists from within and outside of the continent. For example, Ubud in Bali has built an international reputation for yoga studios. Several cities in India are popular for Ayurveda treatments. Traditional Chinese medicines (TCM) are attracting more visitors to Chinese cities as well.

Taken together these new and improved attractions and activities are one of the major reasons for the upswing in tourism in Asian cities. They have greatly expanded their offers to regional and international markets, as well as stimulating higher levels of domestic travel.

6. *Appearance*

The impressions that cities make on visitors, when they first arrive and throughout their stays

There is an old saying that "you only get one chance to make a good first impression". There is a second one that suggests that great places to live are also great places to visit. Many city planners seem to agree with these sentiments. Urban beautification has occurred in many Asian cities. In a comprehensive study by Carlino and Saiz (2019), conducted in US cities and not in Asia, it was found that government investment in public recreation facilities drew more tourists to their cities. Singapore, which often refers to itself as *"the garden city"*, is one of the world leaders in urban beautification (National Geographic, 2017), especially in making it greener.

Another aspect to appearance and first impressions is the transportation terminals and other gateways through which visitors arrive in cities. Once again, the new airports, cruise and ferry terminals recently built or under construction in Asian cities are undoubtedly enhancing these initial perspectives on cities. New airports are being built in Ulaanbaatar, Ho Chi Minh City, Mumbai and Istanbul at this time, and there are other airports that are expanding.

One of the paradoxes of Asian cities in this era of rapid urbanisation is the juxta positioning of gleaming new buildings and residences in close proximity to run-down older areas and slums. In the latter was the inspiration for slum tourism, which has been associated with the popular movie, *Slumdog Millionaire*, that was set in Mumbai's major slum area. The popularity of slum tourism can create a dilemma for city tourism as it draws greater attention to the unsightly urban areas. This runs contrary to the modern and clean images that many cities wish to project.

7. *Appreciation*

The perceived levels of welcome and hospitality encountered in cities

This has to do with the feelings about the warmth of the welcomes and the friendliness of people within cities. Also included are the steps that government authorities and others in cities have taken to make visitors feel more comfortable such as quality assurance programmes.

Some Asian countries have actively promoted their friendliness, and Thailand is one of them with the slogan of the *"land of smiles"*. This is somewhat confirmed in recent results with Chiang Mai ranked as the 11th most friendly city in the world. Kuala Lumpur was in second place and Taipei was fourth (Big Seven Travel, 2020).

Realistically it is difficult to accurately measure friendliness, and the evidence for cities tends to be anecdotal rather than robust and accurate. However, there are related indicators that may be influences on friendliness such as liveability, happiness and quality of life. In a ranking of happiness in world cities for 2020, Helsinki, Aarhus, Wellington, Zurich and Copenhagen were the top five (De Neve and Krekel, 2020). Taipei (#47), Singapore (#49), Bangkok (#56), Almaty (#68) and Tashkent (#75) had the best scores for Asian cities among the total of 186 cities that were ranked.

A global ranking system based on quality of life scored Japan, Singapore, Taiwan, South Korea and Malaysia highest among Asian countries (Numbeo, 2020). Japan ranked 17th in the world on this index.

For city liveability, there are a number of ranking systems. The *Mercer Quality of Living Ranking* for 2019 had Singapore in 25th place and Kobe and Tokyo tied at 49th. The Economist Intelligence Unit (2020) showed Osaka (fourth at 97.7%) and Tokyo (seventh at 97.2%) in its top ten in the world.

Do these ranking schemes definitively indicate the level of appreciation in Asian tourism cities? The answer is probably in the negative as they do not specifically measure the construct. There are countries and cities that consistently rank at high levels, including Japan and Tokyo as well as Singapore. However, poorer and lesser-developed countries tend to score poorly on these systems, and it could be said that the rankings do not account for the natural sense and cultures of hospitality among their residents.

8. *Assurance*

The perceived levels of safety and security within cities

Many Asian cities have taken steps to assure higher levels of safety and security for visitors. Chapter 5 mentioned the introduction of special tourism police units, and these are in place in Thailand, Turkey and South Korea.

Sweet tweet 91

Food safety improving in Asia

One of the frequent worries and concerns of those travelling to Asia cities is about food safety. The FAO notes the increasing threats and what is being done to ensure higher standards of food safety within Asia:

> Fast urbanization, rapid growth of population, new technologies in the production and changing environmental conditions trigger the emergence of new food safety threats.
>
> Member countries in the region are modernizing their food safety systems to ensure the availability of safe and nutritious food for the projected five billion inhabitants in 2050.

Source: FAO (2020).

If we can assume that the safest cities for travel are in the safest countries, there are rankings available that suggest levels of assurance. One of these is the *Global Peace Index* prepared by the Institute for Economics and Peace. Four Asian countries were in the top 20 most peaceful in 2020 (Singapore, Japan, Bhutan and Malaysia). For its safety and security domain, Singapore ranked second and Japan ranked third best in the world (Institute for Economics and Peace, 2020). Thailand, Myanmar, the Philippines and North Korea received the lowest overall rankings within Asia.

9. *Action*

The pre-planning actions by cities for tourism

There is evidence that city destination management is advancing in sophistication in Asia. For example, there is a comprehensive system for tourism planning in Mainland China and major cities all have tourism master plans (Wu, Li, Ma and Wang, 2021). Elsewhere, cities including Kuala Lumpur also have tourism master plans. Moreover, the high level of professionalism in destination marketing is evident in several Asian cities, including Hong Kong, Macao, Seoul and Singapore.

10. *Accountability*

The performance evaluation with respect to tourism planning, development and marketing by cities

As described in Chapter 5, accountability is an element of city destination management governance and involves openness and continuous performance evaluation. While the lack of transparency and accountability remains an issue in several Asian countries, due mainly to hierarchical government structures, there are some refreshing examples of good tourism governance in some countries and cities. For example, Hong Kong and Singapore are widely recognised as having two of the best CDMOs in the world across several roles. Also, the DMOs in Macao and Taiwan are regarded as exemplars.

It can be argued that action and accountability have not directly influenced the growth of Asian city tourism; however, they indirectly affect the performance of city tourism destinations. It must be acknowledged that the other eight As have had more significant direct effects.

Overall, and based upon the foregoing, by performing well on all the 10 A factors Asian cities have enjoyed significant tourism growth. This success cannot be attributed to one single reason; rather, a combination of several factors has played a role. Performance across all Asian tourism cities has not been even, and some have fared better than others. Often external events have conspired to thwart the great efforts of Asian CDMOS, such as with the civil unrest in Hong Kong and the terrorist attacks in Colombo, Sri Lanka. It also must be recognised that there are great swaths of the Asian continent that are relatively undiscovered, and which attract many fewer Asian and non-Asian tourists. These include, for example, Mongolia and the Central Asian Republics (Kazakhstan, Kyrgyzstan, Tajikistan, Turkmenistan and Uzbekistan), and the Asian portion of Russia. Current awareness levels internationally are also very low for many parts of China and India. Finally, there are parts of Asia that are essentially "off-limits" for tourism due to political issues and wars and these are Afghanistan and Iraq.

Major growth markets

Having reviewed the reasons for the expansion of Asian city tourism, it is of great importance to now pinpoint the principal sources of this upward trend and to review the growth of tourism.

Regional tourism

The recent successes of Asian tourism cities are mainly the result of inter-regional travel. Now, the majority of international tourist arrivals in Asian countries are from other Asian nations. Post-COVID, this regional tourism trend is likely to become more pronounced. The factors fuelling regional tourism expansion have been identified in this and other chapters; however, increasing household incomes and more convenient transportation have been two of the main stimulants.

Domestic tourism

International inbound tourism is miniscule when compared to the volumes of domestic tourists in several Asian countries. Now, Asian cities have significant potential for growing domestic tourism due to improving household incomes, better internal transportation networks and expanded and improved tourism offerings. Moreover, in the wake of COVID-19, it is inevitable that there will be a much greater emphasis on closer-to-home markets in the short and medium terms.

The Mastercard city rankings and UNWTO statistics are based on international tourists and no account is made of domestic travel. This can be quite misleading as domestic tourism is much larger than international inbound tourism in most Asian countries. Also, the global data fail to adequately report on all major trip purposes for travel and especially business, VFR and personal.

All five of the most populated countries in Asia – China, India, Indonesia, Pakistan and Bangladesh – have large domestic tourism volumes. The Ministry of Tourism, Government of India for 2019 reported 2.32 billion domestic visits, a 23.5% increase over 2018. Inbound foreign tourist arrivals to India were 10.93 million, with an increase of 3.5% over 2018 (Ministry of Tourism, Government of India, 2020). According to WTTC economic data, domestic spending accounted for 83% of all travel and tourism spending in India in 2019 (World Travel & Tourism Council, 2020). Domestic tourism volumes are even higher in China, at an estimated 6.1 billion tourists in 2019 (China Internet Watch, 2020), up 8.4% over 2018. WTTC estimates that domestic tourism spending represents 86% of all travel and tourism spending in China. The statistics for Pakistan and Bangladesh indicate an even greater dependence on domestic tourism. Indonesia, with domestic tourism estimated around 250 million tourists, is more dependent on international tourism than the other four most populated Asian countries.

It is proposed, therefore, that domestic tourism, and not international tourism, has been the main catalyst for the tourism growth in Asian cities. However, it is acknowledged that tourists from abroad have a more beneficial economic impact through increasing foreign exchange earnings as well as in some instances having higher per capita daily expenditures. Then there is the "glamour factor" allowing politicians and tourism officials to tout their growing attractiveness to foreign visitors.

Business and MICE tourism

Economic growth has been relatively rapid in Asia, and many cities have been focussing on expanding GDP. As a result, business travel has had significant growth as has MICE (Newport, 2019) Domestic business travel in most Asian countries is much greater than inbound international travel. Statistics on international arrivals often do not differentiate between business and leisure travellers and now the trend towards more bleisure trips is blurring this distinction even further. Nevertheless, it appears that business travel is being under-reported in tourism statistics, and this could be the case for Asia as well.

With respect to the staging of international conferences, Singapore and Tokyo rank in the top ten cities in the world based on the statistics published by the International

Congress and Convention Association (ICCA, 2020). Bangkok, Seoul and Taipei are in the top 20, while Beijing, Hong Kong, Kuala Lumpur and Shanghai are also highly ranked. All of these Asian cities have made significant investments in convention and exhibition centres. Greater business and MICE tourism has been greatly assisted by improved transportation networks that have provided faster and more convenient accessibility to cities.

SHORT BREAK 11

Singapore, a city with a passion for tourism

The city state of Singapore is among the Asian urban areas that has enjoyed significant success in tourism. It is ranked 17th in the *Travel and Tourism Competitiveness Index 2019* edition by the World Economic Forum. In this ranking, Singapore was placed in the top ten in the world for its business environment (second), tourist service infrastructure (second), international openness (third), human resources and labour market (fifth), prioritisation of travel and tourism (sixth), safety and security (sixth) and ground and port infrastructure (seventh). There are many superlatives that can be attached to Singapore's tourism capacity, including the number-one airline and airport in the world in Singapore Airlines and Changi, respectively, and a portfolio of great hotels, resorts, attractions and shopping. There is also a large and well-equipped convention and exhibition centre. The Singapore Tourism Board (STB) is generally considered to be one of the best CDMOs in the world, and its programmes are comprehensive and innovative.

Singapore had 19.1 million visitor arrivals in 2019, and the average occupancy rate of hotels was at a very high 86.9% (Singapore Tourism Board, 2020a). As a result of COVID-19, these statistics have taken sharp downturns. According to WTTC figures on economic impact, Singapore is quite dependent on international visitor spending (71% international vs. 29% domestic), and a significant portion (46%) of total spending is from business tourism.

Singapore's tourism appeal and capacity were significantly increased with the development of two integrated resort projects on Sentosa Island – Marina Bay Sands and Resorts World Sentosa (Figure 11.3). Importantly, these brought gaming and a number of new themed entertainment attractions into the mix that Singapore had to offer.

Singapore has placed a priority on its role as a cruise port and hub. According to the Singapore Tourism Board, 414 cruise ships called on Singapore during 2019 (Singapore Tourism Board, 2020b). According to CLIA, Singapore was the top port in Asia hosting 991,000 passenger destination days (PDD).

Changi Airport reported 68.3 million passenger movements for 2019, which confirms its role as an important hub airport for Asia. However, this also signals that many air passengers go through Singapore without experiencing the city. To deal with this issue, Singapore came up with a creative solution – a free Singapore tour for those with 5.5 or more hours between flights at Changi. A 2.5-hour city tour can be booked as a result of this cooperation among Singapore Airlines,

Figure 11.3 Sentosa Island in Singapore (Courtesy: Unsplash.com, Hu Chen).

Changi Airport and the Singapore Tourism Board. Three varieties of tours are available – Heritage, City Sights and Jewel.

Discussion points:

1. What have been the factors contributing to the growth of tourism in Singapore?
2. How important was it for Singapore's tourism to add the two integrated resorts?
3. Are Singapore's location and its transportation influential in its tourism growth and competitiveness and, if so, in what ways?

Sources: Changi Airport (2020); Cruise Lines International Association. (2019); Singapore Airlines (2020); Singapore Tourism Board (2020a); Singapore Tourism Board (2020b); World Economic Forum (2019); World Travel & Tourism Council (2020).

VFR travel: The "under the radar" market

So far, this chapter has talked mostly about leisure and business travel growth for Asian cities. Medical tourism was also covered, and that is a form of personal travel. Then, what about the masses of people travelling home or to other locales to see their family and friends – the VFR travel market? Each year in China there are three annual "migrations" of millions of people from cities back home. Then, there are the constant movements of nannies and housemaids from the rich cities like Hong Kong to poorer countries such as the Philippines and Indonesia. These VFRs are often counted within tourism numbers, but somehow not recognised or given the credit they deserve – they are thus the "under the radar" market.

Unique features of Asian tourism cities

The exoticism of the East has long been perceived by Western travellers. The so-called Orient has also been a magnet for trade and industrial expansion. However, before highlighting the alluring positives of Asian tourism cities, the authors choose to first focus on what some foreigners do not like when they visit these urban areas.

Rodgers (2019) identifies factors he believes that foreigners do not like about Asian cities. Two of these are the crowdedness along with heavy traffic congestion and reckless driving. The data from INRIX (2020) confirms the traffic issues, with Jakarta and Bangkok being rated among the worst in the world for congestion. Scams and beggars are other encounters within Asian cities that foreign visitors dislike (Gowreesunkar, Serafin and Nazimuddin, 2020; Li and Pearce, 2016). These are a result of some of the urban issues discussed later in this chapter. There are other cultural and personal interactions and values that some international visitors find difficult, including being perceived as rich, always being stared at and the "face" culture of the East. Then there is the litter, widespread use and careless disposal of plastic and the non-Western-style toilets. To this, one can add the high noise levels and constant neon glare in many Asian cities (Figure 11.4), and the difficulties in communicating in languages other than European

Figure 11.4 The neon landscapes of Tokyo (Courtesy: Unsplash.com, Jezael Melgoza).

ones. Last but by no means least is the worsening air pollution in many Asian cities, discussed later. It is fair to say that many of these negatives can be ascribed to Western cities, and to developing regions of the world, including those in South America and Africa. Paradoxically, some of these negatives may be attractive to Western visitors such as the liveliness and cacophony of Asian cities.

Despite these negatives and perhaps some others, Asian cities increasingly intrigue people from other continents as well as other Asians. There are many features that visitors like and find different within Asian urban areas. These include the cuisine, unique religious and other heritage structures, contemporary architecture, relative inexpensiveness, interesting markets and shopping experiences, health and beauty treatments, arts and crafts, festivals and performances and several others (Figure 11.5).

Impacts of the COVID-19 pandemic

Tourism suffered greatly within Asia as a result of the COVID-19 pandemic. It is widely believed that the virus originated in Wuhan, a large city in Hubei Province, China, around the beginning of 2020. From there, the disease spread worldwide and seemed destined to last as a global threat until 2021 or longer if a proven vaccine was not discovered and introduced with wide distribution. An unprecedented public health and economic crisis was evident, and travel and tourism experienced catastrophic setbacks for the first time since 2001 (SARS) and 2008–2009 (global economic crisis).

UNCTAD (2020) modelled three scenarios of the impacts of the pandemic on country economies. In its moderate scenario, Thailand, China and Malaysia would suffer the greatest in terms of GDP reductions; Japan, Indonesia and South Korea would also be among the most adversely affected.

Sweet tweet 92

Tourism in Asia plunges in the first half of 2020

The COVID-19 pandemic originated from Asia and as a continent it was the first one to experience the negative impacts of the resulting public health crisis on travel and tourism. UNWTO released its *World Tourism Barometer* statistics in September 2020 showing that international tourist arrivals in the Asia and the Pacific region had decreased by 72% in January–June 2020 when compared with the same period in 2019. North-East Asia (–83%) had the largest decline among sub-regions in the world.

Source: UNWTO (2020).

In the aftermath of COVID-19, many tourism workers lost their jobs and businesses were closed down. The airlines and cruise lines were among the most affected. Large conferences and exhibitions were cancelled, some for the first time in their history, including ITB Berlin. Popular destinations in Asia became almost deserted. City tourism marketing changed its themes and focus to more of a "see you later" stance. A sense of uncertainty and a loss of confidence were prevalent in Asian city tourism from dealing with such unprecedented circumstances.

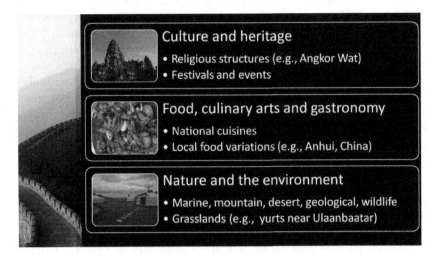

Figure 11.5a Features that attract visitors to Asia (Author photos).

Figure 11.5b Features that attract visitors to Asia (Yunnan photo by authors; other photos courtesy: Unsplash.com, Jernej Graj and Sunyu Kim).

Issues and challenges for Asian tourism cities

Up until the end of 2019, cities in Asia were experiencing record tourism growth. However, these cities experienced major declines in tourism during the COVID-19 pandemic in 2020 and 2021. Nevertheless, the future promises unprecedented opportunities that will be accompanied by significant issues and challenges, which are now discussed.

Urbanisation

Chapter 3 describes urbanisation as one of the demographic mega-trends in the world. The United Nations (2020) states that Africa and Asia are the least urbanised regions of the world at the current time with around 50% of the Asian population residing in cities. However, Asia is the fastest urbanising area of the world (World Bank, 2020). As Asian cities grow in size, it is inevitable that their infrastructure, amenities and attractions for tourism will expand. That is the good news; however, it is also likely that current issues will be exacerbated such as pollution, urban poverty and traffic congestion.

Urbanisation has been shown to spur economic growth and increase income levels, spawning a larger middle class in cities. Also, it leads to greater emphasis on service sectors (Luo and Lam, 2021). This huge growth in urban areas has produced more than 200 cities in China with populations over one million (McKinsey Global Institute, 2018). It has also created major increases in domestic and outbound tourism by Chinese citizens. As mentioned before, more convenient transportation through a vastly improved highway system and an enormous high-speed railway system has been another catalyst for domestic tourism growth in China.

Air pollution

According to an IQAir report (2020), all of the 30 cities with the highest levels of air pollution in the world in 2019 were in Asia. Based on PM2.5 data, 21 of the world's most polluted cities were in India and six more in other South Asian countries. The research on the impact of air pollution on tourism is growing (e.g., Li et al., 2016). Heavily polluted cities are beginning to develop somewhat negative destination images (e.g., Ulaanbaatar in Mongolia, Beijing in China, Jakarta in Indonesia, Lahore in Pakistan and Delhi and Agra in India).

A study conducted with visitors to East and South Asian cities found that exposure during travel to increased PM2.5 adversely affected cardiopulmonary health (Vilcassim et al., 2019) and suggested that this should be of particular concern for people with pre-existing heart or lung problems. The high-pollution cities that respondents visited in the study were Ahmedabad and New Delhi (India), Rawalpindi (Pakistan) and Xi'an (China).

There can be little doubt that COVID-19 will sensitise travellers to health issues in the places that they plan to visit. Thus, issues such as air and water pollution will be of greater concern in the future.

Globalisation

The world is becoming more interconnected in different ways. Despite offering many benefits, one of the major challenges it is bringing is that cities are starting to look more like one another in what Chapter 3 referred to as homogenisation. The most popular fast food and coffee shop brands, along with famed designer clothing stores, can be found in almost all major cities across the world. The familiarity of surroundings such as expansive shopping malls will attract some groups of tourists; however, as the old saying goes "familiarity breeds contempt". In other words, those seeking differences and authenticity will be repelled by the sameness that is creeping into many Asian city destinations.

Increasing globalisation has positives and negatives for Asian tourism cities. On the plus side, through the greater amount of information available, there is potentially more awareness of what they offer. However, many Asian cities are starting to look more like their Western counterparts and are losing their distinctiveness.

Sweet tweet 93

Is Asia seventh heaven or 7-Eleven?

7-Eleven is a convenience store chain that spans the world after starting business in the USA. Where are the most 7-Elevens now is an interesting question to answer. According to data from Statista, Japan has the most stores at 20,904; Thailand is second with 11,299; and South Korea with 9,485 is in third place. The USA is fourth and Taiwan is fifth. Other Asian countries in the top ten for 7-Elevens are China, the Philippines and Malaysia.

You could say that these have become the new "corner stores" of Asia, or then again you could propose that 7-Elevens are a shining symbol of globalisation in the East. Of course, there are more family members in brands such as KFC, McDonald's, Starbucks, Pizza Hut – and lest we forget, Family Mart.

Source: Statista (2020).

Commodification

Turning a city's tangible and intangible culture and traditions into commodities that can be purchased by tourists represents the commodification of these assets (Xie, 2003). This has positive and negative connotations and potential outcomes. Monetising culture creates income and employment for urban areas and produces entrepreneurial opportunities. However, mass production and presentation often cheapen and distort the cultural treasures of cities.

Again, this appears to be an issue that especially plagues cities where there is poverty. These situations tend to create many copy-cat vendors and those selling fake goods and souvenirs. In fact, the fake goods trade is a major problem in many Asian cities, yet it does attract tourists to visit the vendors and buy their goods.

Sharing economy

The commercial success of sharing economy providers in tourism has produced some unique issues and challenges for cities. From bedrooms to bicycles, consumers have rapidly demonstrated acceptance for the value and convenience of these offers. The rise of person-to-person sharing of accommodations through platforms like Airbnb has been linked to the increasing popularity of social media, as well as being singled out as one of the causes of overtourism.

There are differing opinions on the impacts of sharing economy providers in Asian cities. Ride-sharing and shared bicycle suppliers have enjoyed success in many cities and created additional economic benefits. However, some see it as adding to traffic congestion, greater safety concerns and, in the case of shared accommodation rentals, intrusion into residential areas (Ramizo, 2019). Generally, there appears to be support for greater government regulation of sharing economy providers in Asian cities in the future.

Overtourism

Crowding within Asia is inevitable given the population sizes and densities of many of its cities. Overcrowding at certain tourism attractions and destinations in Asia is already a significant issue, including at the Great Wall and the Taj Mahal. While the term was coined based upon experiences in Europe, it also applies to Asia's increasingly crowded and traffic-laden urban areas. There can be no doubt that Asian city tourism officials must pay greater attention to visitor management systems through smart destination applications.

Crises

Crises and disasters tend to frequently occur in or near Asian cities and present significant problems for tourism development and marketing. Natural disasters are numerous in Asia and often result in significant loss of lives given the living conditions. Political, security and financial crises are also recurrent, including acts of terrorism. Crisis management planning is essential for Asian tourism cities as is building resilience to crisis events.

Unsavoury forms of tourism

Asia and Asian cities share a reputation for types of tourism that many consider not to be wholesome or unsavoury from a general public view. These include sex tourism, orphanage tourism and tourism that harms animal welfare. Forced shopping tourism is a fourth category that is commonly frowned upon.

Sweet tweet 94

Under the red lights of Bangkok

There are several areas within Bangkok that make up the city's Red Light District. They are adjacent to one another and populated by sex workers who have moved from rural areas to find work under the bright lights of the city. This makes Bangkok a major hotspot for sex tourism in Thailand.

Source: Stanton (2020).

Readers may have noticed that there are two sweet tweets about Bangkok in this chapter. The first one is about international tourists going in increasing numbers to Bangkok hospitals for medical care. The second is on tourists risking their health to engage in sex tourism. Can you see the paradox in this?

Other issues, challenges and opportunities

There are several other issues, challenges and opportunities for tourism in Asian cities, and these are just some of the more prominent ones. For example, urban poverty is producing more slum development, and slum tourism has become an issue of considerable debate. Asian cities also face huge challenges in providing transportation and infrastructure, as well as in assuring security and food safety.

Tourism in many Asian cities is at an earlier development stage than the mature urban tourism destinations in Europe and North America. As we move forward, the fragility of tourism in Asian cities has been laid bare by the COVID-19 pandemic and also in the unfortunate circumstances of specific cities, including Wuhan and Hong Kong. The latter, long one of tourism's iconic Asian destinations, has been rocked by months of civil unrest and political wrangling. Wuhan, allegedly the epicentre of the virus, may never recover from the damage to its destination brand. This has taught us at least one important lesson and that is to be more cautious and measured with respect to tourism growth in the future.

Summary comments

Asian tourism cities have prospered during the past two decades and until the global COVID-19 pandemic took hold. A combination of factors contributed, while urbanisation along with increasing incomes was at the core of the growth. Tourism has had positive and negative impacts on Asian cities, many of which were already struggling with overcrowding, poverty and traffic congestion.

The increasingly attractive tourism cities welcomed more international tourists and even more from their own countries, and business and MICE tourism expanded as well. An unevenness has persisted in the performance and awareness levels of cities within Asia, and some are still awaiting a tourism boom.

Many paradoxes exist in Asian city tourism – rich versus poor, new versus old, sex tourism versus medical tourism and ugly versus sublime. It can also be argued that globalisation is slowly eroding what makes Asia so special as authenticity is often being sacrificed for performance and entertainment.

There is great future potential for Asian city tourism to grow even more in the future. Mistakes have been made in tourism development, which hopefully yield lessons for CDMOs to do things with greater care and professionalism. While the cities of Europe and North America ponder a continuance of tourism growth after the COVID-19 pandemic, it is likely that Asian tourism cities will be keener to return to "business as usual".

Thought questions

1) Why have Asian cities enjoyed such great growth in tourism during the past decade?
2) Do you feel the growth in Asian city tourism is sustainable for the longer term and why or why not?
3) Many positives were discussed in relation to Singapore tourism in this chapter. In your view, what makes Singapore stand out from other Asian tourism cities?
4) People are flocking to Asia for health and medical tourism, yet the continent has been the source of several global health issues. Why does this paradox exist?
5) Another paradox is that some people decide to avoid the crowdedness and congestion of Asian cities; others are drawn by their intensity and hustle and bustle. Why do you think there is this contradiction?
6) With the greater onset of globalisation, do you believe that Asian cities will lose some of their distinctiveness? Why or why not?

7) There are several major cities in China and India of which many people are unaware. How should these cities create greater awareness for tourism purposes?

8) For Asian cities, what are the relative advantages of domestic and international tourism?

9) In your opinion, what are the most serious issues and challenges facing Asian tourism cities in the future and why?

10) The huge and expanding volume of travel from Mainland China has fuelled a significant proportion of tourism growth for Asian tourism cities before COVID-19. Is it a wise strategy for cities to be very reliant on one market source or should demand be more diversified? Why or why not?

References

Ampersand Travel. (2019). Top 20 most visited cities in Asia. https://www.ampersandtravel.com/blog/2019/top-20-most-visited-cities-in-asia/

ASEAN. (2020). Joint statement of the ASEAN Tourism Ministers on strengthening cooperation to revitalise ASEAN tourism. https://asean.org/storage/2020/04/ENDORSED-Joint-Statement-of-the-ASEAN-Tourism-Ministers-on-COVID_19-29Apr20.pdf

Big Seven Media. (2020). The 50 friendliest cities in the world. https://bigseventravel.com/2019/08/the-50-friendliest-cities-in-the-world/

Carlino, G. A., & Saiz, A. (2019). Beautiful city: Leisure amenities and urban growth. *Journal of Regional Science*, 59(3), 369–408.

Centre for Aviation (CAPA). (2019). LCCs in Asia Pacific: Two decades of steady market share gains. https://centreforaviation.com/analysis/reports/lccs-in-asia-pacific-two-decades-of-steady-market-share-gains-456096

Changi Airport. (2020). Traffic statistics. https://www.changiairport.com/corporate/our-expertise/air-hub/traffic-statistics.html

China Internet Watch. (2020). China domestic tourism grew 11.7% in 2019, but to lose 1.18 trillion yuan in 2020. https://www.chinainternetwatch.com/tag/outbound-travel/

Cruise Lines International Association (CLIA). (2019). 2019 Asia cruise deployment & capacity report. https://cruising.org/-/media/research-updates/research/2019-asia-deployment-and-capacity---cruise-industry-report.pdf

De Neve, J.-E., & Krekel, C. (2020). Cities and happiness: A global ranking and analysis. https://happiness-report.s3.amazonaws.com/2020/WHR20_Ch3.pdf

Economist Intelligence Unit. (2020). The global liveability index 2019. https://www.eiu.com/topic/liveability

Food and Agriculture Organization (FAO). (2020). FAO regional office for Asia and the Pacific. http://www.fao.org/asiapacific/perspectives/one-health/food-safety/ar/

Gowreesunkar, V. G., Seraphin, H. & Nazimuddin, M. (2020). Beggarism and black market tourism: A case study of the city of Chaar Minaar in Hyderabad (India). *International Journal of Tourism Cities*, 6(4), https://doi.org/10.1108/IJTC-12-2019-0210

Health-Tourism.com. (2020). Medical tourism to Thailand. https://www.health-tourism.com/medical-tourism-thailand/

Henderson, J. C. (2021). Outdoor and indoor markets in tourism cities. In Alastair M. Morrison, & J. Andres Coca-Stefaniak (Eds.). *Routledge Handbook of Tourism Cities*, pp. 293–303. London: Routledge.

Hong Kong Tourism Board. (2020). Hong Kong tourism board annual report 2018/19. https://www.discoverhongkong.com/eng/hktb/about/annual-report.html

HZMB. (2020). Project uniqueness. https://www.hzmb.hk/eng/about_uniqueness.html

INRIX. (2020). INRIX 2019 global traffic scorecard. https://inrix.com/scorecard/

Institute for Economics & Peace. (2020). Global peace index: Measuring peace in a complex world. https://www.economicsandpeace.org/reports/

International Congress and Convention Association. (2020). *ICCA Statistics Report Country & City Rankings: Public Abstract.* Amsterdam: ICCA.

IQAir. (2020). 2019 World air quality report. https://www.iqair.com/world-most-polluted-cities?continent=&country=&state=&page=1&perPage=50&cities=

Kokkranikal, J., Morrison, A. M., & Gowreesunkar, V. G. (2020). India's incredible cities: Anticipating the future, respecting the past. *International Journal of Tourism Cities,* 6(3), 495–490.

Li, J., & Pearce, P. L. (2016). Tourist scams in the city: Challenges for domestic travellers in urban China. *International Journal of Tourism Cities,* 2(4), 294–308.

Li, J., Pearce, P. L., Morrison, A. M., & Wu, B. (2016). Up in smoke? The impact of smog on risk perception and satisfaction of international tourists in Beijing. *International Journal of Tourism Research,* 18(4), 373–386.

Loi, W. H., Kong, K. L., & Bandeira, H. R. (2021). Macao as a city of gastronomy: The role of cuisine in tourism product bundle. In Alastair M. Morrison, & J. Andres Coca-Stefaniak (Eds.). *Routledge Handbook of Tourism Cities,* pp. 569–577. London: Routledge.

Luo, J. M., & Lam, C. F. (2021). Urbanisation and its effects on city tourism in China. In Alastair M. Morrison, & J. Andres Coca-Stefaniak (Eds.). *Routledge Handbook of Tourism Cities,* pp. 76–86. London: Routledge.

McKinsey Global Institute. (2018). World urbanization prospects 2018. https://population.un.org/wup/Publications/.

Macao Government Office of Tourism. (2020). MGTO representatives. https://industry.macaotourism.gov.mo/en/about_us/aboutus_content.php?id=2

Mercer LLC. (2020). Mercer quality of living city ranking. https://mobilityexchange.mercer.com/Insights/quality-of-living-ranking

Ministry of Tourism, Government of India. (2020). India tourism statistics at a glance: 2020. http://tourism.gov.in/sites/default/files/2020-09/ITS%20at%20a%20glance_Book%20%282%29.pdf

Miniwatts Marketing Group. (2020). Internet usage statistics. *The Internet Big Picture. World Internet Users and 2020 Population Stats.* https://internetworldstats.com/stats.htm

Moodley, C. (2019). REVEALED: Top 100 city destinations for 2019. *IOL.* https://www.iol.co.za/travel/travel-news/revealed-top-100-city-destinations-for-2019-38525917

National Geographic. (2017). This city aims to be the world's greenest. https://www.nationalgeographic.com/environment/urban-expeditions/green-buildings/green-urban-landscape-cities-Singapore/#:~:text=Singapore%20calls%20itself%20the%20Garden,and%20even%20into%20its%20heights.

Newport, A. (2019). Asia's top ten cities for meetings & events. *Travel Daily.* https://www.traveldailymedia.com/518647-2/

Numbeo. (2020). Quality of life index by country 2020 mid-year. https://www.numbeo.com/quality-of-life/rankings_by_country.jsp

Park, E., Kim, S., & Yeoman, I. (Eds.). (2019). *Food tourism in Asia.* Singapore: Singapore.

PwC. (2018). Health tourism today and into the future. http://dihtf.com/wp-content/uploads/presentations/DrTim%20Wilson%20-%20Health%20Tourism%20today%20and%20into%20the%20future.pdf

Ramizo Jr., G. (2019). Why Asia needs to rethink the 'sharing economy'. East Asia Forum. https://www.eastasiaforum.org/2019/10/29/why-asia-needs-to-rethink-the-sharing-economy/

Rodgers, G. (2019). 10 things travelers hate about Asia. https://www.tripsavvy.com/things-travelers-hate-about-asia-1458317

Singapore Airlines. (2020). Free Singapore tour. https://www.singaporeair.com/en_UK/us/plan-travel/privileges/free-singapore-tour/

Singapore Tourism Board. (2020a). Quarterly tourism performance report. https://www.stb.gov.sg/content/stb/en/statistics-and-market-insights/tourism-statistics/quarterly-tourism-performance-report.html#

Singapore Tourism Board. (2020b). Tourism statistics. https://stan.stb.gov.sg/portal/tourism-statistics.html

Stanton, H. (2020). Sex tourism in Thailand: What where and why? https://tourismteacher.com/sex-tourism-in-thailand-what-where-and-why/

Statista. (2020). Number of 7-Eleven stores worldwide in 2019, by country. https://www.statista.com/statistics/269454/number-of-7-eleven-stores-worldwide-in-2010-by-country/

TEA/AECOM. (2019). Theme index and museum index: The global attractions attendance report. Burbank, CA: Themed Entertainment Association (TEA).

United Nations. (2020). World urbanization prospects: The 2018 revision. https://population.un.org/wup/Publications/Files/WUP2018-KeyFacts.pdf

United Nations Conference on Trade and Development (UNCTAD). (2020). COVID-19 and tourism: Assessing the economic consequences. https://unctad.org/system/files/official-document/ditcinf2020d3_en.pdf

UNESCO. (2020). Creative cities network. https://en.unesco.org/creative-cities/home

UN World Tourism Organization. (2013). Tourism visa openness report. Visa facilitation as means to stimulate tourism growth. https://www.e-unwto.org/doi/pdf/10.18111/9789284415731

UNWTO. (2020). International tourist numbers down 65% in first half of 2020. *UNWO Reports*, https://www.unwto.org/taxonomy/term/347

Vilcassim, M. R. J., Thurston, G. D., Chen, L.-C., Lim, C. C., Saunders, E., Yao, Y., & Gordon, T. (2019). Exposure to air pollution is associated with adverse cardiopulmonary health effects in international travelers. *Journal of Travel Medicine*, 26(5), 1–8.

World Bank. (2019). China's experience with high speed rail offers lessons for other countries. https://www.worldbank.org/en/news/press-release/2019/07/08/chinas-experience-with-high-speed-rail-offers-lessons-for-other-countries

World Bank. (2020). East Asia and Pacific cities: Expanding opportunities for the urban poor. https://www.worldbank.org/en/region/eap/publication/east-asia-and-pacific-cities-expanding-opportunities-for-the-urban-poor

World Economic Forum. (2019). The travel and tourism competitiveness report 2019. https://www.weforum.org/reports/the-travel-tourism-competitiveness-report-2019

World Travel & Tourism Council (WTTC). (2020). Economic impact: Country/region data. https://wttc.org/Research/Economic-Impact

Wu, B., Li, Q., Ma, F., & Wang, T. (2021). Tourism cities in China. In Alastair M. Morrison, & J. Andres Coca-Stefaniak (Eds.). *Routledge Handbook of Tourism Cities*, pp. 508–519. London: Routledge.

Xie, P. F. (2003). The bamboo-beating dance in Hainan, China: Authenticity and commodification. *Journal of Sustainable Tourism*, 11(1), 5–16.

The future for world tourism cities

This chapter focuses on the ever-changing environment we live in, and how this impacts world tourism cities. It highlights the opportunities brought by these changes.

Chapter 12 summarises the main recommendations from the previous 11 chapters. After this, a brief review is made of studies and reports on the future of cities, tourism and tourism cities. Then, a PESTEL-RVS framework is employed to more specifically identify future opportunities within nine categories.

Unique concepts in Part IV:

PESTEL-RVS

Short breaks: Part IV

12. Shanghai

Sweet tweets: Part IV

 95. More applications of technologies in future cities
 96. Food diplomacy initiatives from Thailand
 97. Crowdfinancing a pop-up cinema in Ealing, London
 98. What are pop-ups?
 99. Connected and autonomous vehicles
100. The City Brain project
101. What is the circular economy?
102. The Netherlands wants fewer tourists
103. How best to govern the night-time city?

DOI: 10.4324/9781003111412-15

Chapter 12

Future opportunities for world tourism cities

Abstract

This chapter focuses on the ever-changing environment in which we live, and how this impacts world tourism cities. It highlights the opportunities brought by external factors and changes. The main recommendations from the previous 11 chapters are summarised first. After this, a brief review is made of studies and reports on the future of cities, tourism and tourism cities. Then, a PESTEL-RVS framework is employed to more specifically identify future opportunities within nine categories. This is an extension of the PESTEL-RV model used in Chapter 2, with the addition of stakeholders to residents and visitors.

Governments will be introducing many new policies and guidelines in cities in the next ten years to adapt and cope with several urban issues, including quality of life (QoL), climate change and sustainability, and to accommodate technological innovations. This chapter emphasises the need for cities to "plan from the inside out" by making them better places to live and visit.

A multidisciplinary approach is used in Chapter 12 to uncover the latest research and future projections across a variety of fields including artificial intelligence, computer science, engineering, geography, public administration, sociology, transportation, urban planning and landscape architecture and others. The need to blend multiple disciplines is stressed to realise future opportunities for urban tourism.

Keywords: Artificial intelligence (AI); big data; citizen engagement; connected and autonomous vehicles (CAVs); crowdsourcing/crowdfunding; COVID-19; degrowth (tourism); resilience; urban greening.

DOI: 10.4324/9781003111412-16

Learning objectives

- Identify the recommendations and suggestions from Chapters 1 to 11.
- Describe how previous studies and reports characterise the futures of cities, tourism and tourism cities.
- Explain the PESTEL-RVS framework and why it is worthwhile to apply the model for pinpointing world tourism city opportunities.
- Identify potential government policy initiatives to capture future opportunities.
- Discuss the implications of the economic recovery from the COVID-19 pandemic.
- Describe how societal and cultural changes will affect tourism cities.
- Review how new technological advances will change and benefit world tourism cities in the years to come.
- Explain how city environments can be enhanced in the coming years.
- Envision where new laws and regulations will be introduced.
- Pinpoint future opportunities for city residents, visitors and stakeholders.

Introduction

The authors wanted to deliver the contents of the final chapter of *World Tourism Cities* in a positive tone. Therefore, opportunities was the term used rather than issues, problems or challenges. Despite the doom and gloom accompanying the COVID-19 pandemic and its economic trail of destruction, there is a bright future ahead for tourism cities. This future is inextricably tied to the scenarios for cities in general. As such, it is essential to use a foundation of expected future conditions in the world's urban areas for this chapter.

It is easy to become dazzled by the future and particularly by the exciting new technologies that are ahead. However, it is more realistic to have a feet-on-the-ground approach and think ahead just five to ten years from now. If the COVID-19 pandemic has taught us one lesson, it is not to assume that business will always be as usual. Thus, this chapter begins by recounting the major recommendations and suggestions contained in Chapters 1–11.

A recurrent theme in this chapter is the need for cities to build greater resilience so as to be able to better withstand future crises and shocks. Along with this topic, another phenomenon that is persistent is the need for more engagement and involvement of different parties in destination decision-making, particularly local residents and visitors. These two themes receive significant attention in this chapter due to their future relevance.

Previous chapter recommendations and suggestions

The authors have provided several recommendations and suggestions within the previous 11 chapters to enhance city destination management in the future. A brief summary of these is given now.

What is a world tourism city? Chapter 1

- There is a need for more work on criteria for world tourism cities so that comprehensive measurements and evaluations can be made in the future.

- World tourism cities must be elevated to a higher priority level in academic research and teaching.
- City governments and practitioners must have greater recognition of the concept of tourism cities and world tourism cities.

Globalisation and world tourism cities: Chapter 2

- Globalisation must be balanced with localisation to better assure uniqueness and authenticity.
- Careful consideration needs to be given to resident and visitor needs and expectations.
- City destination managers should be aware of all the advantages and disadvantages of globalisation.

Growth of the urban tourism phenomenon: Chapter 3

- Greater attention should be paid to the rapid changes that urban environments have gone through over the past decades.
- The importance of the phenomenon of urban tourism and its contribution to the development of towns and cities needs greater recognition.
- More interdisciplinary research is needed to better understand the inter-relationship between cities and tourism.

City destination management: Chapter 4

- Cities must adopt all seven-plus-one destination management roles.
- Visitor management needs to be given a higher priority in urban destinations.
- Cities should pay greater attention to crisis management and resilience planning.

Planning and development of world tourism cities: Chapter 5

- Regular tourism plans and strategies should be prepared.
- Participative tourism planning processes need to be adopted.
- Broad participation from all stakeholder groups should be invited.
- Overall tourism product development strategies should be designed.
- The application of the 10 As model should be considered.

Marketing and branding of world tourism cities: Chapter 6

- Professional destination marketing planning needs to be adopted.
- A higher priority should be assigned to research data collection.
- A systematic brand development process must be followed.

Quality of life and resident well-being in world tourism cities: Chapter 7

- World tourism cities must give a greater priority to resident quality of life and well-being.
- Greater emphasis should be assigned to sustainability within world tourism cities.
- Overcrowding issues need to be tackled.

- For visitor management purposes, the ADVICE framework should be considered.
- Visitor management programmes must be implemented.

Sustainability in world cities: Chapter 8

- A strong political will is needed to help cities commit the necessary resources to manage tourism sustainably.
- World tourism cities should contribute towards achieving the SDGs, especially SDG11.
- Cities must more actively address climate change.

Smart cities and smart tourism in cities: Chapter 9

- City destinations should have the right infrastructure and knowledge in place to be able to implement fast-evolving new technologies.
- Policy-makers in cities need to be aware of both the benefits and limitations of ICTs and have a better understanding of how these can affect visitors and local residents.
- Smart cities must do more to improve the living conditions of their residents through the use of new technologies.
- Urban destinations should be prepared to rapidly adapt to the new realities and implement smart solutions to improve their efficiency, enhance visitor experiences and remain competitive in the global marketplace.

World tourism cities in crisis times: Chapter 10

- It is paramount for city destinations to be well prepared to face crisis events.
- Crisis communication is a vital aspect of crisis management and efforts should be made by destinations to engage proactively in communication with their stakeholders during all stages of a crisis.
- Cities must develop greater resilience in the future.

Rise of the Asian world tourism cities: Chapter 11

- Asian cities need to deal more effectively with issues including urbanisation, pollution and traffic congestion.
- Urban safety and security levels must be improved.
- Local governments are required to clean up or terminate unsavoury forms of tourism.
- City destinations should continue to emphasise regional travel.

Several of the authors' recommendations and suggestions are reiterated in the remainder of the chapter, and this provides further evidence of the need for world tourism cities to follow the advice.

Future of cities

Several governmental and consulting company reports have been written on the future of cities. For example, the European Commission (EC) (2019) published the report, *The future of cities: Opportunities, challenges and the way forward* with a focus on cities in Europe. The United Nations Economic and Social Commission for Asia and the Pacific (UNESCAP) (2019) produced the report on *The future of Asian and Pacific cities: Transformative pathways towards sustainable urban development.* The EC identifies eight major urban challenges as affordable housing, mobility, provision of services, ageing (population), urban health, social segregation, environmental footprint and climate action. It sees the solutions being in space and the city (well-designed public and green spaces), tech and the city (new and emerging technologies), cities as innovation hubs, the citizen's city (greater citizen participation), urban governance (strengthening urban governance) and the resilient city (planning and preparing for all hazards). The UNESCAP report highlights four pathways to laying the foundation of a sustainable future for Asia-Pacific cities: (1) urban and territorial planning; (2) urban resilience; (3) smart and inclusive cities with the best technological applications; and (4) financing tools.

Sweet tweet 95

More applications of technologies in future cities

The EC report included this observation on technology,

> Cities will increasingly apply new technologies and innovation across a wide range of sectors, from transport and mobility to citizen engagement. This technology will need to be interoperable and integrated, and its implementation done in an inclusive way to benefit the overall functioning of cities.

Source: European Commission (2019).

These two reports have some common themes in planning, sustainability, resilience building, better governance, technology applications and smartness and citizen participation and inclusiveness.

Future of tourism and tourism cities

Several scholars and industry observers have discussed and prognosticated about the future of tourism and tourism cities, and a brief recounting of their ideas is useful here.

Bock (2015) pinpoints experiential travel and social acceleration as key reasons why urban tourism is changing and becoming more popular. These are being prompted by the increased use of information communication technologies and a faster pace of life. Social acceleration is "an attempt to realise as many options as possible in our lifetime" and causes visitors to seek out memorable experiences when visiting cities.

Postma, Buda and Gugerell (2017) note the substantial growth in city tourism, which they attribute to spatial, social, economic and technological factors. The OECD (2018) identifies four megatrends in tourism – evolving visitor demand, sustainable tourism growth, enabling technologies and travel mobility. Govers (2019) suggests that cities need to foster "imaginative communities" in the future. Coca-Stefaniak (2020) suggests that city tourism destinations should become "wiser", meaning that urban areas need to consider the growing inequalities between host communities and visitors, wellness, resilience and mental health. He described "post-smart tourism destinations" as ones that use a more people-centred approach to the use of technology. Francis (2021) recommends that city destinations must prioritise residents and businesses, invest in desirable, sustainable living and manage tourism well. Peacock (2021) also emphasised the need for a closer alignment of city tourism and more engagement with local residents in the future.

UNWTO (2020) made three overall, significant recommendations on urban tourism in the future, and these were the following:

- Promote the integration of tourism in the wider urban agenda.
- Foster sustainable policies and practices in urban tourism.
- Create cities for all: Building cities for citizens and visitors.

Much more has been written on this topic; however, several common themes appear to run through these commentaries on the future of tourism and tourism cities. These include technology applications, changes in visitors and their needs, sustainability and the requirement for greater consideration and involvement of local residents. A cautionary label is attached to some opinions regarding a consumer backlash against too much technology, that is the so-called need for a digital detox.

Review of future opportunities for world tourism cities

The PESTEL-RVS framework (Figure 12.1) is now used to identify and explain future opportunities according to nine factors.

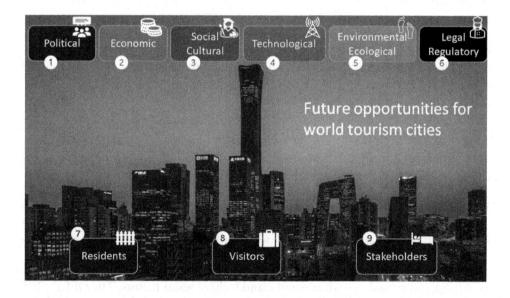

Figure 12.1 PESTEL-RVS framework of opportunities (Photo of Beijing: Courtesy: Unsplash.com, Henry Chen).

Political and governmental opportunities

There are many novel situations within urban areas that require the attention of governments and politicians. The authors have singled out globalisation (Chapter 2), urbanisation (Chapter 3), destination management (Chapters 4–6), quality of life (Chapter 7), sustainability (Chapter 8), smart technology (Chapter 9), crises (Chapter 10) and the rise of Asian cities (Chapter 11) as crucial urban issues and challenges; however, these eight factors are also replete with future opportunities for city administrations.

There are several movements within city and other governments that must be acknowledged first as these are changing how the public sector operates now and will perform in the future. They are the concepts of "new public management" and "open government". Paddison and Walmsley (2018), in a case study on the city of York in England, defined new public management as local government adopting characteristics more commonly found in the private sector, including competition, efficiency, quality, human resource management and entrepreneurship. Attard et al. (2015) documented how governments were becoming more transparent by opening up their data to the public for three reasons: (1) transparency (openness); (2) releasing social and commercial value; and (3) participatory governance. This then reflects the idea of open government.

Following on from these two movements, in general, the theme within this chapter is "planning from the inside out" and that essentially means making world tourism cities better places in which to live and work in the future. Cities that are more liveable will also be more attractive to visitors, while providing greater leisure and recreation opportunities for their citizens. Governments will need to craft new policy directions and guidelines for a raft of novel developments within municipalities. Urban planners will be required downstream to implement the new policies and guidelines on the ground.

The new policy directions and guidelines will be as a result of expected developments within the other eight components of the PESTEL-RVS framework. Some of these policies will be articulated through new laws and regulations, and these are explained later. Short break 12 on Shanghai that follows demonstrates how large cities with rapid economic growth policies must also engage in initiatives that enhance quality of life and conserve their cultural and industrial heritage. This is a very good example of urban regeneration and planning to improve the lives of local citizens.

SHORT BREAK 12

Better city, better living – in Shanghai

The slogan for Shanghai Expo 2010 was "Better City, Better Life" and we pick up on that in Short break 12. With a population of over 27 million in 2021, Shanghai is one of the world's mega-cities.

> Shanghai, the Oriental Paris, is China's biggest and most prosperous city … The city rivals New York or Paris in terms of modernity and boasts a blended culture of the East and the West. Shanghai is a tourist destination famous for historical landmarks as well as modern, ever-expanding skylines.

Figure 12.2 Shanghai old and new – Yu Garden (*Yu Yuan*) and Pudong from the Bund (*Waitan*) (Courtesy: Unsplash.co m, Vista Wei and Terry).

This is an apt description of today's Shanghai, which on first exposure can strike one as a kaleidoscope of ambitious skyscraper construction. However, like every world tourism city, there is a need to look further and dig deeper to discover the true essence of Shanghai. The Shanghainese (*ning*) are immensely proud of their city and for good reasons.

The Shanghai Municipal Government has initiated many urban regeneration initiatives, especially in waterfronts, former industrial areas (brownfields) and older neighbourhoods. These have meant that whilst Shanghai has further internationalised and urbanised, becoming a formidable financial and commercial centre in Asia, it yet still remains a great place to live.

Chapter 1 mentioned the *Shikumen* structures that have been preserved in Shanghai in *Xintiandi* and other neighbourhoods (see Figure 1.6). One much visited area in the city is the *Waitan* also known as the Bund, where magnificent buildings were erected in the late 1800s when Shanghai was the financial centre of Asia. The classical structures housing banks and customs houses were built in grand styles by the British, Americans and Russians and were a symbol of Shanghai's economic prowess. Fast-forwarding to the 1990s, the Bund had a ten-lane road separating the grand buildings and the city from the river and waterfront promenade. However, in preparation for Expo 2010, the Shanghai government restored the 1.8-kilometre-long boulevard along the west bank of Huangpu River, to a beautiful and walkable public space (Figure 12.2).

Shanghai is a city of stark traditional and modern contrasts as depicted in Figure 12.2, where the Qing-Ming structures of the Yu Yuan tourist area have a view of the futuristic skyline of Pudong on the east side of the Huangpu.

In 2005, the Shanghai Municipal Government launched the Shanghai Creative Industry Centre which recognised cultural and creative industries as a key sector to be developed in the city. This led to the readaptation of several industrial heritage sites (Niu et al., 2018) and culture and tourism-led peri-urban transformation (Li, 2020). The former included the Shanghai M50, and the Songjiang and Lingang New Towns were in the latter category.

Overall, Shanghai is an exemplary example of urban regeneration within a mega-city. This has been as a result of visionary government policies and with substantial investment by the public sector.

Discussion points:

1. What are the major challenges for urban regeneration faced by a city that is growing very rapidly?
2. How has Shanghai's history and culture benefited its urban regeneration?
3. How can cities like Shanghai assure the sustainability of urban regeneration projects in the future?

Sources: Chen (2020); China Highlights (2021); Li et al. (2014); Li (2020); Niu et al. (2018); Weng et al. (2021); Zhong and Chen (2017).

What about seeing urban futures through the eyes of those that will be inheriting them? Children's involvement in urban planning is a topic generating considerable debate; however, it is hardly ever mentioned in the context of destination management. Nordström and Wales (2019, p. 507) suggest that children contribute (to urban planning) with new perspectives on the environment; they challenge existing power relations through the creation of new adult–child relationships; and their participation requires changes in planning practices and the establishment of new routines in order to plan cities which meet the needs of children. Seraphin and Green (2019) conducted a study in which children were asked to draw, communicate and display their view on their Winchester (England) of the future.

Some have suggested that governments need to think "outside of the box" in the future in policy-setting, establishing relationships with external parties, and with place branding. For example, Suntikul (2019) discusses gastrodiplomacy as a strategic use of (local) cuisine in influencing perceptions of a destination. Linardaki and Aslanides (2020), using Greece as a case, suggest incorporating local poems and songs in place identity building and branding.

Sweet tweet 96

Food diplomacy initiatives from Thailand

Suntikul demonstrates a national-level gastrodiplomacy programme through the example of Thailand.

The Thai government's 2002 "Global Thai Program" aimed to increase the number of Thai restaurants abroad from 5,500 to 8,000 by the following year. The subsequent "Thai Kitchen to the World" programme was designed to inform domestic and foreign publics about Thai food and its history, including granting "Thailand's Brand" certificates to restaurants fulfilling criteria set by the Thai Ministry of Commerce.

She also cites Rockower's definition of gastrodiplomacy as "a form of public diplomacy that combines cultural diplomacy, culinary diplomacy and nation branding to make foreign culture tangible to the taste and touch".

Source: Rockower (2014); Suntikul (2019).

The UNESCAP report cited earlier suggested that financing tools needed to be a priority for cities in the future. Here, therefore the crowdfunding approach is relevant within the broader concept of crowdsourcing. Both techniques use technology via online platforms. Brabham (2013) addressed crowdsourcing by governments in proposing "a four-part, problem-based typology, encouraging government leaders and public administrators to consider these open problem-solving techniques as a way to engage the public and tackle difficult policy and administrative tasks more effectively and efficiently using online communities". The four approaches are as follows, with examples added by the authors:

- Knowledge discovery and management: For example, local residents report overcrowding incidents, excessive noise or other incidents involving visitors to their cities.
- Distributed human intelligence tasking: Such as using Amazon Mechanical Turk to assign foreign language translation tasks to members of the community.
- Broadcast search: This is an approach that has already been used by several DMOs in gathering photos, stories and recommendations from people about their places of residence that thereafter are shared with potential visitors. These searches can be set up as contests with prizes and awards for the best materials.
- Peer-vetted creative production: This involves asking citizens to propose potential solutions to complex problems. For example, a city government could ask residents to suggest ways to distribute visitors more evenly or to propose methods to reduce pollution and curb climate change.

Civic crowdfunding is defined by Stiver at al. (2015) as "a sub-type of crowdfunding through which citizens, in collaboration with government, fund projects providing a community service". There are several online crowdfunding platforms that enable this fund-raising, including Ioby.org (USA) and Spacehive.com. The latter platform, operating in the UK, has several projects for the restoration of historic buildings and structures.

Sweet tweet 97

Crowdfinancing a pop-up cinema in Ealing, London

The project idea here is to convert a historic but now unused library building into a pop-up cinema. According to Spacehive.com,

This will house a single screen viewing area and a bar/café that will have independent traders present. The project will have distanced seats and will be "Covid-19" prepared from the beginning. This will allow us to expand and add more seats, as the situation changes and evolves. It will also demonstrate the viability of the project, strengthening the proposed full development of the cinema. It will allow us to establish revenue streams with a minimal outlay and costs. We will be operating the pop-up cinema.

This project is one under the auspices of the Mayor of London.

Source: Spacehive.com (2021).

Economic opportunities

In 2021, the economic future of the world seemed bleak after the ravages of the COVID-19 pandemic. Economic recovery was the priority for world tourism cities in mid-2021 after the sharp downturn in visitor arrivals and spending in 2020 and 2021. This has led to a reassessment of markets and destination marketing for the near-term future.

The World Economic Forum published two reports on the future of the fast-growing consumer markets in China and India (WEF, 2018a; WEF, 2018b). Prior to the unexpected events in early 2020, the burgeoning outbound tourism market from Mainland China was receiving significant attention from world tourism cities. Also, cities such as Singapore and Bangkok were receiving increased volumes of visitors from India. In tourism parlance, these are often referred to as "emerging markets" that in future will produce much greater economic impacts. COVID-19 abruptly ended the rapid growth in outbound tourism from China and India from early 2020 to mid-2021, when recovery began at least in the case of China.

Price Waterhouse Coopers (PwC) (2019) contributed *Chinese cities of opportunity 2019* in which the company identified 38 urban areas of which it ranked ten as "major regional cities" (Shanghai, Beijing, Hong Kong, Guangzhou, Chongqing, Shenzhen, Chengdu, Hangzhou, Wuhan and Xi'an). The ranking was based on the degree and influence of the cities' external relations measured by star-graded hotels, length of stay per capita of international inbound visitors, inbound and outbound flights, passenger capacity and exhibition/convention economy development index. This bears a close resemblance to the features of world tourism cities identified in Chapter 1. However, the main point here is that these ten cities and the 28 others are prime potential sources of visitors from China.

Cities must carefully evaluate the future economic opportunities from these two emerging source markets and other origin regions including Southeast Asia, Middle East and North Africa (MENA) and the rest of Africa, Latin America and elsewhere. Also, growing market segments and new forms of tourism need to be assessed, some of which are now discussed within social and cultural opportunities.

Social and cultural opportunities

Societies are changing and cultures are evolving, and perhaps no more so than within world tourism cities which are on the front edges of transformation. New concepts for leisure, recreation and tourism within urban areas are emerging, some of which are introducing the rural into the urban. Also, there is greater concern for delivering cultural authenticity in visitor experiences, avoiding the cultural homogenisation mentioned in Chapter 2 on the effects of globalisation. Here, some but not all of the urban experiences and concept opportunities are reviewed.

Nikoo, Farsani and Emadi (2020) tested domestic tourist reactions to trompe l'œil, a 3D street art painting form, in Shiraz, Iran. They found that domestic Iranian tourists were very enthusiastic about art tourism in general and trompe l'œil in particular. Zuma and Rooijackers (2020) reviewed the use of "urban culture" in creative placemaking including hip-hop and breakdancing with Heerlen and Eindhoven in the Netherlands as examples. They also discussed other activities that are enjoyed by youth, including BMX, skateboarding, free-running, DJ-ing and graffiti. Dos Santos (2021) examined four film cities that are part of UNESCO Creative Cities (UCCN) (Galway, Bradford, Busan and Sydney). The four cities since receiving the designation have been successful in focusing on creativity to support sustainable development, which is their mandate from UCCN. Skinner, Sarpong and White (2018) advocated using geocaching as an activity within urban areas. This is a type of gamification using mobile phones to find hidden caches.

The nanofication of objects seems to be an ever-present trend as engineers and scientists try to make things smaller and more compact. Haynes and Egan (2019) discussed the miniaturism concept of hospitality and tourism by citing microbars as an example. Space limitations within cities and people's increasing desires for micro-breaks were cited by them as reasons for this trend. An allied idea here is pop-up attractions, restaurants, retailing and landscapes in urban areas. The Dinner in the Sky concept is an excellent example of a pop-up attraction and dining venue that was originated in Belgium (EITS BvBa, 2021). Pop-ups are widely used in retailing and especially in fashion retailing. Street food stalls, night and farmer markets are earlier prototypes of the idea.

Sweet tweet 98

What are pop-ups?

Pop-ups are a great idea for cities.

> Translated into the spatial language of urban planning and geography, the term implies installations or design interventions that burst onto the scene for a limited time. The idea is to stimulate curiosity in a particular site. In this context, using the pop-up terminology introduces the idea that sites present opportunities to seize urban space, to arrest peoples' attention, and to possibly alter their sense of space and time. Pop-ups thus break through the routine time that people experience in the space of the city.

Source: Schaller and Guinand (2017).

Flash mobs, including branded ones, are more fleeting calls to attention within cities. They been used by DMOs in the past, e.g., by VisitBritain and British Airways in Moscow. Grant, Botha and Kietzmann (2015) examined the branded flash mob trend and its use in video-based advertising on YouTube and similar platforms. They found it to be an increasingly popular form of viral advertising that takes advantage of social media.

Slow food and slow tourism in general are not new concepts; in fact, they have been around for decades. However, the interruption in normal behaviours as a result of COVID-19 caused people to journey closer to home and focus more deeply on local experiences. Fusté-Forné and Jamal (2020) concluded that slow-food tourism (SFT) is "a pathway to contribute to locally based agricultural and food practices for sustainable development, food security, social sustainability and community well-being". As such this undoubtedly should be on the menu for world tourism cities to implement in the future.

Zmyślony and Wędrowicz (2019) suggest that existing and novel urban leisure formats (ULFs) will become more popular in the coming years. They specifically identify art and cultural festivals, day/evening socialising spots, open-air cinemas, serious leisure events, outdoor dance zones, local fan zones, culinary events/food festivals, urban beaches/waterfront areas and street parades and marches.

Griffin and Dimanche (2017) reminded everyone of the importance of the VFR market, and this surely was driven home further in 2020–2021 during the global public health crisis.

Coca-Stefaniak (2020) suggested that "wise" future tourism cities must have wellness on their agendas. Lee, Lam and Lam (2020) agreed and suggested that urbanisation was one of the reasons why city wellness tourism deserved a higher priority in the future.

Technological opportunities

There is a huge amount of research and other written contributions on how technologies will affect the cities of the future. As well as being the context for many sci-fi movies, this is a topic area that seems to fascinate scholars, within and without tourism. The following is a brief discussion of some of the technological opportunities, presented in an alphabetical order.

5G is the fifth-generation mobile network, and it is expected to have a transformational influence on how people use smartphones and the Internet. It is faster, has much more connectivity and lower latency (delays) and will become widely applied in leisure, entertainment and travel. In terms of connectivity, the Internet of Things will greatly enhance the value and applicability of 5G networks. Simply put, IoT means connecting everything to the Internet. More technically, Atzori et al. (2010) say that IoT takes things that are around us "such as radio-frequency identification (RFID) tags, sensors, actuators, mobile phones, etc. through unique addressing schemes, are able to interact with each other and cooperate with their neighbours". Xia et al. (2012) describe the IoT as the networked interconnection of everyday objects.

Whilst the authors are trying to disentangle concepts for ease of understanding, designers of new technologies are doing their best to combine and network tools and applications, such as just described with 5G and the IoT. Also, Allam and Dhunny (2019) discuss the combination of artificial intelligence and big data, along with the IoT, in smart cities. They note the analysis of big data through AI within cities for issues related to the environment and climate change, energy conservation, mobility and transportation, culture and other aspects. More specifically, artificial intelligence and service robots are gradually being incorporated into world tourism cities and within individual tourism businesses. Service robots in urban hotels are becoming more popular and received a boost in the "no touch" conditions during the COVID-19 pandemic.

Sanchez-Anguix et al. (2021) identified major current city issues as being in management, security, transportation, public health, distribution of resources, sustainability, energy efficiency and other areas. They predicted that these would become more acute as cities grew larger. However, AI was expected to contribute positively to public health, informed people and public participation, city management and economic development, energy efficiency, transport and CO_2 emissions, security and emergency services and water and waste management.

Augmented (AR) and virtual reality (VR) are two technologies that are already in use in world tourism cities and are expected to experience much greater application in the next five to ten years. Yung and Khoo-Lattimore (2019) define AR as the enhancement of a real-world environment using layers of computer-generated images through a device (usually a smartphone or pad) (Figure 12.3). The same authors describe virtual reality as the use of a computer-generated 3D environment, that the user can navigate and interact with, resulting in real-time simulation of one or more of the user's five senses.

Big data will play an even more crucial role in city tourism in the times ahead and be integrated with several of the technologies discussed here. McAfee and Brynjolfsson (2012) in a much-cited *Harvard Business Review* article stated that big data was different due to its volume, velocity and variety. In other words, it is massive, instantly available and present in many sources in dissimilar formats. They projected that big data would revolutionise management, and it will certainly change city destination management through the 2020s. Li et al. (2018a) and Mariani et al. (2018) produced literature reviews on the use of big data in tourism.

A blockchain is a digital recording of transactions made in cryptocurrency such as bitcoin. It is an application of big data. Several researchers have recently been studying

Figure 12.3 Augmented reality enhances visitor experiences (Courtesy: Unsplash.com, Patrick Schneider).

the application of blockchain approaches in cities and in tourism. Sigala (2017) discussed this as a type of collaborative commerce. Kwok and Koh (2019, pp. 2248–2249) suggested that blockchain will bring four benefits to tourism in enhancing tourist experiences and allowing operators to identify and match tourist preferences, quick and hassle-free cross-border remittances, providing a means of diversification and eliminating commission fees. Bagloee et al. (2021) called this a "distributed digital ledger" and suggested that this technology could become "an underlying operating system that governs the way our cities function in the future". They associated blockchain adoption with smart city initiatives.

Connected and autonomous vehicles (CAVs) and electric cars are likely to change urban transport in the years ahead (Figure 12.4). They are among the many future opportunities to transform transportation and transit systems within cities. Several cities have recently introduced new light-rail and subway networks to ease the pressures on roads in urban areas, including Bern (Switzerland), Bergen (Norway) and Copenhagen, all in Europe, and Macao in China. However, perhaps an even more transformational prospect for surface transportation is the emergence of CAVs.

Sweet tweet 99

Connected and autonomous vehicles

Automated vehicles (AV): "Autonomous (or automated) vehicles" are those in which operation of the vehicle occurs without direct driver input to control the steering, acceleration and braking and are designed so that the driver is not expected to monitor constantly the roadway while operating in self-driving mode.

Connected vehicles (CV): "Connected vehicles" are vehicles that use any of a number of different communication technologies to communicate with the driver, other vehicles on the road, roadside infrastructure and to other systems and services via the cloud.

Source: Transport Scotland (2019).

Several scholars have looked at the impacts of CAVs on cities and tourism and the market acceptance of this form of transportation. For example, Prideaux and Yin (2019) speculated on the impacts of CAVs and electric cars on tourism and particularly in the context of climate change realities and the need to switch from the use of fossil fuels. They suggested that these will be a disruptive (transformational) force in tourism in the future (Cohen and Hopkins, 2019). However, Acheampong et al. (2021) suggested that drivers' attitudes in preferring to use private, fossil-fuelled cars will need to change, and that new government policies and legislation may be needed to support greater adoption of CAVs. Also, Ribeiro et al. (2021) suggested that actions need to be taken to reassure travellers about the safety and risks in using these vehicles.

Electric vehicles (EVs) are also advancing technologically and are already very evident on urban highways and roads. The introduction of these vehicles poses new challenges to cities, not the least being the provision of recharging stations. Wu et al. (2021) evaluated the policies of the Chinese government in encouraging its citizens to make greater use of EVs to improve urban environmental quality. The sales of EVs in China went

Figure 12.4 Driving a CAV (Courtesy: Unsplash.com, Roberto Nickson).

from 18,000 in 2013 to 1,225,000 in 2019 when supported by the government policies which included financial subsidies. It is highly likely in the future that other countries like China will have many more EVs on the road through the 2020s.

Tracking visitor movements within city destinations is likely to become much more important for a variety of reasons, including visitor management. The use of global positioning system (GPS) apps on mobile phones is one of the ways to follow the tracks of people as they move around (Hardy et al., 2017).

Chapter 9 provides a detailed explanation of smart cities and smart tourism. Most of the above-mentioned technologies will be implemented in these "smartness" efforts within cities.

Sweet tweet 100

The City Brain project – Hangzhou

Hangzhou has built a "City Brain" which runs the government on a huge amount of data. Using analytics and artificial intelligence, it has helped cut traffic congestion, road accidents and crime. City Brain can detect and predict traffic flows ten minutes in advance with 90% accuracy and it then sends reports to the monitoring centres. Cameras across the city monitor the traffic conditions at all times. If an accident happens, road users and authorities are alerted quickly, and traffic flows are managed accordingly. Through camera systems across the city, Alibaba tracks road conditions in real time.

Source: SmartMyCity (2021).

It must be realised that there are negatives to technology in addition to their many positives. While many people cannot survive without Wi-Fi, a growing number of others crave "digital detox" (Li, Pearce and Low, 2018b), (temporarily) giving up their wired devices.

Environmental and ecological opportunities

There is a growing level of concern in cities about the environment and particularly with respect to climate change. This was a topic broached in Chapter 8 as well as in other chapters, including Chapter 11 on Asian cities. City exemplars have been identified, including Copenhagen in Chapter 5 and Singapore in Chapter 11.

Sweet tweet 101

What is the circular economy?

There is much talk these days about circular economies, although many still do not completely comprehend what the term means. Here is a definition: the

circular economy is an economy constructed from societal production-consumption systems that maximizes the service produced from the linear nature-society-nature material and energy throughput flow. This is done by using cyclical materials flows, renewable energy sources and cascading-type energy flows. Successful circular economy contributes to all the three dimensions of sustainable development. Circular economy limits the throughput flow to a level that nature tolerates and utilises ecosystem cycles in economic cycles by respecting their natural reproduction rates.

Source: Korhonen, Honkasalo and Seppälä (2018).

Climate change threats have already inspired city governments and tourism businesses to implement potential solutions in the fight against global warming and urban pollution. Moreover, actions are being taken to make many cities better and healthier places to reside by greening them. Next follows a selection of these initiatives.

Green buildings, walls (vertical gardens), and roofs are becoming more noticeable in cities across the globe. Clar and Steurer (2021) explored the green roof concept and its application in Copenhagen, Hamburg and Vienna. They found that local governments preferred offering fiscal incentives rather than mandatory policies on green roofing. Zhang and Yong (2021) demonstrated that green buildings in Singapore provided a supportive and educational environment for motivating and educating residents to behave in a pro-environmental manner (Figure 12.5).

The nature-based strategies (NbS) for cities are varied; however, they usually have the twin goals of improving environmental conditions while enhancing the quality of life and well-being of residents. Additionally, they tend to beautify urban areas and make cities more attractive to visitors. Frantzeskaki (2019) analysed 15 cases of NbS implementation in European cities and extracted seven lessons for their planning. Lehmann (2021) discussed renaturalisation and rewilding as strategies for cities. He argued that green spaces improve the health and well-being of residents, and linked NbS with urban resilience. Puskás, Abunnasr and Naalbandian (2021) examined community participation in the planning and definition of NbS for their cities.

Among the NbS, parks and other green spaces are especially crucial to urban greening and the lives of local residents. This was highlighted in Chapter 7 with the example of Kings Park in Perth, Australia. Another city greening concept is the community gardening approach. Milbourne (2021) and Kou et al. (2019) review community gardening as a strategy in cities. The first author examined community gardening across 15 cities in Australia, Canada, the UK and the USA. The second author analysed the community gardening initiative in Shanghai and studied the phenomenon as a form of community engagement in building healthier urban environments.

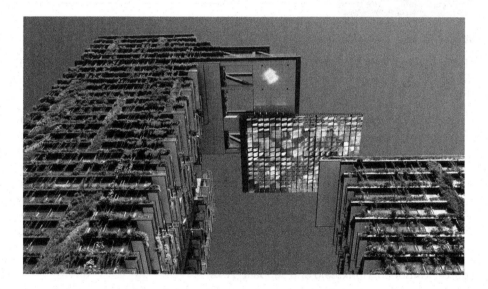

Figure 12.5 A green building, Blancas One Central Park vertical gardens, part of a larger regeneration programme in the Central Park zone of Sydney, Australia (Courtesy: Shutterstock.com, SAKARET).

Legal and regulatory opportunities

As mentioned earlier, new laws and regulations will be needed in the future in world tourism cities. Most of the five foregoing factors will be covered, as will be the interests and rights of residents, visitors and stakeholders. For example, with technological adaptation, there will be more controls on data security and modes of transport. Tighter laws and regulations are expected to achieve climate change goals and curb urban pollution. Greater protection of citizens and visitors from public health crises may also be on the agendas of lawmakers, given the results of recent history. New policies and rules might be needed to rekindle flagging economies. In addition, several specific issues in tourism will be addressed, including overtourism and tourism degrowth, sharing economy providers and night-time economies.

As a consequence of overtourism, the debate over the "degrowth" of tourism in urban and resort areas is intensifying. The images of deserted destinations during the COVID-19 pandemic added to the viewpoints in this discussion, as environments bounced back from the pressures brought by tourism. A special issue of the *Journal of Sustainable Tourism* in 2019 was titled "Tourism Degrowth". Essentially, this means controlling or cutting back on the number of visitors. Degrowing tourism is not a new concept as ten years before the special issue, Hall (2009) discussed the need to reconsider continued tourism growth due to the adverse environmental and climate change that it was creating. At the present, several destinations, including cities, have or are considering introducing laws and regulations to more strictly control or limit visitor numbers. For example, Valdivielso and Moranta (2019) used critical discourse analysis to examine the debates surrounding overtourism, tourism pressure and gentrification on Spain's Balearic Islands, and the solutions to these issues. Higgins-Desbiolles et al. (2019) suggest a variety of degrowth initiatives for destinations, including localising the tourism economy, shifting the values of tourism away from excessive commodification and exploitation and restructuring production from multinational domination.

Sweet tweet 102

The Netherlands wants fewer tourists

In the Netherlands,

> A strategy document suggests solutions including actively dissuading people from visiting certain areas through means such as closing down some attractions to imposing a tourist tax. It aims to future-proof development of destination Holland, as a loved, valuable and liveable destination.
>
> The nuisance factor to locals of tourists in parts of the Netherlands means that the tourist board is encouraging regions to take up a policy of "develop and discourage" by stopping new hotels or extra airport capacity being built.

Source: LaingBuisson (2019).

Linked to the degrowth movement, there will be more legislation and regulation of sharing economy providers in cities. Palgan, Mont and Sulkakoski (2021) point out that many cities want to mitigate the negative effects of sharing economy providers, while also enhancing their positive impacts. Brauckmann (2017) examined the resident housing and visitor accommodation markets in Hamburg, Germany. He suggested that in future city administrators should use global information system (GIS) data and mapping to identify potential conflicts between sharing economy accommodation and urban housing needs.

For many cities, the night-time economy is of great value economically, while presenting a variety of issues, particularly related to safety and security for visitors and residents. Roberts and Eldridge (2009) blamed alcohol-related entertainment for problems in city and town centres in the UK. Unfortunately, this is a pattern played out across the world and has become a headache for city administrators. Chapter 4 highlighted the issues with drunk tourism in Prague, for example. Various solutions have been advanced, and changing the approach to night-time city governance is one of them (Seijas and Gelders, 2021).

Sweet tweet 103

How best to govern the night-time city?

The answer according to select cities is to appoint a night mayor or create night-time advocacy organisations. "More than 40 cities have appointed night mayors or individuals responsible for maintaining nocturnal vibrancy, while mediating between those who wish to work, party or sleep". The cities mentioned in this study include Amsterdam, Berlin, London, New York, Washington DC and several other cities in the Netherlands. These approaches appear to be quite effective.

Source: Seijas and Gelders. (2021)

Policies, laws and regulations will also be needed to support changes in transportation modes and usage. Earlier in the chapter, the government role in encouraging greater adoption (and manufacturing) of CAVs and electric vehicles was discussed.

Resident opportunities

This book so far has placed considerable emphasis on city residents in terms of their quality of life (Chapter 7), sustainability (Chapter 8) and the need for visitor management (Chapter 4). It is envisaged (and recommended) that overall local city residents will be given a much higher priority in world tourism cities, having been somewhat neglected for the past 30 years. The lack of consideration of local people resulted in protests and are a symptom of overtourism.

Vergara, Papaoikonomou and Ginieis (2021) discussed the idea of a "sharing city" using the example of Barcelona. They state that contemporary cities are typically plagued with a variety of difficult issues that include social inequality, affordable housing, traffic problems, environmental pollution and others. Using frame analysis, these scholars investigated Barcelona's version of a sharing city that was introduced by the city council to: (1) promote the sharing city as a combination of a top-down approach and citizen participation; (2) put forward the notion of sharing as an opportunity for the city's future; and (3) generate trust in the local administration. In essence, this is a strategy to listen to resident voices in guiding urban planning.

Through reviewing the six PESTEL factors in terms of opportunities several potential resident benefits are evident. These include open government (access to data), more equitable economic growth strategies, greater inclusivity and citizen participation, greening of cities and enhanced legislative and regulatory protection.

Visitor opportunities

Several new visitor activities and experiences were previewed earlier under social and cultural opportunities. There are yet still other opportunities that can create win-win-win (triple-win) propositions for cities, stakeholders and visitors. Rong (2020) describes one of these in Amsterdam through the deployment of waterborne autonomous vehicles (WAVs) for museum visits. Boat tours and museums are extremely popular with Amsterdam's visitors, which WAVs combine. This will take some traffic off of the city's streets (a win for the city), provide a variety of interesting sightseeing boat itineraries for visitors (a win for the visitors) and supply more traffic for the museums (a win for the stakeholders).

Overall, it is argued that making world tourism cities better places to live (for the residents) will also make them better places to visit. Thus, there is the suggested mantra of "planning from the inside out" and the more considered stewarding of the precious resources within urban areas.

Stakeholder opportunities

How will tourism stakeholders benefit from these various opportunities? Once again, cities must be looking for multiple-win (rather than one beneficiary) projects or initiatives where the winners include the stakeholders. The following are some ways in which stakeholders may benefit from opportunities according to each of the PESTEL dimensions:

- Political and governmental: Policies that support the creation and operations of SMEs; strategies that reduce crimes and scams.
- Economic: New types and sources of guests and visitors; reductions in seasonality of business.
- Social and cultural: New concepts that provide product expansion and diversification opportunities for the private sector.
- Technological: New service concepts such as robots and other AI applications; more efficient payment and transaction systems; new and speedier online connectivity and communication.
- Environmental and ecological: Improvement of local neighbourhoods, and policies and incentives that encourage green practices.
- Legal and regulatory: Legislation and regulations that provide greater protection for existing tourism businesses.

Resilience

Adger (2000), in the social and ecological contexts, defined resilience as the ability of communities to withstand external shocks to social infrastructure as well as the ability of groups or communities to cope with external stresses and disturbances as a result of social, political and environmental change. Resilience can be evaluated at the micro (individual residents or visitors), meso (individual companies or organisations) and macro (cities or nations) levels.

The advent of COVID-19 heightened the call for resilience within cities and destinations. Cochrane (2010) suggested a sphere of tourism resilience with the three principal elements of harnessing market forces, leadership and stakeholder cohesion. She also highlighted the need for learning, flexibility and adaptability. McCartney, Pinto and Liu (2021) examined the recovery and resilience of Macao against the COVID-19 pandemic. They identified five determinants of economic resilience and tourism recovery as the tourism industry structure, labour market conditions, financial environment, governance arrangements and decision-making process. Other scholars identified the importance of big (and small) data in helping cities make better decisions leading to enhanced tourism resilience. For example, Janusz, Six and Vanneste (2017), when considering the historic centre of Bruges, uncovered resident concerns through using the photo elicitation technique. Simone et al. (2021) analysed online comments by residents and visitors about specific points of interest in Rome.

Chelleria and Baravikova (2021) studied the perceptions of European scholars and practitioners of the meaning of urban resilience, which they connected with sustainability. They identified perceived barriers and characteristics to resilient cities, and the most cited characteristics were adaptive capacity, inclusivity, integration, diversity and flexibility. A distinction is made between "bouncing back" (returning to a previous normal) and "bouncing forward" (finding a new normal).

Summary comments

There are multiple opportunities ahead for world tourism cities despite the global difficulties in 2020 and 2021. "Planning for the inside out" needs to be the mantra of city destinations in grasping these opportunities, which means helping to make their communities better places to live. The Short break for this chapter on Shanghai echoed this proposition that better cities make for better lives (and visits too).

Building the future resilience, economically and environmentally, of world tourism cities must be a top priority to better withstand the challenges that certainly are ahead. This means broadening portfolios of tourist sources and markets, the greening of public and private spaces and building stronger communities.

Careful attention must be paid to the needs of city residents, visitors and tourism stakeholders in the 2020s. Top-down, authoritarian approaches by city governments must give way to more resident engagement and input to urban planning and decision-making. Serious questions must be asked about continually growing visitor numbers and degrowth strategies may be in order.

Technology will reshape the face of urban tourism through the 2020s. However, not all technological advances improve the well-being of people and considered, balanced strategies are needed. Detoxification from technology might well become a more pressing social need.

The authors predict that world tourism cities in 2032 will be much different than they were in 2022. As evidenced in this final chapter, charting the best future for these cities requires taking a broader and multidisciplinary view of urban tourism.

Thought questions

1. How should world tourism cities take the fullest advantage of technological innovations in the future?
2. What new products, activities and experiences should world tourism cities contemplate for future visitors?
3. In what ways can cities build greater resilience into tourism?
4. How can world tourism cities best engage with local residents and involve them in destination planning for the future?
5. This chapter advocates a "planning from the inside out" approach for urban tourism in the years ahead. What key principles should be defined to guide the implementation of this strategy?
6. How will the lessons gained from the COVID-19 pandemic influence the future of city tourism during the 2020s?
7. In which ways do local governments need to change in the future to take advantage of the several opportunities highlighted in this chapter?
8. How can artificial intelligence (AI) be employed to address some of the major issues present in world tourism cities, including with transportation and climate change?
9. What should cities do to involve children and other youth in imagining and visioning the future of leisure and tourism within cities?
10. Can you suggest an issue or a project that could be crowdsourced or crowdfunded in your community or another? How can this be accomplished?

References

Acheampong, R. A, Cugurullo, F., Gueriau, M., & Dusparic, I. (2021). Can autonomous vehicles enable sustainable mobility in future cities? Insights and policy challenges from user preferences over different urban transport options. *Cities*, 112, https://doi.org/10.1 016/j.cities.2021.103134.

Adger, W. N. (2000). Social and ecological resilience: Are they related? *Progress in Human Geography*, 24(3), 347–364.

Allam, Z., & Dhunny, Z. A. (2019). On big data, artificial intelligence and smart cities. *Cities*, 89, 80–91.

Attard, J., Orlandi, F., Scerri, S., & Auer, S. (2015). A systematic review of open government data initiatives. *Government Information Quarterly*, 32(4), 399–418.

Atzori, L., Iera, A., & Morabito, G. (2010). The Internet of things: A survey. *Computer Networks*, 54(15), 2787–2805.

Bagloee, S. A., Heshmati, M., Dia, H., Ghaderi, H., Pettit, C., & Asadi, M. (2021). Blockchain: The operating system of smart cities. *Cities*, *112*, https://doi.org/10.1016/j .cities.2021.103104.

Bock, K. (2015). The changing nature of city tourism and its possible implications for the future of cities. *European Journal of Futures Research*, 3, 20.

Brabham, D. C. (2013). Using crowdsourcing in government. IBM Center for the Business of Government, http://www.businessofgovernment.org/

Brauckmann, S. (2017). City tourism and the sharing economy: Potential effects of online peer-to-peer marketplaces on urban property markets. *Journal of Tourism Futures*, 3(2), 114–126.

Chelleria, L., & Baravikova, A. (2021). Understandings of urban resilience meanings and principles across Europe. *Cities*, 108, https://doi.org/10.1016/j.cities.2020.102985.

Chen, Y. (2020). Financialising urban redevelopment: Transforming Shanghai's waterfront. *Land Use Policy*, https://doi.org/10.1016/j.landusepol.2020.105126

China Highlights. (2021). Top 7 reasons to visit Shanghai. https://www.chinahighlights.com/shanghai/top-reasons-to-visit.htm

Clar, C., & Steurer, R. (2021). Climate change adaptation with green roofs: Instrument choice and facilitating factors in urban areas. *Journal of Urban Affairs*, https://doi.org/10.1080/07352166.2021.1877552.

Coca-Stefaniak, J. A. (2020). Beyond smart tourism cities: Towards a new generation of "wise" tourism destinations. *Journal of Tourism Futures*, http://dx.doi.org/10.1108/JTF-11-2019-0130

Cochrane, J. (2010). The sphere of tourism resilience. *Tourism Recreation Research*, 35(2), 173–185.

Cohen, S. A., & Hopkins, D. (2019). Autonomous vehicles and the future of urban tourism. *Annals of Tourism Research*, 74, 33–42.

De Andrade, N., & Forte dos Santos, S. (2021). Crossroads between city diplomacy and city branding towards the future: Case study on the film cities at UNESCO Creative Cities Network. *Place Branding and Public Diplomacy*, 17, 105–125.

EITS BvBa. (2021). Dinner in the sky: The concept. https://www.dinnerinthesky.com/the-concept.

European Commission. (2019). *The Future of Cities. Opportunities, Challenges and the Way Forward*. Brussels: European Commission.

Francis, J., & Responsibletravel.com. (2021). The future of city tourism. https://www.responsibletravel.com/copy/future-of-city-tourism

Frantzeskaki, N. (2019). Seven lessons for planning nature-based solutions in cities. *Environmental Science and Policy*, 93, 101–111.

Fusté-Forné, F., & Jamal, T. (2020). Slow food tourism: An ethical microtrend for the Anthropocene. *Journal of Tourism Futures*, 6(3), 227–232.

Govers, R. (2019). The future of tourism: Imaginative destinations. https://www.imaginativecommunities.com/the-future-of-tourism/

Grant, P., Botha, E., & Kietzmann, J. (2015). Branded flash mobs: Moving toward a deeper understanding of consumers' responses to video advertising. *Journal of Interactive Advertising*, 15(1), 28–42.

Griffin, T., & Dimanche, F. (2017). Urban tourism: The growing role of VFR and immigration. *Journal of Tourism Futures*, 3(2), 103–113.

Hall, C. M. (2009). Degrowing tourism: Décroissance, sustainable consumption and steady-state tourism. *Anatolia*, 20(1), 46–61.

Hardy, A., Hyslop, S., Booth, K., Robards, B., Aryal, J., Gretzel, U., & Eccleston, R. (2017). Tracking tourists' travel with smartphone-based GPS technology: A methodological discussion. *Information Technology & Tourism*, 17, 255–274.

Haynes, N. C., & Egan, D. (2019). The implications of "miniaturism" for urban tourism destination futures: From micropubs to microbars. *Journal of Tourism Futures*, DOI:10.1108/JTF-10-2019-0105.

Higgins-Desbiolles, F., Carnicelli, S., Krolikowski, C., Wijesinghe, G., & Boluk, K. (2019). Degrowing tourism: Rethinking tourism. *Journal of Sustainable Tourism*, 22(1), 31–49.

Janusz, K., Six, S., & Vanneste, D. (2017). Building tourism-resilient communities by incorporating residents' perceptions? A photo-elicitation study of tourism development in Bruges. *Journal of Tourism Futures*, 3(2), 127–143.

Korhonen, J., Honkasalo, A., & Seppälä, J. (2018). Circular economy: The concept and its limitations. *Ecological Economics*, 143, 37–46.

Kou, H., Zhang, S., & Liu, Y. (2019). Community-engaged research for the promotion of healthy urban environments: A case Study of community garden initiative in Shanghai, China. *International Journal of Environmental Research and Public Health*, 16, 4145, DOI:10.3390/ijerph16214145.

Kwok, A. O. J., & Koh, S. G. M. (2019). Is blockchain technology a watershed for tourism development? *Current Issues in Tourism*, 22(20), 2447–2452.

LaingBuisson. (2019). Netherlands wants less tourists. https://www.laingbuissonnews.com/imtj/news-imtj/netherlands-wants-less-tourists/

Lee, L. Y.-S., Lam, K. Y.-C., & Lam, M. Y. C. (2020). Urban wellness: The space-out moment. *Journal of Tourism Futures*, 6(3), 247–250.

Lehmann, S. (2021). Biodiverse urban futures: Renaturalization and rewilding as strategies to strengthen urban resilience. *Sustainability*, 13, 2932, https://doi.org/10.3390/su13052932.

Li, J. (2020). Culture and tourism-led peri-urban transformation in China: The case of Shanghai. *Cities*, 99, https://doi.org/10.1016/j.cities.2020.102628.

Li, J., Xu, L., Tang, L., Wang, S., & Li, L. (2018a). Big data in tourism research: A literature review. *Tourism Management*, 68, 301–323.

Li, J., Pearce, P. L., & Low, D. (2018b). Media representation of digital-free tourism: A critical discourse analysis. *Tourism Management*, 69, 317–329.

Li, P., Braae, E., & Liu, J. (2014). Expo 2010: Strategic transformation of former industrial areas by means of international events. *Journal of Urban Planning and Development*, 140(2), 05013004.

Linardaki, C., & Aslanides, A. (2020). From poem and song to cultural diplomacy: Challenges and opportunities for place branding and tourism promotion. *Place Branding and Public Diplomacy*, 16, 304–315.

Mariani, M., Baggio, R., Fuchs, M., & Höpken, W. (2018). Business intelligence and big data in hospitality and tourism: A systematic literature review. *International Journal of Contemporary Hospitality Management*, 30(12), 3514–3554.

McAfee, A., & Brynjolfsson, E. (2012). Big data: The management revolution. *Harvard Business Review*, 90(10), 60–68.

McCartney, G., Pinto, J., & Liu, M. (2021). City resilience and recovery from COVID-19: The case of Macao. *Cites*, 112, https://doi.org/10.1016/j.cities.2021.103130

Milbourne, P. (2021). Growing public spaces in the city: Community gardening and the making of new urban environments of publicness. *Urban Studies*, https://doi.org/10.1177/0042098020972281.

Nikoo, Z., Farsani, N. T., & Emadi, M. (2020). Trompe l'œil: An approach to promoting art tourism (Case study: Shiraz city, Iran). *Journal of Tourism Futures*, http://dx.doi.org/10.1108/JTF-09-2019-0090.

Niu, S, Lau, S. S. Y., Shen, Z., & Lau, S. S. Y. (2018). Sustainability issues in the industrial heritage adaptive reuse: Rethinking cultureled urban regeneration through Chinese case studies. *Journal of Housing and the Built Environment*, 33, 501–518.

Nordström, M., & Wales, M. (2019). Enhancing urban transformative capacity through children's participation in planning. Ambio, 48, 507–514.

Organization for Economic Cooperation and Development (OCED). (2018). Megatrends shaping the future of tourism. In *OECD Tourism Trends and Policies*, pp. 61–91. Paris: OECD.

Paddison, B., & Walmsley, A. (2018). New public management in tourism: A case study of York. *Journal of Sustainable Tourism*, 26(6), 910–926.

Palgan, Y. V. , Mont, O., & Sulkakoski, S. (2021). Governing the sharing economy: Towards a comprehensive analytical framework of municipal governance. *Cities*, 108, https://doi .org/10.1016/j.cities.2020.102994

Peacock, D., & Destinations International. (2021). The future of tourism. https://destina tionsinternational.org/future-tourism

Postma, A., Buda, D.-M., & Gugerell, K. (2017). The future of city tourism. *Journal of Future Tourism*, 3(2), 95–101.

Prideaux, B., & Yin, P. (2019). The disruptive potential of autonomous vehicles (AVs) on future low-carbon tourism mobility. *Asia Pacific Journal of Tourism Research*, 24(5), 459–467.

Puskás, N., Abunnasr, Y., & Naalbandian, S. (2021). Assessing deeper levels of participation in nature-based solutions in urban landscapes – A literature review of real-world cases. *Landscape and Urban Planning*, 210, https://doi.org/10.1016/j.landurbplan.2021.10 4065.

PwC. (2019). *Chinese Cities of Opportunity 2019*. Beijing: PwC China.

Ribeiro, M. A., Gursoy, D., & Chi, O. H. (2021). Customer acceptance of autonomous vehicles in travel and tourism. *Journal of Travel Research*, https://doi.org/10.1177%2 F0047287521993578

Roberts, M., & Eldridge, A. (2009). *Planning the Night-time City*. Abingdon, UK: Routledge.

Rockower, P. (2014). The state of gastrodiplomacy. *Public Diplomacy Magazine*, Issue 11. Winter.

Rong, H. H., Tu, W., Duarte, F., & Ratti, C. (2020). Employing waterborne autonomous vehicles for museum visits: A case study in Amsterdam. *European Transport Research Review*, 12, 63, https://doi.org/10.1186/s12544-020-00459-x.

Sanchez-Anguix, V., Chao, K.-M., Novais, P., Boissier, O., & Julian, V. (2021). Social and intelligent applications for future cities: Current advances. *Future Generation Computer Systems*, 114, 181–184.

Schaller, S., & Guinand, S. (2017). Pop-up landscapes: A new trigger to push up land value? *Urban Geography*, 39(1), 54–74. http://dx.doi.org/10.1080/02723638.2016.1276719.

Seijas, A., & Gelders, M. M. (2021). Governing the night-time city: The rise of night mayors as a new form of urban governance after dark. *Urban Studies*, 58(2), 316–334.

Seraphin, H., & Green, S. (2019). The significance of the contribution of children to conceptualising the destination of the future. *International Journal of Tourism Cities*, 5(4), 544–559.

Sigala, M. (2017). Collaborative commerce in tourism: Implications for research and industry. *Current Issues in Tourism*, 20(4), 346–355.

Simone, C., Iandolo, F., Fulco, I., & Loia, F. (2021). Rome was not built in a day. Resilience and the eternal city: Insights for urban management. *Cities*, 110, https://doi.org/10.1016 /j.cities.2020.103070.

Skinner, H., Sarpong, D., & White, G. R. T. (2018). Generation Z: Gamification in tourism through geocaching. *Journal of Tourism Futures*, 4(1), 93–104.

SmartMyCity. (2021). City Brain: What happens when we connect a city's traffic lights to Alibaba. https://www.smartcitylab.com/blog/digital-transformation/city-brain-what-ha ppens-when-we-connect-a-citys-traffic-lights-to-alibaba/

Spacehive.com. (2021). The action pop up. https://www.spacehive.com/theactonpopup

Stiver, A., Barroca, L., Minocha, S., Richards, M., & Roberts, D. (2015). Civic crowdfunding research: Challenges, opportunities, and future agenda. *New Media & Society*, 17(2), 249–271.

Suntikul, W. (2019). Gastrodiplomacy in tourism. *Current Issues in Tourism*, 22(9), 1076–1094.

Transport Scotland. (2019). *A CAV roadmap for Scotland*. Glasgow: Transport Scotland.

United Nations Economic and Social Commission for Asia and the Pacific (UNESCAP). (2019). *The Future of Asia & Pacific Cities: Transformative Pathways Towards Sustainable Urban Development*. Bangkok: UNESCAP.

UN World Tourism Organization (UNWTO). (2020). *UNWTO Recommendations on Urban Tourism*. Madrid: UNWTO. UNWTO Recommendations on Urban Tourism | World Tourism Organization (e-unwto.org)

Valdivielso, J., & Moranta, J. (2019). The social construction of the tourism degrowth discourse in the Balearic Islands. *Journal of Sustainable Tourism*, 27(12), 1876–1892.

Vergara, J. I. S., Papaoikonomou, E., & Ginieis, M. (2021). Exploring the strategic communication of the sharing city project through frame analysis: The case of Barcelona sharing city. *Cities*, 110, https://doi.org/10.1016/j.cities.2020.103082.

Weng, J., Ding, Y., & Yu, L. (2021). Measuring demand spillover of vacation town: A case of Shanghai Disney Resort. *Asia Pacific Journal of Tourism Research*, 26(2), 95–108.

World Economic Forum (WEF). (2018a). *Future of Consumption in Fast-Growth Consumer Markets: China*. Geneva: World Economic Forum.

WEF. (2018b). *Future of Consumption in Fast-Growth Consumer Markets: India*. Geneva: World Economic Forum.

Wu, Y. A., Ng, A. W., Yu, Z., Huang, J., Meng, K., & Dong, Z. Y. (2021). A review of evolutionary policy incentives for sustainable development of electric vehicles in China: Strategic implications. *Energy Policy*, 148(Part B), https://doi.org/10.1016/j.enpol.2020.111983.

Xia, F., Yang, L. T., Wang, L., & Vinel, A. (2012). Internet of things: Editorial. *International Journal of Communication Systems*, 25, 1101–1102.

Yung, R., & Khoo-Lattimore, C. (2019). New realities: A systematic literature review on virtual reality and augmented reality in tourism research. *Current Issues in Tourism*, 22(17), 2056–2081.

Zhang, D., & Yong, T. (2021). Green building, pro-environmental behavior and well-being: Evidence from Singapore. *Cities*, 108, https://doi.org/10.1016/j.cities.2020.102980.

Zhong, X., & Chen, X. (2017). Demolition, rehabilitation, and conservation: Heritage in Shanghai's urban regeneration, 1990–2015. *Journal of Architecture and Urbanism*, 41(2), 82–91.

Zmyślony, P., & Wędrowicz, K. A. (2019). Cities in the experience economy: The rise and the future of urban leisure formats. *Journal of Tourism Futures*, 5(2), 185–192.

Zuma, B., & Rooijackers, M. (2020). Uncovering the potential of urban culture for creative placemaking. *Journal of Tourism Futures*, 6(3), 233–237.

City index

City index

City index

Subject index

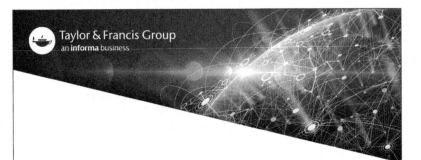

Printed in the United States
by Baker & Taylor Publisher Services